D1453321

Kearny's Own

Kearny's Own

THE HISTORY OF THE FIRST NEW JERSEY BRIGADE IN THE CIVIL WAR

BRADLEY M. GOTTFRIED

Rutgers University Press
New Brunswick, New Jersey, and London

Library of Congress Cataloging-in-Publication Data

Gottfried, Bradley M.
   Kearney's own : the history of the First New Jersey Brigade in the Civil War /
Bradley M. Gottfried.
      p. cm.
   Includes bibliographical references (p.   ) and index.
   ISBN-13: 978–0–8135–3661–3 (hardcover : alk. paper)
  1. United States. Army. New Jersey Brigade, 1st (1861–1865). 2. New Jersey—
History—Civil War, 1861–1865—Regimental histories. 3. United States—History—
Civil War, 1861–1865—Regimental histories. 4. United States—History—Civil War,
1861–1865—Campaigns. I. Title.
E521.4.G68   2005
973.7'449—dc22

                                    2005002524

A British Cataloging-in-Publication record for this book is available from the British
Library.

To the Men Who Fought in the First New Jersey Brigade

To the Modern Writers Who Have Devoted Countless Hours to the Study of New Jersey in the Civil War, Including Joseph Bilby and John Kuhl

CONTENTS

Illustrations follow page 130.

MAPS

PREFACE

This book marks my second Civil War brigade history. Although my real specialty is the Gettysburg Campaign, I feel compelled to produce histories of units that hailed from my current surroundings. I wrote my first unit history, *Stopping Pickett: The History of the Philadelphia Brigade,* when I lived in the Philadelphia area. Within a year or two of moving to New Jersey, I felt a need to write a book on the First New Jersey Brigade. I wish I could better articulate the urge to write these books, but let me leave you with the impression that it is a very strong feeling.

This book, like the Philadelphia Brigade volume, is told primarily through the eyes and voices of the men who experienced the war. These first-person accounts eloquently describe what it was like to join the army, become a soldier, and fight for the Union. The hopes, fears, and sorrow come through so vividly and, I believe, truly help the reader understand what it was like to live during those difficult days.

I have dedicated this book to two sets of New Jerseyans. First, and most obvious, I dedicate this book to all of those men who lived and died fighting for the preservation of the Union. No words can ever make up for their sacrifices. I also recognize those individuals who have dedicated their lives to helping us understand the sacrifices that the soldiers made. These are men like John Kuhl and Joe Bilby, Bill Styple and Dave Martin. They have devoted their lives to the study of New Jersey in the Civil War and have truly broadened our perspectives.

Many people helped this idea become a reality. Melanie Halkias, the history and Asian American studies editor at Rutgers University Press, enthusiastically supported the project and shepherded it to fruition. John Kuhl and Joe Bilby were generous with their time and resources. John opened his extensive collection to me and patiently answered all of my questions, even the stupid ones. Joe lent me his archives used to write his wonderful *Three Rousing Cheers* and his *Remember You Are Jerseymen!* epic. Quite simply, this book could not have been written without their support. I also want to thank Wayne McCabe, who was generous with his time and archives. So many archives and libraries opened their repositories to me, and the book is much richer because of it.

Special thanks go to Linda Nieman for patiently reviewing an early draft of the manuscript and finding a myriad of errors. She also did a masterly job of preparing the maps.

Kearny's Own

CHAPTER 1

Forming the First New Jersey Brigade

"The First and Second Regiments were on the ground before us . . . holding, or attempting to hold, a dress parade. Their uniforms had not been issued to them and their rags were fluttering in the breeze." Such were the observations of a visitor to Camp Olden, just outside of Trenton, in the spring of 1861. The recruits, arriving in droves, first learned what soldiering was like here. Expecting to receive their uniforms upon arrival, the men wore their worst clothes. So began the formation of the First New Jersey Brigade, a unit that was destined to fight with great distinction.

The April 17, 1861, attack on Fort Sumter jolted the state of New Jersey out of its complacency regarding its militia. A serious analysis found that it was sadly ill-prepared for the upcoming conflict. According to one observer, it was not much more than a "system of shreds and patches, without organic unity, and almost entirely worthless." However, Governor Charles S. Olden had little choice but to look to his militia when President Lincoln issued the call for seventy-five thousand men for a three-month term. New Jersey's allotment was just over three thousand. Olden could immediately call upon the 1,863 men in the active militia, but he needed a total of four regiments, with 780 men in each. On the same day that Sumter fell, he wrote to Richard Stockton, New Jersey's adjutant general, about how the militia regiments should be organized to bring them up to the prescribed size. If not enough volunteers came forward, men on the rolls of the reserve militia would be called into duty. Almost eighty-two thousand men were in this pool. This action was not needed, however, as thousands of men, consumed with a patriotic ardor, came forward to enlist, and the number in each regiment quickly swelled to over a thousand men.[1]

Olden actually had the opposite problem—the state's quota was not high enough to accommodate the thousands of Jerseymen strongly interested in enlisting in the militia. Many of these men milled around the Trenton area, waiting for an opportunity to arise. Others, like Charles Hopkins of Boonton, left the state for New York to try their luck. He intended to enlist in the Second New York Militia, but was dissuaded by newspaper accounts of their mutiny. Visiting one military unit after another without success, Hopkins returned to New Jersey in May, where he ultimately joined the first regular three-year regiment formed in the state, the First New Jersey Volunteers, which was now forming at Trenton. Many years later, Hopkins reflected on the fact that he took the action "with more patriotic ardor than good sense."

A depression settled over the hordes of men left behind when the First, Second, Third, and Fourth New Jersey Militia departed for Washington on May 3, 1861. Robert McAllister, a forty-six-year-old railroad construction contractor from Oxford Furnace in Warren County, had brought his "Warren Guards" company to Trenton as part of the Fifth New Jersey Militia. He wrote home on May 3, 1861, "we are all in doubt here as to what will be done with us . . . [the governor says] that he has no orders for any more troops, dampens our feelings very much. We fear that we may be sent home." McAllister was especially depressed because he had lost the command of the Fourth New Jersey Militia when he arrived in Trenton too late. He rationalized that it was just as well, as "there was trouble—and is still trouble among them in Bordentown. One company fought their captain."[2]

Concerned about the growing number of highly disappointed men wanting to help end the rebellion, Governor Olden sought assistance from Secretary of War Simon Cameron on May 1, 1861. He noted that he was "exceedingly embarrassed by the fact that, besides the four militia regiments called for by the President's requisition, there are already in this State, organized or nearly organized, enough volunteer companies who have expected to make a part of our four regiments, now about moving, to make four additional regiments. I must now either encourage these men that they will have an opportunity of entering the U.S. service, and speedily, or I must advise them to disband."

Olden was not in favor of the latter course of action because "the spirit and enthusiasm of our people are excited to the highest pitch, and the consequences here of disbanding these men would be extremely injurious." He therefore requested that at least two additional regiments be accepted from New Jersey. He also delicately broached a subject that had been a growing source of irritation—the Federal government's inadequate equipping of the volunteers. "We have had great difficulty in equipping the four regiments we are now sending. The arms furnished to them by the United States are of inferior quality, being flint-lock muskets percussioned. It is earnestly desired that they may, if possible, on arriving at Washington be provided with arms superior to those they now have. The United States have provided us with little besides these arms, yet our troops are on their way, prepared to defend the Government of their country."

Governor Olden received a response two days later, on May 3, but it was not what he wanted to hear. Cameron was unable to accept additional troops, but added that the president was contemplating another requisition of troops from the states. He promised to inform Olden of his allotment, if and when it was determined. As for the equipment, Cameron wrote, "the arms furnished your troops may not be the best, but they are the best the Government at the present time is able to furnish them."[3]

Many men milled around the camp, which according to McAllister was a "barracks, enclosed by the State Arsenal on one side and a heavy stone wall on the other side. All around the inside of which are temporary barracks made for sleeping and large sheds for eating" that was located opposite the state prison, just south of Trenton, near the Delaware and Raritan Canal. This was apparently a militia camp. It was not until later that the men transferred to Camp Olden.

The men spent considerable time drilling while waiting to be inducted into Federal service. Oscar Westlake wrote home that the men were primarily between the ages of twenty and twenty-eight years old, and drilled five and a half hours each day. Because the men did not have uniforms, they presented a crazy quilt array of dress. "Many were shirtless, except the nether shirt, shoeless, hatless, and pantless—in fact, were quite 'less' in every way," Charles Hopkins noted. Those who did have clothes, according to Hopkins, "were fantastic—some self-made paper hats, tri cockade, square and round, as fancy designed; others for pantaloons, had their blankets folded over a string much like the Kilt of the Scot, bound to the waist by a knotted cord, or a wooded skewer for a pin."[4]

Men continued flooding into Trenton. Some arrived individually; others in groups. For example, David Hatfield brought what would soon be Company A, First New Jersey Volunteers, to Trenton on May 16, 1861. Arriving there in the early afternoon, the men were received by a full band and were escorted through the streets to the State House, and then to Camp Olden. When Charles Tay brought his Company B of the Newark City Battalion to Trenton it was initially quartered in the Council Chamber of City Hall, but it trudged back to the arsenal for its meals. The company, which would become Company K of the Second New Jersey Volunteers, moved to Camp Olden on June 1. Men and women lined the streets as the company marched to its new quarters. Isaac Howell of Newton, New Jersey, who arrived alone on May 21, was not happy with his tent, hard ground, and scarce straw to cushion him, so he rented a room at the Eagle Hotel until he was mustered into Federal service.[5]

The men's anxious wait ended on May 3 when President Lincoln issued a call for forty-two thousand additional volunteers. There was, however, a hitch—these troops would not be considered militia and their terms of enlistment would increase to three years. This requirement caused the men to entertain second thoughts, and many headed home. Robert McAllister lost his company, as all but twenty men decided to leave. The remaining men were dispersed among other companies. McAllister was chagrined, writing to his daughter, "[T]hey ought to have staid. I done all I could but they would not go into it for three years." Those who accepted these terms would later be inducted into the First, Second, or Third New Jersey Volunteers.[6]

Governor Olden apparently doubted the Federal government's sincerity in needing additional troops, for he wrote to Cameron on May 11, 1861, "these men ought not to be subsisted and withdrawn from their ordinary pursuits unless they are really to be received by the General Government, nor ought the State to be subjected to the burden of their maintenance if they are not needed." He volunteered to quarter them near Trenton if not needed in Washington. Major Theodore Laidley, who had arrived to officially muster the troops into Federal service, may have caused Olden's concerns because he was "without instructions to proceed to muster in the volunteers for three years." Olden reasoned that these new three-year troops "could be thoroughly drilled here in camp, and equipped and uniformed at leisure. They would then be ready for active service whenever needed, and they could be transported hence with great facility, either by land or water, to any point to which the Government might at any time order them."

Olden walked a fine line. He needed the Federal government to accept the men who wanted to enlist so future recruits would not be dissuaded from joining the army, but he realized that the authorities were not satisfactorily caring for the men already mustered into service.[7]

On May 16, Olden received official notification that the Federal government would indeed require a trio of three-year regiments, and two days later he was able to write that "the three regiments are now ready, and only await orders to the mustering officer, Major Laidley, who is now here awaiting orders." He continued, "I have not called out more than the three regiments, because I have not been authorized to do so by you; but if the occasion required their services this State would willingly furnish twice as many regiments to serve during the war." Olden also outlined his plan to retain the three regiments in Trenton until called south. As soon as they were mustered in, he would begin furnishing them "with clothing, camp and garrison equipage, pursuant to my contract recently entered into with the Quartermaster-General of the United States." He also assured the secretary of war that they would be "drilled daily and systematically." Many of the men joining these regiments were already in militia companies that enlisted as a unit. Such was the case of the Second NJV, which contained the City Battalion of Newark as its nucleus.

Governor Olden and his staff appointed the regimental field officers (e.g., colonel, lieutenant colonel, major). Robert McAllister hoped to receive command of the First New Jersey, as he had lost the Fourth New Jersey Militia. This was not the case. Olden summoned McAllister to his office and explained that he was appointing William Montgomery to the post because of his decades of service in the U.S. Army. Since Montgomery was no longer in the service "for political reasons," Olden felt compelled to find a suitable position for him, and besides, he told McAllister, Montgomery would soon become a brigadier general. The governor told McAllister that he would receive the rank of lieutenant colonel, and assured him that the regiment would be surely his upon Montgomery's promotion. McAllister agreed to become the second in command of the First NJV and tried to make the situation a positive one, writing home, "I am perfectly satisfied, as I have one who is fully competent over me, and I will learn more under him than anyone else."[8]

William Montgomery was officially appointed colonel of the First NJV on May 21, 1861, the same day that the regiment was mustered into Federal service. The governor commented that Montgomery had "some thirty years' service [and is] still in the vigor of life." Born in Monmouth County in 1801, Montgomery had graduated from West Point and served with distinction during the Seminole War and the Mexican War. Stationed at Fort Riley, Kansas, after the Mexican War, he had gotten into trouble with his antislavery views, and was ultimately forced from the army by then-Secretary of War Jefferson Davis on a trumped up charge of misappropriating funds. A resident of Bucks County, Pennsylvania, Colonel Montgomery began his command on the mend for several weeks, as he was thrown from his horse on May 26 and confined to bed at his home in Bristol, Pennsylvania, with a fractured rib.

The First NJV was prepared to go to war on May 18, and was mustered into U.S. service three days later by Major Theodore Laidley of the regular army. The regiment numbered 1,034 men, which included a full complement of thirty-eight officers. Most of these men hailed from Camden, Hudson, Middlesex, Mercer, Union, and Warren counties.[9]

Governor Olden wanted his three-year regiments led by men who had served in the regular U.S. Army, so he appointed George McLean to lead the Second NJV. This regiment was fully equipped and officered by May 18, and was mustered into Federal service on May 26 by Major Laidley. It numbered 1,044 men, including the requisite thirty-eight officers, who primarily came from Essex, Passaic, Sussex, and Union counties.

The Third NJV was led by Colonel George Taylor, and it mustered into service on June 4, 1861. Born in Hunterdon County in 1809, Taylor was a product of a local military academy before serving as a midshipman in the U.S. Navy. He resigned in 1831 and returned to New Jersey to farm. Taylor joined the Tenth U.S. Infantry during the Mexican War, but did not see action. Returning to New Jersey, he entered the business of mining and manufacturing iron. Reserved and haughty, Taylor was never popular with his men, but he garnered their respect and was considered an effective infantry officer. The regiment was fully organized, equipped, and ready for war on May 18, but was not mustered into Federal service until June 4 by Captain Alfred Torbert. The regiment, raised in Burlington, Camden, Cumberland, Gloucester, Somerset, and Union counties, boasted 1,051 men, including thirty-eight officers.[10]

Prior to being sworn into the army, the men were checked by physicians. According to Wallace Struble of the First NJV, "there was but seven thrown out of our company. Three of them was not tall enough and two was not old enough."

The men enlisted for many reasons. Some, particularly those joining immediately after Fort Sumter's demise, were fueled by intense patriotism. The newspapers teemed with stories about putting down the rebellion, and Jersey towns and cities were decked out in flags. The war was the main issue on everyone's tongue. More than a few without this patriotic fervor were propelled into the army by their ardent wives, parents, or friends. For others, it was the prospect of adventure—the ability to leave the drudgery of home behind and be involved in life-changing events. This was especially prevalent among the younger men. Enlistment allowed some men to leave their difficult experiences behind. Perhaps trouble with the neighbor or boss, and certainly intolerable marriages, could suddenly be cured by a man's absence. Money also played a role. The economy struggled in 1861, and the $11 a month from the Federal government and another $4 the state promised were too good to turn down. For most, it was a combination of factors. For example, some units, particularly those from Hudson and Essex counties, were almost completely composed of recent immigrants, who joined en masse to show support for their new homeland, because of peer pressure, and because of the need for cash.[11]

The lack of uniforms, the bland food, and, most importantly, the homesickness caused many to regret their decision to enlist. According to Private Charles Reid of the Third NJV, "there are many among us who would prefer to be home and regret that they went along." Reid did not include himself in this group—"[while] it is rather skimpy here, but I am satisfied because I knew full well how it would go . . . I have no complaints, as I like it pretty well." Some of the men did not agree, and deserted when given the opportunity. The opposite point of view was voiced by John Perdick of the Third NJV, who noted, "our only fear is we wont get our shear [*sic*] of fun with the Rebels."

Financial matters also weighed on the soldiers. Uncertainty of when the paymaster would arrive caused many to openly worry about their families. Private Reid expected that his family would get monthly funds, and when he realized that they had not, he wrote, "[I]f you do not get anything I will not remain in the army. This is sure, because I counted on it that you would be provided for; you may say this publicly." Reid was naive in thinking that he could ask for his release from the army.[12]

The men were sworn into Federal service at the State House, which Charles Hopkins described as an "unpretentious, quaint little octagon shaped, or six sided building . . . on the Delaware River." Military supplies finally arrived after the men were sworn in. The men were particularly excited about the uniforms that replaced their rags and ill-suited clothes. Unfortunately, many received ill-fitting uniforms. "The variety of fits and misfits was laughable to any one except those most concerned," noted Hopkins. Tall men received pants that were too short and the short men received grossly large ones. The men traded parts of their uniforms until all had reasonably fitting ones. The men's hats were universally hated. Hopkins described it as "the Regulation hat—black, stiff-rimmed, disagreeable to wear at any time . . . and ornamented with a brass excutcheon of the United States covering nearly one side of [the] crown." A long black feather finished the decor. "Really, we looked very fierce and warrior-like!" Hopkins noted, but admitted, the "boys rebelled at wearing the hat in that climate and found ways of disposing of them." The men who discarded them were forced to repay the government and were then issued identical copies. Governor Olden visited the camp on May 27 and must have been impressed by what he saw.

Camp Olden teemed with life. Hacks constantly plied their trade between the camp and Trenton for the "moderate" sum of twenty-five cents each way. Visitors approaching the camps could see "a number of shanties and wagons in which a thriving business . . . selling cakes, pies and refreshments to the soldiers on furlough and [to] their friends . . . ," reported the *New Brunswick Fredonian*. Guards posted at the camp entrances barred unauthorized entry. The men slept in large Sibley tents, which housed as many as sixteen soldiers. Each company had six tents—five for its enlisted men and one for its noncommissioned officers. Each commissioned officer had his own tent, the size of which related to his rank. The enlisted men often honored their officers by planting evergreen trees at the entrance of their tents. Adjacent to each company's tents was a 150 by 40-foot parade ground. Each line of tents ended with a rough shed, where the company's food was prepared. The men were fed boiled ham, bread, and coffee. Sometimes they received beef rations twice a day. While the men could not complain about the quality of the food, they felt that they were not given enough. Wallace Struble complained about not having butter for his bread. A large hospital tent in the rear of the camp ministered to the sick.[13]

The men quickly settled into a routine. Drilling was the most prominent activity, taking up at least three to four hours each day. One newspaper noted, "it is generally thought best to drill the three year's troops well before sending them off." Reveille sounded at daybreak, and five minutes later the men were lined up for roll call. Drilling on empty stomachs followed for the next hour or two, depending on the "humor of the commanding officer." The men then formed single file for breakfast before policing the area around their tents. "Guard mounting" occurred at about 10:00 A.M., when ten men from each company were detached for guard duty. The men occasionally drilled at 11:00 A.M., and then broke for their midday meal at 12:30 P.M., followed by two additional hours of drilling. Free time was provided between 4:00 and 6:00 P.M., followed by supper. This was by far the best meal of the day, as the men sometimes received a beefsteak. Supper over, the men next participated in a "drum parade," where they heard reports about each company's progress in becoming soldiers. This took about half an hour. They were then dismissed and given free time until tattoo sounded at 9:30 P.M., when the men again assembled for roll call. Taps finally sounded at 10:00 P.M.

The routine changed on Sundays, as drilling ceased and the men were given more free time. Wallace Struble wrote home, "we go to church every Sunday once up to Trenton and in the afternoon we have preaching in the Camp."[14]

The men initially drilled with ancient flintlock muskets before being mustered into service. When not in use, the men jammed them into the soft ground, muzzle first, until their barrels were fully caked with dirt. With the new uniforms came newer arms. Charles Hopkins recalled that "our arms were of good make for those times, being smoothbore, caliber fifty-eight, Springfield pattern, and four pounds lighter than old 1776, formerly used." While the new arms were good for drilling and morale, the scarcity of ammunition caused not one to fire.[15]

On June 4, 1861, Olden took up his pen again to inform Secretary of War Cameron of the condition of the state's first three three-year regiments. "The regiments are all full and are here in camp. They have tents and camp equipage, but we have not undertaken to provide ambulances or wagons. The regiments have the best officers it was in my power to obtain. . . . The troops themselves are hardy, able men. This State was authorized by General Sibley, acting quartermaster, to furnish these regiments with clothing, uniforms, knapsacks, &c. . . . our troops will be equipped in two weeks." He ended his letter with perhaps its most important line—"I consider it very desirable that these regiments should not be separated, but that they serve in the same brigade."

With the ranks of the First, Second, and Third NJV full, and the men chafing to be sent south to end the rebellion, Governor Olden wrote to Secretary of War Cameron on June 21, 1861, that the three regiments were equipped and could break camp and move south as early as June 27, 1861. Colonel William Montgomery of the First NJV was in charge of them.[16]

Colonel Montgomery finally issued the orders to prepare for the journey south on June 26, 1861. The company commanders were told to ensure that every man was properly equipped and ready for the move. Each soldier received five days worth of rations in his haversack and ten rounds of ammunition in his cartridge box "with strict orders not to be used except under special instructions from their commandants." Tents were to be struck immediately after reveille and the men prepared for travel.

The three regiments received word on June 27 that they would depart the next day, so the men spent considerable time packing their belongings and preparing for the trip. Governor Olden appeared on June 28 to review the troops and see them off, as the band played "Hail to the Chief." The governor was accompanied by a large number of spectators to see "so large a body of New Jersey troops [that] has never before been assembled, and reviewed together, on any one occasion," noted a newspaper columnist. The writer also observed that during the time the men were in camp "they have been drilled several hours daily and have attained a degree of discipline admirably fitting them for active service." This definitely was not the case, as a month of lackluster drilling under lax officers had in no way prepared them for the future rigors of soldier life.[17]

Tired of the monotony of camp, the men enthusiastically embraced the orders to break camp and entrain for Washington. They were surprised to see the throng of civilians at Trenton waiting to see them off. Wallace Struble wrote home, "was two hours going through the crowd. Their [*sic*] was over 15 thousand people to bid us farewell. Woman screeching and screeming [*sic*], waiving of hankerchiefs [*sic*], throwing hats and every thing." The men boarded a two-locomotive train pulling thirty-two cars on the Camden and Amboy Railroad. Each train could carry one regiment at a time, so the First NJV left Trenton at 9:00 A.M., the Second NJV at 1:00 P.M., and the Third NJV at 7:00 P.M. "As the trains moved off, the troops were loudly cheered by the voices of the multitude and the waving of handkerchiefs. The wives, mothers, brothers, sisters and other relatives of many of the troops were present to bid them adieu, and on many of them could be seen the tear trickling down their cheeks, and they one and all looked as though they were sad at parting thus," reported the *Trenton State Gazette and Republican*.

The departure was not without some excitement. Several civilians scrambled atop a shed to get a better view, but were unceremoniously thrown to the ground when the excess weight caused it to topple. A child was injured when an officer's horse slipped and trod on his foot. The men were also excited. According to Oscar Westlake of the Third NJV, the men had a "first rate time . . . only one drawback . . . a good many of the boys got drunk as the devil and were pretty noisy." Three girls smuggled onto the train were quickly expelled when found by the officers.[18]

The train arrived in Burlington about an hour after it departed from Trenton, where another large group of civilians gathered. During the half-hour stop here, women entered the cars distributing water, lemonade, oranges, cakes, and flowers. This ended when the "iron horse, with a wild scream, again hurried us forward," noted one of the men. The train did not reach Camden until two and a half hours later, as there were halts at each station along the way to permit the townspeople to express their gratitude. The troops detrained at Camden and boarded a boat that crossed the Delaware River to Philadelphia.

"I cannot describe the scene here," wrote a soldier in the Third NJV. "We marched through a perfect jam of citizens, more than 10,000 in number." The first stop was the Cooper Shop for refreshments. A number of New Jersey women were there to help the men remove their knapsacks and to serve them food and hot coffee. The next stop was the train station at Broad and Pine streets, and despite the time (1:00 A.M. for the Third NJV), the route was lined with thousands of cheering citizens.[19]

While in Philadelphia, the men heard the news of a civil disturbance in Baltimore, so they were ordered to load their muskets, but not place a percussion cap on them. Reaching Wilmington, Delaware, the men received waves of applause from appreciative citizens who had flocked to the train depot. A newspaper reported, "Flags and handkerchiefs in the hands of men, women and children, waved by the hundreds, while the hearty cheers given by the multitude proved that their hearts were fully in the good work." The men noted that every bridge was guarded by troops. Detraining in Baltimore, the Jerseymen marched to another depot on the south side of the city. Along the way they received both cheers and jeers. The newspaper reported that "Every gun was loaded, and every officer walked with drawn sword, so that had an attack been made upon the Regiment it would have been promptly and efficiently met." A Trenton newspaper noted that "both Regiments [Second and Third] marched through Baltimore by daylight, and, by the magnificent display they made [progress] . . . towards quelling this rebellion and insuring the perpetuity of the Union than ten thousand such private 'peace meetings.'" Wallace Struble was equally dramatic: "[T]hey said they was agoing to fire into us at Baltimore but when they saw three thousand of us they backed down."

After waiting at the depot for two hours, the men of the First NJV entrained into forty-six cars drawn by two huge locomotives for the final leg of the trip to Washington, D.C. The regiment finally reached Washington at 3:30 A.M. on June 29, or approximately eighteen and a half hours after the men broke camp. This trip normally took about nine hours during peacetime, causing the *Trenton State Gazette and Record* to explain that "large bodies move slow." Because trains were limited, the Second NJV arrived at 1:00 P.M. and the Third NJV at 4:30 P.M.[20]

The trip south was not without some accidents. Private Frederick Warner, who apparently had been asleep by an open window, suddenly awoke and thrust his arm out the window, only to have it broken on contact with a pole on a bridge the train was crossing. A second, more serious incident occurred when a soldier, Henry Stout, was accidentally shot in the breast when picking up a musket that had fallen to the floor. The bullet apparently exited his body and the wound was not fatal.

The First NJV arrived in Washington in the midst of a rainstorm, so the men quickly marched to the Treasury Building. When the rains ended they stretched out on the rapidly drying sidewalks. However, the sun superheated the sidewalks, forcing them to stand. Realizing that they needed a more suitable location, the officers ordered the men back into column and put them again in motion. According to Charles Hopkins, "we were seesawed and repeated again and again, marched and countermarched (all this time in the sun, at from ninety-five to a hundred degrees) with woolen suits." The march continued late into the afternoon of June 29, when the regiment finally ground to a halt at what was to be called Camp Monmouth. The enlisted men did not know that some of the regiment's field officers had scouted this location during the time they were resting near the Treasury Building. Tents were soon up, and Lieutenant Colonel McAllister was able to brag that they "look so much better than those around us." Water availability became a problem, forcing teams of horses to deliver barrels of it to the men.[21]

The Second NJV also had a difficult time with the location of its first camp. Following a government officer, the men halted at the designated place. However, the lack of water forced the column to reform and move to another area. They named it Camp Pennington. The men were chagrined when they realized that the tents had not arrived, forcing them to sleep under the stars the first night in camp. The tents appeared the next day, but now the men were disappointed about the lack of straw to line the floors.

The Third NJV was initially quartered in large buildings in Washington. Almost half of the regiment was quartered at Abolition Hall on the corner of Pennsylvania Avenue and 4th Street. Inspected at 3:00 P.M. on July 1, the men marched toward the Potomac River, where they halted about two miles from Washington. This would be the site of their camp. A storm soon passed through the area—"the wind howled fearfully and the rain fell in torrents," noted one of the men. Because the tents did not accompany the column, the men sought whatever shelter they could find. Four hundred found it in a brewery, a hundred and fifty in a large cow shed, two hundred were in an open shanty, and the rest dispersed into hen houses and barns. The tents arrived the next day and were quickly erected.[22]

The men were not impressed with their capital. One wrote, "I am some-what disappointed in Washington [as] it is not as fair a city as I expected to find and everything is in an unfinished state." The men were impressed by the number of other troops in the region. One soldier from the Third NJV could count eleven camps within sight in Virginia, Maryland, and around Washington. He estimated that they contained approximately eighty thousand men. New Jersey had seven regiments in the field—four nine-month militia and three three-year volunteers. Four were stationed near the Long Bridge, two at an aqueduct, and one at Arlington Heights. More ominous were the Rebels, who could be seen in the distance making their rounds.

July 3, 1861, was a special day for the three regiments, for President Lincoln reviewed them from a stand constructed at the north portico of the White House. The men spent considerable time preparing for the review, shin-ing their shoes, cleaning their uniforms, and oiling their guns. The three regi-ments left their respective camps and met at the "eastern terminus of Pennsylvania Avenue" at 3:30 P.M. and then marched directly to the White House. Oscar Westlake complained that the day was "as hot as the very devil—two or three of our boys almost gave out from the heat." Forming in sections, the column stretched over half a mile. Colonel George McLean of the Second NJV commanded the brigade in the absence of Colonel Mont-gomery. Lincoln was delighted with the display. Major David Hatfield of the First NJV reported, "Mr. Lincoln looked well and pleasant; the regiments looked well and marched fine." The men chipped in the following day and bought fireworks to liven up the celebration of the nation's birthday.[23]

Major Hatfield noted that the weather was very hot in the early part of July. The men could "wring our shirts out every day." Comparing the current conditions with those in Trenton, Hatfield observed, "we do not live as pleas-antly here as at Camp Olden; however, we can bear all necessary hardship for the sake of our country." Many men would later look back on these early days and wish that they had experienced such "hardships" throughout the rest of the war.[24]

New Testament Bibles were distributed prior to leaving Camp Olden, which the men received with "seriousness and expressions of gratitude." Now, with time on their hands, many soldiers participated in regular prayer meet-ings and discussions.

The Jerseymen spent most of the early days of July drilling and trans-forming themselves into soldiers. According to Lieutenant Colonel McAllister, "we have company drill in the morning, battallion [*sic*] drill at half past nine o'clock, target firing by the right wing before dinner, target firing by the left wing after dinner, battallion [*sic*] drill at 5 o'clock, and dress parade at six." The men were usually tired because of the many false alarms during the night. Sentries fired their guns every time they heard a sound, causing the men to rush out of their tents and form into line of battle. McAllister reasoned that the "alarms, though false they be, serve a good purpose to acustom [*sic*] our men to fall in double quick time." His regiment could assemble in less than five minutes. These relatively quiet and safe days would soon end, as preparations were being made to move into Virginia.[25]

CHAPTER 2

Into Virginia

*J*uly 11, 1861, brought a mix of emotions to the Jerseymen, as they received orders to prepare to break camp and march into Virginia at 5:00 A.M. the next day. Peeking out of their tents on July 12, the men saw torrential rains falling on the area and were relieved to learn that the march would be postponed until 8:00 A.M. The rains continued, so the march was postponed until 5:00 P.M. The rains finally let up as the men were breaking camp, and all were in column by 6:00 P.M., and the march finally began. Crossing the Long Bridge into Virginia, the column finally halted between 9:00 and 10:00 P.M. after a twelve-mile march. The men were miserable. Not only were they unaccustomed to marching such long distances, they were initially soaked to the skin. The rain was replaced by hot, muggy conditions, causing the men to sweat excessively, and then it rained again, soaking them once more. The rains also turned the roads into muddy quagmires, making marching exceedingly difficult. According to Charles Reid, "we were up to our knees in mud. You may perhaps know how the roads are in Virginia." When the column halted for the night, the men were not permitted to pitch their tents, but instead were told to lay out their rubber blankets on the grassy field filled with moss and sleep under the stars. No one grumbled when told they would rest the following morning. Hot coffee arrived at 11:00 A.M., and then the column marched another mile to Roach's Mill, where the men pitched their tents in what was to be called Camp Trenton.

Now in enemy territory, the men were initially nervous. However, they felt a measure of safety from the large number of other Federal troops nearby. Charles Reid estimated that they numbered twenty thousand. Many were also reassured when they were assigned to General Theodore Runyon's Fourth Division of Major General Irwin McDowell's Army of Northeastern Virginia. Runyon's Division also contained the New Jersey Militia Brigade. There was little time to visit with their fellow Jerseymen, as they were given axes and told to chop down trees that obscured their view, to prevent the enemy from sneaking up on them.[1]

The initial days in Virginia were fairly carefree. Oscar Westlake of the Third NJV wrote home that "we have it lazy enough when we are in camp but when we are on the march you bet it is work." He complained about the heavy knapsack, weighing twenty-five pounds, the ten-pound musket, and everything else, which added up to forty or forty-five pounds. Westlake could not complain about the food, though. For breakfast the men were given bread without butter, pork or fresh beef, and coffee. He had entered the service expecting tough times, but was pleasantly surprised.

The men did not mind that they spent less time drilling, as the enemy was near. After reveille, the men drilled from 5:00 A.M. to 6:30 A.M., followed by breakfast. Two hours of additional drilling commenced at 4:30 P.M., then dress parade, followed by supper.[2]

On July 13, the First and Second NJV were ordered to leave camp with two days' rations and march fourteen miles to Vienna, Virginia, or approximately eleven miles west of Washington, and then nine miles east to Bailey's Cross Roads, where the men were ordered to guard the roads. The officers apparently hoped to find provisions along the way, so they did not bring any with them. Colonel Montgomery arrived in camp just before the march began at 6:00 A.M. Sore ribs prevented him from riding a horse, so he remained behind. Colonel George McLean was also ill, so Lieutenant Colonel McAllister took command of the two regiments. The Third NJV remained behind at Burke's Station and worked on the Orange and Alexandria Railroad.

Knowing that the enemy occupied Fairfax Court House, a mere three miles away, the men of the First and Second NJV were especially vigilant. Lieutenant Colonel McAllister wrote home on July 18, "we lay on our arms all night, expecting every minute to be attacked, but the morning dawned without the enemy appearing." Their close proximity to the enemy unnerved the men, and few slept that night. McAllister wrote home, "I am very well but very tired." The troops felt a measure of relief when the Rebels abandoned Fairfax Court House, but there were still plenty of them at Manassas Junction, about eighteen miles away.[3]

Discipline continued to be a problem, as is illustrated by an incident occurring at Roach's Mill while most of the men marched to Vienna. A lieutenant and a small squad of men were left behind to guard the camp. Learning that the enemy was only three miles away, they immediately slipped away, along with a sutler, who reluctantly left his goods behind. Some of the men doubled back and broke into the sutler's store, stealing as much as they could carry.

At least two soldiers were hit by "friendly fire" during this period. The most serious incident occurred on the night of July 17, when John Ellis of the Third NJV was on the picket line. Samuel Middleton of the same company was on Ellis' right. Middleton apparently fell asleep, and when he suddenly awoke at 11:00 P.M. he saw someone approaching him. Yelling "Halt," Middleton fired when the shadow continued to approach. The bullet hit Ellis, who was merely walking his route, killing him instantly. He was the first fatality of the First Brigade. Ellis was sent home to Germantown, Pennsylvania, and Middleton was sent to the guardhouse. The latter was released a short time later and permitted to return to duty. The following night another private, John Biedeman of the First NJV, was shot by a sentry. He never recovered sufficiently to return to his unit and was discharged in November 1861.[4]

Despite the danger, Lieutenant Colonel McAllister reported that his men wanted to be even closer to the Rebels, as they were growing tired of the inactivity. They envied the Third NJV, which was closer to the enemy at Manassas Junction. The men did not get their wish, for on July 18, after forty-eight hours at Bailey's Cross Roads, the two regiments were ordered back to Vienna.

Grumbling escalated, as none of the men had been paid since joining the service. Many wrote letters home requesting financial assistance. Charles Reid wrote, "dear wife, if you can, send me not more than one dollar; for when marching it is good to have a few cents." Robert McCreight, also of the First NJV, wrote home asking for some postage stamps, saying, "[T]he colonel says that if we don't get paid soon he will disband the regiment and go home." The paymaster finally arrived on July 26, 1861, with two months' pay for the enlisted men, but the officers were not paid until the following day. Wallace Struble of the First NJV received $22, but complained, "we are where we cannot spend a cent of our money. We cannot get any little thing we realy [sic] need very bad such as tobacco [sic]."[5]

Although the men were kept busy drilling, digging entrenchments, and walking the picket line, there was still plenty of time to spread rumors. Chaplain George Darrow of the Third NJV wrote home, "among the thousand men there are many whose love of the marvellous [sic] is so strong, that no regiment will long lack for astounding news." The men also spent time bathing and washing their clothes in a nearby canal.

On July 21, 1861, McAllister dashed off a letter to his wife at 9:30 A.M., "All is bustle and excitement in preparing to move to the conflict. We have to march . . . we leave knapsacks and trunks all here to be sent down to

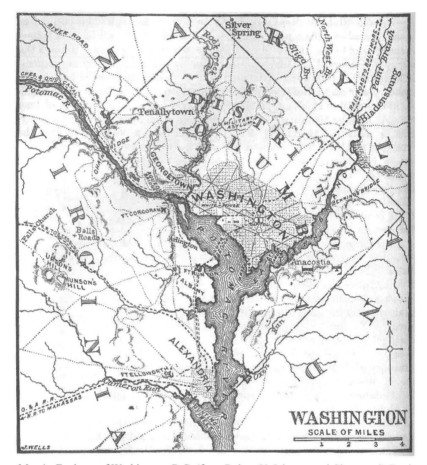

Map 1. Environs of Washington, D.C. (from Robert U. Johnson and Clarence C. Buel, *Battles and Leaders of the Civil War* [New York: The Century Co., 1884]).

Camp Trenton. . . . You will hear of the battle before this reaches you." McAllister was referring to the First Battle of Bull Run, which was well un- der way as the lieutenant colonel penned his note. The men were disappointed that their brigade was designated as a reserve unit. Captain Henry Ryerson of the Second NJV wrote that "we almost wept because we were to be kept here to protect the rear."[6]

Taking seven companies of his First NJV and eight of the Second NJV, Colonel Montgomery left Vienna and dashed toward Centreville. General Runyon had sent Montgomery his orders at about 8:00 A.M., but the column did not move out until noon. The men did not need much encouragement, as they had waited months for this moment and were not about to miss an opportunity to destroy the Rebels. The distant booming of cannon helped put spring in their steps.

Initially joyful, the men's mood began to change when the column came within four miles of Centreville. Citizens began appearing with conflicting accounts of the battle. Needing additional information, Colonel Montgomery sent Major David Hatfield galloping ahead. Within half a mile, Hatfield reported seeing: "United States regulars, mounted citizens, soldiers and baggage wagons coming thundering down the hills . . . a more frantic set of people I never saw. There seemed to be a perfectly wild panic among them. Some of them were bareheaded, and the hair standing on their heads. Shovels, spades, axes, bags of oats, boxes of hard bread . . . were flying out of the wagons. A gentleman came running up to me and lifting up both hands, exclaimed, 'For God's sake stop them, there is no cause for this panic.'"[7]

Hatfield immediately returned to Montgomery and suggested that he form the fifteen companies across the road in an effort to halt the retreat and rally the troops. Montgomery promptly complied, and the men did not have long to wait before the disorganized throng approached. "We were compelled to draw our swords and pistols and also to charge bayonet on them, and in some instances we had to threaten to shoot them before they could turn back, not only the soldiers but the officers as well, and when they found that we were determined to stop them, some of them jumped from their horses, others who were on foot threw away their guns and overcoats, and started across the fields and through the woods," reported Hatfield.

Realizing the folly of these efforts, Montgomery again put the column in motion toward Centreville and the advancing enemy. The bright moon illuminated the landscape as the men arrived. Leaving his troops, Montgomery rode in search of General Irwin McDowell, commanding the troops at Bull Run. McDowell told him to post his men in as good a position as he could find and prepare to beat off any enemy advance. Upon returning, Montgomery was shocked to learn that Colonel McLean had taken his eight companies back toward Vienna. Two days later, Montgomery was still fuming about McLean's actions, and wrote in his official report that he "ascertained [that] it had retired and was on the retreat, and continued to do so, for reasons doubtless its colonel will duly explain." Captain Ryerson reported that the eight companies were in danger of being cut off by large bodies of enemy cavalry during the movement to Centreville. The regiment periodically halted and deployed to face the threats, only to realize that they were hoaxes. Nevertheless, McLean initiated the retreat, despite the protests of several company commanders, including Ryerson, who felt the unit should remain with the First NJV.[8]

Major Hatfield noted that "Colonel McLean showed the white feather and swore that he was not going to have his men killed. So he wheeled his regiment about and started back towards Vienna." It was actually worse than Montgomery and Hatfield intimated. After McLean about-faced his regiment, he disappeared, allegedly to seek further orders, much to the disgust of his junior officers. Lieutenant Colonel Isaac Tucker was left to guide the column to safety. Ryerson believed that his commander was a coward, and that Tucker was not much better. Even Major Samuel Buck left the column to ride to Vienna to order the regiment's two remaining companies to retreat. He too, then turned and galloped off toward Washington.

Realizing that he could not do much about the Second NJV's missing companies, Montgomery marched the seven companies of the First NJV through Centreville and formed them into a line of battle on a hill beyond the town. Here Montgomery and his green troops awaited the victorious horde. Lieutenant Colonel McAllister recalled that "we prepared for battle, expecting every minute to have an attack. We waited in silence." Compounding the men's dread were the moans and screams coming from a nearby church, filled with wounded men. Feeling uncomfortable about his isolated position, Montgomery rode back to McDowell's headquarters, only to find them deserted.[9]

Montgomery now rode about the town looking for other organized Federal units. He soon found the Eighth and Twenty-ninth New York of Colonel Louis Blenker's Brigade. Here began the pettiness that seems to accompany all wars. For several weeks after this affair, the two units bickered over who had the "honor" to be the last to leave Centreville. Colonel Blenker reported that he was ordered by McDowell at about midnight to begin his retreat. Montgomery claimed that he extended his line to the right, where he expected the enemy attack, but then realized the folly of remaining in this isolated position, so he finally ordered his men to pull back to safety at about 2:00 A.M. on July 22. So fearful were the officers that the enemy was nearby that the orders were whispered to the troops. The men marched all night back to Fairfax Court House, and then spying Major Henry Hunt's Second U.S. Artillery, Battery M, accompanied it to Arlington Heights, which it reached about noon. A drenching rain hit the area during the long march, turning the road muddy, which added to the men's misery. According to Major Hatfield, his men had marched forty miles "without sleep or rest, and no refreshments except dry bread and water." He was on his horse for thirty hours, and at times became so tired that he laid his head on the neck of his mount and fell asleep.

The march finally ended at Fort Albany, southwest of Washington, in Virginia, where the men encountered the Third NJV.

The First NJV arrived without its surgeon, Edward Taylor. Although every pew and aisle in the old stone church at Centreville was filled with wounded Federal soldiers, only a young man from Massachusetts who had worked in a drugstore before the war tried to minister to them. Realizing how desperately his services were needed, Taylor immediately pitched in to help. As the seven companies were preparing to depart, Taylor approached McAllister and said, "Colonel, will you let me stay with the sick and wounded? All of the other surgeons have left. I can't think of leaving them here to die." McAllister did not like the idea, as he knew that Taylor would be captured and the regiment deprived of his assistance when needed most. Rather than denying the request, McAllister sent Taylor to see Colonel Montgomery, who approved it. McAllister was correct—Taylor was captured by the enemy, but was paroled three weeks later and returned to the regiment.[10]

Although the Third NJV did not play a role in the battle, it did march from Burke's Station toward Bull Run that morning. Realizing the futility of the march, Colonel Taylor turned his men around and marched back to Alexandria, reaching there at about 10:00 that night. "This was haled [*sic*] with a frown by every man. Almost all of us was willing to stay till we were attacked . . . but we had to obay [*sic*]," wrote John Perdick to his family. As the regiment had marched off toward Bull Run, Taylor had left a twenty-seven-man detachment behind at Burke's Station to guard the ammunition. Despite the disorganized mass of the army storming by, Lieutenant E. Burd Grubb refused to depart until he received orders to do so from his commander. When these arrived, Grubb and his men destroyed thirty thousand rounds of ammunition rather than allow them to fall into the enemy's hands.

While the center of the three regiments' activities after Bull Run were at Fort Albany, the right wing of the First NJV was sent to Arlington Mills, about a mile closer to Washington, where it replaced a three-month regiment that was on its way home. The men called this Camp Princeton. While the higher authorities believed that it was superior to Fort Albany, McAllister did not agree, fearing the spread of "fever and ague." But the first order of business was, in McAllister's words, to get "this dirty, filthy camp cleaned up." The men spent considerable time resting after their difficult exertions.[11]

There was still the matter of Colonel McLean's actions during the march. According to McAllister, McLean rode directly to Willard's Hotel in Washington while his men were still marching back to their camps. "Everybody has become perfectly disgusted with him," noted McAllister. McLean's officers were among the colonel's greatest detractors, but he still had the support of the enlisted men.

McAllister accurately predicted the future to his wife on July 26, 1861—"I don't think Washington will be attacked at all. Little will be done on either side until fall, when our army will be swelled to a tremendous size and will be well-drilled. Then we will take up our line of march and see Centreville again." Major General George McClellan, fresh from his victories in what is now West Virginia, assumed command of the army on August 15, 1861, and immediately began building it into a magnificent fighting force. However, McAllister could not have predicted that the army's commander was overly cautious and would not take the offensive until the spring of 1862. The daily masses of reinforcements pouring into Virginia from Washington relieved the men and swelled the army, making a Confederate attack on the capital less likely.[12]

The debacle at Bull Run had a profound impact on the North. Perhaps most importantly, it showed the folly of thinking that the rebellion could be put down after a short conflict. It also impacted the ardor of male civilians who had been clamoring to join the army, making recruiting activities more difficult. No one was more shaken than President Lincoln, who immediately ordered additional troops from each state. Governor Olden received his request, dated July 29, 1861, for five additional regiments, "if tendered within a reasonable time." The letter from Secretary of War Simon Cameron indicated an uncharacteristic urgency—"I trust you will lose no time in equipping and forwarding these regiments, as the Government needs them at the earliest moment."

After consulting with his aides, Olden responded on August 3, 1861: "The State of New Jersey will furnish, equip, and forward as soon as possible five additional regiments of infantry, to serve during the war, in accordance with the request of the President and your instructions. The regiments will be reported separately as each is equipped and ready to move." The units formed during this period were the Fourth through Eighth New Jersey Volunteers. The Fourth would be incorporated into the future First New Jersey Brigade.[13]

The August 2, 1861, issue of the local New Jersey newspapers announced the opportunity to its readers and summarized General Order #15, which stated that preference would be given to men who had served in now-mustered out three-month militia regiments. Further, each of these "veterans" was entitled to a bounty of $40. To further entice interest, the readers were informed that each man would receive $100 when he was mustered out after the additional three years of service. The monthly pay for each unmarried volunteer was raised by $4 to $15 per month, and married men, and those with widowed mothers, received an additional $6 to help their families left behind. The latter caused great anguish to the New Jersey men who had enlisted in New York or Pennsylvania units, as they would not be entitled to this compensation. Hoping to ease the process, Trenton indicated that any company enlisting en masse would be permitted to retain its officers, "if adjudged qualified by a Board of Examiners appointed by the Governor."

Unlike the first of New Jersey's three-year volunteer regiments, which each mustered just over a thousand men, these regiments had trouble filling their ranks and each contained about nine hundred men. When the Fourth NJV was mustered into Federal service on August 19, 1861, by Captain Alfred Torbert and Captain David B. McKibbin, it contained 38 officers and 871 noncommissioned offices and men, for a total of 909. Colonel James Hervey Simpson, an engineer with the regular army, was placed in command of the regiment.[14]

Believing that the three original three-year regiments were not to be broken up, the July 18, 1861, edition of the *Somerset Messenger* speculated on the future commander of the brigade. Among the candidates mentioned were Philip Kearny, "highly complimented for his gallant conduct," wrote the paper, but it pointed out, "there are however objections to this candidate, and for ourself, would rather not see him appointed." The paper thought more highly of Robert Stockton, adjutant general of New Jersey, calling him a "young man of decided ability and well booked up in the routine of military duty and the theory of military tactics, with courage enough to face a battery or charge upon a battalion if needs be. . . . His administrative ability fits him for the position." The paper also liked General Theodore Runyon, commander of the New Jersey Militia Brigade in Virginia. "He will make a good officer," the paper predicted. The paper also thought that Colonel William Montgomery "would make an excellent Brigadier," and would be the compromise choice.

Back in Virginia, the three regiments had a dress parade on August 4, 1861. At its conclusion, the men were read General Order #4, which formed the First New Jersey Brigade. The brigade was initially composed of the First, Second, and Third NJV, Battery G of the Second U.S. Artillery, and Company G of the Second U.S. Cavalry. The men also learned that their new commander was Brigadier General Philip Kearny. Kearny was already a legend. Having had inherited a million dollars soon after graduating from Columbia University's law school, Kearny had been able to pursue his first love—the military. He served with the First U.S. Dragoons in the Mexican War, where he lost his left arm at the Battle of Churubusco. With the war won, Kearny resigned from the army and settled down on his New Jersey estate. Still craving an active military life, Kearny ventured to France, where he joined Napoleon III's army. He got his share of action, holding his horse's reins in his clenched teeth while swinging his sword with his remaining arm. Contemporaries described him as "all flame and color and ardor, with a slim, twisted streak of genius in him" and said that he "went under fire as on parade, with a smile on his lips." He was also a strict disciplinarian, "making no exceptions, accepting no excuses." General Winfield Scott, who held so much power during the early part of the Civil War, called Kearny "the bravest soldier I ever saw and a perfect soldier." With the outbreak of the Civil War, Kearny returned to the United States and was given the rank of brigadier general and the First New Jersey Brigade. The Jerseymen were most fortunate to have a commander with extensive battlefield experience. While this would serve them well, it was his training as a leader off the battlefield that would cause the unit to become a first-rate fighting force.[15]

The brigade moved west and established a new camp near Munson's Hill on August 5. It was called Camp Edgehill or Camp Advance, because of its proximity to the enemy. Major Hatfield of the First NJV noted in his diary, "this time we will be in the advance, instead of the reserve, and perhaps ere long we will smell gunpowder." The march to their new camp was a difficult one, beginning at 10:00 A.M. and ending at dusk. Many men had trouble keeping up. The brigade's historian recalled that the men "straggled along . . . some on one side of the road, some on the other, singly and in squads, muskets carried as most convenient, some of them decorated with various delicacies—pretzels, sausages and other things dear to a soldier's heart."

As the men "marched" to their new camp they spied a peach orchard, and many broke ranks and attacked the trees. General Kearny, who had taken a large house nearby as his headquarters, closely watched his new command from his piazza. He observed many men breaking off tree limbs while trying to get at the half-ripened peaches. Then looking down the road and seeing the nonchalant approach of the rest of the brigade, Kearny exploded and sent a torrent of oaths at the men. He later called the men his "damn band of thieves." Kearny was dressed "like an old farmer," so the men did not know who he was, and responded in kind. This only made Kearny angrier. Finally seeing a junior officer casually carrying his sheathed sword by the tip of the scabbard, Kearny glared at him and shouted, "Who the ____ ____ ____ are you?" The lieutenant calmly told him, and then asked who he was. Kearny again exploded, yelling, "I am General Kearny, commanding this Brigade of ____." The unfazed young officer merely said, "General Kearny, I am glad to make your acquaintance and wish to introduce to you the commissioned officers of the First New Jersey Regiment." Piercing them with his look, Kearny replied, "Lieutenant, you and these commissioned officers go to your quarters and consider yourself under arrest." The officers complied with the order, but requested a meeting with their new commanding officer at his earliest convenience. Kearny also sharply reprimanded a First NJV sergeant who ignored him and then yelled, "Who the hell are you." He quickly yelled, "I am General Phil Kearny, you damned thieving Jersey scoundrel, you . . . get in the ranks or I will have you shot."[16]

Realizing that the officers would be vital in whipping the brigade into shape, Kearny essentially declared war on them to make them effective. "Kearny made it very plain that he was in command, and would have [them impose] discipline or [have their] heads," noted Charles Hopkins of the First NJV. McAllister was among those arrested, but he consoled his wife on September 16, writing, "as to my character being injured by Kearny's arresting me, that is all moonshine—nothing to it. He is arresting officers every few days." Kearny was still at it two weeks later, for McAllister wrote to his wife on October 1, "Lieutenant Col. Tucker is under arrest by Kearny. I condemn Kearny for doing it. . . . Kearny will soon have all of our officers under arrest. Some are always in that fix."

Kearny vented his frustrations in a letter to a New Jersey politician. "The worst of a volunteer command is the unmitigated indifference of the officers to their men." He was also frustrated by their "absolute non comprehension of the simplest military axioms," and felt that volunteer officers often shirked their duties and too often played favorites. Kearny would have none of this, so he arrested the officers as their indiscretions came to his attention. While the officers had misgivings about their new commanding officer, Henry Callan, one of his orderlies, understood him well. "The Gen. is pretty easy to get along with if you only mind your own business and obey orders. He is busy all the time sending orders, listening to reports, etc. He does more with his one arm than most of his officers ever thought of doing with two. If any one neglects a duty he will give him the full extent of the law but if he deserves praise he will get it. Altogether I am very well satisfied with him."[17]

The close proximity to the enemy caused the men to be roused almost every night when the still inexperienced sentries sounded the alarm. There were also exciting times during the day. For example, a company of the Third NJV coming back to camp after scouting the area encountered four Confederate cavalrymen reclining by a fence. Opening fire, the Jerseymen watched the enemy horsemen jump on their horses and speed away, but at least one of them was wounded. Then another group of thirty enemy cavalry emerged from nearby woods and, seeing the Jerseymen, quickly galloped to safety.

The brigade moved again on August 13, this time only a mile, to Alexandria's Episcopal Theological Seminary. The men immediately took to their new surroundings, which they called Camp St. John. They appreciated its abundance of water, beautiful grounds, and spacious buildings. It also provided fine views of the Potomac River and Washington.[18]

The men could tell that they now had an experienced brigade commander. One of Kearny's first actions was to lay out the camp. "The regiments were separated by short intervals. The company tents were placed in straight rows, leaving spaces between for company streets. Another space was left between the ends of rows of the tents and the line officers' quarters, and still another beyond for the field and staff officers," noted the brigade's historian. The men also spent more time drilling, policing their camps, and on Sundays undergoing a thorough inspection. In addition to inspecting the men's weapons, clothing, and accouterments, the inspectors noted the men's cleanliness. This became a priority for Kearny when he realized that most of the men were infested with lice and other vermin. Kearny personally inspected the men at times. "Lieutenant, there's a louse on the breast of your coat," Kearny said in a harsh tone. The young officer saluted and replied, "General, there's one on your collar." Continuing down the line, Kearny looked down at a soldier's shoes and bellowed, "What do you mean by coming to inspection with your toes polished and heels muddy?" The man replied, "General, you told us a good soldier never looks behind." Kearny also insisted that every uniform fit correctly, and the regimental tailors repaired those that did not.

Although they initially grumbled, most of the men quickly learned to appreciate Kearny's experience, abilities, and generosity. John Perdick of the Third NJV noted, "our Colonel [Taylor] is the Devil. He is not fit to command a lot of dogs, much less much, but we have a General now and he will make a few changes in camp. . . . He is a good man I think and knows his business." Isaac Clark of the same regiment agreed. "We got a good general. He often goes in [to the] hospittle [*sic*] and gives the women fifty dollars for to get things for the sick." It took longer for the men of the First NJV to warm to their new commander as he had called them "a set of thieves" after several of them broke into a private home, robbing it and insulting the women living there. Orderly Henry Callan tried to reassure his family by writing, "he looks out for the comfort of his men before his own—he is strict but not more so than is needed and if a man does his duty he gets credit for it and if he neglects any duty he gets credit for that too but in a little different manner from what he expected."[19]

Lack of supplies continued to plague the army. Captain Henry Ryerson of the Second NJV was disgusted with the government's inability to furnish shoes to twenty men in his company, who therefore had to be confined to camp. Kearny, however, was not as limited, and used much of his own wealth to help equip, clothe, and ensure that his men were ready for the rigors of war. According to one contemporary, "his talents as an organizer, his fervid enthusiasm for his profession, his close study of the art of war, his intuitive perception of character, his strategic genius, his generosity and lavish expenditure of his large wealth . . . from the outset, distinguished his career. In a little while his brigade was confessedly the best disciplined in the army." Charles Hopkins noted that "from a dirty unshaven, long-haired, misfit clothed mob we were now to have someone to make us over into disciplined, well trained, well fed, well dressed soldiers." Although the men appreciated what Kearny was trying to do, most grumbled about how hard they were being worked. Hopkins recalled that "some swore, some prayed—not very reverently— to be delivered from the thralldom of Phil Kearny." However, on August 21, a newspaper could proclaim "the troubles of this Regiment [Second NJV] are being gradually overcome, under the discipline of Gen. Kearney [*sic*]."

The brigade was about to become about 25 percent larger, as the Fourth NJV broke camp in Trenton and journeyed south. The regiment was joined by Captain William Hexamer's Battery A of the First New Jersey Artillery. The journey to Washington began on August 19, when the men entered railroad cars bound for Philadelphia. Once in the City of Brotherly Love, the men marched to the Cooper Shop Volunteer Refreshment Saloon where hearty hot food awaited them. Cheering citizens lined the streets waving handkerchiefs and flags. A problem arose when the men reached the saloon and tried to stack their muskets—something they had never undertaken before. "A sorry old mess we made of it," noted Frank Gaul. Each company visited the washrooms, and then supper was served at 5:30 P.M. The men retrieved their weapons two hours later and reformed their column. Before moving out, Colonel James Simpson read the men an account of how the Sixth Massachusetts had been attacked as it marched through Baltimore several months before. The men were now ordered to load their guns, but not cap them. The men boarded railroad cars drawn by teams of horses. A locomotive was attached after the train was pulled across the Schuylkill River, and then it was on to Baltimore. Detraining, the men recalled their officers' admonishments to keep together and not straggle. There was little need to worry, because it was 3:00 A.M. and the streets were empty. Marching through the quiet city without incident, the men boarded trains for the final leg of the journey to Washington. There was only one occurrence that relieved the monotony of the trip—one of the soldiers went to sleep on the steps of a car and fell out of the train, but he was able to regain his composure and equipment fast enough to jump back on the slow-moving transport, much to the merriment of his comrades.[20]

The men reached Washington at 10:30 A.M. on August 21, where they ate and rested. Back in column again by 4:00 P.M., the regiment marched through the city, crossed into Virginia, and joined the rest of the First New Jersey Brigade at the seminary at about 9:30 P.M. From the window of his hospital ward, a sick Wallace Struble watched the Fourth NJV arrive. "They are a hard looking set. I think New Jersey is very near played out, the First Regiment takes them all down in every thing, the best drilled, and better officers," he noted.

Colonel William Montgomery's promotion to the rank of brigadier general was announced on August 24, 1861. Montgomery, whose commission was backdated to May 17, became the military governor of Alexandria. However, he lingered for at least three days as commander of the First NJV because of his anxiety for the safety of the regiment. This is odd, given the fact that Lieutenant Colonel McAllister, who had commanded the regiment frequently in Montgomery's absence, was in camp. This may have suggested Montgomery's true feelings about his subordinate's abilities or his ambivalence about his new role. General Kearny was happy to see Montgomery go, noting in a letter dated August 29, 1861, "I doubt if he was ever good, but he is certain now as complete as an old woman, as an old maid."[21]

Speculation grew over who would lead the First NJV. As second in command, McAllister naturally assumed that he would receive the post, but he bitterly wrote home on September 10 that twenty-eight-year-old Alfred T. A. Torbert of the U.S. Army would get the command. "I have been treated badly in this manner," McAllister steamed, and he considered resigning from the army. He later wrote that it would all depend upon how he was treated by the "young Colonel." McAllister could not deny Torbert's credentials. A West Point graduate, he had seen active service against the Seminoles.

Kearny desperately wanted a steady hand to lead the regiment, which he considered "the worst as to men and officers that I have yet met among the volunteers." He spent additional time with the regiment and reported, "with much care [it is] becoming healthier, and I hope to bring it to order." He hoped that Torbert would be the officer to whip it into shape.[22]

Although initially upset with Torbert's appointment, McAllister came to respect him, calling him the best drill officer he had ever seen. To the enlisted men, Torbert was gentlemanly, handsome, a strict disciplinarian, and a martinet while on duty. Edward Hollinger noted that, "it does one good to hear Col. Torbert give orders, his low ringing voice echoes over the field like a brass trumpet, and the men and officers feel more alacrity and cheerfulness when commanded by such a man."

Kearny also had problems with the Second NJV, and these disputes often found their way into the local newspapers. For example, the *Paterson Daily Guardian* noted that "all the difficulties which have heretofore existed within the organization, have been healed. It was generally believed that when McLean had been taken from the jovial bar rooms about Washington, the discipline of the Second would improve. Not that it is to be inferred from this that Gen. McLean is a bummer . . . but his love of jovial society and his fondness for the chance of telling good stories while in the immediate reach of Washington, kept him away from his command most of the time, and introduced a lack of discipline, which, whilst it made him popular with the mass of his troops who like the life of inertia." The paper also announced that a correspondent from the *Trenton True Democrat* was imprisoned for printing the truth about the regiment.[23]

Despite the problems with its leadership, Kearny respected the Second NJV's enlisted men. "It is a most noble Regiment—altogether the finest as to its companies." He also respected the Third NJV, but knew that "it has been altogether made by its noble Colonel [Taylor]." Kearny admitted that he did not know enough about the Fourth NJV to judge it, but called Colonel Simpson "too old, too slow, and too fussy to ever have it as it ought to be— nor do I think much of the major [William Hatch]—he has been ruined by having been previously in a bad Regiment."

Many Jerseymen became sick during the middle part of August and the early part of September. Chills and fever were the most frequent symptoms, filling the hospitals and forcing Kearny to designate additional hospital space in the seminary. Most of the men recovered, but some succumbed to their illness, which was probably typhoid fever. Among the first to die was musician Daniel Brower of the First NJV, who departed on September 6. General Kearny, sickly all of his life, also spent long periods of the time indisposed with a variety of maladies.[24]

The men could easily see the enemy soldiers diligently throwing up entrenchments "under our very nose," and most anticipated that it would be but a matter of time before they were called out to drive them away. The Jerseymen also spent considerable time augmenting their own defenses. According to Charles Reid of the First NJV, the men spent about six hours a day building Fort Taylor, later called Fort Worth, and a long line of breastworks when not on picket duty. The fort, which was located on the Little River Turnpike, about three miles northeast of Alexandria, was constructed with heavy timbers surrounded by heaps of earth that could resist even the heaviest artillery shells. Trees growing in front of the fort were cut at chest high, and the trunks left where they fell, to retard an enemy attack. All brush around the fort was also removed to prevent undetected enemy movements. Kearny was in so much of a hurry to finish the fort that he had twelve hundred men working on it in six hundred–man shifts. The men worked seven days a week and were often given two rations of whiskey "to make them work well." The men also learned more about the art of being a soldier during this period. One soldier from the Third NJV called his camp a "second home" and noted, "all of us enjoy ourselves very much. . . . We think we are perfect in military life." They were less happy about the frequent drills, which McAllister called "the hardest kind of style—men carrying their knapsacks to prepare them for long marches." Kearny knew what was ahead for his men and he prepared them for the challenge.

The period between supper and tattoo, when the men turned in for the night, was usually a most interesting time. According to Robert McCreight, "sometimes we sing songs and then we have a speech on women's rights, and then we have a sensation[al] speech about our country, and then we have a regular theater spouting. Then we have a political speech about President Lincoln." Because the Newark newspapers reached camp less than a day old, the men often discussed and debated war-related events and personalities.[25]

Kearny created an elite "light battalion" soon after he assumed command, detaching two companies from each regiment and arming them with .58 caliber Springfield rifles. The men were overjoyed to get rid of their less accurate smooth-bored muskets, which also had shorter ranges. Lieutenant Colonel Isaac Tucker of the Second NJV commanded the unit, but it never quite lived up to Kearny's expectations because in his view Tucker constantly missed opportunities to engage and best the enemy.

Although no pitched battles were fought from the late summer through the late winter of 1862, the proximity of the enemy forced constant vigilance. Kearny used the situation to his advantage. Understanding the need to forge his men into soldiers who were unafraid of the enemy, Kearny continually launched patrols against them. Every twenty-four hours he sent out four companies from each regiment on picket duty near Camp Advance with orders to attack any enemy encountered. Sometimes entire regiments were sent out on patrol. Kearny's aggressiveness caused the loss of several men as early as late August. The enemy reciprocated in kind, launching attacks on Kearny's pickets in October.[26]

This aggressiveness is illustrated by an event occurring during the last week in August, when Kearny sent out the entire First NJV on picket duty, halting it at the junction of Seminary and Leesburg roads. The unit spent several days here waiting to be attacked. The Rebels did not take the bait, but the unit was rushed to Bailey's Cross Roads, where some New York pickets had been driven in by the enemy. The light battalion was also in the vicinity, and its men were ordered to capture some Confederate cavalrymen in the area. Seeing enemy cavalry, one of the companies from the First NJV advanced to a fence, but then "turned and ran like sheep with their bayonets fixed on us and the other companies. The captain and the first sargeant [*sic*] was the only ones stood out of the whole company," wrote Robert McCreight to his brother.

Accompanied by two cannon and about forty cavalrymen, the First NJV formed into line of battle and waited. It rained constantly during the next three days. The men stayed relatively dry in makeshift huts made from bushes, except when they were periodically ordered out to form line of battle. The men were most miserable during the cold nights, as they were not permitted to build fires, lest the enemy pinpoint their location.[27]

A story dated September 2, 1861, in the *Trenton State Gazette and Republican* began with the following lines: "The Third N. J. Regiment were [*sic*] thrown into quite an excitement on Saturday morning by the return of a small scouting party with two dead and four wounded of their own men." Intent on putting an end to the continual harassment of his pickets along Little River Turnpike by Confederate pickets and sharpshooters, Colonel Taylor took forty volunteers from two of his companies toward Cloud's Mills on August 31. Using the woods to mask his men, Taylor hoped to circle around and capture some of the enemy troops who had been troublesome to his pickets. The newspaper account noted that while Taylor's men crossed a cornfield "all of a sudden a whole company opened fire on them," hitting three of his men in their initial volleys. Since the enemy could not be seen, Taylor wisely pulled his remaining men back to safety. The *Somerset Messenger* reported that "the band of the 3d Regiment played the solemn march of the dead behind the hearse which bore them away to Alexandria. . . . The hearse was guarded by eight of the Company to which the deceased belonged, while behind marched a platoon with their arms reversed, and the Company followed without arms." According to Major Hatfield of the First NJV, Taylor's mission was overly rash, as he had been warned that large bodies of Confederates were in the area.

Boredom began setting in as most of the men remained in camp. Oscar Westlake considered his Third NJV in reserve. "They call this a post of Honor but our Boys had Rather go in and have a good fight—they are getting tired of laying around and having nothing to do." Most of the men hoped that the Rebels would attack them, as they believed their position to be almost impregnable. Westlake was surprised to see that many African Americans were doing picket duty and other activities on the enemy side. He wanted to shoot them, as "I don't believe in fighting Niggers."[28]

General Kearny created quite a stir on September 26 when he caused the Confederates to vacate Munson's Hill. The hill had served as the headquarters of General Jeb Stuart and his Rebel cavalry, and was often the jumping-off point for attacks on the Federal line. Although he did not think he had the manpower to take the hill, Kearny decided to feign a full-scale attack. The four regiments left camp on September 24 and quietly marched toward the hill. On the skirmish line, Captain William Siddon's Company B of the Fourth NJV encountered the enemy and forced them to withdraw up the hill to the fort. Siddon's men, with the rest of the brigade advancing behind them, entered the fort, which they found abandoned. McAllister complained that "night came. We had no dinner and no blankets, as we had not intended to remain after dark . . . it was a queer move, for it was not intended to advance our lines. But the enemy heard we were moving our whole force and commenced a retreat." The men were not impressed with the poorly constructed fort, which contained Quaker guns—tree trunks painted black to resemble cannon barrels.

Further loss of life occurred in October. As brigade field officer of the day on October 12, McAllister heard his picket line firing shots, and rushing over, learned that the Third NJV spied the enemy. Looking through his field glasses, McAllister could see only Federal troops belonging to the Sixty-eighth New York. The Jerseymen apparently killed and wounded a number of New Yorkers, causing McAllister to confide in his wife the next day, "I really fear that the deadly fire was from our own men. But I have not said so publicly." A Second NJV picket post along the Little River Turnpike was boldly attacked by twenty Confederate cavalrymen on October 15. The six Jerseyans opened fire, emptying several saddles before rushing to the safety of the rear. The

Rebels surrounded Private Jordan Silvers, who shot one and was in the process of pulling out his bayonet to deal with the others when he was shot and killed. Three days later, Sergeant-Major Thomas Bonney of the Fourth NJV was killed on the picket line when he either did not hear the order to halt or ignored it and was killed by one of his own men.[29]

The four regiments had marched to war without flags. This changed during the middle of September–early October. The *Somerset Messenger* on September 26, 1861, reported that the First NJV received a stand of colors on September 15. The Third NJV received its colors, along with the Fifth NJV, on October 4 while President Lincoln and a number of cabinet officers and other officials watched. Drawn up in line of battle, the Third NJV heard a presentation by Joseph Bradley of Newark, who spoke for about twenty minutes "in a highly patriotic and appropriate manner," noted the Trenton *State Gazette and Republican.*

The intense drilling continued into November. McAllister noted that Kearny insisted on conducting daily brigade drills. Although McAllister had been in the army for five months, he confided to his wife that "there is so much to learn and so much to do." Regular army officer Colonel Torbert also pushed his First NJV very hard, causing considerable resentment among the men. The routine during this period was a dress parade at 8:00 A.M., and then companies drilled in the fine art of skirmishing from 10:30 A.M. through noon. Sometimes the men had target practice during this time slot. The midday meal was served at 1:00 P.M., and brigade drill went from 3:00 P.M. until sundown.[30]

Gambling was an ongoing problem. Because of little cash, the men often used I.O.U.s, and it was not unusual for a soldier's entire pay to go toward settling these debts. The officers worked diligently to stop gambling, as it injured morale. Colonel Simpson of the Fourth NJV made it known that he would take swift action against any of his commissioned and noncommissioned officers who permitted gambling. Thievery was another problem. Although thievery was found in all armies, Private Charles Reid was especially incensed when he saw his leaders doing it. He wrote home, "so much cheating goes on that one cannot believe it; the whole war is nothing but money. Our officers steal wherever they can; even our pastor allowed wheat to be stolen so that he would not have to pay for it." Some of the men formed an association in which "all Christians and those that like to associate with pious people [can associate] rather [than with] the wicked vile men," noted Jacob Wycoff of the First NJV.

The men became expert foragers. Their motivation ranged from providing supplements to their daily rations, breaking the tedium of camp life, and penalizing the citizens of the Confederacy. David Samson of the Second NJV wrote home that the men were living well off of the land. The citizens "have to suffer a scourge of which old Virginia will never recover."[31]

The men began settling into a life of little initiative. For example, Sergeant Oscar Westlake admitted that "this life is calculated to make any one lazy[,] if anything will[.] [W]e never do any thing of any account without orders to do it and then it is hard work to get us to do it without growling half an hour about whose turn it is." Drilling and most other activities were not conducted on Sundays. Instead, the men were encouraged to participate in religious services. Those who did not attend "have to stand two hours and a half and have the articles of war read to us which is not very pleasant." Most of the men got the message, according to Westlake, and attended the services instead.

The paymaster arrived again at the end of October, and McAllister informed his wife that it cost the Government $35,000 to pay a regiment for two months. The men were sending about half of their pay home and keeping the rest. The mail service was becoming more efficient by this time, and it took only two or three days for letters to arrive from home. The men lived and died by the mail call. David Samson wrote home that "I have watched the effect the receival [*sic*] of letters would have upon the countenance of comrades . . . that acts as an electric fluid to his countenance."[32]

New uniforms were distributed in November. In addition to their blouses and pants, the men received dress coats, which Robert McCreight described as "real dark blue and fit tight to the body, and a little tail that don't cover my backside and have little slits on it bound with blue. And we have brass epaulets on the shoulders."

Colder weather, combined with flimsy tents, caused considerable grumbling. Most men were able to compensate by sleeping in pairs, with two blankets over them. Under them was a board with a rubber blanket on top of it. By November, many of the tents had stoves in them. However, the tents were not stable and often toppled in high winds. During one such incident, John Judd of the Third NJV reported that the men did not care, as he estimated that half were drunk. The men could not complain about the food. They received meat rations four days out of seven and desiccated vegetables, which the men made into soup. The men were becoming veterans and realized it when a New York unit arrived. Oscar Westlake wrote that they are "as green as you please [and] we stuff them up with all the stories we can think about the secesh and it is fun to see them open their eyes."[33]

The Fourth NJV received orders to form into column in November and then marched to Washington. The Second NJV's band took its place at the head of the regiment as it marched through Washington to the Navy Yard, where the infantrymen received modern Springfield rifles. Colonel Simpson arranged for the music, as he was fond of saying, "Good music makes good soldiers."

November 20 was a special day for the army, as it conducted a grand review for General McClellan, President Lincoln, and some of his cabinet members. Perhaps not coincidentally, the review took place at Bailey's Cross Roads, which had been so hotly contested during the late summer and early fall. The First NJV and eight other companies of the brigade missed the review, as they were sent to the picket line near Edsall's Hill.[34]

Colonel George McLean never recovered from his actions during the Bull Run Campaign. Although his enlisted men generally supported him, his officers did not, nor did the men in the other New Jersey regiments. The *Somerset Messenger* reported on September 26, 1861, that McLean was given a leave by General Kearny a few days earlier, but it was revoked by division commander General William Franklin. McLean finally resigned in November, and Lieutenant Colonel Isaac Tucker was promoted and given command of the regiment. General Kearny did not believe that McLean was a coward as much as a man of limited mental abilities. Once, Kearny was furious when he learned that each of McLean's men had only ten rounds of ammunition when they left camp to engage the enemy. In another incident, McLean compromised Kearny's line of defenses by permitting a company to withdraw from the picket line without first telling his commanding officer.

Most of the men were homesick on Thanksgiving. Given a reprieve from drilling, many went to the seminary, where they played checkers and other games.[35]

Clashes between the two forces continued into December, with the level of aggressiveness actually increasing as the cold weather set in. Major Hatfield noted that the enemy was "getting quite saucy and impudent," but so too were the Federals. For example, Colonel Taylor ventured out again on December 4 to lay a trap for the Confederate cavalry who were tormenting the Federal pickets in the area. Taking fifty men from his Third NJV out beyond Springfield, he divided them into three groups. The first group was hidden along the road that Taylor knew would be used by the enemy. The other two were deployed farther down the road. When the band of cavalry appeared at midnight, they passed the first group without incident. Then the second group opened fire, emptying eight saddles. The rest of the Confederates scattered, and those turning back were met by a volley from the first group. Taylor lost one soldier killed and three wounded. Some officers ordered rifle pits and breastworks constructed to protect the pickets.

When not on picket duty the men remained close to camp, as the enemy constantly lurked nearby. Some could not resist temptation, however. Six men ventured out in mid-December to fill their knapsacks with ill-gotten goods. Spying geese in a pond, the men attacked. So intent were they on their mission that they did not hear the screams from the soldiers of the Second NJV on the picket line, and all six were gobbled up by Confederate cavalry who dashed in among them.[36]

The brigade turned out on December 13 to observe the execution of Private William Johnson of the First New York Cavalry, who had deserted from the army. He became the first of many men to meet this fate. Orderly Henry Callan noted that there was "no laughing or joking" among the men, but "they spoke in low tones or whispers." David Sampson wrote home that it was the first and "I hope it may long be the last" execution of a deserter.

With winter setting in, the men finally received new tents. Each company received five large Sibley tents, and the men quickly built furnaces between them, complete with tall chimneys of brick and mortar, for additional warmth. "We sleep comfortable in the tent," wrote Robert McCreight to his brother. As the temperatures continued falling, the men began surrounding their tents with logs, boards, and any other materials they could find to keep out the cold. Mud was slopped between the materials to hold them in place. The men also fashioned raised floors and bunks to avoid sleeping on the cold, hard ground. Some even added a stove or oven for additional warmth.[37]

The temperatures moderated, but then came the rains. Day after day it soaked the tents, men, and ground. The latter became waterlogged, and mud was found everywhere, halting drilling and making the days even more monotonous. Lieutenant Colonel McAllister noted that "it is raining almost every day and we have mud without limit. This prevents us from getting around . . . it is next to impossible to step outside the door without plunging into it ankle deep." News of a Federal victory at the Battle of Mill Springs in Kentucky on January 19, 1862, brought jubilation. "Such cheering and yelling you never heard. Some of the boys were hopping around as if they [were] crazy."

Discussions, reading, and games filled the days. Bibles were abundant in camp, and the men made good use of them. McAllister noted, "religious duties, feeling and interest are on the increase in our New Jersey regiments." After supper, the sounds of men singing filled the camps until about 9:00 P.M. Clubs, like the "Platform of Human Blood," formed to help the men while away their idle moments. "When we initiate a member, he gets two cracks on the backside with a thin piece of board from each of us. And then we sing a song. After that is done, we lay him down on a blanket and roll and pinch him for about five minutes. And then he becomes a member," wrote Robert McCreight to his brother. Some men even formed thespian corps that traveled from camp to camp providing plays. According to Josiah Brown of the Second NJV, "story telling for which of course there was much material and song filled up pleasantly many an otherwise idle hour."[38]

The brigade was ordered to picket near the recently destroyed Benton house in January. Each regiment provided five companies that remained in the area for an entire week. Therefore, each company was sent back every nine weeks. The men hated this duty because of the cold, wet conditions. They constructed thick pine "bush houses" that were dense enough to keep out the wind and allow fires to be built without the enemy seeing them. Mid-January brought the paymaster and jubilation to the men.

Snow in late January offered some lively entertainment when two of the regiments fought a sham battle, complete with skirmish line and line of battle. A colonel became so excited that he mounted his horse to lead his men's attack, only to be hit by hundreds of snowballs thrown by the opposing regiment, forcing him to beat a hasty retreat. "Two thousand men snow balling is a sight worth seeing," noted Henry Callan.[39]

The monotony of camp was broken on February 7, as "salutes [were] fired from all the forts & batteries. Great cheering," noted John Judd of the Third NJV when news of the fall of Fort Donelson reached them. A few weeks later, on February 22, the men celebrated George Washington's birthday. Each regiment formed a square, and its colonel stood in the middle reading Washington's farewell address to his troops. Batteries also fired throughout the day.

Charles Tripler, the Army of the Potomac's medical director, filed a report on February 6, 1862, that addressed the general health of the army. He noted that, as a general rule, the ratio of sick to healthy was inversely related to the military age of the unit. Most prevalent were measles and typhoid fever. The number sick in each regiment was fairly consistent. First NJV: strength = 1,000, total sick = 34, percent sick = 3.4; Second NJV: strength = 1,027, total sick = 33, percent sick = 3.2; Third NJV: strength = 1,040, total sick = 32, percent sick = 3.1; Fourth NJV: strength = 884, total sick = 28, percent sick = 3.2. The brigade's totals were: strength = 3,951, total sick = 127, percent sick = 3.2.

The monotonous days were about to end with a bold initiative developed by General McClellan. Within a relatively short time the men would finally experience battle.[40]

CHAPTER 3

On to Richmond!

With March came the return of winter weather. The once muddy and miserable ground now froze, much to the relief of the men. Drilling broke the monotony of camp life, and the men appreciated just being able to move easily around their camp. Rumors of pending battle intensified and the men of the First New Jersey Brigade savored the idea of seeing real action. "The Boys are not much pleased at the Prospect of their [*sic*] being a fight close by and our not having a hand in . . . just the same way [as] at the other Battle of Bull Run," wrote Oscar Westlake of the Third NJV.

During the third week of the prior month, General Joseph Johnston, commander of the Confederate army in front of Washington, met with President Jefferson Davis and his cabinet. Concerned that General McClellan would launch an offensive against Richmond once the weather moderated, Johnston told the gathering that his forty-two thousand troops were too dispersed to be effective. He advocated pulling back to better defensive ground closer to Richmond. The problem, however, was not in pulling back the men, it was the enormous task of moving the 3.24 million pounds of supplies accumulated at Manassas and the heavy guns needed to defend Richmond. News of movements of Federal troops on both of his flanks sped up the preparations. Pulling out as many supplies as he could, Johnston moved his troops out of Manassas, Centreville, and the surrounding areas during the weekend of March 8 and 9.[1]

Rumors of the enemy's pending withdrawal flew during the early days of March. The brigade was ordered out to guard railroad repair crews, but when Kearny received corroborating information on March 6, he put his men on the road toward Burke's Station the following day. Before leaving, each man received a shelter tent, six days' rations, and forty rounds of ammunition. The quartermaster carried thirty additional rounds for each man. After the monotony of camp, the men were ready. Major Hatfield recorded in his journal that "the sight of the enemy does not frighten our men. They seem eager for a fight." The column reached Burke's Station, a stop on the Orange and Alexandria Railroad, at about 1:00 A.M. on March 8 after a fourteen-mile march. The Fourth NJV, which had been guarding the baggage train, arrived just after daylight that day. It was a tough, tedious march. While his men rested, Kearny threw out scouts to gather information. Receiving word that the Rebels were indeed on the move, General Kearny ordered a reconnaissance in force toward Sangster's Station on the Orange and Alexandria Railroad. Kearny was much less cautious than McClellan, and if there was an opportunity, he was going to exploit it.

Kearny's first objective was Fairfax Court House, about four miles away. The brigade marched along the railroad, with the light battalion acting as both the advance guard and the flankers to prevent a surprise attack. Taylor's Third NJV led the advance, followed en echelon to its right by the Second and then the Fourth NJV. After reaching Fairfax Court House, the column pushed onto Sangster's Station. The Jerseymen could see scattered bands of Confederate pickets, but met no real resistance. Two companies of the First NJV under Major Hatfield were sent north to occupy Farr's Cross Roads on Braddock Road, while the rest of the regiment, under McAllister, remained at Burke's Station until ordered by General Kearny to join Hatfield at the crossroads. McAllister again commanded the regiment, as Colonel Torbert was debilitated with a bout of rheumatism. By evening, the brigade occupied Fairfax Court House, Sangster's Station, and Farr's Cross Roads.[2]

Bigger prizes, Centreville and Manassas, awaited them. Colonel Taylor ordered Lieutenant Harry Hidden to scout the area with thirteen men from his First New York Cavalry. Hidden was told he could attack any enemy force smaller than his. Leaving camp on the morning of March 9, the cavalrymen soon saw an enemy picket line approximating their numbers. Hidden ordered an attack, which drove the pickets before it. Out of nowhere about 150 enemy infantry materialized and surrounded the small band of cavalry. It was surrender or try to cut their way through, and the New Yorkers decided on the latter. Each horseman grabbed an enemy soldier and dashed for safety. The band suffered but one casualty—Lieutenant Hidden—who was killed by a musket ball.

No one knew what was happening in Centreville, so Lieutenant Colonel McAllister was ordered to send a small detachment there to reconnoiter on March 10. McAllister ordered Lieutenant W. H. Tantum and fourteen men from Company B toward Centreville. Cautiously approaching the town at about 11:30 A.M., the detachment found it empty of Confederate soldiers. The remainder of the company reached the town about forty-five minutes later. The brigade's historian proudly wrote, "Thus to the First Regiment of New Jersey Volunteers fell the honor of being the first infantry to occupy the field of Bull Run battle in this movement, as well as the last troops of any army to leave it, after that battle." The remaining nine companies of the First NJV began marching to the town between noon and 1:00 P.M. and arrived three hours later, with the Fourth NJV in support. McAllister wrote home that the "enemy's fortifications here are immense. Thousands of lives would have been lost in taking them." Robert McCreight disagreed, writing home on March 16, "when we came up to the forts they did not look so formidable. They were not built as good as ours." McCreight was, however, impressed with the enemy's winter quarters, which he considered far superior to their own. Oscar Westlake thought the Rebels were cowards "for they leave their very Stronghold and Run without even firing a Gun."[3]

While the First and Fourth NJV secured Centreville, the brigade's other two regiments continued their advance toward Manassas. Eight companies of Taylor's Third NJV led the column, which reached Union Mills late on March 10. They were closely followed by the Second NJV. The march continued through the night and ended at 4:00 A.M. on March 11, when the column reached Bull Run. The enemy had partially burned the bridge, so Taylor put his men to work repairing it for the next hour. Then it was on toward Manassas Junction, which the two regiments reached at 9:30 A.M. Taylor formed his regiment into line of battle and, with skirmishers in front and flankers on either side, entered the town. It was already abandoned, much to the relief of the men. After hoisting a U.S. flag up a flagpole, the men again took to the road, this time bound for Centreville, which they reached at sunset, reuniting with the rest of the brigade. The morning of April 12 found the brigade in motion again, this time headed for Fairfax Court House. The Second NJV led the march and entered the town with its band playing. The column began its trek back to its camp at Fort Worth during the early evening of March 14, arriving there at about 1:30 A.M. on March 15. The Jerseymen encountered General McClellan during this march and "cheer after cheer rent the air. The General took off his hat and smiled very pleasantly," noted Major Hatfield.

Although the campaign accomplished little, it broke the monotony, and it gave the men a taste of what lie ahead. Sergeant Westlake wrote home, "the Boys are all in the Best of Spirits at the thought of leaving and going where there is something to do—you must know that we are tired of doing nothing." Colonel Isaac Tucker of the Second NJV concluded his official report by stating that his men "returned [to camp] in good health and full of enthusiasm." Lieutenant Colonel McAllister chose to end his report by complimenting his senior officer—"permit me to say that General Kearny deserves a great deal of credit by this bold push towards the enemy lines, and by the energy and bravery thus displayed caused the enemy to leave in great haste, leaving many valuables behind them."[4]

McAllister was only partially correct. In actuality, General Johnston had fully planned to retreat well before Kearny began his movement, but McAllister was correct that the Confederates left a tremendous array of supplies behind. In his haste to withdraw, Johnston shipped as many supplies as he could, and then each regiment marched to the supply depot and the men helped themselves. The retreating troops tried to burn the rest, but plenty remained for the Federals to capture. Although McAllister was disappointed that his men bagged only one enemy soldier and one "Sesesh flag," they did secure "a large amount of ammunition and some flour."

There was one fatality during the operation, when Private Thomas Spriggs accidentally shot himself in the head as he was removing his musket from an arms stack. According to Colonel Tucker, "he expired in a few moments."[5]

Kearny had done a miraculous job of whipping his undisciplined and slovenly soldiers into an effective fighting unit. In time, the general's expectations became quite evident, causing a precipitous drop in the number of arrests compared with his early tenure as brigade commander. Tensions still arose at times, leading to more arrests. Such was the case in early April when Major Hatfield was arrested for disrespectful behavior toward Colonel Simpson during a brigade drill. According to McAllister, Simpson "is easily excited and gets very angry."

The men of the First, Second, and Third NJV replaced their old muskets with new rifled Springfields in late March and early April. Private Charles McCreight was excited about the new weapons because of their greater accuracy and ease of use. "Before . . . when we would fire three rounds out of them, they would get so hot they would almost burn your hand. . . . [They are a] light and handy piece and the boys like them first rate," he wrote home.[6]

This was a time of great excitement and anticipation, as the men could see the fruits of General McClellan's activities over the past few months. Their commander had spent considerable time planning an offensive against Richmond, one whose scope has been rarely matched in military history.

McClellan's plan involved transporting 121,500 men, 14,592 animals, 1,150 wagons, 44 artillery batteries with over 250 cannon, 74 ambulances, pontoon bridges, and tons of supplies aboard 389 steamers, barges, and schooners, sailing down the Chesapeake Bay to Fort Monroe at the tip of the peninsula, just seventy-five miles southeast of Richmond, and, with Johnston's army far to the north, capturing the capital without much difficulty.

Part of McClellan's plan involved the army's reorganization. The army, now called the Army of the Potomac, was divided into six corps, each composed of two or three divisions. Each division contained three brigades. Kearny's Brigade had the distinction of being designated the First Brigade, First Division, I Corps. General Irwin McDowell commanded the corps and General William Franklin the division.[7]

Every day, Kearny's men watched a steady stream of troops heading for Alexandria, where they embarked on the journey to Fort Monroe. As day followed day without orders to embark, the men became demoralized. Oscar Westlake wrote home, "I am beginning to get almost Discouraged and think we will never leave it but the Officers all say we will get of[f] soon."

Orders to pack up their belongings and prepare for a march excited the men. The march began at 1:30 P.M. on April 7, but it was *away* from Alexandria. Reaching Burke's Station on the Orange and Alexandria Railroad, the brigade boarded cars and headed for Bristoe Station, on a mission to divert the Confederates' attention from Alexandria. The train stopped periodically and the men hopped out to help repair the tracks and bridges destroyed during the Confederate retreat. Wallace Struble reported, "we cannot goe [sic] very fast for we have to repair up the railroad as we goe [sic] along [sic] that the Secessia [sic] tore up when they left Manassas." The train finally reached Bristoe Station at 9:30 P.M., where the men camped for the night. The next morning it was back on the trains, this time bound for Catlett's Station, which the brigade reached that day. A wintry mix of rain and snow turned the ground into a muddy quagmire, causing the brigade to remain in camp until the evening of April 11, when the column reformed and marched back to Bristoe Station, reaching there around midnight. Peter Goetschins noted that it was "one of the hardest times," as he had to lay in the three-inch deep mud for three days while it rained and snowed. "We laid down tired, supperless, and tentless in the open air," added McAllister. John Judd of the Third NJV recorded in his diary on April 10: "mud knee deep—gun covered with rust. Knapsacks & clothes wet through." Reveille sounded at 4:00 A.M. on April 12, and the Jerseymen marched to Fairfax Court House, reaching it about thirteen hours later. The men marched approximately forty-one miles during this short campaign.[8]

The men did not know it, but McDowell's I Corps was to be left behind to protect Washington. But McClellan desperately wanted additional troops and was able to pry Franklin's Division away from McDowell. Kearny's men reached Alexandria on April 13 and awaited transport vessels. Because the unit would finally see action, many men wanted to get to Alexandria for "recreational" purposes. Wallace Struble had a hard time performing guard duty during this period. "We lay so close too Alexandria that it is almost impossible too keep the soldiers in camp. When they get out they most all get drunk." Wallace noted that a soldier trying to get past the pickets on April 14 was shot and his leg was later amputated. "We have orders to shoot every man that attempts to run the guard," he noted.

An excited McAllister wrote to his wife at 4:00 A.M. on April 17, "we are on board the *Hero,* an old North River boat. We are much crowded." The Second NJV, along with General Kearny and his staff, embarked on the *Elm City,* the Third NJV scrambled aboard the *J. A. Warner,* and the Fourth NJV hopped onto the *Arrowsmith.* The small flotilla finally departed at 12:45 P.M. on Friday, April 18. Within half an hour, the men heard bands playing for their benefit as they steamed past Fort Washington, across from Mount Vernon. The Jerseymen responded with wild cheers. They could see each boat pulling three to six barges loaded with cannon, horses, and equipment behind it.[9]

Steaming down the Potomac River, the flotilla entered the Chesapeake Bay. The convoy reached the mouth of the York River at about 8:00 P.M. on April 19 and dropped anchor. To prevent grounding, the ships steamed south only during the daylight hours. The journey continued the next morning, and a short time later the ships reached the mouth of the Pequosin River. A storm hit the area that night, and continued for the next several days. The adverse weather, combined with the cramped conditions, made the men miserable. They could not complain about the food though—coffee and ham rations. The debarkation point at Cheeseman's Creek was approximately twelve miles north of Fort Monroe—close to the enemy, who had entrenched around Yorktown, just to the northwest. The sounds of artillery and the rattle of small arms fire could be heard in the distance.

The weather finally moderated on April 22 and the men disembarked and planted their feet on firm earth once again. The region yielded an abundance of oysters, clams, and crabs, which the men ate to their hearts' content. This was a welcome supplement to their regular fare, once off the boats, which consisted of a piece of raw meat that the men had to cook and eat with hardtack for breakfast, bean soup and cooked beef for dinner, and coffee and salt beef for supper. The men were using "shelter tents" now, which were six feet square pieces of canvas with regularly spaced buttons and button holes along the sides. Each man was also provided with a ridgepole and forked upright. When two men combined their equipment, they could make an inverted V-shaped tent; three could make a shelter with three sides enclosed. The tents were lightweight and portable, as opposed to the much larger Sibley tents that had to be transported by wagons and were cumbersome to erect.[10]

It was not totally heaven, for the sounds of artillery could be heard day and night. The enemy were entrenched at Yorktown, a mere six miles away, and it would take a bloody fight to eject them. The weather turned cold and wet, causing a number of men to become sick with measles and colds. Discipline was still a problem. For example, about half of the noncommissioned officers of the Third NJV decided to strike out on their own to see the countryside. When they returned they were slapped with three and a half hours of additional drill for being absent without leave.

A cautious commander, General McClellan decided not to launch a full-scale attack on the Confederate defenders at Yorktown until he brought up his siege guns. This gave General Johnston's army valuable time to get between McClellan and Richmond. McClellan was finally ready to begin the offensive on May 4, but he then learned that the enemy had withdrawn from Yorktown the day before.[11]

The men were ambivalent about the Confederate withdrawal. While they realized that any attack on the enemy's works would result in high casualties, they hoped that a decisive action could end the war. They were less ambivalent about the departure of General Kearny to command the Third Division in General Samuel Heintzelman's III Corps. This was not the first time that Kearny had been offered a division command—he had rejected an earlier offer because he wanted to combine the two New Jersey brigades into a new division. The men knew he had turned down an earlier offer, but they thought it was because he wanted to stay at their head. The loss of Kearny devastated them. Robert McCreight wrote to his brother, "I don't believe there was a [man] in the brigade that was not sorry when he left us, for he was to us more like a father."

Colonel George Taylor of the Third New Jersey was promoted to the rank of brigadier general and given command of the brigade; Lieutenant Colonel Henry W. Brown became a colonel and took over the regiment. Many men were not happy with Taylor's ascent. McAllister wrote home, "he is the most unpopular man or officer I know, and all hope that he will not be assigned [to lead] our brigade." Robert McCreight disagreed, writing home that the men supported Taylor's promotion.[12]

Realizing that he had missed a great opportunity to defeat the Confederate army, McClellan took the offensive once more. He again attempted a bold move—putting half of his army back onto transports and dropping them behind the retreating Confederates. Attacked in front and rear, the enemy would be forced to surrender.

McClellan decided that Franklin's fresh division would lead the offensive movement. Taylor's Brigade reembarked on the transports on May 4, but because it was difficult getting artillery aboard, the transports did not begin their movement up the York River until the next morning. The transports halted near Yorktown, permitting officers and men to inspect the Confederate fortifications. McAllister noted that they were much better constructed than the ones at Manassas and Centreville and "had they not evacuated, we would have lost a grate [*sic*] number of men." The sounds of battle to the north told the men that the Federal advance was clashing with the Confederate rearguard at Williamsburg. The convoy finally got under way on May 6, arriving near West Point at 4:00 P.M. that day. Gunboats threw shells into the woods, and seeing no response, General Franklin ordered his men off of the transports at Eltham's Landing. Taylor's Brigade was the second one off the boat, beginning at 9:30 P.M. It took virtually all night for the four regiments to disembark and march the half-mile to West Point. The night was a harrowing one, as continual picket firing proved that the enemy lurked nearby. Few got any real sleep that night.[13]

Franklin's thrust was about forty-eight hours too late. Instead of confronting the van of General Joe Johnston's army, he encountered the rearguard, composed of General Chase Whiting's Division, which was sent to distract Franklin while the rest of the Confederate army made its way to safety. Franklin wisely decided to wait until he was joined by the three other divisions still at Yorktown.

Learning that large numbers of Confederate infantry were in the area, Franklin had his men fell trees during the night and redouble their vigilance. He held a strong position with both flanks protected by creeks that prevented a Confederate turning movement. Franklin's men did not know it, but in front of them was one of the most aggressive fighters in the Confederate army. General John Hood, commanding a mixed brigade of Texans and Georgians, was ordered to merely "feel the enemy gently and fall back." Hood had his own four regiments and another six from other brigades. He responded to his orders by barreling into General John Newton's Brigade at 9:00 A.M. on May 7. To Newton's left were the Third and Fourth NJV of Taylor's Brigade, and behind them was Hexamer's Battery, supported by the First and Second NJV. Casualties walking and being carried to the rear in increasing numbers added to the Jerseymen's anxiety, as they had never been in a pitched fight before.[14]

Whooping and hollering, Hood's men threw the Federal skirmish line back on Newton's main body, and then pushed the Thirty-second New York and part of the Ninety-fifth Pennsylvania to the rear. General Franklin quickly responded by sending reinforcements to seal the breech. This included six companies from the First NJV and four from the Second NJV, all under the command of Lieutenant Colonel McAllister, who retained command of the former regiment because Colonel Torbert was officer of the day. The line held until 3:00 P.M., when Hood finally withdrew. McAllister recounted his experiences to his wife after the engagement. Never referring to the Second NJV, he noted that he advanced his entire regiment and, when he encountered the enemy, ordered his men to lie down to avoid taking casualties. Hearing the Federal order to charge, McAllister had his men on their feet and moving toward the enemy. Crossing a worm fence, McAllister drove the enemy before him. Wallace Struble proudly wrote after the battle, "our Colonel gave the command Charge. At them we went and the way they went was a sin. We run them through the woods over the ditches, and fences, with the bayonet so close to them that they did not dare stop to look around." Surprised to see that no other Federal troops had advanced, McAllister quickly walked back to the fence, where he encountered the commander of the Thirty-first New York, who told him that his orders were to remain behind the fence. McAllister quickly pulled his men back to the fence and awaited another attack, which never came.[15]

General Newton, who was in a good position to view the battle, complimented McAllister and his men, writing that they had "gained an advantageous position, which . . . they heroically maintained until the end of the action against greatly superior numbers of the enemy." The losses were light—three wounded in the First NJV. The men acquitted themselves well during this, the first serious action for the First Brigade.

Needing to determine the whereabouts of the enemy, Franklin threw Taylor's Brigade forward on the morning of May 8. "He performed his work well, though without an engagement, and occupied a position 2 miles in advance early next morning," Franklin noted. Thinking he saw enemy soldiers in the woods to the left, Taylor requested artillery support, and soon the gunboats were tossing solid shot into the area. Charles Harrison of the Second NJV noted that the shot "made a hole large enough to bury 20 men."[16]

The movement toward Richmond continued on May 9, when the column marched to New Kent Court House, about four miles from West Point. The brigade remained here until May 12, when it marched to the town of White House on the Pamunkey River with General George Stoneman's cavalry brigade. While the distance was relatively short, the spring rains had turned the roads into muddy quagmires, making movements difficult. The mud was knee deep in some places. The distance to Richmond melted each day—it was now less than twenty-five miles away. The men were in column again on May 13, when they marched to Slaterville and then to New Kent Court House. Stoneman finally allowed the infantry to return to their camps at White House on May 14. McAllister explained to his daughters that his brigade was following the enemy toward Richmond. "Our camp fires are in sight of each other. Where they camp one night, we camp the next." The men received a reprieve at White House, where they rested, washed their clothes and bodies, and prepared for the remainder of the campaign.

The brigade was back on the road at 5:00 A.M. on May 18, trudging to Tunstall's Station on the Richmond and York Railroad at 9:00 A.M. No one complained when ordered to pitch their tents and go into camp. They did not immediately know it, but the army was reorganized again on this day, and the brigade became the First Brigade of the First Division of the VI Corps. General William Franklin was given the corps and General Henry Slocum took his place as commander of the First Division. The men marched to Paysley's Farm the next day, where they spent the night, and then they marched to Cold Harbor on May 20. The brigade, along with the rest of the VI Corps, camped at Old Cold Harbor on May 21. During this march the men could see the devastation wrought by the Confederates, who burned their discarded materials rather than permit them to fall into Yankee hands. The brigade remained at Old Cold Harbor until May 25, when it was back on the road and marching toward Gaines' Mill on the Chickahominy River. It remained here for several days. Many men fell sick and all felt the misery of not being well supplied, as the ongoing rains made it all but impossible for wagon trains to make their way along the roads. The brigade was now about twelve miles from Richmond.[17]

Confederate gunners periodically trained their guns on the Federal camps. Such was the case on May 29, when sixty-nine shells rained down on the First New Jersey Brigade. Charles Harrison noted that only nineteen exploded and no one was injured. A shell passed through the hospital tent, which was filled with the sick.

Speculation about the Rebels' plans was rampant. Would they attack or simply abandon Richmond, which was now less than ten miles away from their positions? General Fitz John Porter's V Corps thoroughly defeated a small Confederate force defending Hanover Court House to their right on May 27.

Almost inexplicably, McClellan divided his army, separated by the Chickahominy River—the II, V, and VI Corps were north of the river; the III and IV Corps, making up the left of the army, were on the south side. Between the two sets of Federal units rushed the raging Chickahominy, swollen by the recent heavy rains. While a number of bridges crossed the river, most were old and rickety. General Johnston took advantage of the Federals' poor dispersion by attacking the two corps south of the Chickahominy on May 31 and June 1 in the Battle of Fair Oaks. The attacks were ultimately repelled with help from the II Corps, which was able to cross the turbulent river. Generals Fitz John Porter and William Franklin agreed that to cross it was "impracticable." While McClellan was not happy with their assessments, he did not order them to attempt it. Losses were heavy on both sides, and included General Johnston, who was wounded. President Jefferson Davis, who was on the battlefield, immediately elevated Robert E. Lee to army commander. The Federal VI Corps was merely a spectator to this intense battle.[18]

Slocum's Division marched three miles to Mechanicsville on June 6. The Jerseymen were now the right-most unit of the army, and they remained here for over a week. Less than five miles from Richmond, the men climbed cherry trees to see the Confederate capital's church spires. The brigade's campground was an old Confederate camp that had most recently been used by the Ninety-sixth Pennsylvania. The filth and lack of sanitary conditions of both groups disgusted the New Jerseyans. "The 96th Pennsylvania squatted down right on top of the Rebel dirt, a thing you won't get the 1st New Jersey to do," wrote McAllister. He noted that the Pennsylvanians had a large number of men on the sick rolls and that he could understand why. Picketing and bridge repair occupied most of the men's time, while Confederate batteries continued lobbing shells at the Federal troops, harassing them and inflicting some injuries. McAllister wrote home, "we often find them [shells] whizzing overhead." The men were chagrined to learn that many of the Confederate guns firing at them had been captured at Fair Oaks. Siege guns opened such an accurate fire on the camps at 5:00 P.M. on June 12 that the men had to quickly scatter. They returned after the guns fell silent and soon after received orders to move their camps to less exposed locations. The close proximity of the enemy also caused the men to be constantly on the alert, as a Confederate attack could be launched at any time. The stress mounted with each passing day, and so did the sick list, as dysentery and typhoid fever ravaged the regiments. Sickly Colonel Torbert of the First NJV fell ill, and during one stretch at least one Fourth NJV soldier was dying from illness each day.

The entire corps was on the march on June 19, when Franklin's men crossed the river and took up positions on the Fair Oaks battlefield. The brigade began its march at 7:00 A.M. and rested two hours at noon before crossing the river. The men were relieved to be reunited with the bulk of the army, as they expected an attack at any time. Most of the men toured the great battlefield and soberly examined the thousands of Federal graves marked by head— and foot—boards; the enemy were piled into common graves. A stench from the poorly buried dead permeated the area. Skirmishes and artillery fire escalated in frequency and intensity, and all knew that the decisive battle would be soon in coming.[19]

While McClellan was content to wait, General Robert E. Lee carefully crafted a plan to drive the enemy from the gates of Richmond. The plan was complicated. While his army would take on the front of McClellan's army, Stonewall Jackson's units arriving from the Shenandoah Valley would attack the Federal right and rear. However, the Seven Days battles did not begin with Lee's thrusts, but rather with McClellan's, who threw General Joseph Hooker's Division (III Corps) against the Confederates on June 25. Charge and countercharge marked the Battle of Oak Grove, but the Confederate line held. The New Jersey Brigade was in the third line and was not involved in the fight.

While four Federal corps were concentrated near Fair Oaks Station, Fitz John Porter's V Corps remained on the north side of the Chickahominy River, near Mechanicsville. An isolated corps was too tempting for Lee, who decided to destroy it on June 26. After waiting all day for Jackson's troops to appear, Lee could wait no longer and launched a desperate frontal attack against Porter's almost impregnable position. The Confederate losses were heavy, and none of the attacks were successful in driving Porter's men from their defenses.[20]

Although Porter wanted to hold his ground along Beaver Dam Creek, McClellan wisely ordered a retreat. It was too dangerous to try to cross the Chickahominy, so Porter retreated eastward. Arriving almost due north of the rest of the army, Porter carefully arranged his twenty-seven thousand men along Boatswain's Swamp near Gaines' Mill and waited for the enemy.

McClellan quickly put Slocum's Division in motion at about 8:45 A.M. to reinforce Porter, but then countermanded the orders, fearing that by moving troops he might encourage an enemy attack south of the river. The men trudged back to camp at about noon, no doubt grumbling about the ineptitude of their officers. General Taylor had a feeling that his men would be engaged that day, so he ordered his aide, Captain E. Burd Grubb, across the river to sketch the terrain.

Lee decided to attack Porter's new position, and as with the day before, his plan was to hit the Federal center while Stonewall Jackson found the enemy's right and rear. General A. P. Hill's Division, which had opened the bloody fight at Mechanicsville, again initiated the action. General Maxcy Gregg's Brigade attacked at 2:30 P.M., but was repulsed with heavy losses. A second brigade attacked and met the same fate. Hill's other brigades appeared and they too attacked the almost impregnable Federal line. By the time it was fully repulsed, Hill's Division had lost over two thousand men in this vicious fight.[21]

Porter did not know it at the time, but McClellan threw caution to the wind and ordered Slocum's Division across the river at Woodbury Bridge to reinforce the beleaguered V Corps. General Newton's Brigade crossed at about 2:30 P.M., and Taylor's and Bartlett's followed about a half-hour later. The First NJV had the honor of leading the brigade, followed by the Third, Fourth, and four companies of the Second (D, H, I, and K)—the remaining six companies (three hundred men) were on picket guard on the south side of the river. The march took about an hour, the latter part at a trot. This exhausted the men, as the day was hot and humid. Slocum's Division initially took position on Turkey Hill, with Newton's Brigade on the right of the line and Taylor's to its left near the Watt house at the center of the Federal line. Taylor quickly deployed his brigade in two lines in a clover field about five hundred yards from the front line at about 4:00 P.M. The Third and Fourth NJV fingered their muskets on the front line; the First and the four companies of the Second were behind them. Because of stray shots, Taylor ordered the men to lie down. They did not know that the four units would be fed into the battle piecemeal, from left to right, starting with the Third NJV and ending with the Second NJV.

The brigade initially supported Hexamer's Battery, but the men had barely settled into their position before Colonel Henry Brown was told to advance his Third NJV into the woods near Newton's line, where A. P. Hill's men were making their desperate thrusts. Swinging behind Newton's Brigade, the regiment took position behind the Ninety-fifth Pennsylvania. The latter

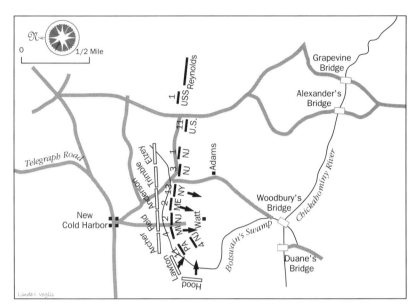

MAP 2. Battle of Gaines' Mill (June 27, 1862).

regiment had advanced and taken a murderous frontal and flank fire that mortally wounded two of its field officers and scores of its men. The remaining field officer saw the Third NJV behind him and ordered the remnants of his regiment to form behind it. The Third NJV was now in the front line, and looking to their right, the men could see some of Newton's Brigade, probably the Eighteenth New York, and the Eleventh U.S. of Sykes' Division. The Jerseymen initially encountered elements of General Lawrence Branch's North Carolina brigade, but the Third NJV held its ground.[22]

A gap in the line to the right of the Third NJV caused Taylor to receive orders to send the First NJV to its support, about a half hour later. Because Colonel Torbert was still unwell, McAllister led the First into what was essentially its first pitched battle. As the troops marched toward their position they passed a steady stream of wounded men. With only the four companies of the Second NJV in reserve (the Fourth NJV had already left—see below), Taylor decided to accompany the First NJV and take personal command of the two regiments. Wading across a waist-deep swamp, the men carefully picked their way along so they would not step on the large number of dead and wounded soldiers from Porter's Corps. McAllister's men finally reached the right of the Third NJV, where they were ordered to lie down behind one of Porter's regiments to avoid taking unnecessary casualties. When the regiment gave way, the Jerseymen stepped forward and fired at the enemy. McAllister tried to get his men to charge, but the undergrowth was just too thick, so he and his men were content to maintain their positions and blaze away at the enemy. Where available, the men used the shelter of trees. The First and Third were up against two Confederate brigades of Ewell's Division (Stonewall Jackson's Corps): Elzey's Brigade, now under Colonel James Walker, and General Isaac Trimble's Brigade. With Ewell's troops in front of them and to their right, and General James Archer's, General Charles Field's, and J. R. Anderson's brigades of Longstreet's Division to their left, the First and Third NJV were caught in a deadly crossfire and casualties mounted.

General Taylor proudly noted in his report that the "First Regiment . . . exposing themselves to the leaden hail of an often unseen foe, advancing with the Third Regiment, and stood steadily under a most galling fire until the close of the fighting." Taylor wrote that the Third NJV began giving ground when its ammunition was all but expended. The two regiments were placed in even more difficult straits when the Second Maine and Thirteenth New York to their left were forced to withdraw, exposing their left flank to the enemy. The troops on their right also withdrew, forcing the Jersey boys to retreat as fast as their feet could carry them.[23]

Captain Grubb of Taylor's staff recalled another reason for the forced withdraw of the First and Third NJV. The smoke was so thick that there was no more than twenty yards visibility. Lying down, the men continued blazing away at the unseen enemy. Taylor ordered his men to cease firing to let the smoke clear so he could ascertain the whereabouts of the enemy. As the smoke cleared, the men did not see any enemy soldiers, so many got up to stretch their cramped limbs. They did not realize that enemy soldiers occupied a sunken road in front of them. Grubb and Taylor both heard clear orders being given by enemy officers—"Aim" and then "Fire." "The volley that fell upon the brigade was the most withering I ever saw delivered, for the men were totally unprepared for it," noted Grubb. The regiments now "broke all to pieces," as the survivors headed quickly for the rear. Quickly mounting his horse, Taylor was finally able to rally his men about a quarter-mile in the rear by swinging his sword in the air.

While Taylor was gone, General Porter threw the four companies of the Second NJV forward to a belt of thick woods about five hundred yards to the left-front of their original position near Hexamer's guns to support the Fourth Michigan. Colonel Isaac Tucker purportedly said to another officer as he moved his small unit into position, "Things are rather hot in there, and I rather think some of us will never come out." Quickly pushing hay bales into position along the edge of the woods for protection, the outnumbered unit opened fire and held its own. However, the woods were so thick that the men did not notice that a hole had opened on their left. The enemy informed them of the fact when they opened a crossfire on them. Looking back, the men could see Federal troops, possibly the Fourth Michigan, rushing to the rear. One soldier recalled that the "balls whistled around me like hail stones." Sergeant Abram Paxton noted, "we had not fought over half an hour before the rebels flanked us right and left and they was coming up on the left of our company front, marching by the flank as close as I ever saw troops." Realizing that the position was now untenable, Colonel Tucker ordered the flagbearer to move to the rear—the signal to withdraw. A bullet thudded into Tucker as he gave the order. A number of men ran to help the colonel, and this attracted the enemy's attention, resulting in additional men going down. Tucker received another wound, this time mortal. Realizing that he had little time to live, Tucker insisted that his men leave him and run for safety.[24]

Major Henry Ryerson took command and led the Second NJV through the woods in what Captain Edwin Bishop called a "perfect storm of bullets." Reaching the top of a hill, Ryerson rallied his men into a line of battle. Sergeant Paxton was saddened to see that "we had no reserve to fall back on, they skedaddled before we got to them. I tell you it was a regular stampede." Looking around and seeing how few men he had to take on the growing horde of enemy troops, Ryerson wisely ordered a retreat to the next hill, where other Federal troops were assembling. The enemy closely followed, opening a deadly crossfire, which felled Major Ryerson and a number of his remaining men. To make matters worse, the Federal troops on the hill mistook them for the enemy and fired two volleys into them. The unit's flag attracted considerable attention. A Confederate lieutenant demanded the flag, but was shot down at point-blank range by Private Joseph Hodgkins. To try to save the colors, Color Sergeant James Marshall ripped the flag from its staff and wrapped it around his body. Neither he nor the flag were accounted for when the unit's report was filed on July 11.

Captain William Hexamer could only helplessly watch the stampede without firing because the fleeing Federal troops covered his front. Once the field cleared, he opened fire, first with case shot, and then with canister. The Confederates were not to be denied, forcing Hexamer to quickly limber his guns and gallop them to the rear. The rapidly approaching enemy infantry shot down many of the horses, forcing a gun to be left behind.[25]

Also lost were seven "coffee-mill" guns. These crank-operated precursors of machine guns could fire sixty rounds per minute from a hopper maga-zine feeding into a single barrel. Pennsylvania governor Andrew Curtin equipped several regiments with them, and it appears that Taylor's men used them for part of the battle in the form of a battery under the command of Sergeant James Dalzell of the Third NJV. These guns may have been given to Taylor's Brigade because the men were using the same type of ammuni-tion—patent cartridges that did not need to be bitten during the loading pro-cess. One soldier recalled that "after the pieces had become warm it was only necessary to insert the cartridge, give the piece a slight shock, and it was home, thus greatly facilitating the rapidity of loading." The use of these car-tridges could dramatically increase the men's firepower but would also rap-idly deplete their ammunition supply.

The remaining regiment, the Fourth NJV, had a fight that it would never forget. General Taylor had initially decided to send it toward the Third NJV, but before he could put the men in motion a French aide to General McClellan, either the Duc de Chartres or the Comte de Paris, approached Colonel Simpson and ordered the regiment to a different location, farther to the left (west). Clearly agitated, the aide was sent to General Taylor while Simpson waited. The aide galloped up to Taylor and issued a stream of French words. Taylor turned to his aide, E. Burd Grubb, and asked, "Who the devil is this, and what is he talking about?" Grubb replied, "This is the Comte de Paris . . . and he has come to you by General Porter's orders, under which you are to give him one of our regiments." Taylor was not happy about this and asked his aide, "Do you know him?" and Grubb indicated that he did. "Very well, then, give him the Fourth Regiment and go and see where he puts it and come back and report." Grubb saluted and rode away with the young French officer.[26]

After conversing with the aide in French, Colonel Simpson formed his regiment in column of fours and led it toward a swale. Captain Grubb saw Federal troops heavily engaged with the enemy on the right of this position, but there were no troops in this sector, so a concentrated enemy push here could roll up the Federal line. The Jerseymen realized that they were not alone—the Eleventh Pennsylvania Reserve was nearby, also waiting to be de-ployed. Grubb watched as Simpson quickly deployed his men into line of battle, but not before his right was attacked by swarming Confederates. Grubb did not see what happened, for he was in the process of returning to report to General Taylor.

Colonel Simpson told a slightly different, and probably more accurate, story. He noted that his regiment was placed about fifty yards in the rear of the Third Pennsylvania Reserves. Striding forward, Simpson met its commander, Colonel Horatio Sickel, and informed him that he could relieve him when needed. Simpson then returned to his regiment. Sickel appeared about fifteen minutes later and told him that his men were on the verge of exhaustion, and asked to be relieved. Simpson agreed and the Fourth advanced to the front, remaining there from 4:30 P.M. to 7:00 P.M. During this period, Simpson's men continually poured gunfire into the enemy. The men were periodically told to cease firing to allow the smoke to clear so Simpson could see the whereabouts of the enemy.[27]

After almost three hours of fighting, Colonel Simpson became increasingly concerned about the men's muskets, which were becoming so fouled that charges could not be rammed home. Simpson walked back to Colonel Thomas Gallagher to request that the Eleventh Pennsylvania Reserve regiment advance to relieve the exhausted Jerseymen. Gallagher, who had volunteered to do this twice before, was happy to oblige, and the two regiments exchanged places. Looking to his left and rear, Simpson discerned a long line of battle. Not certain about its identity, Simpson asked his men. He finally sent Lieutenant Josiah Shaw to definitively identify the troops. Shaw bounded back a short time later and showed Simpson the bullet holes in his clothes as evidence that the unknown soldiers were Southerners, probably from Lawton's Brigade of Jackson's Corps. Simpson quickly redeployed his regiment to face this threat, which almost immediately received damaging volleys. Looking behind his new position, Simpson saw yet another line of troops and this time sent his adjutant, J. S. Studdeford, to identify them. To reduce losses, Simpson ordered his men to lie down. Looking up, Simpson saw the Eleventh Pennsylvania Reserve retreating, and to his right he could see Confederates approaching and passing his front at the double-quick. Simpson quickly ordered his men to their feet and, wheeling his regiment around, fired into the Confederates, probably the Fifth Texas of Hood's Brigade, who were chasing the Eleventh. General Isaac Trimble remarked that the charge against the Pennsylvanians and Jerseymen "could not be surpassed for intrepid bravery and high resolve."

Realizing that further resistance was folly, Simpson ordered his men to the rear. They had not gone far when they saw "a large body of the enemy, drawn up in several lines, and a battery directly in our rear, to cut us off." Simpson realized that his men were all but surrounded and reluctantly ordered them to drop their arms and surrender, which the Eleventh had already done. About eighty men were not willing to give themselves up to the enemy, and were able to escape. Seeking to surrender, the officers sought out a suitable enemy officer to proffer their swords. They encountered Lieutenant Colonel J. C. Upton of the Fifth Texas, who had entered the battle wearing an undershirt and carrying a frying pan rather than a sword. When the Jerseymen became convinced that he was indeed an officer, they gave him about twenty swords. Seeing some of his men were trying to prevent several Jerseymen from escaping, Upton yelled, "Let 'em go! We'd a damned sight rather fight 'em than feed 'em." Colonel Simpson, who had predicted to his men, "We should go into Richmond tomorrow," the day before the fight, was correct, but not in the way he had imagined.[28]

To surrender almost his entire regiment was quite a stigma, and Simpson needed to justify his actions, so in his report he noted, "we had done our whole duty in keeping at bay the enemy for an hour after every other regiment on our right and left had fallen back," and attributing the mishap entirely to the fact that "I received no orders from the brigadier-general commanding or any other authority to retreat (being in the woods it was impossible for me to see what was going on the flanks), I cannot reproach myself or my regiment with any fault on account of our capture." He also noted that his men's actions "showed an obstinate courage . . . which must relieve them of any blame on account of the misfortunes of the day." In fairness to Simpson, neither he nor his men had combat experience, the dense woods confused them, and they were up against some of the best troops in the Confederate army. Similarly, Taylor cannot be criticized because he gave up the unit and expected others to care for it. The following day, a detail was sent to bury the knapsacks of the captured members of the Fourth. Other equipment was burned.

Taylor, who rallied the First, Second, and Third NJV in the rear, was soon joined by the Irish Brigade and by French's Brigade. The growing darkness, coupled with the disorganization of their troops and the sounds of cheers heralding Federal reinforcements, caused the Confederates to halt their attack and contentedly rest on the hard-fought battlefield.[29]

Although the men of the First, Second, and Third NJV could feel proud of their actions in repelling attack after attack until nightfall, they mourned the loss of their comrades. For McAllister the worst was that they had to leave their dead and desperately wounded behind in the hands of the enemy. The losses to the brigade were horrendous. The Fourth NJV sustained the greatest losses (585), exceeding the total losses for the other three regiments (487), and was all but destroyed during the battle. Excluding the Fourth, the Third NJV had the highest actual casualties (215), but on a percentage basis none lost more than the four companies of the Second (113, or 38 percent). Overall, the First New Jersey Brigade, which carried approximately 2,300 men into battle, lost almost 1,100 (47 percent) in a span of a few hours. If the number of captured and missing from the Fourth are deducted, the losses were much more modest (28 percent). Indeed, McAllister wrote home, "it is a wonder to me that it was not three times as many—standing as we did for one and a half to two hours under a storm of lead and hail." Modern historian Joseph Bilby noted that a large number of the injuries were caused by "buck and ball" ammunition, with a round ball and three buckshot. Buckshot wounds were often not serious.

The brigade also lost the services of several good field officers. Colonel Isaac Tucker, who had taken over command of the Second NJV when Colonel McLean left the army, was killed. Also lost was Major David Hatfield of the First NJV. Many soldiers writing home thought that Hatfield had sustained a minor head wound, but it was more serious than that and he died on July 30. Major Henry Ryerson of the Second NJV was the reverse. Trying to rally his troops by conspicuously swinging his sword near the regiment's flagbearer, Ryerson was severely wounded and left behind to die. Exchanged, he quickly recuperated and returned to the brigade.[30]

Charles Hopkins of the First NJV became the brigade's first Medal of Honor winner for his actions during the regiment's retreat. Although wounded twice, Hopkins grabbed hold of a fallen comrade and carried him twelve hundred yards to safety, despite having to run a gauntlet of hostile fire. After placing his comrade down in what he thought was a safe spot, Hopkins was later shot in the head, and both were captured.

The brigade crossed the river and returned to its former camp near Fair Oaks that night. Captain Grubb called the bridges "small, frail things, not much wider than to allow four men to march abreast." During the crossing, Lieutenant Thomas Howell of the Third NJV, at seventeen the youngest officer in the brigade, commented on how glad he was to be alive. The words had barely left his lips when a cannon ball struck him, ripping him in half.[31]

Slocum's Division reached its camp near Fair Oaks by 11:00 P.M. The men were so tired that they threw themselves on the ground and immediately went to sleep. There would be time the next day, and for many days after that, to think about and mourn the heavy losses of friends and comrades. The men, depressed about not being able to bury their dead, were pounded awake the next day as Confederate artillery shells exploded all around them. General Slocum moved the men to a more sheltered wooded area nearby, and the men spent the day resting, washing, and writing home. The reprieve ended that night when Slocum received orders to move his men to Savage Station. They did not know it at the time, but McClellan had finally given up hope of capturing Richmond. His only goal now was to save the army by withdrawing to the James River, where gunboats could protect it.

The retreat began at 11:00 that night, June 28. However, the march ground to a halt after only three miles as troops clogged the narrow roads. The men rested until the early morning hours, when the march resumed. The column reached Savage Station at 5:00 A.M., in time for breakfast. The Jerseymen could see troops attempting to destroy the vast amount of supplies stored here, and some may have seen General McClellan arrive and enter into discussions with General Slocum. The latter was ordered to take his division to White Oak Swamp, which it reached at 2:00 P.M. on July 29. Three hours later, the division was again on the move, this time to relieve two divisions, which then began their retreat to the James River, and safety. The division reached its destination by 7:00 P.M., and Slocum threw out half of his units as pickets—Taylor's men were permitted to stack arms, have supper, and go to sleep, until they were rudely awakened by ammunition blowing up at Savage Station. All were furious at the news that hundreds of their wounded comrades would be left behind at Savage Station to be captured by the enemy. Wounded in the arm at Gaines' Mill, John Judd of the Third NJV was told to leave the hospital or be captured. He decided on the former, but his strength gave out after walking for four hours, so he lay down by the side of the road and waited for an ambulance to come by.[32]

With daylight on June 30, Slocum pulled in his pickets and marched his men to the Charles City Road, where McClellan anticipated an attack. Slocum was charged with guarding Brackett's Ford, on the Federal right. The men fired into Confederate general William Mahone's Brigade, which was demonstrating in the area but gave no indications of attacking. The situation was different just to the left of the division, where A.P. Hill's and Longstreet's divisions, consisting of twelve brigades, attacked Hooker's, McCall's, and Kearny's divisions, consisting of nine brigades, in the late afternoon in what was called the Battle of Glendale. Stonewall Jackson was ordered to hit the rear of the Federal line after crossing White Oak Bridge, but he was late in arriving and did not play a major role in this battle.

The Battle of Glendale was going badly for the Federals, as the front line was pushed back and several batteries were captured. Riding along his lines, General Phil Kearny was shocked to find a gap and immediately communicated a need for reinforcements to his corps commander, Samuel Heintzelman. The latter rode over to Slocum and asked for Taylor's Brigade.

Slocum agreed, and soon the three regiments were trotting toward the front. Darkness was falling as the Jerseymen arrived. One historian dramatized the situation when he wrote, "they dashed at the double quick toward the point of danger . . . cheering as they went with the wildest enthusiasm." A contemporary newspaper reporter accurately noted, "the Jersey troops took no active part of it, although they were under a tremendous fire all the afternoon." However, a modern historian noted, "the brigade filled a breach in the Federal lines. . . . Though its fighting was minor, the unit's timely arrival on the field was providential for McClellan's successful retreat."[33]

Lieutenant Colonel McAllister took time to describe the battle to his daughters: "at nightfall we were called forward to assist Genl. Kearny and charge the enemy . . . we hurried on amidst a shower of balls and then laid down to be ready to charge. The balls passed over our heads. After a hard struggle the Rebels went back into the woods, the officers trying in vain to rally them." McAllister attributed the behavior of the enemy to the three loud cheers that his men gave as they approached Kearny's line. The Jerseymen could hear the enemy soldiers yelling, "Rallying is played out! Don't you hear the Yankees cheering. . . . They have got reinforcements. There is no use now trying to get them. They can whip us!" The men were relieved that they were not fed into the battle. According to McAllister, "it saved us fighting another battle which, I can assure you, we had no wish to do."

E. Burd Grubb, a captain at the time, and a member of Taylor's staff, told a different story. Captain Moore of Kearny's staff galloped up and, waving his hat, yelled to the men that Kearny had lost a battery and needed his "pets" to recapture it. Before Taylor could stop them, they were off. Grubb quickly mounted his horse as Taylor yelled, "Keep ahead of them and keep them from going too far." As they arrived in the vicinity of the battery, the Jerseymen could see that other troops had recaptured the guns, and Grubb told the officers to stop the men from going any farther.[34]

During the day's actions, General Slocum was impressed by all of his artillery, except for a section of Hexamer's guns. He wrote in his report, "Hexamer's battery has usually been well served, but on this occasion the two pieces under command of a lieutenant (since resigned) were poorly handled, and proved of but little assistance."

The march toward the James River continued until just after midnight. The men were tired and were not adverse in expressing their grumpiness about their fatigue and the wounded they left behind. McClellan was worried about saving his army, and nothing was going to stop him from moving toward the

James River. The division reached Malvern Hill at 7:00 A.M. on July 1, where the men were permitted to halt at the brow of the hill for breakfast. The troops then marched down the hill and toward the York River at about 10:30 A.M., thereby missing the great battle that would be fought here in which Lee would experience one of his worst defeats. Marching another four miles, they halted and threw up breastworks. Surprised when roused at midnight, the men took up the march again toward the James River. They finally reached their destination, Harrison's Landing, at 8:00 A.M. on July 2. The brigade's first camp was in a wheatfield with "mud knee deep and very little wood for fire," complained Charles Harrison. The brigade moved the following day, and was soon joined by the Second New Jersey Brigade, much to the delight of all. The men were ordered to yet another campsite on July 7.[35]

The rest of July was spent resting and waiting to be called back into service. Swarms of mosquitoes and pathogen-filled water felled many men. With plenty of time on their hands, the troops spent considerable time writing to their relatives and receiving old correspondence. The great variety of available food cheered the Jerseymen, who had had only hardtack to eat during the retreat.

Several changes in command occurred while the army camped at Harrison's Landing. Lieutenant Colonel McAllister, who for almost a year had felt slighted about not having been given the First NJV, was promoted to the rank of colonel and assigned command of the new Eleventh NJV on June 30. He knew that his promotion was just a matter of time, for he had written to his wife in early July, "there are plenty of chances for promotion—in fact, too many, as so many of our brave officers have fallen."[36]

The Fourth NJV was exchanged during the second week of August, and it immediately returned to the brigade, still encamped at Harrison's Landing. On the night of their capture, the men of the Fourth NJV had marched through Richmond. Charles Currie wrote that "in going through the streets . . . we were subjected to all sorts of indignities, the worst of which was trailing our colors through the streets in front of us." Robert Aitken also observed this indignity and wrote, "it was a bitter pill to swallow, to stand to see the Damned Rebels take our colors. It made my blood boil, but we could do nothing." The men first occupied Libby Prison, but after several weeks the enlisted men were sent to Belle Isle. There was not much to do. Offered additional food if they would clean the captured Yankee guns, all but one man declined. When he returned that night, his comrades shaved his head and beat him. Five hundred men of the Fourth NJV were exchanged and returned to Harrison's

Landing, but many were too weak for the rigors of active campaigning. Per-haps their greatest indignity occurred when they returned and their valued Springfield rifles were replaced with old smoothbore muskets.

Colonel Simpson relinquished his command immediately upon the regiment's return. Governor Olden probably exerted pressure on Washington to get rid of Simpson, who was now an embarrassment. Olden got his wish, for Simpson resigned his commission on August 27, 1862, noting the "leave of absence granted me by the War Department to enable me to command the 4th Reg. N.J. Volunteers having been recalled." Simpson resumed the rank of major in the topographical engineers and left the army. Lieutenant Colo-nel William B. Hatch replaced him.[37]

With plenty of time on their hands, the men speculated about the fu-ture. No one could have anticipated the brigade's devastation before the end of August.

CHAPTER 4

The Summer and Fall of 1862

$\mathcal{W}$hile the Army of the Potomac rested near Harrison's Landing, events were unfolding farther north that promised to have a profound impact on the First New Jersey Brigade. A new army, the Army of Virginia, comprised of the Federal units defending Washington and those holding the lower Shenandoah Valley, was formed under General John Pope. He was ordered to drive south toward Richmond and relieve the pressure on McClellan's army. While Pope's units maneuvered, McClellan was ordered on August 3, 1862, to transport his army back to northern Virginia. Franklin's Corps was the third major component to make the journey. The brigade marched south to Newport News, where the men embarked on transports on August 23. This would not be the same type of leisurely journey as the trip south, for Lee had slipped away from Richmond and was heading toward Washington. The ships docked at Alexandria on August 24 and the men marched two miles south to Fort Worth at Cloud's Mills, where they waited for events to unfold. They did not have long to wait.

Telegraph transmissions from Manassas Junction, Pope's supply depot, abruptly stopped on August 26—soon after the operator sent an urgent message that Confederate cavalry were in the area. Suspecting that enemy raiders had hit the well-stocked depot, the Federal high command ordered a brigade to the area to ascertain the situation and recapture the depot. General Taylor received orders at 2:00 A.M. the next morning to take his brigade toward Bull Run Bridge and drive away the Confederate raiders. Taylor conveyed this information to his four regimental commanders an hour later with orders to get their men immediately in line and ready to board trains on the Orange and Alexandria Railroad. Due to casualties and illness, the brigade's strength had fallen to approximately two thousand men. General Taylor and his officers did not know that they were about to engage the enemy in what would be the first action of the Second Bull Run Campaign.[1]

Knowing Confederates were somewhere ahead of them, the Jerseymen understood why the train inched cautiously forward. A quarter-mile east of Bull Run Bridge, the train halted and the men hopped off with their belongings. They soon saw why. Two trains had collided head on the night before, and mangled bodies of soldiers killed in the crash lay all around. The brigade marched along the railroad to Bull Run Bridge and crossed it. Here the men dropped their accouterments, except for their rifles, ammunition, and canteens, and formed into line of battle. Taylor threw out a line of skirmishers, and five hundred yards behind it marched the First NJV, in line of battle, on the right side of the road. The Second NJV formed on its left, and the Third NJV marched about two hundred yards behind its sister regiments. Ominous artillery fire could be heard in the distance. The Fourth NJV, whose men had recently been freed from Rebel prison camps, was left behind at the bridge with orders to hold it at all costs. A more pleased set of men could not be found in the brigade, as they were not overly eager to engage the enemy again.

A good many Jerseymen had misgivings about their venture into the open Virginia countryside, but General Taylor brushed off their concerns. He was sure that only guerrillas faced them and that they could easily be pushed aside. Josiah Brown called his commanding officer a "brave, but not over[ly] prudent man." The men began seeing knots of enemy troops as they advanced. Then they saw a small body of Confederate cavalry with a battery to their front-right, and then another small force on their left. Taylor did not know it, but he was advancing against Stonewall Jackson's entire wing, or half of Lee's army. Jackson had been ordered to sweep around the Federal right to cut its line of communication and create as much havoc as possible. Jackson's vanguard of two full divisions now advanced toward Taylor. It was a terrible mismatch of two thousand Jerseymen against over fifteen thousand veteran Confederates.[2]

Compounding the problem of an overconfident brigade commander was that three of his four regiments were commanded by officers who had never led their units in battle. Colonel Torbert was ill yet again, so Lieutenant Colonel Mark Collet led the First NJV. The Second was led by Lieutenant Colonel Samuel Buck, and the Fourth was commanded by Captain Napoleon Aaronson in Lieutenant Colonel William Hatch's absence. Only Colonel Henry Brown of the Third had experience at the regimental level.

Believing decisive action could drive away the enemy, Taylor ordered a charge. The Confederate horsemen watched Taylor's advance first with disbelief, then with great admiration. One called it a "grand sight," and another claimed that it was "the prettiest line I ever saw." Stonewall Jackson arrived and told his men, "Don't shoot, men. Stand steady and let them come on." This was a difficult order for some of them, and they had to be reminded not to raise their guns. Some of the Confederate artillery opened fire, sending shells screaming toward Taylor's men. Other artillery units galloped up and dropped trail on both sides of the Jerseymen, and they too opened fire with shell and then canister. When within three hundred yards of the batteries, the Jerseymen could clearly see large masses of enemy infantry and cavalry in front of them and on either flank.[3]

Stonewall Jackson watched the charge with growing fascination and admiration. In his report, Jackson noted that the Jerseymen's "advance was made with great spirit and determination and under a leader worthy of a better cause." After watching the senseless loss of life for awhile, he halted his artillery's fire and waved a handkerchief, calling for Taylor's men to surrender. A Federal infantryman raised his gun, took careful aim at Jackson, and fired—the ball zoomed close, but did not hit the legendary Confederate commander. Jackson had no choice but to order his men to continue firing, which became more destructive with every step forward the Jerseymen took. Taylor steadfastly believed he could be successful, so he continued urging his men forward despite being enveloped by a broad semicircle of Confederate troops.

A Confederate officer recalled that "we brought our batteries, four in number, to bear, shot and shell from which began to plow through their ranks before we opened up on them with our infantry. They closed the gaps and marched towards us in the most perfect line of battle that I had seen during the war, and it was only when General Jackson's Corps enveloped them front and flank that they broke." Major William Henry of the First NJV agreed, noting that when Taylor finally realized that he was up against large numbers of cavalry and infantry and "it was apparent our brigade was entirely inadequate to cope," he wisely decided to quit the attack and to order his men back to the bridge.[4]

The order filled the men with relief, but then there was the mile and a half of open ground to traverse to get back to the bridge. Looking behind them, the men could see enemy soldiers and artillery in rapid pursuit. Major Henry noted that "column against cavalry was formed and the Brigade marched in good order to the rear." The day was exceedingly hot, causing

Collet and Buck to fall from sunstroke, and both had to be carried to safety. Back at the bridge, the commander of the Fourth NJV, Captain Napoleon Aaronson, was also stricken by the same malady, forcing him to relinquish command to another captain.

The situation worsened when the men of the First and Second NJV reached a steep hill near the bridge. Because the ground was hard and the men's shoes slippery, many had trouble climbing up the slope. Seeing the delay, the Confederates unlimbered some artillery pieces and fired at close range, causing panic in the ranks and a rapid disintegration of the neat column. The narrow bridge was ahead and it was essentially each man for himself. The Third NJV, which had been following its sister regiments, came to a stream and attempted to cross it. However, the banks were too steep, and many men slid into the cool water. Gathering themselves and their belongings, they crawled up the opposite bank only to be hit by enemy shells at close range. "Fatigue of incessant marching over bad roads and continuous fire of the enemy had thinned my ranks, and many men had fallen out, unable to march . . . these stragglers were captured by the enemy," noted Colonel Brown. The Rebels saw the growing disorganization of the Jerseymen and swept in from three directions, scooping up about two hundred men. Quickly sizing up the situation, Taylor gathered as many men as he could and, with the Eleventh and Twelfth Ohio under Colonel Edward Scammon, who had just arrived on the train, attempted to make a stand. Some Ohio officers attempted to stem the retreat of other Jerseymen without success. A bullet slammed into Taylor's lower right leg, throwing him from his horse. Because of the seriousness of the wound, Taylor was placed on a stretcher and rushed to the rear for medical treatment. As he passed the adjutant of the Ohio regiments' brigade, Lieutenant Robert Kennedy, Taylor yelled, "For God's sake, prevent another Bull Run." Taylor told his enlisted men to "stand and make a fight for the bridge."[5]

With Taylor out of action, Scammon took command of the brigade. As the last Jerseymen crossed the bridge, Scammon waited for the lead Confederate regiment to traverse it, and then screamed, "Open fire," and his Ohioans' fire cleared the road. The surviving Confederates jumped into year-old rifle pits on the west side of Bull Run Creek, while the Midwesterners scrambled behind an embankment. The Jerseymen reorganized their ranks and found a good defensive position behind a railroad embankment around a bend in the road, and anxiously awaited the appearance of their tormenters. They did not need to worry, as the Ohioans held off the Confederate attacks. Not knowing the strength of the Federal forces in front of him, Jackson exercised caution and ordered his men to cut off their pursuit. This permitted the brigade to continue its retreat toward Fairfax Station, reaching there at 6:00 P.M. The men marched to a church near the station at 7:30 P.M. and remained there until 11:30 P.M., when Colonel Scammon ordered them to board cars bound for Burke's Station. Learning that the enemy occupied the railroad station, the men disembarked and took the road to Fairfax Court House and marched all night, finally reaching their old camp near Alexandria by 9:00 A.M. on August 28. It had been a very long twenty-nine hours with little rest, but at least the brigade was still intact.

The brigade set off with about two thousand men, and returned with 337 fewer in the ranks, or losses of about 17 percent. As expected, the losses to the First (132) and Second NJV (129) were almost identical, as both occupied the front line. The Third's was considerably less (64), as it marched in the rear of its two sister regiments. The Fourth NJV, which remained near the bridge, sustained negligible losses (11). Appendix A contains the regimental breakdowns of losses.

Added to these losses were General Taylor and his son, who was a staff officer. A third Taylor, a captain in the Third NJV, was also wounded. General Taylor's crushed leg bones required amputation. Considerable blood loss, combined with his already weakened condition from a bout with malaria during the Richmond Campaign, caused Taylor to succumb on September 1 in Alexandria. The official cause of death was listed as "exhaustion." Taylor's body, minus his amputated leg, which was donated to the medical corps for study, was returned to Hunterdon County for burial.[6]

The unpopular Taylor's death was not deeply mourned. Many were openly angry with him because of the handling of the brigade during the Second Bull Run Campaign. Robert McCreight of the First NJV wrote to his brother that "there is not a man in the brigade that is sorry for him, for he not only caused his own death but that of other brave men." McCreight indicated that the men had pointed out the Rebels on their flanks to Taylor, but he said nothing and just continued the advance. "I never read or heard tell of such a thing in all my life; marching men up on three batteries without any artillery or cavalry to support them, marching us up like sheep to be slaughtered. If he had given us an order to charge or to fire it would have caused some satisfaction. But then marching us up to within 300 yards of their batteries and then march us right back without giving us any order; it was awful," he wrote.

The brigade had lost yet another battle, and after more than a year in the service the men had yet to taste victory. They had also lost a second brigade commander. A few days later the men mourned the loss of their first brigade commander, Phil Kearny, killed at the Battle of Chantilly. Reactions to Taylor's actions near Bull Run Bridge were mixed. The brigade's historian obviously had mixed feelings about the matter, noting that Taylor "had gained for himself the reputation of being absolutely without fear. He never hesitated in carrying out an order . . . he must have believed that the work given him to do was not a very difficult task, as shown by the bold and rapid march towards the enemy, without even a single piece of artillery or any support. It is well within reason to believe that, had he even suspected any superior force to confront him, he would have conducted the affair on quite different lines. One regiment sent out as a reconnoitering force could have developed the number of the enemy's force." Another distinguished historian was more blunt, noting, "he did precisely as he was ordered, and the responsibility of the blunder, if blunder it was, rests elsewhere than with him." In actuality, Taylor's behavior is indefensible, as he almost destroyed his brigade by blindly throwing it against an unknown force without the information necessary to make intelligent command decisions.[7]

Speculation on Taylor's replacement was the order of the day. Colonel Torbert of the First NJV was the obvious choice. He had both seniority and the most military experience, as he was a West Point graduate and a veteran of the prewar army. Torbert, however, was sickly and rarely with his regiment, and because of this, had never commanded it in battle. These problems were surely considered, but his prewar experience probably carried the day, so he was given the brigade. Promotion to the rank of brigadier general did not come, however, until November 29, 1862.

Meanwhile, the brigade, now about sixteen hundred strong, had little rest after the fiasco at Bull Run Bridge, for the day after its return, August 29, the officers told their men to stop complaining and get into column. The brigade's destination was Benton's Tavern on the Little River Turnpike, about seven miles away. It reached Fairfax Court House the next day. The men did not know that they were given the vital task of guarding the approaches to the court house. According to author David Welker, "General Slocum must have believed that if any of his brigades was capable of singlehandedly covering the army's retreat, it was Torbert's New Jersey Brigade." The brigade thus missed the savage fighting that occurred during the Second Battle of Bull Run on August 29 and 30.[8]

Leaving four companies of the First NJV behind to picket the roads running into town, Torbert took the rest of his brigade, and Hexamer's Battery, out of town about two miles on the Centreville Turnpike. Not certain about the location of the enemy, Torbert threw out a picket line composed of companies from all four of his regiments about a half-mile in advance of the brigade. Six companies from the Second NJV relieved them on August 31. Learning that Confederate cavalry had clashed with their Federal counterparts nearby, Torbert ordered half of the Fourth NJV out to reinforce the picket line. That evening, Torbert received orders from General Pope to send two regiments and a section of Hexamer's Battery to guard the wagon trains rolling slowly past them toward Alexandria. He selected the First and Third NJV for this duty, which left him only two regiments and four guns in his exposed position. Confederates suddenly appeared about three hundred yards from Torbert's picket line at 8:00 P.M. and quickly unlimbered three cannon that fired six shots into the long line of wagons and the Jerseymen's camp. Torbert reported that "drivers deserted their wagons and the greatest confusion existed." He quickly dispatched his infantry to round up the drivers and force them back to their wagons, even if they had to resort to the bayonet. After awhile, the wagon train was again under way. At the same time, Torbert sent his picket line, reinforced by the Second NJV, against the Confederate guns. It was like shooting mosquitoes with a shotgun, so the Confederate gunners limbered their pieces and galloped to safety.

The following day, September 1, the day that General Taylor died, Confederate cavalry dashed toward the Jerseymen's picket line at 9:00 A.M., wounding one man in the process. General Pope ordered the brigade to Germantown that afternoon, where Torbert was to report to General Joseph Hooker. Fearing an attack, Hooker ordered the Jerseymen to form into line of battle, and they remained in this manner through a drenching rain all night. Pope ordered the brigade back to the seminary the following day, where the men rested for several weeks. During this time the quartermasters busily replenished the equipment lost at Bull Run Bridge.[9]

As the Yankees rested, Robert E. Lee was already planning his next offensive—an invasion of the North. Craving Harper's Ferry and its garrison of eleven thousand Federal troops, Lee boldly divided his army and sent Stonewall Jackson's Corps, along with Lafayette McLaws', John Walker's, and Richard Anderson's divisions of Longstreet's Corps, to reduce it. Lee's movement into Maryland caused General McClellan, back in charge of the Army of the Potomac, to break camp and cross the Potomac River. The VI Corps began its movement on September 6, crossing the Potomac on Long Bridge later that day. The end of September 7 found the corps beyond Tenallytown, Maryland, and at Muddy Water the following day. Passing through Darnestown, Barnesville, and Urbana, the corps finally reached the foot of Catoctin Mountain on September 13. The VI Corps, along with General Darius Couch's Division of the IV Corps, now formed the left wing of the army. McClellan needed to break the siege of Harper's Ferry, and he needed to get through the mountain passes to do it, but Confederates guarded them. General Franklin's Corps was ordered to break through Crampton's Gap and then quickly advance on McLaws' rear on Maryland Heights overlooking the town. "Having gained the pass, your duty will be first to cut off, destroy, or capture McLaws' command and relieve Colonel Miles [commander of the Harper's Ferry garrison]," were McClellan's orders.

General Franklin's men broke camp at Buckeytown at 6:00 A.M. on September 14 and marched into the small village of Jefferson by midmorning. Pressing on to Burkittsville, the corps' advance drove Rebel cavalry out of town by noon. The Federals then rested for about ninety minutes while Franklin pondered his options to clear the passes in front of him.

Franklin decided that Slocum's Division would lead the attack, deployed on a three-brigade front. Colonel Joseph Bartlett's Brigade, which led the division, began its deployment at about 4:00 P.M. General John Newton's Brigade was second, and it formed on Bartlett's left. Torbert's Brigade brought up the rear and formed on the left of Newton. Each brigade deployed in two lines. The First NJV formed on the left of the first line, and to its right was the Second NJV. Approximately 150 paces behind them were the Third and Fourth NJV. The men advanced about half a mile through fields of clover and corn, climbing over high wood and stone fences, all the while being pounded by Confederate artillery on the heights. Slocum halted his men approximately three hundred yards from the enemy positions at the base of Crampton's Gap. Although none of the Jerseymen noted it in their letters or reports, General William Brooks' Vermont Brigade formed on their left.[10]

Confederates behind a stone wall along Burkittsville Road loomed before them. The Sixteenth Virginia was strongly posted directly in front of them, and to the Jerseymen's right were the Sixth and Twelfth Virginia. All three regiments belonged to Mahone's Brigade, now commanded by Colonel William Parham. Also in the vicinity were the Tenth Georgia and the Second and Twelfth Virginia Cavalry. General Paul Semmes' Brigade guarded Brown's Gap, far to the Jerseymen's left. Realizing that an attack on Crampton's Gap was imminent, McLaws ordered reinforcements from Semmes' and Cobb's brigades, including the Sixteenth and Twenty-fourth Georgia, and Cobb's Legion.

The First and Second NJV were initially ordered to lie behind a stone wall. Unable to restrain themselves, many men leaped upon the wall, shak-

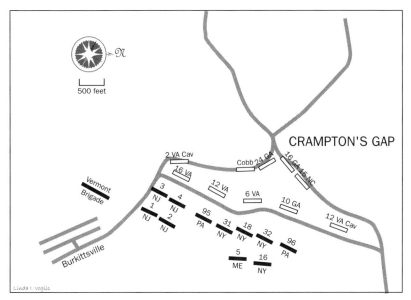

MAP 3. Battle of Crampton's Gap (September 14, 1862).

ing their fists at the enemy, taunting them and telling them to come out and fight. The Confederate response was rapid, opening fire, hitting several Jerseymen and causing the others to scramble behind the stone wall for safety. They returned fire for about twenty-minutes. General Slocum now realized that he should have brought up his artillery—he had not done so because the terrain seemed too rugged for his guns. Now he saw his division being blasted by at least eight enemy cannon, and the only thing his men could do was snuggle against the stone wall in front of them. Slocum quickly ordered up his guns, but it was too late.[11]

Colonel Bartlett, whose brigade was to lead the charge, rode over to confer with Colonel Torbert. Both realized that "nothing but a united charge would dislodge the enemy and win the battle," so they agreed to work together in the attack.

While bringing up his second line, Torbert told the First and Second NJV on the first line to hold their fire. Leaping over their comrades, the men of the Third and Fourth NJV entered the open fields between the two forces. Double-quicking, the men of the Fourth NJV excitedly yelled, "Remember Belle Island and Richmond." After the two regiments were about 150 yards into their charge, Torbert ordered the First and Second NJV to stand and sprint after them. The men let out a cheer before rushing forward, and many yelled, "Avenge Kearny." Torbert explained in his report, "the enemy, although holding a very strong position, and having the advantage of artillery, could not stand these charges, so broke and fled up the mountain side in great disorder, closely pursued by our men, who drove them through the pass, and some distance in the valley on the other side, when night put an end to the pursuit." According to Lieutenant Oscar Westlake of the Third NJV, the enemy occupied a strong position behind a stone fence with rails on top. "They stood their ground until we got [to] within 150 yards of them when they Broke and Run in every direction." Reaching the fence, the Union men halted for about five minutes to catch their breath. "Balls whistling around our heads like hail," Westlake recalled. As the men continued their charge up the mountain they yelled, "Remember Manassas and Gaines' Mill."[12]

Colonel Brown's report suggested that his Jerseymen might have exceeded their orders. "The Third and Fourth were ordered in to relieve the first line, and the men, springing up, went in with a cheer up to, over, and through the high fence held by the enemy at the base of the wooded heights and strongly lined by his sharpshooters, who delivered their fire with great rapidity. But nothing could withstand the onset of our men." Colonel Hatch of the Fourth NJV added, "I advanced across a plowed field for 400 yards in extent under a heavy cross-fire from the enemy's artillery, which was planted on the mountain slope, driving him from every point in front of us. We leaped the walls and continued in pursuit over the mountain into the gorge and up the next ascent to its summit, the enemy retreating in disorder into the valley below." The Virginians abandoned their defenses when the Jerseymen's line of battle was about twenty yards away. They "broke and run like sheep, and we after them," wrote a soldier to his local newspaper.

The First and Second NJV in the second line were not about to let their comrades claim all the glory, so they quickly closed the distance. Colonel Samuel Buck claimed that his Second NJV advanced so rapidly that it reached the stone wall shielding the Sixteenth Virginia at about the same time as the Fourth NJV in front of it.[13]

After firing a few rounds after the enemy, who were now rushing up the mountain, the Jerseymen followed, mad with the excitement of victory that had eluded them in the past. Additional Confederate reinforcements arrived, and some of the Jerseymen wheeled to the right to face them. Closest was Cobb's Legion of General Howell Cobb's Brigade, numbering approximately 250 men. The most vulnerable period for a fighting unit is when it is deploying, and this is precisely the time that the First New Jersey Brigade fired into Cobb's men. While the Second and Fourth NJV took on the front of the regiment, the First and Third NJV hit its flank. According to Colonel Brown, "we changed front forward and delivered a destructive fire on his half-formed line, followed up by a renewal of the charge, when he broke utterly and the pursuit continued." Colonel Buck added, "they could not stand our fire, and without getting into position, broke and fled, we following them down the hill and along the road a distance of about a quarter of a mile."

A quick-thinking Colonel Brown sent his acting adjutant, David Fairly, and twenty men of Lieutenant Baldwin Hufty's Company E around the Legion's right flank and into their rear. The party moved so quickly that by the time it reached their destination, only five enlisted men remained. Still, it was enough to capture five officers and "many of their men." While Cobb's Legion suffered only 33 killed or wounded, an additional 156 men were captured, for a total loss of 76 percent. In all, General Cobb admitted losing over eight hundred of his brigade.[14]

Exalting in their victory, the men in the Third and Fourth NJV could not halt and savor it. Instead, they scrambled down the opposite side of the mountain into the valley below, where they spied a baggage train in full retreat, protected by two cannon. The guns from Carlton's Battery opened fire, instantly killing Adjutant Josiah Studderford of the Fourth NJV. With the growing darkness and the men's increasing fatigue, the officers cut off the attack.

After major setbacks at Gaines' Mill and Second Bull Run, the First New Jersey Brigade had finally tasted victory. Eugene Forbes of the Fourth NJV wrote home, "Well, we licked 'em," and Major Henry Ryerson of the Second NJV, who had recently returned after recuperating from his Gaines' Mill wounds, noted, "our men distinguished themselves above all others that day." He also wrote in the same letter, "they charged like an avalanche upon the frightened foe with cheers and shouts of 'Kearny Kearny.'"[15]

While the charge was both gallant and effective, the Jerseymen were assisted by the ineptitude of General Cobb, who commanded the Confederate troops at Crampton's Gap. Instead of overseeing the troops personally, he chose to remain at Brownsville, leaving Colonel Thomas Munford of the Second Virginia Cavalry to command the vital Crampton's Gap sector. A flurry of urgent messages finally got Cobb to the gap, but by then the battle was already lost. Colonel Munford's report was unusually blunt in his assessment of two of Lee's general officers—"General Semmes certainly knew the condition of things, as his artillery had been used, and he could see what was going on from his gap [Brownsville Gap]." He added, "had General Cobb come up in time, the result might have been otherwise." Munford also noted that Cobb's men "behaved badly." Cobb, a political-general, tried to rally his broken troops without success. A soldier wrote to a New Jersey newspaper after the battle, "we found them strongly posted in the mountains, a position which our men could have held against tremendous odds." While the news media accurately described the Federal charge, they wildly distorted the odds, incorrectly noting that the Confederate defenders dramatically outnumbered Franklin's Corps. One account had the Confederates outnumbering the Federal attackers five to one.

The majority of the exhausted men grabbed supper and then fell into a deep sleep on the battlefield. Such was not the case for all—Chief Musician Montreville Williams of the Third NJV and his men worked until 1:00 A.M. scouring the battlefield for their wounded comrades and carrying them to aid stations for treatment.[16]

The Confederates quickly stabilized their defenses during the night with additional troops. General McLaws, whose division manned Crampton's Gap, admitted in his report that he had not paid much attention to the gunfire he was hearing at the gap, for he knew there were three infantry brigades and several cavalry regiments that should have defeated any force thrown against them.

With the morning, Torbert's men took stock of their losses. Despite the charge over open ground, the casualties to the brigade were remarkably light, 171, or about 10 percent. The losses among the regiments were fairly uniform, ranging from 36 in the Fourth NJV to 55 in the Second NJV. Appendix A contains the regimental breakdowns of losses.[17]

In addition to the luxury of sleeping on the battlefield, the men collected about seven hundred valuable Springfield rifles. Most of these were given to the Fourth NJV, who were still equipped with the smoothbore muskets issued to them after their return from captivity. The brigade had also captured three stands of colors during the fight. Torbert wrote, "I am happy to state that the Fourth . . . which lost its colors before Richmond, captured two colors during this engagement."

Colonel Torbert took time to prepare a congratulatory note to his men— "you dashingly met and drove the enemy at every point. Your advance in line of battle, under a galling artillery fire, and final bayonet charge, was a feat seldom if ever surpassed. . . . You have sustained the reputation of your State, and done great credit to your officers and yourselves."[18]

The VI Corps was poised to continue driving northwest to save Harper's Ferry the day after the battle, September 15, but the garrison had already surrendered. The men instead remained on the battlefield, caring for the wounded, burying the dead, and resting. General Franklin received orders on September 17 to quickly march toward the town of Sharpsburg, by Antietam Creek, where the two armies were slugging it out in what would be the bloodiest one-day battle in American history.

The First Division arrived on the battlefield at 11:00 A.M. Slocum quickly deployed Torbert's and Newton's brigades east of Hagerstown Turnpike, near the infamous Miller's cornfield, relieving a portion of the II Corps and plugging a gap between Sedgwick's and French's divisions. The men expected to attack the enemy in the West Woods in front of them, but minutes and then hours passed without orders to do so. II Corps commander General Edwin Sumner decided that the fresh troops should instead be used to repel an expected enemy attack. The brigade spent the next six hours supporting the Federal artillery in the sector and being pounded by counterartillery fire from the Confederate guns. Two men were killed and seventeen wounded during the deadly artillery barrage. Oscar Westlake noted that the "shells flew thick and fast around us as we lay Drawn up in three or four lines of Battle." Reuben Brooks of the same regiment called it a "very unpleasant situation."[19]

The brigade, with the rest of the VI Corps, remained on the battlefield until September 21, when it marched to Williamsport and then to Bakersville on September 23, where it remained through October 31. McClellan used this time to refit his worn-out army, which had continually campaigned since early April. Shoeless men in uniforms that at best could be called rags were commonplace. The brigade camped in a large woods during this period, "doing nothing but eat, drink and sleep," noted Reuben Brooks. The Second NJV was down to about three hundred men. "Nearly four hundred are away wounded or sick. The rest are dead," Major Henry Ryerson wrote to his sister. A frustrated Ryerson noted in a subsequent letter that "nearly four weeks this brigade has been lying here doing nothing except picket duty and no effort is made to supply them with necessary clothing for the want of which the men are sadly suffering." He steamed that "this want of forethought on the part of the Government is shameful. There is no life, no enemy, no system anywhere." Some men were not unhappy with this carefree life, particularly when fifty gallons of whisky found its way to the Second NJV. Ryerson counted about half the regiment as being drunk—"the men were boisterous & very noisy but not uproarious."

New uniforms finally began arriving by the end of October. Oscar Westlake wrote home, "our Brigade have all just been getting their new Uniforms and they look first Rate again. It Put me in mind of the old times at

Ft. Worth [late 1861] only there is not more than one quarter as many men now in the Brigade as there was when we left there for the Peninsula."[20]

The brigade swelled in size by almost two thousand men during early October with the addition of two additional units—the Fifteenth and Twenty-third New Jersey Volunteers.

The Fifteenth NJV was the last of the five new three-year regiments formed in New Jersey during the summer of 1862 in response to President Lincoln's call for an additional three hundred thousand men. Concerned that men might not volunteer, there was ongoing talk about a draft. This led the *Phillipsburg Standard* to write, "Don't talk about drafting. . . . Let the army be filled with *brave men* not *cowards*. That day should never dawn when our country's honor should be placed in the hands of forced defenders."[21]

The Fifteenth NJV, composed of hearty men from the northwestern portion of the state, mustered into service at Flemington, one of four sites in the state where new regiments were forming. Three companies hailed from Sussex County, two each from Hunterdon, Morris, and Warren counties, and one from Somerset County. Governor Olden selected Samuel Fowler of Franklin Furnace, Sussex County, to lead the new regiment. Fowler received his commission on July 10, 1862. "His personal influence, and the magnetism of his presence and words, were everywhere felt," noted Reverend Alanson Haines, the regiment's postwar historian. Haines surely exaggerated when he exuberantly wrote, "never was a regiment so quickly enlisted in the State." Unlike the other four initial regimental commanders of the First Brigade, Fowler did not have prior military experience. A prominent lawyer and politician, he was also an inventor and entrepreneur, and seemed to be successful at everything he tried, so Olden reasoned he had good prospects as a military leader.

Olden achieved geographic harmony when he selected Captain Edward Campbell of the Third NJV, who hailed from Belvidere, Warren County, as lieutenant colonel, and Captain James Brown of the Seventh NJV, from Morristown, as major. They also balanced Fowler's inexperience. While the latter provided "fine abilities, and [was] endowed with a stern sense of duty," Campbell supplied the "drill and discipline that Colonel Fowler could not."[22]

Most of the regiment was composed of men accustomed to the wilds and farms of northwestern New Jersey. Reverend Haines considered them to be "of fine physique, mostly young and in excellent health and spirits." However, Lieutenant Ellis Hamilton, at just shy of seventeen years old, the youngest officer to serve New Jersey during the war, wrote his father, "I have seen a lot of Sussex boys here in camp and they are all about the hardest cases around there, so I suppose Newton must be pretty well cleaned out."

The volunteers were uniformed, equipped, and drilled as they arrived at the Flemington Fairgrounds, and the men named it "Camp Fair Oaks." Mustered into Federal service on August 25, the regiment consisted of 38 officers and 909 enlisted men. Each enlisted man received his first month's pay of $13 the following day, along with a $2 "premium" from the state of New Jersey and the first $25 of the $100 bounty promised from the Federal authorities. The men had also been promised Springfield rifles, but were disappointed to receive Enfields. At least one man did not find soldiering to his liking and immediately deserted to Philadelphia after receiving his bounty.[23]

The men were caught by surprise at midday on Wednesday, August 27, when they were told to be ready to break camp for passage to Washington on Friday. About two hundred were on furlough and had to be quickly recalled, and about a hundred were left behind when the regiment struck camp. They had to find passage the following day and on Monday.

Just about everything was different in the Twenty-third NJV, which was born of President Lincoln's August 4, 1862, call for another three hundred thousand men. Worrying that New Jersey would not be able to fill its quota, Olden reluctantly agreed to a draft for September 3, 1862, if the State's 10,478 commitment was not reached. The state clearly announced that ablebodied men had until September 1 to enlist, and by September 3 it proudly stated that it had reached its quota without resorting to a draft. The Twenty-third NJV was a nine-month regiment, and its men hailed mostly from Burlington County. Because many Quakers resided in the county, the regiment was initially called the Quaker Regiment. However, its nickname was changed to "The Yahoos" because the men were "a very noisy, boisterous set of fellows."[24]

Mustered into Federal service at its camp in Beverly, New Jersey, just south of Trenton, on September 13, 1862, the Twenty-third NJV was composed of 39 officers and 955 enlisted men. Colonel J. S. Cox commanded the regiment, which broke camp and headed for Washington on September 26, 1862.

While the route to the war zone was similar for both regiments, much more is known about the Fifteenth's trip. Friends and family members descended upon the camps in droves to hear patriotic speeches and bid a fond farewell to their loved ones. The men then hopped aboard the trains on August 29. The first stop was Lambertville, where a large crowd waited at the depot. Civilians entered the cars, passing out food and good wishes during the half-hour stop, then it was on to Philadelphia, where the trains ground to a halt at about 7:00 P.M. The men left the train and marched to the Union Volunteer Refreshment Saloon (the Twenty-third arrived at about 4:00 P.M.

on September 26). A large cannon stationed on one of the Philadelphia streets signaled their imminent arrival. When fired, women of all ages gathered food together and rushed to the saloon, where the soldiers were as excited about their reception as they were by the food. The *Hackettstown Gazette* noted that it was "astonishing to see the people . . . in one solid column on each side of the line, all anxious to greet us as we passed, and as many as possibly could grasped our hands and those who could not would bid us good-bye and God speed; the scene was affecting and at the same time inspiring." Quincy Grimes added that the "boys would stop and shake hands and then run to catch up, the officers just the same." Young Jonathan Hutchinson recalled that pretty girls made up most of the crowd.[25]

Fed and rested, the Jerseymen boarded trains bound for Baltimore. The Twenty-third NJV had to board cattle cars, as no passenger cars were available. The latter regiment reached Baltimore at 3:00 A.M. the next day, September 27, while the Fifteenth arrived at 6:00 A.M. on August 30. The men again took breakfast at a saloon established for the soldiers. Edmund Halsey of the Fifteenth NJV noted that Baltimore was "not so clean or neat as at Phila." The march through the streets of Baltimore to the train station for the final leg of the journey was also quite different from that in Philadelphia. "With fifes and drums sounding, we marched through Philadelphia; but Baltimore heard only our footfalls upon her pavement," recalled Chaplain Haines.

The trip from Baltimore to Washington became tedious because the train halted frequently on the sidings to permit passenger trains to pass. Outside of Washington, the men of the Fifteenth NJV could hear the sounds of cannon fire signaling the Battle of Second Bull Run. The Fifteenth finally reached Washington at dusk on August 30; the Twenty-third reached there at noon on September 27. Both regiments marched immediately to the Soldiers Rest, a huge barn-like building, to be fed. Dayton Flint of the Fifteenth complained that the men were not fed supper until 9:00 P.M., and it consisted of a "piece of bread with a little salt meat with coffee, without sugar or milk." The Fifteenth NJV spent the night in a barracks in Washington, where Hutchinson noted, "we were packed so close that some laid on top of one another." They were so exhausted that it really did not matter. The next day the men ate dry bread and tough salt pork washed down by coffee, then they were ordered back into line and marched through the pouring rain to Fort Pennsylvania at Tennallytown, northwest of Washington, but still within the confines of the District of Columbia. The march was mostly uphill, and despite three rest stops, scores of men fell from the ranks. The march ended at 4:00 P.M., but the officers' confusion about where to pitch their tents south of the fort caused the men to stand in the rain for an additional four hours. The Twenty-third marched to East Capital Hill in a blazing sun, and there its men went into camp.[26]

Upon arriving at Tennallytown "we were put right into the service as if we were old soldiers," Dayton Flint wrote his father. This meant companies going out on picket duty to help ensure the safety of Washington. While here the green Jerseyans first saw the veterans of the Army of the Potomac, who were often filthy and ragged. Edmund Halsey observed that the "contrast between these troops and our men was striking . . . [the veterans were] browned by the sun almost to blackness—no baggage but a blanket each—& not appearing to need any—a cup or tin plate their only cooking utensil." Flint added, "such a rough-looking set you never saw in your life." It quelled the Jerseymen's grumbling, for Flint admitted, "'I thought we were having it pretty tough, but after listening to the stories they tell, I think we are faring pretty well . . . some are without shoes, others without regular uniforms, and all very dirty as water is scarce." Reverend Haines also observed the condition of the troops, but noted, "their arms and accoutrements were in splendid order."

The Army of the Potomac left the confines of Washington for Maryland to take on Lee's invading hordes on September 4, but the Fifteenth NJV remained behind to defend Washington. The regiment moved its camp to a new location, dubbed Camp Morris, and stayed here for the remainder of September. Meanwhile, McClellan's army battled Lee's in Maryland and new regiments were being formed in New Jersey.[27]

The Fifteenth NJV built Fort Kearny, cut down timber, and constructed new military roads during this period. Details of twenty-five men from each company were sent out daily to work on the fort. Lieutenant Ellis Hamilton commanded one detail and told his father, "it was pretty hard work as they were all green hands in military affairs and don't know how to mind yet, but as they are fresh from the woods and mountains of North Jersey they chopped away right hastily." The area abounded with woods that could hide the enemy's approach, so the men were detailed to cut a half-mile-wide swath through it on all sides of the fort. Martin Grassman complained to a friend back home, "there is a great amount of labor that we soldiers have to perform that amounts to just nothing at all, but it all belongs to soldiering." Companies continued picketing during the regiment's stay here.

While not building, clearing, or picketing, the men drilled during their time at Camp Morris. Complaining that he was too busy to write home regularly, Quincy Grimes informed his family, "we have to drill six hours every day beside dress parade, and meals three times a day, and roll call morning and night." By September 21, Lieutenant Hamilton could write home, "the regiment is in splendid trim now and drills beautifully . . . [it is] the best disciplined, the best drilled and the best behaved of all the Regiments which compose the Defences [*sic*] of Washington."[28]

The sudden discharge of a private's pistol startled the men, but no one was more surprised than Major Brown when the bullet entered his tent and grazed his leg. Realizing the danger of these weapons, Colonel Fowler ordered the men to relinquish them to their offices and carry only rifles, much to the chagrin of the affected men.

The men could not complain about the food, however. They received a loaf of "good" bread daily, meat rations three times a day, and coffee twice. Saturday and Sunday brought rice, beans, potato "mush," and soup made with fresh vegetables. The men generally rested on the weekends, but they spent Saturday washing their bodies and clothes.[29]

As with those who had enlisted before them, the new soldiers from the Fifteenth NJV had to adjust to military life. There were many temptations, and while some men willingly succumbed to them, others, like Paul Kuhl, fought against them. He wrote home, "there are a great many temptations in that I have to contend against and I find it much harder to withstand them than I thought it would be but I hope that through the help of God and the thought that the prayers of my Mother and Sisters . . . [I] will be purified by the temptations through which I have to pass." Not accustomed to an austere life, many spent lavishly at the sutlers' wagons. John Laughton wrote home to his father, "I have spent pretty much all my money . . . send me some for I can't live here without money."

The peaceful days near Washington abruptly ended at 10:00 P.M. on September 28, when the regiment was ordered to be ready to march at a moment's notice. Rubbing the sleep from their eyes, the Jerseyans prepared two days' rations and trudged out of Camp Morris at 4:00 A.M. on September 30 with a mixture of excitement and dread. They grumbled when informed that they had to leave everything behind but their haversacks, canteens, and weapons. Tramping down the road toward Washington, the Fifteenth began singing "We'll Hang Jeff Davis to a Sour Apple Tree." The regiment reached Washington at about 8:00 A.M., where the men spent several hours resting. The column marched to the railroad depot during the early afternoon. They found the depot choked with soldiers also seeking passage, so the Jerseymen had to wait. Space on the train to Baltimore was finally available on October 1, but quarters were cramped, as there were not enough cars. Some men climbed atop the cars, giving them a panoramic view of Maryland and making more space for the ones remaining inside. Switching trains, the regiment finally reached Frederick, Maryland, at about 8:00 P.M., where the men jumped out of the cars and marched to an open field outside of town. The stench of decomposing horses from the Antietam Campaign was too much for some men, and without tents, they spent their first night sleeping under the stars. Shelter tents arrived the next day.[30]

The Fifteenth NJV waited outside of Frederick until 3:00 P.M. on October 2, when it was called back into line to take the hilly road toward South Mountain, marching about seven miles before halting for the night. Up early the next day, the column struggled over hills, mountains, valleys, and ravines. The sixteen-mile march to Keedysville, then to Bakersville, was very difficult for veteran soldiers and torture for inexperienced ones. Sergeant Phineas Skellenger wrote home, "I have stood the march very well but it is just about as hard work as I have ever done." Men fell from the ranks in droves. Up early on October 4, and expecting the worst, the regiment was relieved to march only two miles, to the camp of the First New Jersey Brigade. The men of the Fifteenth NJV were overjoyed to learn they were to join this esteemed unit. One reported, "the [men in the] old regiments say ours is so large it seems more like a brigade, being larger than all the four regiments composing the first."

Lieutenant Colonel Edward Campbell finally joined the regiment from his stint with the Third NJV during this period. The men's enthusiasm for him soon turned to disdain, as he moved quickly to make them into soldiers. That meant strong discipline, the type Colonel Fowler had never imposed. Lieutenant Ellis wrote home that he was "very stern and very green although I may be mistaken about the latter." Benjamin Hough's first experiences were much more negative when some men in his company fell out of line during the march toward Bakersville. Campbell rode over and drove them after the column, hitting one who had stopped to get some water with the flat of his sword. One soldier became so incensed that he loaded his gun and pointed it at Campbell. Hough also noted that Campbell had choked a guard because he would not present arms to him. "If we ever Get in to a fight I pitty [*sic*] hi's [*sic*] case."[31]

The journey to join the First New Jersey Brigade was shorter for the Twenty-third NJV. Remaining in camp on East Capital Hill for two days after its journey from New Jersey, the regiment found itself back in column and marching back to Washington on September 29. Before breaking camp, the officers inspected the men's weapons. "They were condemned," noted Forrester Taylor. They received new weapons, Model 1842 smoothbore percussion muskets, which one modern historian has called "third rate." The march from Washington on September 30 was a miserable one on the hot, dusty road. Taylor noted that the dust was so thick, "I could not see the first men in our company from the position I occupied near the rear." Because they left their tents behind, the men grumbled about sleeping under the stars. Just getting comfortable at 11:00 that night, they were told to collect their meager belongings and get back into column. Now the men were too tired to grumble. Marched to the train station, they boarded trains bound for Frederick, Maryland. Upon arriving, the men fashioned shelters for the night comprised of fence rails and corn stalks. The regiment remained here until October 8, when it marched to Bakersville and joined the First New Jersey Brigade. Lieutenant E. L. Dobbins would never forget the first time he spied his new unit. "Where were the rest?" he asked.

The men soon realized that their commander, Colonel Cox, was a problem. Taylor wrote home, "our colonel is drunk the greater part of his time and we were in consequence neglected." He added that the men were on the verge of mutiny on more than one occasion, and one enlisted man even threatened Cox, screaming that he "would be riddled with balls [at] the first fire." Assistant Surgeon Robert Elmer recorded in his diary, "there is considerable dissatisfaction on account of the manner in which the men are fed & provided for." The last straw occurred during an inspection on September 29, when Colonel Cox whacked several of his officers with the flat of his sword. A court-martial convened on October 13 with General John Newton presiding. Cox faced two charges—"conduct unbecoming an officer and a gentlemen" and "drunkenness on duty." While found not guilty of the first charge, Cox was found guilty of the second. He was permitted to resign, citing health reasons as the cause.[32]

The relations between the old and new regiments were strained, particularly with the nine-month regiment. Wallace Struble of the First NJV wrote home, "of course not a very good feeling prevails between the new and old Regiments. of [sic] course old Soldiers come out Without much prospects of ever getting more than $12 a month, and we have been in more hard fighting than they ever dare goe [sic] into and yet they are jealous about something."

Realizing that he needed a Jerseyman with combat experience to lead the Twenty-third NJV, Colonel Torbert selected Major Henry Ryerson of the Second NJV. Ryerson was not so sure. He wrote to his sister, "I dislike the idea of taking command of one of the 9 month regiments—at the expiration of their term I would be mustered out of service, which I do not desire." He finally relented and assumed command of the regiment on November 12.[33]

While the newly invigorated First New Jersey Brigade remained in Maryland, there were strict rules against stealing from civilians. Dayton Flint noted that most obeyed this order unless the civilians were suspected of being "secession in principle." The new recruits realized that they were becoming real soldiers now. Gone were the high-quality food and the spacious Sibley tents. In their place were hardtack and small shelter tents. Halsey wrote home, "now we are content to wash occasionally and dress as warm as possible without any great regard to features."

The brigade settled into a routine during its stay at Bakersville. Roll call followed reveille, and then the men prepared their breakfast, which usually consisted of salt beef and hardtack with coffee. Sometimes the beef was omitted, much to their disdain. They also became accustomed to breaking the hardtack into pieces so they could pull out the worms infesting them. Next came equipment cleaning, and squad drill at 8:00 A.M., followed by company drill. These drills continued until 11:30 A.M., when "recall" sounded and the men prepared for their midday meal. "Battalion drill" followed at 1:00 P.M., with the entire regiment drilling as a unit. Supper followed at about 5:30 P.M., followed by free time until 8:30 P.M. Roll call sounded, and then taps half an hour later.[34]

Dayton Flint wrote home that "we live in a city of tents." The new soldiers were anxious to engage the enemy and put down the rebellion, causing their veteran comrades to smile. The latter had encountered the enemy countless times and valued the periods when they could luxuriate in camp without the prospect of battle. Considerable excitement occurred on October 17 when wagons appeared with the knapsacks left behind by the Fifteenth NJV. Up to this point they had gone shirtless after washing their only shirts in the river. Because many of the knapsacks were not identified, there was "a good deal of 'smouching' and a good many things were lost," noted Halsey. Jonathan Hutchinson's was never returned and he bemoaned the loss of his extra shirts, socks, and other valuable belongings.

The men of the First New Jersey Brigade hoped that they would soon go into winter quarters. None could have imagined the agony that awaited them before they were permitted to do so.[35]

CHAPTER 5

Fredericksburg, Terrible Weather, and Sickness

The serenity of the post-Antietam period near Harper's Ferry ended at 3:30 A.M. on October 31, 1862, when reveille sounded and the brigade broke camp and headed toward the Potomac River. This move was no surprise, as the brigade had been under marching orders for a week. Despite this knowledge, the men were still disappointed when the orders finally arrived. "We had lain in camps so long we hated to move but it couldn't be helped," noted Orderly Henry Callan. Another volunteer wrote home, "once the order came to be ready to start at 5 minutes notice; again we were ordered to be ready at 6 hours notice, thus we were kept in suspense until Thursday night when we were ordered to be ready to start the next morning at 4 o'clock." The Fifteenth NJV marched away with Lieutenant Colonel Campbell in command. Colonel Fowler remained behind, too ill with typhoid fever to accompany his men.

The first day's march was a tough one for the veterans and new recruits alike—fifteen miles, to within a mile of the old Crampton's Gap battlefield. The officers permitted only four stops of five minutes each during this march. By the time the ordeal finally ended in the early afternoon, about a third of the brigade had fallen out of the ranks. The totals were disproportionately higher in the two new regiments. The latter did their best to keep up, throwing away items previously thought to be indispensable. Dayton Flint of the Fifteenth NJV described what he carried during this phase of the war: "First our gun, cartridge box with forty rounds inside, haversacks with three days rations, canteen holding about three pints of water. My knapsack contains a blanket, overcoat, rubber blanket, one piece of tent cloth, two shirts, one pair drawers, one pair socks, and a box of writing paper. Besides this I have in my cupboard, a tin plate, cup, knife and fork, and part of the time I carry the frying pan." Many new soldiers threw away important items, such as blankets. The men of the Twenty-third NJV had a particularly tough time maintaining the pace, and by the time the brigade reached its bivouac only a handful of men remained in the ranks. "Not having enough men to stack arms," a local newspaper reported. The regiment straggled so badly that Colonel Torbert sent Major Charles Wiebecke of the Second NJV with two companies to correct the situation. Already resentful of the "bounty men," Wiebecke carried out his orders "with a vengeance . . . [he] drove them along like sheep." When a group balked, the major ordered his men to fix bayonets and charge. The green troops "ran for their lives," strewing the road with their accouterments. Realizing that the veterans meant business, the new troops returned to pick up their equipment and then continued their march without straggling.[1]

Wallace Struble of the First NJV was not a fan of the Twenty-third NJV, and he wrote after this march that when the new regiment arrived in camp, "they had but one Company left, the rest lay strung out along the road. While not a man in our regiment fell out."

The brigade did not stay long at the Crampton's Gap battlefield, but pushed ahead to Berlin, five miles below Harper's Ferry, the next day. November 2 found the Jerseymen crossing the Potomac River into Virginia on pontoon bridges. The column continued about five miles, where it bivouacked. Because it was the Sabbath, the men participated in religious services all afternoon and into the evening.[2]

The new week brought no reprieve to the weary, for the VI Corps was on the road on Monday, November 3, for a fairly easy eight-mile march to Purcellville. A soldier reported to his local newspaper that five men were "drummed out of the brigade this afternoon. The whole brigade was drawn up in two lines, and they were marched at the point of the bayonet from one end of the line to the other, having their heads uncovered, and hair cut short. The cause was cowardice." Another soldier reported that the men's heads were shaved. Eight more miles along the east side of the Blue Ridge Mountains on November 4 brought the Jerseymen to Philomont, near Bloomfield. The seven-mile march to Carrville on November 5 ended on the road leading to Ashby's Gap. With the supply wagons far to the rear, the men worried about getting rations, but they solved their problem by cleansing the area of every chicken and pig they could find. One wrote to a local paper, "we have bloody swords but through God they are not stained with human blood. Pig blood will make its mark." Back on the road the next day, the men marched eleven miles, through White Plains, to near Thoroughfare Gap. The routine after each halt for the night was the same—many men slipped away from their units to forage. To try to stop the looting, Lieutenant Colonel Campbell court-martialed seventeen men in the Fifteenth NJV for absence without leave and "marauding." They were reduced in rank and fined. The weather had been pleasant up to this point, but the Jerseymen awoke on November 7 under a layer of snow and with the storm still blowing. It was a "bargain to keep warm in our little muslin houses," Paul Kuhl of the Fifteenth NJV noted. Robert Elmer of the Twenty-third NJV reported that it was "a very trying day indeed." No one complained when the brigade remained in camp for two days until the storm blew itself out.

The storm over, the brigade was back on the road on Sunday, November 9. There would be no prayer services on this day, as the column marched to New Baltimore, which Edmund Halsey called "as mean and wretched a place as ever I saw." Camp was in a thicket with the tents pushed close together for warmth. The weather was "very cold & blustery all day," according to Elmer.

The following afternoon, Generals George McClellan, Ambrose Burnside, and William Franklin reviewed the brigade. Fed up with McClellan's cautious nature, Lincoln had finally replaced him with Major General Ambrose Burnside, commander of the IX Corps. Burnside did not want the assignment but felt that he had no choice but to accept. "As he [McClellan] rode by each Regiment he was greeted by such cheers as only soldiers of the union army can give . . . we gave him three times three cheers and then three for Gen. Franklin and after that three more for Col. Torbert," reported Kuhl. He reported that Burnside "looks exactly like all the portraits you see of him in the papers." Oscar Westlake of the Third NJV wrote home that if their "Pet" was removed, "it will not be long until I take my farewell of the army also." Not all the men showed their support for McClellan. According to one account, "many were loud in their denounciations [*sic*] of him—Burnside was the favorite of many and the men cheered lustily as he passed by; his common appearance, having no mark of distinction, with a slouch hat on effected much merriment among the boys." Quincy Grimes claimed that McClellan "cost the country more treasure and lives than any other [general]."[3]

The entire army was now concentrated near Warrenton. Lee, always the gambler, had again divided his army, and a concentrated Federal thrust against any component could lead to serious consequences. Because Burnside insisted on waiting for the arrival of pontoon brigades, the army waited to cross the

Rappahannock River to take on the relatively few enemy units in front of it. Perhaps because of the transition in leadership, the entire Federal army remained near Warrenton for a week, frittering away an opportunity to crush Lee. There was not enough wood for fires, not enough blankets, and the men had only flimsy canvas shelter tents to keep out the extreme cold. The brigade broke camp again on November 16, marching forty miles over the next three days to reach Stafford Court House. These were very harsh marches through rain, snow, and the ever-present mud. Edmund Halsey described the latter as being clay, "blue, yellow & red—greasy and sticky." John Judd of the Third NJV added in his diary, "took a straight course through the fields, woods. . . . Marched 14 miles." The exceedingly muddy roads may have forced this overland route. Meals consisted of only hardtack and coffee, so on the evening of November 16, Judd reported, "all of brigade went to catching rabbits. Very plentiful."

The march on November 17 was easier—only ten miles—but the men were unhappy about camping in a thicket. "Had to cut our way through before we could camp," noted Charles Harrison of the Second NJV. The first Federal troops reached the Rappahannock River on this day, but Burnside would not permit them to cross until pontoon boats arrived.[4]

A brigade flag arrived from some New Jerseyans living in California on November 21. The grateful unit accepted the banner during a formal ceremony. About two thousand men gathered for prayer services on Sunday, November 23, which entailed formal sermons in the morning and prayer meetings in the evening. "It seemed much more like a Jersey sabbath than any I have spent for a long time," Kuhn noted. Many men went out gathering persimmons, which were abundant in the region. For John Judd it was an interesting experience. "Got lost in the woods. Found my way out just at dark," he recorded. Judd spent spend additional time hunting persimmons and ate so many that he became sick.

Not many men discussed their activities on Thanksgiving. Judd noted in his diary, "No work no drill. Divine service in all the camps." Adequate rations continued to be a problem, partially because the enemy tore up the railroad tracks. "Railroads are torn up and a regiment ten miles from its supplies with only its two or three teams to haul the food would starve to death," Edmund Halsey recorded in his diary on this special day.[5]

Sickness and desertions grew by the day, and discipline remained harsh. Private Henry Rockefeller of the Third NJV was court-martialed for sitting down while on picket duty. The penalty was forfeiture of $20 in pay and twenty tours of additional guard duty.

Typhoid fever broke out while the men were near Stafford Court House, filling hospital tents and decimating the ranks. The men were actually relieved to be on the road again at 6:00 A.M. on December 4. The sick were left behind to avoid exposure. The march, with few halts, was a long one on muddy, slippery roads. The column finally camped for the night near King George Court House after the sixteen-mile march and remained here for several days because the ubiquitous mud finally put a halt to all movement until the temperature dropped. The camp was so miserable it was dubbed the "Devil's Hole." It was a period of extreme hunger, sickness, and death. Wood was scarce, so the men were cold most of the time. Jonathan Hutchinson and his comrades in the Fifteenth NJV were furious to see the officers posting guards around large piles of fence rails while the men shivered under the frigid conditions. "While in Maryland the boys could burn all the fences they wanted—they were Union people. But down here where they are all rebels, they post guards over every house . . . it is too bad." The scarcity of clothing also worsened the situation. All the men had to protect themselves from the cold were meager clothes, blankets, and the thin canvas shelter tents when the temperatures fell well below freezing at night. They often huddled together to share their body heat and blankets. The sick left behind to be properly cared for arrived soon after, many in bad shape. There were surprisingly few deaths during this harsh period.[6]

Although the daily ration was supposed to be one and a quarter pounds of beef or three-quarters of a pound of pork, it was usually salt pork. While hardtack was a staple, additional rations of a pound of rice, beans, sugar, and coffee were now scarce. The arrival of the brigade's brass band relieved some of the misery. If the music did not ease the pain, the periodic whiskey rations certainly did.

Pontoon bridges to span the Rappahannock River finally arrived on December 10, and with them came marching orders for the next day. No one grieved leaving "Devil's Hole." Actually, "orders came in by the dozen of every kind," noted Halsey. More pleasing to the men, particularly those of the Fourth NJV, was the presentation of a new set of colors from the state of New Jersey to replace those lost at the Battle of Gaines' Mill. The state flag was inscribed with the legend:

Presented by the State of New Jersey

To her Fourth Regiment

For Gallant Conduct at Crampton's Pass, Maryland

September 14th, 1862

The men cheered and saluted as they received the colors. Colonel Hatch gave a speech in which he called upon his soldiers to never desert their colors and told them that they had shown as much valor as any other troops at Crampton's Gap and Antietam. The stain of Gaines' Mill was finally erased.[7]

All the brigade's regiments were now commanded by veterans: Lieutenant Colonel Mark Collet (First), Colonel Samuel Buck (Second), Colonel Henry Brown (Third), Lieutenant Colonel Edward Campbell (Fifteenth), and Colonel Henry Ryerson (Twenty-third).

General Burnside reorganized the army into three Grand Divisions during this period. The Right Grand Division was commanded by General Edwin Sumner; General Joseph Hooker led the Center Grand Division; and General Franklin led the Left Grand Division, composed of the I and VI Corps. The VI Corps was commanded by General William Smith, and General William Brooks continued leading the First Division. Burnside planned to throw his army across the Rappahannock, seize Fredericksburg and the heights overlooking it, secure the railroad leading to Richmond, and then drive south to capture the Confederate capital before Lee could stop him. Although the army was in the vicinity of Falmouth as early as November 17, and could have crossed the river and captured Fredericksburg before Lee could bring up his entire army, Burnside chose to wait until the pontoon bridges arrived. Because of the delay, Lee accumulated his entire army just south of Fredericksburg and awaited his foe's next movement.[8]

Franklin's Left Grand Division, reinforced with three divisions, sixty thousand men, would storm the heights in front of him. This accomplished, it would turn to its right and attack Marye's Heights behind the town which was being attacked frontally by Sumner's Right Grand Division. Because Burnside's orders were somewhat ambiguous, Franklin construed them to mean that only one well-supported division was to make a reconnaissance in force—the rest of his massive "Grand Division" would essentially be observers to the great battle occurring to the north.

Burnside first had to get his army across the Rappahannock River. Not all the men were anxious to be driving southward, particularly in the winter. Colonel Henry Ryerson of the Twenty-third NJV wrote "every step we take beyond the Rappahannock River carries us further from our supplies and if the roads continue as they are now our supply trains will not be able to follow us." The veterans of the original four regiments were not happy about the prospects of meeting Lee's legions again, especially in this weather. "I am not in the least anxious to meet the Rebels again, [and] am perfectly satisfied with what I have seen of them, but if I have to, [I] will do my best to pay off old scores," Orderly Henry Callan wrote home.[9]

Reveille sounded at 4:00 A.M. on December 11, and the brigade was on the road two hours later for the eight-mile march to Stafford Heights, overlooking the Rappahannock River. It was a relatively slow march because of ankle-deep mud, but the brigade reached its destination at about 2:00 P.M. and the men were told to pitch their tents. The Jerseymen could see the town of Fredericksburg about a mile upstream. Down below they could see the bridge-builders trying to complete their task. However, Mississippians on the opposite side opened fire, killing and wounding a number of builders, and harassing the others. Burnside ordered his artillery to open fire, but it provided little assistance, as the guns' barrels could not be depressed enough to hit the pesky marksmen. The shells instead devastated the town. Federal infantry poured into pontoon boats in a new attempt to force the defenders from the town. Rowing rapidly across the river, the small force dispersed the enemy sharpshooters, and the bridge-building continued.

The bridges now completed, the Federal troops immediately crossed. Torbert ordered his men to break camp and march down to the riverbank at "Franklin's Crossing" at about 7:00 P.M., where they waited their turn to cross. It was clogged with troops, so Torbert brought the brigade back to its original halting place, about a half-mile away, where it spent the night with the rest of the VI Corps. Fog enshrouded the area on December 12. After a predaybreak breakfast, Torbert led his men back to the river and crossed between 8:00 and 9:00 A.M. So thick was the fog that the soldiers literally groped their way across the bridge and onto the adjoining land. The First New Jersey Brigade formed the division's third, or last, line and was deployed into two lines of battle, with the fresh Twenty-third NJV on the left and Fifteenth NJV on the right, making up the first line, and the original regiments of the brigade in the second, about a hundred yards behind. Although referring to a different situation, Orderly Callan explained the significance of this deployment to his sister. "The new men could not be depended on as reserves for if the old Regt gave way the new would be sure to go—but if the new gave way the old were there for them to rally behind." The men now stacked arms and rested.[10]

The fog lifted between 10:00 and 11:00 A.M., giving way to a beautiful sunny day. Between 2:00 and 3:00 P.M. Torbert double-quicked the men about a half-mile away from the riverbank across the plain toward the ravine that contained Deep Run. The stream angled toward the Confederate positions. The men could see the bodies of dead Confederate skirmishers during this rapid march, which Lucian Voorhees of the Fifteenth NJV noted were "comfortably clad, though their garments were somewhat coarse, being made of a sort of gray cotton jean with U.S. buttons on." Enemy shells began exploding all around the Jerseymen as they approached the shelter of the ravine. "They opened on us with Shell but we got into the Ravine before they done us much damage," noted Lieutenant Westlake. John Laughton likened the shells to hailstones flying over his head. Colonel Ryerson of the Twenty-third NJV marveled at his green regiment's ability to maintain its formation over the thousand-yard march. "I seldom have seen the maneuver better executed by old regiments," he wrote. Finally reaching the ravine, Torbert ordered his men to lie down in it to reduce casualties, which had been light up to this point. The men did not care that their new overcoats became soiled, but they did take special care to put their rifled muskets in safe, dry places. Shells rained down on the ravine, killing and wounding several men and worrying the rest. A shell whizzed by where Colonel Ryerson's head had been as he bent down to see the extent of one of his men's injuries. Ryerson's men marveled at his coolness, but he realized that he was just lucky. Hexamer's Battery dropped trail nearby and took up the enemy's challenge. The brigade remained here all night, and enemy shells continued playing upon the area, wounding several Jerseymen. Later, the men were permitted to make small fires to prepare their suppers.

Ordered to replace the division's pickets on December 13, Torbert selected four companies of the Fifteenth NJV (B, F, G, and K), supported by the remainder of the brigade. The latter were probably reluctant to leave the security of the ravine, but a small knoll in a muddy cornfield protected many of them. Henry Callan, now captain of Company H of the Second NJV, wrote home that they "laid just behind a rise of ground out of sight except when we stood up, which we did not do very often." The initial quiet on the picket line changed when the Confederates decided to reestablish their line beyond the Richmond, Fredericksburg, and Potomac Railroad. The picket line had melted away when General George Meade's Division successfully attacked the Confederates to the left of the brigade. Several companies of the Sixteenth North Carolina (Pender's Brigade) ventured forward, but they did not see the Fifteenth's NJV's picket line. Springing up, the Jerseymen poured a destructive fire into the approaching Tarheels, forcing them back in some confusion. General Dorsey Pender wrote in his report, "these skirmishers become so annoying that additional companies had to be thrown out." The picket line was exposed to a lively artillery fire during this time, which periodically caused the men to throw themselves on the ground for shelter.[11]

The rest of the brigade's inactivity ended at about 3:00 P.M., when their corps commander, William Smith, observed increased Confederate activity in front of him and decided to order an end to it. Division commander General "Bully" Brooks ordered Torbert to move his picket line forward and extend it to the left, to the railroad, which ran parallel to the Federal position. Brooks wrote in his report that Torbert was ordered to "move forward the picket line, supported by one or two regiments." Torbert's report is more expansive, indicating that his orders were to "advance one regiment, supported by another, and drive the enemy from and hold their position, posted in a railroad cut and behind the embankment, just where the railroad crossed a deep ravine, and on the extreme left of my picket line."

Torbert selected the Fourth NJV, with its new flags. Colonel Hatch yelled, "Come on boys, follow me." The regiment "advanced in a handsome manner under a severe fire," reported Torbert. Driving gallantly forward, the Fourth NJV hit the Sixteenth North Carolina in its front, while the four forward companies of the Fifteenth's NJV attacked its left. Mounting the railroad, now held by the Jerseymen, Hatch yelled, "Boys! Three cheers for our side," and the men responded with wild yells. Seeing this aggressive Federal action jeopardizing two of his batteries a mere two hundred yards from the railroad, Confederate division commander A. P. Hill immediately sent General Evander Law's Brigade to blunt the advance. Seeing this threat, Torbert immediately ordered the Twenty-third NJV forward. Two regiments of General David Russell's Third Brigade also ventured ahead.[12]

The men of the Twenty-third NJV had been watching the Fourth's gallant charge until it was lost in the ever-present smoke. Now Ryerson ordered the nine-month men to rise, fix bayonets, and perform a "left face, column right, double quick" maneuver. Ryerson's orders were to advance on the right of the Fourth NJV to take pressure off that flank. Upon approaching the Fourth, Ryerson was to go in "by the flank left in front" and throw three of his companies to the right along the railroad. The four companies on the left were to enter the woods encompassing the Deep Run ravine, near where the Fourth NJV was advancing. Ryerson halted his men as they exited the cornfield and changed their formation from column of four to line of battle. A shell almost immediately screamed into the ranks of Company K, wounding ten men. As the Twenty-third NJV double-quicked across the open plain, it was hit by eighteen enemy artillery pieces. Ryerson called the advance "terrible" and admitted that he did not "think much of it at the time, but I trembled after it was all over." In the excitement of their first battle, the officers neglected to tell the men to shed their knapsacks, which hampered their progress.

When within fifty yards of the railroad embankment, Ryerson yelled, "right face, left wheel" which was intended to drive back those enemy sol-

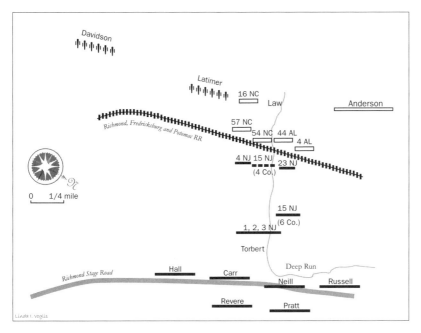

MAP 4. Battle of Fredericksburg (December 13, 1862).

diers on their side of the embankment and capture a number of prisoners in the process. However, performing this complex movement while being pounded by intense artillery and small arms fire was quite different from executing it on the parade ground. "Some confusion ensued, and in fact a slight momentary panic," admitted the regiment's historian. The Twenty-third NJV wavered, and then fell back about fifty steps, but quickly reformed and again moved against the left of Law's Brigade, probably the Fourth and Forty-fourth Alabama, at the railroad. This time they were more successful. Four of the companies entered the wooded Deep Run ravine to their left, where they encountered the right of the Fourth NJV, already slugging it out with the enemy. The remaining companies drove straight ahead.[13]

The Fourth, Twenty-third, and the handful of companies from the Fifteenth NJV were initially successful in driving the enemy reinforcements from the railroad. But worrying that this aggressive act might invoke a larger Confederate attack, General Brooks ordered Torbert to pull his men back from the railroad, leaving the picket line behind to protect it. Meanwhile, near the railroad, a shell exploded near Colonel Hatch, blowing off his lower right leg. Major James Brown, commanding the four companies of the Fifteenth NJV, was also hit, sustaining a painful thigh wound. Because of heavy losses to the Fourth NJV and the loss of its leader, Ryerson halted his regiment's withdrawal until the Fourth NJV pulled back. This is a vulnerable time for any unit, and the situation was worsened because the Twenty-third NJV had never been in battle before. Complicating matters further, Ryerson ordered a complex wheeling movement, yelling "About face—Right Wheel—March" that was intended to get them into the wooded ravine. He also reasoned that he could take a large number of prisoners in this way. However, an officer told him that two enemy regiments, presumably the Fifty-fourth and Fifty-seventh North Carolina, were on the opposite side of the ravine and closing fast. Ryerson noted that the "men not being well drilled, ran the other way." Major E. Burd Grubb was able to get about two hundred men into line, where they fired two volleys into the approaching Confederate infantry, stopping them in their tracks. This permitted the rest of the regiment to withdraw. These actions caused Colonel Torbert to write, "I am pleased to speak in the highest terms of the conduct of the Twenty-third . . . being a nine-months' regiment, and the first time they were under fire." The Confederates continued following the Jerseymen, and one noted that they fled "like wild turkeys." Federal reinforcements advanced and put an end to the Confederate counterattack.

While the Fourth and Twenty-third NJV engaged the enemy near the railroad embankment, the rest of the brigade held its position behind the small knoll. Oscar Westlake of the Third NJV had seen enough of the war to know that "our Regiment was lucky enough to be on the Reserve." John Judd of the same regiment observed the heavy losses in the Fourth and Twenty-third NJV and recorded in his diary, "nothing gained." The Third NJV was called out to perform picket duty that night. Judd described the experience as, "heavy firing all night—no one hurt—lay in the mud all night—no chance to sleep."[14]

The morning of December 14 found the brigade still in a vulnerable position. "On the extreme front all morning laying flat in the mud—every time we raised our heads[,] fired at by Rebel sharp shooters," noted Judd. The Jerseymen were finally relieved by the Second Brigade at about 9:00 A.M., permitting them to slip back to their original positions in the ravine. Seeing the Jerseymen withdraw, the enemy opened fire, hastening the movement. The men were content to lie in the ravine, out of range of the enemy's small arms and artillery fire. General Torbert received notice at about 11:00 P.M. on December 15 that the army was about to recross the Rappahannock River. The men were roused a few hours later, at 1:00 A.M. on December 16, and, under terse orders to be quiet, marched out of the ravine and back toward the river, where they formed a line of battle at about 3:00 A.M. With mixed feelings they observed the rest of the army crossing the river, while they remained behind. Nothing of importance occurred that day, except that the First NJV was sent out on the picket line later that morning. The brigade formed the corps' rearguard and would be among the last Federal troops to cross the river. The men nervously awaited an enemy attack, but none came that night. Before daylight, Torbert was able to send the Fourth, Fifteenth, and Twenty-third NJV. Meanwhile, his other regiments deployed near the bridge. When the First NJV returned from the picket line, it crossed over to rejoin the rest of the brigade. Once on the opposite side of the river, the brigade guarded the engineers as they dismantled the pontoon bridges.

Although the brigade's historian termed the unit's role in this battle as "not much more than a skirmish," it was yet another stinging defeat, and 162 men were lost. As expected, the highest losses were sustained by the Fourth NJV (80) and the Twenty-third NJV (50), which engaged the enemy near the railroad. Appendix A contains the regimental breakdowns of losses.[15]

In addition to losing a number of enlisted men, the brigade lost the valuable services of Colonel Hatch. Carried to the rear, a portion of his leg was amputated, but he lost too much blood and succumbed a few days later. Major Brown of the Fifteenth NJV was also wounded—his second injury of the war. If there was any consolation, it was that the two Confederate regiments attacking along the railroad sustained higher losses (171) than the entire First New Jersey Brigade.

Although an official count of the First NJV's losses is not available, Wallace Struble noted that there were no fatalities. According to Struble, men of the other regiments complained about Torbert's favoritism toward the First. He explained to his sister, "well you see General Torbert is a good Military man, and he knows our regiment has been imposed upon ever since he has been in command of us."[16]

Colonel Ryerson summed up the men's feelings when he wrote, "it was a foolhardy undertaking, I think, to attempt to take . . . the heights, fortified as they were with tier upon tier of guns and forts." Burnside decided to attack Lee's entrenched army again the next day, but was wisely counseled against it by his lieutenants. The men were depressed, and their letters home showed it. Edmund Halsey of the Fifteenth NJV explained that his particularly dark letter reflected that "as an army we had been beaten and were on the retreat. Many men I knew and liked were killed or wounded."

The engineers finished their work, and the brigade pitched their tents about half a mile from the river. Daybreak brought a Confederate artillery barrage, which was quieted when the Federal guns responded. The men could see the enemy scouring the battlefield, and for the three additional days they remained here. December 19 brought orders to pack up and march to White Oak Church.[17]

The camp at White Oak Church was about two and a half miles below Falmouth. A soldier from the Fifteenth NJV wrote home, "the idea of retracing our steps with nothing accomplished, and a less number of men, did not please us exceedingly." Heavy rains fell after the battle, adding to the men's wallowing spirits. They were cheered when told that they would finally go into winter quarters, however. But the very next day, December 20, the men were given additional rations and told to prepare to march. The long roll never sounded, so the men settled into their quarters. The weather remained bitterly frigid, and some men dug holes seven or eight feet under their shelter tents to try to avoid the cold. Wood was scarce, permitting only sporadic fires. Adding to the misery was inadequate clothing and poor food—hardtack and salt pork. The muttering grew in intensity, as the "last sparks of patriotism seem to have disappeared since the conflict and fearful carnage. Some declare their utter indifference as to the final result, while others clamer [*sic*] vehemently for negotiations of peace, on what terms they care not," reported a soldier. Discontent over Lincoln's Emancipation Proclamation also was rampant. Jonathan Hutchinson wrote home, "the men will not fight for niggers." At least the men did not have to spend much time drilling during this period—Oscar Westlake reported that it occurred daily in the Third NJV, but only from 10:30 A.M. to noon.

Christmas day was given over to games and homesickness. Some soldiers, like John Judd, spent the day more intensely—"worked hard all day fixing up tent." He continued perfecting his living quarters the following day as well. The men of the Fifteenth NJV feasted on roast turkey, roast goose, roast beef, and lager beer, leading John Laughton to write, "in all wee [*sic*] had a splendid time." This was not the case in the Third NJV, where Oscar Westlake complained that "we had a devilishly poor Dinner Consisting of hardtack and Beef and what was worse we could get no Whiskey." The burial of a soldier in the Twenty-third NJV put a damper on the day in that unit. This was but a continuation of the string of illnesses and deaths that had begun earlier in the month, particularly among the men of the two new regiments, who had not yet acclimated to the soldier's life. "A disease called the Camp Fever appears to be the prevailing malady," a soldier wrote home, "which seizes upon the vitals of existence and lays its victim prostrate with scarcely a moment's notice." Men were dying at a rate of one a day, and that knowledge took a psychological toll on the sick as well as the healthy. Edmund Halsey noted how differently men handled their illness. Some, he saw, lacked "elasticity." These men "lose their energy—get to brooding over their trials and seem to sink right down." At the other extreme were men who actively fought their disease "as they would a difficulty which *must* be overcome." Another problem was the extreme cold, which sent scores to the hospitals with frostbite, particularly of the feet and hands.[18]

New Year's Day brought a half gill of whiskey, which, according to one soldier in the Fifteenth NJV, "created some merriment among the men, especially those who by traffic and bargain obtained several rations." Dress parade followed, and then each regiment formed into hollow squares, with the chaplain in the middle providing patriotic and religious remarks. The spring-like weather permitted the men to shed their overcoats.

The Jerseymen gradually shook off their depression and made themselves more comfortable. They began constructing more permanent winter quarters of log huts with fireplaces. The scarcity of tools made the work difficult, but the huts rose steadily. These quarters were seven or eight feet long, five or six feet wide, and four feet high. Mud was used to seal the cracks, which Dayton Flint noted "sticks like molasses candy, and answers the place of mortar very well, besides being already mixed." A horizontal ridgepole, supported by two stout saplings at either end of the hut, supported the pieces of shelter tents that acted as the roof. Other pieces provided a door. Fireplaces built with rocks or sticks plastered with mud helped keep the men warm. Drilling took up three to four hours a day. The men were delighted when they received boxes filled with delicacies from home. Quincy Grimes actually called it "high glee." They ate well, having fresh beef every other day, alternating with pork. All was not completely well during this period, however, as the men had not been paid for weeks and the married men increasingly worried about their families.[19]

If the men of the Jersey Brigade thought that they had settled into winter quarters, they were sadly mistaken, for at 9:00 A.M. on January 20, the brigade received orders to fall in and prepare to move out. The men remained on alert until 11:00 A.M., when each regimental commander read them "encouraging" remarks from General Burnside, and then the march finally began. While most of the First New Jersey Brigade gave wild cheers, the Fifteenth NJV remained silent, probably because they were content to remain in camp. Although the road was clogged with marching troops and military vehicles, the brigade could boast that its march ended six miles farther along from where it began. After their long rest in camp, the men quickly tired on the march, and their heavy knapsacks did not help matters. At least the weather cooperated—the temperatures continued to be moderate for mid-January. But the skies were threatening, and rain began falling toward late afternoon, soaking the soldiers as they pitched their tents.

The Jerseymen were up before daybreak and ordered to fall in. It had rained all night, and they grumbled about their wringing wet clothing and exposure to the elements. After marching about thirty minutes, the men halted and prepared breakfast. The wet conditions made fires impossible, so the day began without their beloved coffee. On the road again by 10:00 A.M., the conditions were still passable for the columns, but the roads were sloppy and slippery. This began to change by the hour, as rain continued falling and the myriad feet churned the mixture into almost pure mud. Wagons sunk deep into bottomless mud, and hundreds of horses and mules died from their exertions. Where possible, the infantry avoided the road, marching instead through woods and fields. After two miles, the men were told to fall out and seek whatever shelter they could find for the next four hours. After resting, they resumed the march for another two miles to Banks' Ford, where they bivouacked for the night. Edmund Halsey estimated that the brigade marched a total of ten miles "in a circuitous direction (to avoid being seen by the enemy probably.)" Camping in a wooded area, the men made large fires to warm themselves and dry their clothing. They had been soaked to the skin for days.[20]

The Jerseymen's sufferings were a result of Burnside's attempt to take another crack at Lee's position across the river. Flawed intelligence reported that Lee's army was significantly weakened as parts had left for Tennessee. Burnside also reasoned that Lee would not expect another attack so soon after his enemy's devastating defeat just a month before. The new plan called for a diversionary maneuver in front of Fredericksburg, while the remainder of the army crossed upstream from the town and attacked Lee's flank. Crossing the river on pontoon bridges just below Banks' Ford, General Franklin's Grand Division was to advance toward the Orange Plank Road and attack the enemy entrenched on Marye's Heights. The pontoon boats were supposed to arrive early on January 21, but the hostile weather delayed all but fifteen of the eighty boats. The Yankees spent the day sliding, sweating, and swearing, trying to get the pontoon boats down to the river. Toiling in knee-deep mud, they could move the wagons with the boats only ten feet or so before the wheels again sunk into the deep mud. With the remaining boats still a mile or two away, and the enemy fully knowledgeable about his intentions, Burnside pondered his options.

A more miserable set of men could not be found than the Jersey Brigade soldiers on the morning of January 22. All were encased in muddy clothes, exhausted from their exertions with the pontoon boats, and out of food. They were now ordered to "corduroy" the roads with logs to make them more passable, and these efforts continued into the following day. January 24 was devoted to marching in what they learned later was a circle, causing considerable cursing and dismay. They were then again put to work pushing and pulling the pontoon boats out of the mud. Teams of twenty horses were not able to pull the boats, so entire companies had to accomplish what beasts of burden could not. Taking hold of long ropes, they pulled each boat as much as half a mile until the ground was hard enough for the horses to take over. Sometimes, when two boats were near each other, the men engaged in friendly competition to see who could pull theirs the fastest. The historian of the Twenty-third NJV noted that in some cases it took four hundred men an hour to move a pontoon only one hundred yards in the deep mud. One wag in the Fifteenth NJV yelled out, "We hain't soldiers anymore, we are Burnside's mules!"[21]

Burnside finally decided to abort the mission, which was later called the "Mud March," and on January 25 the Jerseymen marched back to their camps near White Oak Church. The cursing and foul mood returned when the men realized that a cavalry brigade had camped nearby, stripping their camp of firewood, and destroying many of the structures in the process. "The camp was all in disorder, with mud and filth everywhere. Whisky was served out, and profanity and wickedness seemed unchecked," noted Alanson Haines of the Fifteenth NJV.

Demoralization gripped the army, and the pace of desertions reached alarming levels, leading Dayton Flint to proclaim, "the Army of the Potomac is no more an army." Rumors were rampant about the army being broken up and sent to other theaters, attacking the enemy again, or retreating toward Washington. The brigade was also rumored to be Washington-bound for provost duty. The Rebels across the river taunted the men with signs that read, "Burnside's stuck in the mud." The men's clothes were torn and ragged, and those with inadequate shoes remained in camp.[22]

Cooking for each company was performed by two of its soldiers. The all-too-predictable army food was augmented by boxes from home, which cheered the men. In addition to food, the boxes commonly contained clothing and medicine. Glass containers invariably broke during transit, spilling their contents over the other items. The men did not seem to care, however, and rarely complained. Some families sent perishable food—chicken usually spoiled before it arrived, but pies seemed to weather the trip.

Inadequate supplies became a serious problem. Colonel Henry Ryerson of the Twenty-third NJV blasted the Federal authorities in a letter home in mid-January. "Since the battle of Fredericksburgh [*sic*] 181 of my men have been without blankets and tents. A large number are almost shoeless and the whole regiment sadly needs trousers."[23]

Writing to his sisters on a gloomy afternoon in February, Dayton Flint described his routine. "It does not take us long to do our housework in the morning. The first thing we hear is 'fall in line for roll call.' . . . It does not take us long to perform our toilet—we merely put on boots and caps, the only things taken off, when we retire. After that we fold up our blankets and build a fire to make coffee by. We do not make up the beds until night, when we stir up the feathers and spread the blankets over them." Flint explained that the "feathers" were simply pine needles, which the men periodically replaced with fresh ones as they dried out and discolored. He added, we "fall in line" for everything. "It's 'fall in line' for your rations, 'fall in line' for your money, and 'fall in line' for your letters. Yesterday we 'fell in line' to be vaccinated."

Body and head lice were an ongoing problem. While they were old companions to the veterans, the new men of the Fifteenth and Twenty-third NJV began finding them crawling on their bodies just prior to the Battle of Fredericksburg. "We all dove into our tents like so many woodchucks into their holes and such a pulling off of shirts was never seen before," joked Flint. He also noted that "the old soldiers had quite a laugh over us and told us we must get used to these things."[24]

The boredom became unbearable as the winter wore on. Mud was everywhere, limiting outside activities. Sometimes the men were called out to help corduroy roads. Drilling became impossible, except on rare occasions when temporarily falling temperatures froze the ground. Three-day picket duty rotated among the regiments, which helped break the monotony. The only ongoing activities were cooking and gathering wood. There was never enough of the latter, so the men had to trudge farther and farther from their camps to collect it. By the end of February, they walked a mile for wood, and the distance increased each day. During the long days the men also played chess, checkers, cards, and, when weather permitted, baseball and other athletic pursuits.

One day melded into the next until the men were unable to distinguish the day of the week. Sunday was the exception, for it was marked by inspection. With little else to do, the men spent considerable time writing letters and talking to their tent mates. Leaders were a constant source of discussion.

Burnside's Mud March was the last straw, so Lincoln replaced the general with Major General Joseph Hooker on January 26, 1863. A month later, some men were still supporting Burnside. One maintained that, "if Burnside failed it was not his fault; the future will reveal the truth." It did not. Another noted that Burnside failed "through the treachery of subordinates." The Jerseymen knew that Hooker was a tough fighter, but they did not think he was up to the task of army command. For example, Dayton Flint wrote home, "the troops are a little afraid that he won't have the head to carry out the plans for so large an army; otherwise, they have confidence in him." Many of the men who first saw Hooker at a Grand Review in April were disappointed. Edmund Halsey noted that Hooker "looked older and less 'dashing' than I supposed from what I had heard of him." Still, many men expressed optimism that the war would soon be over.[25]

As the dreary winter dragged on, the men became increasingly depressed. Many openly discussed their dissatisfaction with being in the army and wanted to return home. A member of the First NJV admitted to a hometown newspaper that "our Regiment . . . [is] not as disciplined as it should be, principally on account of the fault of some officers, who instead of attending to their business, pass away their time in grumbling and so forth." Edmund Halsey noted in his diary that "we have become disheartened and begin to think we can never succeed."

Periodic visits by the paymaster helped brighten the gloomy days. The more responsible men sent sizable amounts of money home to their families, but all retained at least some currency. One soldier complained that "the sutlers *now* have large stocks at unreasonable profits, and are rapidly accumulating the proceeds of the Paymaster's department . . . such profits are an outrage on humanity."[26]

General Joseph Hooker's first priority was to raise morale and whip his army back into fighting shape. Ovens popped up in every camp, providing fresh bread. Other nutritious food, including potatoes and vegetables, also found their way into the men's diets. According to Wallace Struble of the First NJV, "it makes a great differance [*sic*] after living on salt pork and hard crackers for nearly a year." Quincy Grimes of the Fifteenth NJV referred to hardtack as "shingles." The men also received new uniforms. But it was the ten-day furloughs that they valued most. Married men were given priority. Benjamin Hough of Sussex County was one of the few who rejected a furlough because "I could not more than get home before I would haft to start back."

The men spent considerable time reading their hometown newspapers, becoming spectators to ongoing clashes between Republican- and Democratic-

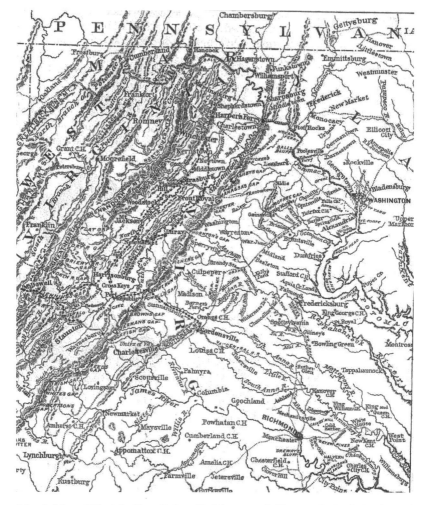

MAP 5. Map of Virginia (from Robert U. Johnson and Clarence C. Buel, *Battles and Leaders of the Civil War* [New York: The Century Co., 1884]).

slanted presses. For example, the January 10, 1863, issue of the *Camden Democrat* slammed the *Sussex Register* and *Morris Jerseyman* for "conspiring together to slander Col. Sam. Fowler . . . charging him with being 'absent from his post of duty,' roving through Sussex County, and abusing the Administration for inattention to the wants of the soldier." The paper noted that Fowler was in New Jersey to accompany the body of his cousin, Sergeant John Fowler, who had been killed at Fredericksburg. The Democratic-leaning newspaper went on to erroneously state that most of the men of the Fifteenth NJV were Democrats and, along with the *New Jersey Herald,* blasted the Federal authorities for taking the large Sibley tents from the Fifteenth NJV and giving them to the "negroes at Belle Plain." This, the papers claimed, led to sickness and discomfort among the men. The Republican-oriented *Camden Press* retaliated by calling the assertions "vile fabrications that none but a traitor would originate or have the baseness to circulate." The *New Jersey Herald* would not relent, writing, "the statement is true, and we make it on the authority of Col. Sam. Fowler and can confirm it by his affidavit and those of any number of his officers and men . . . it is the most villainous outrage upon our soldiers that has yet come to light." The newspaper claimed that the loss of these tents caused many men to fall sick and die. The allegations were false, as the men had not used Sibley tents since they joined the First New Jersey Brigade, because of the impracticality of transporting them during active campaigns. One soldier wrote to the *Sussex Register* that his log house with its roof made of shelter tents was more comfortable than the Sibley tents—"we don't want them," he wrote.[27]

Other newspaper allegations involved inadequate food and clothing, but most of the men told a different story. Benjamin Hough wrote home that "we can get as Many clothes as we want and as to grub we get plenty of that[.] we get ten hardtacks a day[,] pork and fresh beef every other day[,] sugar and coffee[,] rice and beans[,] potatoes and onions[,] and now we get fresh bread every day." He even gained weight—seven more pounds than when he left home. Hough's downfall was the fresh bread. He wolfed down his loaf and then purchased additional ones at five cents apiece. Between the bread and the inactivity, Hough could write home, "I am well and rugged but growing and larger everyday[;] soldiering is a Kind of a lasye [*sic*] life." A member of the First NJV wrote to a local newspaper, "we are well furnished with clothing of a good quality."

Illness continued to be a problem for the new regiments. Dayton Flint estimated that over sixty men from the Fifteenth NJV had died from late December through the beginning of March, and as many as three men were buried in one day. Edmund Halsey reported that seven men died in less than two weeks during mid-February. One soldier wrote home, "Diarrhea, Dysentery and Fevers are the most usual diseases prevalent in camp." John Laughton correctly believed that the bad water was causing the diarrhea. "The less we drink of it, the better we are off I find." Seeking ways to stem the havoc that disease had wrecked on the Fifteenth NJV, the men were ordered to vacate their old camp on March 12 and move to a new one, about a mile away. This meant lugging the logs and other building materials from their old camp to the new site. It snowed during this period, but the temperatures were not cold enough to solidify the mud. "We now have more comfortable quarters than our old ones, but it cost us as hard days' work as I have ever done," Flint reported. At least they were closer to sources of wood, making their daily treks less laborious. A steady stream of returning comrades, who had been sick or wounded, cheered the men.[28]

General Torbert was again away from the brigade because of illness, so Colonel Brown took his place. This did not sit well with Colonel Ryerson, who wrote, "Colonel Brown . . . gets drunk about every other day. He has not been visible for some days now, having fallen off his horse and skinned his nose . . . exceedingly credible for the 1st N.J. Brigade," he wrote sarcastically.

Torbert's return cheered the men. "He is a pride to the boys and to the brigade . . . he delights to dress in fancy uniforms, of which he has a large assortment, and makes as gay an appearance on his gaily companioned horses as any knight of olden times," noted a soldier in the First NJV.[29]

Several changes in command occurred over the winter. Lieutenant Colonel William Birney replaced Colonel William Hatch as commander of the Fourth NJV. Major Charles Ewing replaced Birney as second in command. E. Burd Grubb, who had been an aide to General Taylor during the Seven Days battles, had had a remarkable ascent. Joining the Twenty-third NJV in late November as its major, he was promoted to lieutenant colonel on December 24, 1862, to replace James Brown, who had resigned, and then to colonel of the regiment on March 9, 1863, when Henry Ryerson took command of the Tenth NJV, which was performing provost duty at Washington.

Colonel Samuel Fowler of the Fifteenth NJV, still suffering from a bout of typhoid fever, resigned his commission on February 28, 1863. Lieutenant Colonel Edward Campbell, who essentially commanded the regiment because Fowler was gone so often, deserved the post. One soldier reported, "the Col. is *often absent,* so we scarcely ever miss him." Another noted that Fowler "might as well [resign] for he is no military man." However, Campbell was not popular, because "he is disposed to work the men too hard, and is somewhat imperious in disposition." Another called him a "stern disciplinarian . . . his motto seems to be, every man must do his duty, then all will be well." While the men did not warm to him, they respected the lieutenant colonel and believed he should be given the command. Many of the men shared the sentiments of a soldier who wrote, "if we ever go into a fight, we want to go in under Col. Campbell." Some were openly worried that politics would bring them an unknown leader.[30]

Campbell would not lead the Fifteenth. Instead Lieutenant William Penrose, a Michigander and civil engineer before the war, who had served as the adjutant of the Third U.S. Regulars prior to his promotion, arrived on April 21. One soldier wrote home, "our officers appear much pleased at having a Colonel from the Regular Army, and much improvement in discipline &c., may be looked for." Upon assuming command, Penrose "delivered an inspiring and patriotic address to the officers and men of the 15th, confiding in his ability to see to our well-being and comfort, and asking a hearty cooperation in sustaining him in his efforts." The men soon learned that their new leader was a stern disciplinarian, committed to whipping the regiment into shape. They mistakenly believed Penrose to be a West Point graduate, an idea that he did little to correct.

The long winter of sickness and death had taken its toll on the officer ranks as well, causing a mass of promotions. Selections were not always made on the basis of merit, as one soldier wrote home, "the many promotions made from pure personal motives, without respect to rank, promises or ability, give but little encouragement to the truly patriotic, competent, and worthy . . . an office-seeker here, to be successful, must show kin either direct or indirect, or be a hanger-on at Head Quarters."[31]

The brigade lost its corps commander, William Franklin, after a fight with Burnside. The latter blamed Franklin for losing the Battle of Fredericksburg because he did not adequately deploy his two corps. Franklin responded by sending a letter to Washington declaring that the campaign was hopeless from the start and providing his own ideas for a new one. A furious Burnside demanded, and got, Franklin's removal. General William Smith, who led the corps while Franklin led the Grand Division, was a coconspirator and was also removed. General John Sedgwick assumed command of the VI Corps, and General William Brooks retained command of the First Division.

With spring's arrival came moderate weather, and the sick list shortened by the day. One soldier was able to write home on April 13 that "the [Fifteenth] Regiment enjoys very good health at present." Morale also increased, and gone were the soldiers' grumblings about wanting to return home. Part of the reason for the change was that the men had less free time in which to fret. Another growled, "we drill almost constantly." The officers also began paying closer attention to the men's cleanliness. During the frequent inspections the men's general appearance and rifles were inspected as usual, but now they were also ordered to take off their shoes and socks. The inspectors often scowled, "Dirty as the devil" which sent the offender to the river to wash his clothes and body. Scarcely a dozen men in each company passed inspection. Men continued receiving furloughs, but there were fewer of them and they lasted only five days, rather than ten. Wallace Struble noted that each company received two furloughs at a time. His number was thirty-seven, so his chance of getting one was slim. New ones were not granted until the men on leave returned. Edmund Halsey reported that only three of the twelve men given furloughs reported back on time. He called the offenders "scamps" and noted that their absence "prevents any one else from going."[32]

Torbert, now a brigadier general, assembled his officers together in late March and told them that it was only a matter of time before they broke winter camp and began another campaign. The men were to begin thinking about how they would discard all of the additional belongings they had accumulated during the winter, as storage space in the wagons would be at a premium. During this period, the officers led the men from camp for target practice, further indicating that something was up. As time went on, these activities occurred daily, except for Sunday. Jonathan Hutchinson of the Fifteenth NJV noted that the men each fired five rounds at targets the size of a barrel head, a hundred to two hundred yards away. Quincy Grimes reported with some embarrassment that only twenty-eight bullets out of more than three hundred fired by his company found the target, or one out of every thirteen fired.

Many men now turned to religion when they realized that they were again to tangle with Lee's legions. A soldier noted that "many wicked men are being converted to the faith of the Redeemer." Prayer meetings, which were suspended during the winter because of the adverse weather conditions, started up again, this time with swelled numbers.[33]

Assembly sounded on April 8, and the men were told to prepare for a review by President Lincoln. "He rode in front of the regiments, saluting the colors of each as he passed, the bands playing various airs appropriate to the occasion." The soldier wrote home, describing the president: "the ugliest photograph I have ever seen of him does not make him any uglier than he is. He looked pale, haggard and care-worn, but seemed to have a gleam of happiness about him." Paul Kuhl noted that Lincoln "is very homely quite as much so as his picture represents him to be, but that does not make him any the worse." Quincy Grimes saw Lincoln the following day and reported that he "had a pleasant smile on his face, but is as homely as a brush fence."

The spectacle was awe-inspiring, leading Kuhl to write home, "the soldiers presented a fine appearance. You would not believe what a change there has been in the army in the last few months, instead of the disorganized rabble it presented after Burnside's second failure to drive the rebels from their stronghold, we now have an excellently disciplined army, and one which I am certain will do terrible work when it is next led against the enemy."[34]

April 11 was filled with activity. Battalion dress parade took place at 9:00 A.M., followed by brigade dress parade and review from 11:00 A.M. to 1:00 P.M. After their midday meal, the men watched a baseball game between the Second NJV and the Twenty-sixth New York. The latter won by eight runs.

April 18 brought great excitement to the men of the Twenty-third NJV, for they received a state color that day. As customary, the men had to weather a number of speeches, including one from Colonel Grubb, who was "not an orator," a newspaper reported. Still, he gave a good speech, "full of life, fire and energy characteristic of the man. He spoke to us of the cause that brought this fine Regiment into the service; of our duty to our country, and of his confidence, that . . . the Twenty-third New Jersey will not disappoint the expectations of its friends." Calling Corporal William Price forward, he promoted him to lance sergeant and told him not to defend the flag with his life, but "as your *honor.*" The regiment then let out three loud cheers for the brigade, three more for its commander, and three for Colonel Grubb. The band played between each set of cheers.[35]

The men of the Fourth NJV were relieved of the tedium of camp when they were told to assemble in April for special duty. Three companies under Lieutenant Colonel Ewing performed divisional provost duty, while the remaining seven companies under Colonel Birney guarded the wagons at general headquarters. They would be gone until November, depriving the brigade of their services during two major campaigns.

Governor Joel Parker visited the First New Jersey Brigade on April 26, 1863, with flags for the First, Second, and Third NJV. The deep blue-colored silk flags, fringed with gold, contained the following inscription on one side: "Presented by New Jersey to her ____ [each Regiment properly numbered] Regiment in remembrance of their gallantry at Crampton's Pass, Md., September 14th, 1862." The other side had an American eagle in a halo, with the same inscription. Parker gave a patriotic address during each ceremony, highlighting the deeds of the brigade, and telling the men how proud New Jersey was of them. After the ceremonies, the governor reviewed the troops and received a tour of the brigade's winter quarters. Colonel Penrose of the Fifteenth NJV was not present. According to Paul Kuhl, "I suppose for the purpose of getting a new Cols rig as he had nothing but a Leiuts [*sic*] and a rusty one at that when he came here."[36]

The Jerseymen received seven days' rations on April 27, 1863. All knew that the new campaign against Lee was about to begin. Forming into column at 3:00 P.M. the next day, they marched back toward the Rappahannock River. As the men looked back at their camps, they did so with "apprehension and disappointment." They were about to endure another low and an unexpected high before the summer was over.[37]

CHAPTER 6

Chancellorsville and Gettysburg

𝒩one of the enlisted men knew about General Hooker's aggressive plan to best Lee's army, but if they did they would not have been optimistic because it was similar to Burnside's, which had culminated in the dreadful Mud March. Crossing the Rappahannock River, the I and VI Corps were to make a diversion by preparing to attack Marye's Heights. The remainder of the army, about seventy thousand men, would cross the river farther upstream and fall on Lee's left flank. General George Stoneman's cavalry, galloping around the Confederate army, would destroy the vital railroads just north of Richmond. Opposing Hooker was a considerably weakened Confederate army, as all but one division from Longstreet's Corps was in southwestern Virginia attempting to recapture Suffolk.

Fear and apprehension could probably best describe the Jerseymen's reaction to recrossing the river to take on Lee's army. The heavy rains falling on April 28 soaked the men to the skin. Their woolen uniforms absorbed moisture, making them very heavy. This weight was added to the already heavy fifty pounds of equipment and supplies they carried. To make matters worse, they had not made a march like this for more than three months, so they quickly became exhausted. It was easy to trace the Jersey Brigade's route, for it was strewn with a trail of clothing and other materials thrown away to lessen the load. The superstitious bemoaned the fact that they were traversing the same route they had traveled the previous January during the infamous Mud March. Reaching the river embankment about three miles below Fredericksburg, the brigade was ordered to fall out by acting commander Colonel Henry Brown of the Third NJV, since General Torbert was sick yet again. The men did not care, for they were beyond the point of exhaustion. The men of the First NJV must have loudly complained when told that rest would not be their companion, as they were sent down to Gray's Point to support two batteries. Whether on picket or not, the men spent a miserable night, as they were overtired and not permitted to build fires.[1]

The Jerseymen could see troops slowly trudging toward the river with pontoon boats, but instead of being used to build bridges, the boats were used to ferry troops across the river. Each boat was large enough to carry an entire company across. The First NJV returned from picket duty at about 2:00 A.M. on April 29, and the entire brigade moved toward the riverbank between 4:00 and 5:00 A.M. Russell's Brigade had already crossed, and now it was time for the Jerseymen to climb aboard the boats. According to Halsey, they "double-quicked down the hill and over the plateau and jumping in the boats were rowed over." Most were across an hour later, and assembled in abandoned rifle pits on the river's south side. Forming into line of battle, the brigade moved forward, and then was thrown out on the picket line about four hundred yards from the enemy's defenses. The pickets on both sides affixed their bayonets to their muskets and drove them into the ground as a sign of truce. Trading of newspapers and other commodities, and sometimes animated conversation, filled the quiet hours. It rained all night, causing misery for all. Most would not have slept anyway, as they feared an attack on their vulnerable position with their backs to the river. The brigade remained on the picket line until the evening of April 30, when Bartlett's Brigade relieved it. Then it marched back toward the mouth of Deep Run near the Rappahannock River, where it spent the night. The next day the Jerseyans were read a communication from General Hooker announcing the movements of the III, V, and XI Corps.

The monthly roll of the brigade's effectives who would ultimately be engaged at the Battle of Chancellorsville was as follows:

First NJV	397
Second NJV	436
Third NJV	399
Fourth NJV	on detached duty—three companies on Provost Guard; seven on wagon guard
Fifteenth NJV	583
Twenty-third NJV	549
Total	2,364[2]

With the exception of Major J. W. Stickney, commanding the Third NJV in place of Colonel Brown, the regiments were commanded by their old hands: Collet (First), Buck (Second), Penrose (Fifteenth), and Grubb (Twenty-third).

Lying in their rifle pits all day, the men prepared to storm the heights on the evening of May 1, but Hooker countermanded the order and the First Division merely acted as spectators when the two other VI Corps divisions moved against the heights. Although the men did not know it, their powerful corps faced only ten thousand men under General Jubal Early. The firing halted at one point and the men could hear the Rebel bands playing "Yankee Doodle." The Federal bands responded by playing "Dixie." "Both armies cheered. It was a strange sight, and the sun going down at the moment made a deep impression on everyone," Edmund Halsey recorded in his diary.[3]

Hooker's ambitious campaign was having mixed success up to this point. The heavy storms delayed Stoneman's cavalry raid, but Hooker realized that he must put the rest of his plan into action, for the enlistments of approximately forty of his regiments were about to end, and he needed them to crush Lee. So he launched his flank movement without the vital cavalry diversion. He did not know that Lee was already aware of the Federal troop movements and had guessed that the one against Fredericksburg was merely a ruse.

May 2 found the brigade back on picket duty, but this time the regiments rotated between the line and closely supporting it. Some troops also supported the batteries. The officers assembled the men to hear General Hooker's address outlining the army's initial successes against the enemy. "Now the enemy must either come out from behind his defenses and give us battle on our ground, where certain destruction awaits him, or ingloriously flee," Hooker boasted. While most men cheered, more than a few wondered whether "Fighting Joe" was up to the task. Gunfire to the west indicated that the bulk of the army was taking on Lee.[4]

The Jerseymen were under arms at 2:00 A.M. on May 3, and by daybreak the Fifteenth NJV was in line of battle, slowing approaching the point where the Richmond and Fredericksburg Road intersected Deep Run. As the men approached their assigned positions, an officer of the troops being relieved told Colonel Penrose that the enemy was massing and possibly preparing to counterattack. Penrose quickly sent this information to his division commander, General Brooks, who ordered up the rest of the brigade, along with McCartney's and Hexamer's batteries. The enemy did not attack, but artillery shells rained down on the Yankees for most of the morning. Equally discomforting was the enfilade fire of the enemy pickets that picked off a Jerseyan here and there. The brigade occupied this position until noon, when the enemy troops in front of it melted away.

Colonel Penrose took this opportunity to teach his inexperienced men the nuances of war. Lucien Voorhees wrote home that his commander, "whose intimacy and constant association with the humblest of his command we have been unused to from former commandants, gives us spirit and animation unspeakable. The Colonel tells us personally how to act in emergencies, as he passes up and down the line of battle, as for instance—'Fire low boys'; 'If I order a charge, give three rousing cheers and then be silent.'"[5]

While the New Jersey Brigade slugged it out on the skirmish line, General Hiram Burnham's Light Division and General John Newton's Division, supported by General Albion Howe's, swarmed up Marye's Heights. Twice repulsed, they were not to be denied, and they punched a hole in the Confederate line by driving General Harry Hays' Brigade and half of Barksdale's from their positions. The entire Confederate line crumbled, forcing its men to retreat toward Chancellorsville and the rear of Lee's main army. The Jerseymen could hear the heavy fighting far ahead of them, where Hooker was taking on Lee's main body, as well as to their immediate right, where their corps was attacking Marye's Heights.

An aide galloped up to Colonel Brown at 11:00 A.M. yelling orders to maintain the picket line below Fredericksburg with part of the brigade, and to rush the rest toward the town to rejoin the division. Colonel Penrose was left behind to oversee the activities of the four companies of the Second NJV on the picket line, supported by his own Fifteenth NJV—a force of more than seven hundred men. Brown quickly formed the remaining six companies of the Second NJV in column with the First, Third, and Twenty-third NJV and marched them toward Fredericksburg. With a battle brewing, Brown probably wished he had the services of the Fourth NJV. The reconstituted First Division now marched away from Fredericksburg and toward the hamlet of Chancellorsville and Lee's rear, on the Orange Plank Road. The brigade led the division's advance, with the First NJV in the van.[6]

Hooker was in trouble. After initiating his bold campaign, he lost his nerve and settled into a defensive mode near the Chancellor house. Realizing that he needed reinforcements, he sent for Sedgwick's VI Corps, which was initially ordered to merely demonstrate against Marye's Heights. Now, with the heights taken, Sedgwick was ordered to Chancellorsville.

No enemy soldiers were seen during the first few miles of the advance, but then an enemy skirmish line appeared ahead, supporting a four-gun battery in a garden. These troops were from General Cadmus Wilcox's Brigade, which had been guarding Banks' Ford. When Wilcox heard the gunfire from the direction of Marye's Heights, he put his brigade in motion without waiting for orders. He had to delay Brooks' Division until reinforcements arrived. The six companies of the Second NJV were thrown out on the skirmish line, about two hundred yards in front of the rest of the brigade. The Twenty-third NJV then deployed into line of battle on the left of the road, and the First NJV and Third NJV deployed on the right. The Twenty-third's colors were a tempting sight, and soon Rebel artillery shells rained down on the regiment, killing a member of the color guard. Several other soldiers were wounded and Colonel Grubb's horse was killed, throwing him to the ground.[7]

In his official report, Wilcox reported that the Second NJV's skirmish line did not venture closer than 350 yards to his own. "They seemed reluctant to advance," he noted. But the six companies of the Second NJV did advance, reluctant or otherwise, and by flanking the battery, forced it to withdraw along with Wilcox's skirmish line. The men were aided by Rigby's Battery, which galloped up to the scene of the action, dropped trail, and helped drive the enemy from its position. Still not ready to take on the Federal infantry, Wilcox ordered Major C. R. Collins to take his fifty troopers from the Fifteenth Virginia Cavalry and delay the Second NJV's advance with a running battle. Behind them marched the First, Third, and Twenty-third NJV in line of battle. General Brooks also threw three regiments from Bartlett's Brigade on the left of the Twenty-third NJV, and two regiments from Russell's Brigade formed on the right of the Third NJV. Because the Second NJV's six companies could not completely cover the entire advancing Federal line, two companies of the Third NJV were also thrown out as skirmishers.

None of the men liked the looks of the densely wooded thickets in front of them, but they had no choice but to follow orders and enter. The constant arcing of Federal artillery shells over their heads, seeking to find and destroy the Confederate positions, was somewhat reassuring. The skirmish line was the first to enter the woods. It fired a volley into the enemy, and when it received one in return it "fell back in considerable confusion." The rest of the brigade now entered after unslinging their knapsacks. Bullets flew like swarms of angry bees when the men had advanced about twenty yards. Although the thicket was too dense to see the enemy, it was clear that they were present in heavy numbers. Grubb's Twenty-third NJV on the left of the road could just make out the enemy skirmish line about sixty yards away. Slowly driving them back, the now irregular and disordered Federal line climbed a slight rise, where the woods were more open. The fire was hot here, as Wilcox's men put up a stout defense. The men could make out a couple of structures in the clearing—Salem Church and, to its left (south), an old schoolhouse.[8]

The Tenth Alabama was deployed behind the church, with its left flank resting on the plank road. The Eighth Alabama was to the right of it, behind the school. A company of the Ninth Alabama occupied the church, and another

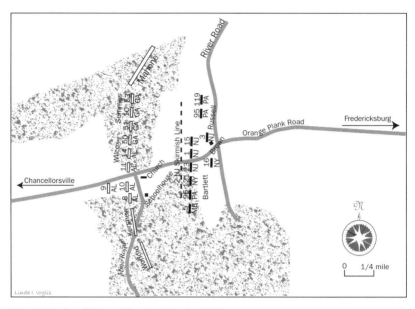

Map 6. Battle of Salem Church (May 3, 1863).

was in the school. The remainder of the regiment was in reserve behind the Tenth Alabama. Kershaw's and Wofford's brigades arrived and formed on the right of the Eighth Alabama, but played only a small role in the coming action. The Twenty-third NJV advanced against these three Alabama regiments, who held the high ground. The One Hundred and Twenty-first New York, Ninety-sixth Pennsylvania, and Fifth Maine of Bartlett's Second Brigade advanced on the Jerseymen's left. Behind them was the Sixteenth New York in reserve. On the opposite (north) side of the road, the First and Third NJV advanced against the Eleventh Alabama, whose right flank touched the plank road. To its left was the Fourteenth Alabama. The Tenth, Fifty-first, Fiftieth, and Fifty-third Georgia of Semmes' Brigade were on the left of the Alabamians. Mahone's Brigade were on the left of the Fifty-first. Two regiments of Russell's Third Brigade were to form on the right of the Third NJV, but instead remained a respectful distance behind its right flank. The Confederate position was a powerful one—eight Confederate regiments on high ground blocked the path of six Federal regiments from Brooks' Division. But Brooks was determined to continue his march to Chancellorsville, so he ordered his men forward to clear the woods. The time was about 4:30 P.M.

Because Russell's two regiments had not extended the line of attack to the right, the First and Third NJV were essentially attacking at least three Confederate regiments in a strong defensive position. They did not know the specifics, but from the amount of gunfire they could tell that they were in an impossible situation. The attack ground to a halt halfway up the hill, as the two regiments could not weather the storm of lead being thrown at them. Most serious was the enfilade fire coming from the right of the Third NJV, which should have been countered by Russell's two regiments. A Confederate soldier on the left of Semmes' line wrote home that the position behind an embankment was a "beautiful position . . . so we could load and fire without exposing anything except our heads and arms." Colonel Brown had anticipated problems, so he ordered Colonel Penrose to bring up his regiment as quickly as possible from south of Fredericksburg.[9]

The Fifteenth NJV had had its share of trouble south of town. Earlier, enemy shells screamed over the men as they took position along Bowling Green Road, causing many to instinctively duck. General Brooks happened to be riding by and tried to calm the men by saying, "test . . . test . . . test . . . test." McCartney's Battery galloped up as the men deployed in a protective depression north of the road. A Confederate picket line advanced to their right, forcing the regiment to fall back across the road, but these Rebels melted away when Marye's Heights fell to the VI Corps. By the time he received the urgent orders to rejoin the brigade, Penrose was on the road. When the Fifteenth NJV reached the scene of the action, Brown immediately threw the regiment into the action on the right of the Third NJV. The brigade commander recalled that the regiment came "into its position in beautiful order."

Brown reported that he had initially wanted the Fifteenth NJV to "support" the Third NJV, but that Penrose had "relieved" the latter regiment as it was "almost worn out by its long march and fight." It appears that the Third NJV had already retreated toward the edge of the thicket when the Fifteenth NJV arrived, thereby forcing the change in the orders. Part of the confusion may have been caused by the fact that Colonel M. W. Collet of the First NJV also commanded the Third NJV. While Collet had commanded the First for awhile, he was inexperienced in commanding more than one regiment at a time, and the thick undergrowth did not help matters. John Judd of the Third NJV merely wrote in his diary that his regiment "encountered a heavy infantry fire—forced to fall back out of the woods with considerable losses. Rallied behind a brush fence." Looking behind them, the men of the Third NJV could see the Fifteenth NJV advance. The latter had never been in battle as a unit before and were exceptionally nervous. The veterans of the Third NJV had to yell, "Throw off your knapsacks. You don't want them here."

"Col. Penrose took the hint and the knapsacks were laid on the ground," noted Edmund Halsey.[10]

Entering the woods, the Fifteenth NJV charged toward the enemy line for approximately a hundred yards. It was eerily quiet, unlike to their left, where the sounds of battle remained intense. The men began wondering if the enemy was even in front of them. Then, as one veteran recalled, "a tremendous roar of musketry met us from the unseen enemy." The Georgians and Alabamians had been ordered to hold their fire until the Jerseymen closed on their position. The effect of the initial volley, fired at eighty yards, is hard to imagine, as hundreds of men fell to the ground—dead, wounded, and just stunned from the sudden eruption before them. The Georgians were armed with smooth-bore muskets that fired "buck and balls," a round lead ball and three buckshot, which were most effective at short ranges. Sergeant Edmund English, whose Second NJV was in the area, wrote home, "never in all my experience have I seen or heard such a fearful fusillade." The officers quickly surveyed the prone men at their feet and ordered a return fire. Men continued falling here and there as the regiment took heavy frontal and enfilade fire. All of the discipline that Penrose had instilled in the regiment now took over, as the Fifteenth NJV held its ground. According to Colonel Penrose, his men "engaged at least four of his regiments, with, as I am convinced, a terrible effect, but without driving him from his well-chosen position." He ordered his men to "fire by file," but these orders were probably unheard in the din of battle, and instead his men blazed away individually at the unseen enemy.

After pulling his men back to reform their shattered line, Major James Stickney attempted to lead his Third NJV back into the fray in support of the Fifteenth. Captain Ellis Hamilton watched the Third's actions, as he was sent by Colonel Brown to bring up the regiment to support his own Fifteenth NJV. Stickney "gave the command 'Attention, Charge' but only about two companies moved forward and they not with an officer." Incensed, Hamilton stepped forward and got a number of others to advance as well. When Hamilton reached the Fifteenth's position, he proudly noted that his regiment was "engaged with the enemy and stood their ground like veterans while all the old Regts. kept back in the rear and fired right through our ranks." Edmund Halsey simply wrote that the "3rd N.J. was relieved and came in to our aid, too. In a short time they moved back." The situation could be best described as a vision of hell, as the day was excruciatingly hot and dry and the men could not see much around them because of the thick woods and billowing smoke.[11]

A bullet slammed into Colonel Brown's thigh at about 6:30 P.M., forcing him to relinquish brigade command to Colonel Penrose. Colonel Samuel Buck of the Second NJV was actually the next senior officer, but in the confusion he probably could not be found, so Penrose took command of the brigade.

The situation initially seemed somewhat better across the road, where the Twenty-third NJV and the three regiments from Bartlett's Brigade advanced against the three Alabama regiments. The Jerseymen "rushed forward with spirit and steadiness," according to the brigade historian, though initially this was not the case. Passing through the skirmish line, the regiment climbed a fence and continued its advance. Although only a nine-month regiment, the Twenty-third NJV had "seen the elephant at Fredericksburg." The fence disordered the Jerseyans' lines, which had already been thrown into disarray by the thickets. Now they were met by "a perfect hail of bullets." To make matters worse, they were receiving contradictory orders, and the combination of these factors caused terrific confusion. General Brooks fortunately appeared at this time and, reordering their lines, sent them forward again.[12]

These Jerseymen, along with the One Hundred and Twenty-first New York on its left, continued advancing toward the church and schoolhouse that housed the isolated companies of the Ninth Alabama. The Alabamians fired from windows and cracks between the logs, converting the simple structures into deadly fortresses. Long after the war, Lieutenant E. L. Dobbins wrote, "I can never forget that little brick church and the firing we heard, the whiz— whit-whung. We knew they were trying to hit somebody." After the battle, the Northerners insisted that the rest of Wilcox's men were in rifle pits nearby, but the Confederates steadfastly denied this claim. Slowly but steadily approaching the buildings, the Jerseymen and New Yorkers were finally forced back by the hail of bullets. Again they charged, this time storming past the buildings, and the Twenty-third NJV captured the company of the Ninth Alabama inside the school.

The Federal line continued forward into the very teeth of the heavy enemy small arms fire. A Confederate officer wrote after the war, "for a few moments everywhere along the line the enemy are staggered, but do not retreat." The battle hung in the balance for a moment, but the two Federal regiments refused to fall back, and finally caused the Tenth Alabama to break and run back to the Ninth Alabama's supporting line. It was tougher going to the New Yorkers' left, where the Ninety-sixth Pennsylvania could not budge the Eighth Alabama on the right of Wilcox's line.[13]

This was the moment of truth. With the Tenth Alabama out of the way, the Twenty-third NJV could have advanced to take on the Ninth Alabama, or turn to the left to hit the flank of the Eighth Alabama. The enemy reacted before a decision could be made. A large company of the Eighth Alabama, which had been on the picket line, suddenly wheeled and smashed into the New Yorkers' flank, causing it to disintegrate. The Ninth Alabama also moved resolutely forward from its reserve position. General Wilcox noted in his report, "the Ninth Alabama . . . sprang forward as one man, and, with the rapidity of lightning, restored the continuity of our line, breaking the lines of the enemy by its deadly fire and forcing him to give way, and following him so that he could not rally." The now reformed Tenth Alabama also sprung forward. Although both the Twenty-third NJV and the One Hundred and Twenty-first New York were fairly inexperienced, they knew a helpless situation when they saw it, and they began scrambling for the rear. Lieutenant Dobbins noted that "they didn't stay there long but came after us and we retired not slowly." The regiment's historian admitted that "we were soon inextricably mingled in one confused mass of fugitives over whom it was impossible to exert any control whatever." The officers finally got enough of the men together from the regiments to make a stand, but it was too little, too late, and the small band was swept away. The last of the Jerseymen's worries were the captured company from the Ninth Alabama, which they left behind.[14]

With the left of Brooks' line rushing for the rear, the Ninth Alabama turned and hit the flank of the Sixteenth New York of Bartlett's Brigade. The regiment was attempting to form along the plank road, plugging the gap between the Twenty-third and the First NJV, but the flank attack quickly smashed the regiment, sending its survivors to the rear. The Alabamians next hit the First NJV's exposed flank, and like dominos, the Federal regiments toppled one by one by the frontal and flank attacks. "The rebs crossed the road at our left and commensed [*sic*] fireing [*sic*] in to us," noted Benjamin Hough of the Fifteenth, which was now the subject of the unstoppable juggernaut. The Third NJV, which was behind the Fifteenth, was also hit. John Judd noted in his diary, "after being in awhile found some one was firing into us from the rear. Went back to see who it was, found the enemy had flanked us and got in our rear. Ordered to surrender, as there was no help for it[,] done so." Comparing the fights on the two sides of the plank road, Wilcox wrote, "the enemy did not assail with the same spirit on the left of the road [north], and were more easily repulsed."

Semmes' men joined Wilcox's, in the whooping and hollering that characterized the Confederate advance as they drove after the badly beaten enemy. Wilcox described the Federal troops at this point as a "confused mass of the discomfited enemy." After fighting for about ninety minutes, it was time for the Fifteenth to pull back from the swirl of disorder closing in on it. Seeing an American flag in the woods, Colonel Horatio Rodgers led his fresh Second Rhode Island forward. He soon encountered a begrimed New Jersey officer who pleaded, "for God's sake colonel, come over and help us out." The new troops helped the Jerseymen make a hasty retreat.[15]

Although anxious to evade the firestorm, many of the Fifteenth NJV stopped to pick up their knapsacks before continuing their retreat. The momentary halt allowed some of the enemy to close on the Jerseymen, killing and wounding a number of them. Not everyone was able secure their knapsacks. Sergeant Kuhl noted that the men "came out with nothing but what they could pick up on the battlefield." Sedgwick was on top of the situation, placing three batteries and Newton's Division within supporting distance. This firepower quickly put an end to the enemy pursuit, but it also caused a number of casualties in the Fifteenth NJV as the newly arrived One Hundred and Thirty-ninth Pennsylvania fired into its ranks. This ended the VI Corps' action on May 3. Brooks' Division lost almost fifteen hundred men during the two and a half-hour fight, which General Brooks called a "brief but sanguinary conflict." Among the killed was Colonel M. W. Collet of the First NJV, who was hit during the withdrawal. Lieutenant Colonel William Henry Jr. replaced him. Colonel Penrose, who briefly commanded the brigade, proudly wrote that "not a man left the line of battle except the wounded . . . my wounded were all brought off during or after the action."

The brigade reorganized its ranks that night, and Colonel Buck assumed command. Company roll calls tallied the losses. Sergeant Skellenger of the Fifteenth NJV wrote home, "our whole Brigade suffered terably [*sic*] our Regt did not suffer any worse than the rest did." Skellenger was right about the brigade's losses, as the Battle of Salem Church took a heavy toll. Of the approximately 2,400 hundred men that marched into battle, 511 became casualties (22 percent). Not since Gaines' Mill had the brigade suffered so heavily. Skellenger was wrong about the Fifteenth, however, as its losses were the highest in the brigade, losing 154 as it slugged it out with several Alabama and Georgia regiments in the open thickets for over an hour, taking frontal and flank fire. One of the regiments facing the Fifteenth, the Fourteenth Alabama, sustained the highest casualties (123) in Wilcox's Brigade. The other regiments in the First New Jersey Brigade also lost heavily, except for the Second NJV (49), which had thrown out some companies on the skirmish line. Most of the missing men were captured during the retreat. Appendix A contains the regimental breakdowns of losses.[16]

Given its untenable position, the brigade had fought well, in a battle General Semmes called "one of the most severely contested of the war." The two newest regiments distinguished themselves, and the *New York Herald* wrote that the men of the Fifteenth NJV handled themselves with the "coolness and *sang froid* of a veteran . . . the conduct of the men has been the subject of the greatest admiration since the fight." Sergeant Andrew Yeomans boasted to his pastor back home, "the 15th is much praised by the old Regiments in the brigade for standing so long under such a heavy fire." Sergeant Kuhl alluded to this in a letter home: "Our Regt. fought bravely and have gained themselves a high name in the Brigade. They have held positions where the other Regts refused to stand." Only the Third NJV's performance was mixed, as some of its men refused to return to the front despite orders to do so. Thirty-three years after the battle, Forrester Taylor, an officer in the Twenty-third NJV, received the Medal of Honor for his efforts to get several wounded men to safety under a hail of Confederate small arms fire.[17]

The men were exhausted, as their day had begun at 2:00 A.M. Most simply fell to the ground and went to sleep. The brigade was broken up on May 4, and each regiment was sent to a different area, sometimes supporting artillery. General Sedgwick knew that the enemy had been reinforced during the night, so he desperately requested additional troops from Hooker. Hooker, stunned by Lee's rapid reaction, which sent Stonewall Jackson's twenty-six thousand men against his vulnerable left flank, and by an artillery shell that knocked the senses out of him on May 2, merely replied that he had no reinforcements to send—Sedgwick must fend for himself. With his back to the Rappahannock River, Sedgwick formed a new defensive line that resembled three sides of a square. The First New Jersey Brigade and Bartlett's Brigade of Brooks' Division faced south, while Russell's Third Brigade and all of Newton's Second Division faced west at right angles with Brooks' right. Howe's Second Division faced east toward Fredericksburg, at right angles with Brooks' left. With a growing host in front of them and a river behind them, the Jerseymen wondered if this was their last action. Little wonder that a soldier in the Fifteenth NJV wrote home, "Gen Brooks appeared very uneasy."

Three large Confederate divisions encircled the VI Corps on three sides and began testing the Federal line, but the attacks were uncoordinated, as the enemy knew that with their backs to the river the Federal troops would fight tenaciously. "Heavy musketry was heard, believed to the right of us— Next in front and then to our left with great anxiety," wrote Halsey. He and the rest of the men knew they were cut off from Fredericksburg. The greatest fighting was on the left, occupied by Howe's Division. Just before dark, each brigade assigned a regiment to the picket line to hold the Confederate advance in check. The men knew it was a dangerous but necessary mission. The massed Federal artillery also opened fire, discouraging the enemy and keeping them at a respectful distance. Pontoon bridges were quickly constructed at Banks' Ford, and the men slipped from their positions that night. The Jerseymen occupied rifle pits while the rest of the VI Corps crossed the river, and they themselves finally crossed just before daylight on May 5. Shells screamed overhead, exploding all around them during the crossing, but few seemed to care, as they were so exhausted from being awake all night. Colonel Samuel Buck, now in command of the brigade, was thrown from his horse into a rifle pit, so command of the brigade reverted back to Colonel Penrose. Reaching the opposite bank, the brigade climbed a bluff, exposing the men once again to the enemy, who opened fire with their artillery. The exhausted Jerseyans threw themselves down about a mile from the river and ate breakfast, paying little heed to the bleached white bones of horses and mules that had perished during Burnside's Mud March scattered all around them. Heavy rains soon descended, and those men still lucky enough to possess their shelter tents quickly erected them. The brigade remained here until 8:00 A.M. on May 8, when it returned to its old camp near White Oak Church. "Footsore—dirty and demoralized" wrote Halsey in his diary.[18]

The first few days back in camp were therapeutic, as the men burned brush, removed stumps, and laid out new camp streets. This physical activity helped take their minds off the terrible battle and lost comrades. Expecting to remain awhile, the men built floors to their tents about a foot off the ground, permitting the cool breezes to pass over, through, and under the shelters. The weather turned warmer as May progressed, but the winds continued. The camps were very dusty, and every time the wind blew, fine particles of dust swirled through, covering men, tents, and supplies with a thin, gritty layer. Men frequently could be seen running through the camp, chasing elusive pieces of paper. The ever-present grit penetrated the eyes, making reading and writing difficult. All wished that rains would soak the area to calm the savage dust. The trees in the region had long been chopped down, exposing the campsite to continual sunlight, causing further distress. Some men arranged pine branches on their tent roofs for cooling insulation.

The men spent time in the usual camp activities—drilling, writing letters home, and whiling away the hours with their comrades. Some of the more popular games were cards, dominos, and quoits. Not happy with his men's performance during the last campaign, Penrose had his Fifteenth NJV spend considerable time on "skirmish drill." By the beginning of June, Quincy Grimes could write, "we understand it quite well." Paul Kuhl noted it was "harder work than farming . . . I can tell you."[19]

Few men took sick during this period, and each day brought the return of comrades who had been sick or wounded, which helped replenish the ranks. Morale was much higher than after the defeat in December. "Last fall the army was demoralized and down-hearted, but now every heart is buoyant with the hope of ultimate success . . . we have become accustomed to defeat, and await the final result, which we are bound to make victory," noted a soldier. Paul Kuhl agreed—"Our army is not as much demoralized by our defeat as might be expected, and if the north will but give us their sincere support, and fill up our thinned ranks, we will yet, by the help of God crush this rebellion."

Realizing that General Brooks had blundered badly at Salem Church, the Federal high command decided to get rid of him. They did so by promoting him on May 23 and sending him to Pennsylvania to command a harmless post—the new Department of the Monongahela. He was replaced with General Horatio Wright. One soldier wrote home, "it is a matter of regret throughout the division, as he was a favorite with all. During an engagement he was always on the lookout, being almost everywhere at the same time." The men knew little of their new division commander, as he had served primarily in South Carolina, Ohio, and western Kentucky. A soldier noted, "we hope he is as good as his predecessor, Gen. Brooks."[20]

The men had not yet sorted out what really happened at Chancellorsville, and many still operated on rumor. A good example is a letter from Sergeant Yeomans, noting that "Hooker is much liked—Sedgwick has lost not a little of his popularity in allowing the heights to be taken from him." Time would reveal Hooker's ineptitude and Sedgwick's impossible position, which forced him to concentrate his forces and ultimately recross the Rappahannock River. Given the condition of the army, Oscar Westlake of the Third NJV was safe in writing, "from all appearances we are not likely to do any thing for some time to come."

The men were not happy about the inspections during this period. In one instance they marched three miles under a scorching sun to be reviewed by General Sedgwick, then marched back to camp. The paymaster arrived on May 28 to pay off the men for two months. The privates received $26, much of which they sent home. Quincy Grimes of the Fifteenth NJV optimistically wrote, "I guess our Government intends to pay its soldiers regularly after this instead of waiting as it has from four to six months and longer."[21]

Facing the enemy in battle was the last thing anyone wanted, but General Lee had other ideas. If the Jerseymen had looked closely during the first week in June they would have seen clouds of dust swirling across the river to the southwest. They did not know it, but Lee was stealthily pulling his troops from their positions near Fredericksburg and marching them toward Culpeper Court House. From there, the Confederate army would enter the Shenandoah Valley, shielded from view by the Blue Ridge Mountains. Hooker knew the enemy camps were abandoned and he could see the dust clouds, but he was still befuddled from his infamous defeat at Chancellorsville.

Hooker sent his cavalry thundering toward Culpeper Court House on June 9 to learn Lee's location. The subsequent cavalry fight at Brandy Station was the largest ever on American soil. While the Federal horsemen experienced initial success, they were unable to break through the Confederate line to see that Lee had massed all but one infantry corps in the region. Prior to the battle, General Sedgwick was directed to move his corps to the river on June 6, crossing if necessary, to see what was going on. Hooker also gave him permission to seize civilians for questioning. Hooker was getting desperate.[22]

Sedgwick moved his entire corps toward the river and threw General Howe's Second Division across. Only General A. P. Hill's thinly stretched corps faced the mighty Federal army. Howe's men initially pushed Hill's men back and captured several prisoners in the process, but the Confederate defense stiffened as reinforcements arrived. Sedgwick reported to Hooker at 10:30 that night that three batteries were in his front and he could not "move 200 yards without bringing on a general fight." Although his orders were permissive, Sedgwick was cautious and wrote Hooker, "before bringing over the rest of my corps, I await orders. I am satisfied that it is not safe to mass the troops on this side."

On June 4, the New Jersey Brigade had been put on the alert about two hours before daylight to be ready to break camp and move. The tents were to remain standing when they left at sunrise. The column formed and moved out of camp at the appointed time, but the march soon stopped, and the men waited all day for orders to proceed. These orders never arrived, nor did they arrive the following day. They finally received orders to proceed at 9:00 A.M. on June 6 and marched to within twenty rods of the riverbank at Franklin's Crossing. They spent the night here in a pouring rain. The men were not reassured when stretchers bearing the dead and wounded from Howe's expedition passed them that night.[23]

This was a tough time for the Twenty-third NJV. With the expiration of their enlistments almost at hand, the regiment's men were unwilling to be ordered against Lee's army. Grumbling gave way to open anger, and they stacked their arms in protest. It was a mutiny—the worst ordeal for an officer. Colonel Grubb assembled his officers in his tent and discussed the options. He told them in no uncertain terms that he expected firmness and support. The conversation over, Grubb ordered "assembly" sounded and marched the men to the parade ground, where they formed a hollow square. The colonel spoke to his men about the reputation they had gained on several battlefields, how it was his duty to maintain this reputation, and asked them how they could meet their mothers, wives, sweethearts, "when the hooting rabble should tell them they had twice been beaten by the enemy and the third time were afraid to meet them?" This approach touched a nerve, for the men began yelling, "We will go" and "We are not afraid." The regiment joined its comrades in preparing to cross the river.

When they rose at 3:30 A.M. on June 7, the Jerseymen could see that it would be a beautiful day. Many attended Sabbath services at 9:00 A.M. A second service was just about to begin at sunset when bugles sounded. It was time for the First Division to cross the river to relieve the Second Division. The men worried that there was still enough light for the enemy's artillery to wreck havoc on their exposed lines, but to their relief no shots were fired. The brigade again occupied the Deep Run region, rotating details for picket duty. That night the First, Third, and Twenty-third NJV were on the picket line. The remaining units did not like having their backs to the river and Lee's army in front of them, so they spent considerable time during the night digging rifle pits.[24]

Although an artillery barrage and attack was anticipated on June 8, none came. Paul Kuhl wrote that "nothing happened to disturb us, except an occasional visitor in [the] shape of a minnie ball coming in close proximity to our ranks." Wondering what this meant, the Jerseyans built fires to prepare their morning coffee, but enemy snipers hiding in nearby houses made them dash for their rifle pits. The Federal artillery on the heights opened fire, smashing houses and sending the enemy snipers scampering to safety. After breakfast, the men deepened their rifle pits and added lunettes of sharpened sticks to discourage an enemy attack. Edmund Halsey noted that the results were "quite like forts." According to Oscar Westlake of the Third NJV, "I don't think they will attack us—we have thrown up some intrenchments [*sic*] and our Corps would be able to hold a large force of them if they should come down [on] us." Sporadic sniper fire continued disturbing the men.

June 8 was an exciting day for the men of the Twenty-third NJV. With its term of enlistment set to expire on June 13, the regiment was told to prepare for the trip home. The three hundred Yahoos bid their comrades a fond farewell and then recrossed the river. As might be expected, those men left behind were jealous of the nine-month regiment's good fortune. Charles Harrison noted that "[we] would have been grateful could we have gone with them." Paul Kuhl grudgingly wrote, the regiment "marched past us on their way home . . . they looked very happy, I suppose at the idea of being at home so soon again. They have done their duty well for a nine months Regt. and I am willing to give them all the honor they deserve."[25]

The remaining soldiers of the now weakened brigade, perhaps twelve hundred strong, were not upset when told they were being relieved by Newton's Third Division on June 9. After recrossing the river, many stripped, bathed, and washed their filthy clothes. Confederate batteries opened fire that night, but most of the shells passed harmlessly overhead. The men rested in camp until June 13, when ordered back to the river to help remove pontoon bridges after Newton's men had recrossed. All knew that something was up. The job took all night and some of the next morning to complete. Fearing that the enemy would appear on the opposite bank and open fire, the Jersey boys worked as quickly as they were able. Their task was made more difficult by a drunken colonel of the engineers who gave conflicting orders and generally hindered their activities. Their task finished, the men marched to the Lacy House on Stafford Heights, where they had breakfast and rested for the rest of the day. Accidentally left behind were two stretcher bearers, asleep in their tents, who later awoke to the "Good morning" of a Confederate officer as they were hustled off to the rear.

By June 13, General Hooker realized that he could no longer wait to move his army north to protect Washington. The army's new concentration point was along the Orange and Alexandria Railroad, and it would take the better part of the next week for the force to arrive. The VI Corps' route was through Dumfries, Greenwood, and Wolf Run Shoals.[26]

Daylight on June 14 found Wright's Division on the march, reaching Potomac Creek at about 1:00 P.M., where the men bivouacked. Many soldiers attended prayer service that evening before retiring to their tents for a well-deserved peaceful sleep. It would not come this night, for the bugles sounded at 9:00 P.M. and the men quickly broke camp. Hospital stores were fired as they left, causing one soldier to write, "I think the destruction of property there was needless, as it could have been easily shipped, had not the hospital functionaries fled in panic." The all-night march was made even more difficult because it was on an old corduroy road with loose logs. "We went stumbling and tripping among them with some hazard to limb and life," Alanson Haines reported. Regiments became intermingled as the men's fatigue heightened. The column finally halted for an hour's rest at Stafford Court House at about 3:30 A.M. on June 15. Some men just dropped where they were and slept in the two-inch-deep dust on the road surface. Then it was up again, and the terrible march continued. Temperatures soared as the sun climbed in the sky. So many men fell from the ranks that by the end of the march regiments were the size of companies. Benjamin Hough bitterly wrote, "they came verry [*sic*] near marched us to death." Sergeant Phineas Skellenger of the same regiment recalled that the "curces [*sic*] that was [*sic*] heaped on our Commanding Gen was awfull [*sic*]." Wright's aides were everywhere, yelling at the men to close ranks and maintain their killing pace. It was easier for them, as they were on horseback. Edmund Halsey began his diary entry of June 15 with, "*Hot,*" and later wrote, "The heat was *intense*. The fine dust being like a cloud in the air and was inhaled at every breath." According to Haines, "the men fell out in squads; some fainted, some were sunstruck." So many men had fallen by the side of the road that General Wright finally halted his command about two miles from Dumfries, permitting many men to rejoin the column. Continuing on, the division reached Dumfries, where it halted for the night in a meadow. June 15 was a day that the men would never forget. They did not know that Hooker, realizing he had dawdled too long in front of Fredericksburg, now had to make up for lost time if he wanted to defend Washington.

The brigade was on the road again at daylight of June 16, this time without breakfast, and the grumbling intensified with each passing mile. After reaching Wolf Run Shoals on the Occoquan River at about noon, the Jerseymen were permitted to rest, bathe, sleep, and eat until 5:00 P.M. Then drums sounded the long roll and they wearily approached their stacked arms. A stack belonging to the Fifteenth NJV fell over, causing a rifle to discharge. The bullet clipped William Kelsey in the neck, possibly nicking his carotid artery. Quick thinking by the regiment's surgeon halted the bleeding and Kelsey survived, but his soldiering days were over.[27]

The late-afternoon march to Fairfax Station was a fairly short one, and the brigade went into camp and remained there the next day. Back on the road on June 18, the column finally reached its destination—on the other side

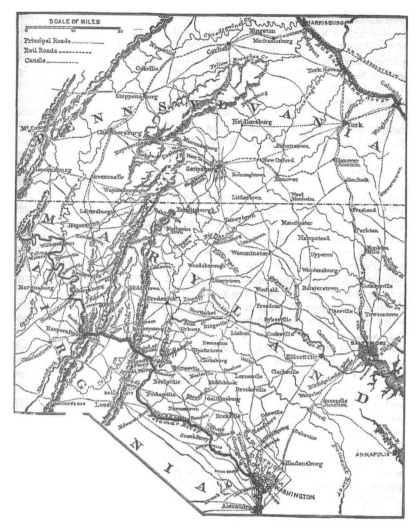

MAP 7. Map of Maryland and Pennsylvania (from Robert U. Johnson and Clarence C. Buel, *Battles and Leaders of the Civil War* [New York: The Century Co., 1884]).

of Fairfax Court House along the Aldie Pike. The brigade would remain here until June 26.

Noting that Confederate cavalry had entered Chambersburg, Oscar Westlake of the Third NJV believed that this was an isolated situation. "My opinion is that Lee wants to get Hooker with his army up into Maryland and then try to take Washington." Events would soon prove Westlake wrong. As the brigade broke camp and marched toward the Potomac River, the Jerseyans marveled at the copious amounts of supplies left behind by the Federal troops marching in front of them. Although efforts were made to destroy the discards, plenty of useful things were there for the taking. According to Haines, "hundreds of thousands of dollars worth of property had been destroyed by the flames, or thrown away, to be gathered by the enemy, should they follow."

The enemy did not follow, as they were already far to the north. In fact, all but three of Lee's divisions were in Pennsylvania by June 26, and the others crossed the state line the following day. Learning of the enemy's advance into Pennsylvania, Hooker ordered his troops into Maryland on June 25. The now reconstituted VI Corps broke camp at 3:00 A.M. on June 26 and marched fifteen miles. Passing through Dranesville, the brigade camped one mile beyond it on the Washington and Leesburg Pike. Reveille sounded at 2:00 A.M. on June 27, but the Jerseyans did not begin their trek until between 9:00 and 10:00 A.M. on the wagon-clogged roads. The brigade finally reached the banks of the Potomac River near Edwards Ferry and waited for the wagon trains to cross. To the band's tune of "My Maryland," the New Jersey Brigade finally crossed back into the Union on the pontoon bridge at 5:00 A.M., and some men sang "Home Again." With Lee in Pennsylvania, the men had much to worry about, yet they remained upbeat. The corps camped for the night about a mile from the river at Poolesville.[28]

Almost completely recuperated from his latest bout with illness, General Torbert returned to the brigade, sending Colonel Penrose back to the Fifteenth NJV. This permitted Lieutenant Colonel Campbell to be assigned to the Third NJV, which was without field officers. Because Colonel Buck was wounded, Lieutenant Colonel Charles Wiebecke commanded the Second NJV. The corps marched through Poolesville and Barnsville, then proceeded along the base of Sugar Loaf Mountain and halted about a mile from Hyattstown, Maryland, on June 28. It was a tiring eighteen-mile march. General Hooker was relieved of command in the early morning hours and replaced with Major General George Meade of the V Corps. Up before daylight on June 29, the men were on the road a short time later. They wondered when they would stop for breakfast, but they never did. The corps marched approximately twenty-four miles that day, through New Market and Riegelsville, before going into camp at New Windsor. Thoroughly exhausted from their long marches, the men threw themselves to the ground. The Jerseymen were not upset when the wagons and the rest of the corps passed them on the morning of June 30 while they continued resting. The reprieve ended at noon, when the brigade set off once more, marching through Westminster and Manchester, reaching the latter at about 10:00 P.M.

No one complained when told they would remain in camp on July 1 and rest their weary bodies. Farmers descended upon the corps in waves to sell their wares, and townspeople came to check out the camps. This all changed as darkness fell. Each regimental commander formed his men and, after conducting an inspection, ordered them into a square. Walking into the center of it, each officer recalled the unit's past bravery and discipline. They also read orders from General Meade about straggling and other expectations of their new commander. The men knew that something must be up, and then heard that they would soon be back on the road, marching instead of sleeping. The column finally began its long march after 10:00 P.M. Although the enlisted men did not know it, the two armies had collided at Gettysburg and the VI Corps was badly needed. The first two-mile march was in the wrong direction, so the corps had to backtrack, wasting four miles and valuable time.[29]

The march now continued through the night and into the next day. The officers knew how badly their troops were needed at Gettysburg, so they halted infrequently, and when they did, it was for about ten minutes or so—just enough time for the men to relieve themselves. The men constantly heard the phrase, "Close ranks and don't straggle" from their officers. Singing and exchanging jokes helped pass the time and take their minds off the misery. The ordeal became more unbearable as the day wore on, however, and the temperatures increased, as did the dust. One officer in Bartlett's Brigade recalled that the "heat was deadly, dust filled our throats; but still the march was kept up . . . no time to rest, no time to eat, no time for any thing but suffering." While the men were clearly suffering, the officer noted the determination in their eyes—a look he had never seen before. The bands and drummers occasionally played to keep the men from falling asleep on their feet.

Civilians lined the road, making the hardships somewhat easier to bear. One Jerseyman wrote home that they "waved flags and in many ways testified their devotion to the cause." Many yelled out, "We thank you for coming." The civilians distributed bread and other delicacies until their supply gave out. Cherry trees lining the road were more generous, and the men gladly stripped them of their fruit. The townspeople of Littlestown, just south of Gettysburg, hoisted buckets of cool water onto horse blocks, and the men gratefully dipped their cups into them as they marched past. The column finally halted at about 1:00 P.M. on July 2. Some men made coffee, but most simply dropped where they were and immediately fell asleep. The march continued an hour later, and the column finally reached the battlefield between 3:30 and 4:00 P.M. The VI Corps had made an epic march of thirty-five miles in sixteen hours.[30]

Resting along the east bank of Rock Creek, the Jerseymen made coffee and threw off their clothes. Many bathed their blistered feet in the cool creek waters. This refreshed them, and one noted that their "patriotic spirit still prevailed." Heavy gunfire soon erupted to the southeast, causing some to jump to their feet. A dusty aide galloped up to the brigade and asked directions to General Sedgwick's headquarters. The men knew what this meant and immediately began collecting their belongings. The march was now at the double-quick toward Little Round Top at the southern part of the field, where two divisions in General Longstreet's First Corps were battering the Federal III and V Corps. "As we went through the woods and over the fields, shells were bursting in the air and minie balls singing close to our heads," Reverend Haines related. Passing a cavalcade of wounded and just plain scared Federal troops, the brigade halted a bit north of Little Round Top, close to the George Weikert house on Cemetery Ridge, where it formed a reserve. The First NJV formed at the foot of a small hill, the Fifteenth NJV formed behind it, and the Second and Third NJV continued the line to the right. The brigade's services were not needed, as the V Corps and part of the Third Division of the VI Corps were finally able to beat back the determined Confederate onslaught.

The men lay on their arms that night, but sleep did not come easily. Thousands of dying and wounded men filled the fields in front of them, and their dreadful cries rent the air all night. Some men ventured out with canteens to help quench the wounded's thirst. The brigade moved southwest toward the northern part of Little Round Top on the morning of July 3. Because his three brigades were dispersed over the battlefield, General Wright turned the First New Jersey Brigade over to General Newton. Sniper fire was a problem, but few were hit, as the men hid behind the numerous rocks and boulders. General Torbert established his headquarters about forty feet behind the main line. Eating lunch, Torbert became annoyed when he realized that his men were throwing pebbles at him. He quickly strode toward his line and bellowed for his men to quit bothering him. This brought a general laugh from the men, and one yelled out, "Them's rebel bullets, General."[31]

The First NJV again formed the first line, with the Third NJV behind it. The Fifteenth NJV was deployed at right angles to the rest of the brigade, and the Second NJV was on the picket line. The men laid out their cartridges

Figure 1. William Montgomery, the initial commander of the First NJV. *Courtesy of John Kuhl.*

Figure 2. Robert McAllister, lieutenant colonel of the First NJV, and later colonel of the Eleventh NJV. *Courtesy of John Kuhl.*

FIGURE 3. Philip Kearny, the first commander of the First New Jersey Brigade. He left to command an infantry division. *Courtesy of John Kuhl.*

FIGURE 4. George Taylor initially commanded the Second NJV and became the second commander of the First New Jersey Brigade. He died of wounds sustained at Second Bull Run, September 1, 1862. *Courtesy of John Kuhl.*

FIGURE 5. James Simpson was the first commander of the Fourth NJV. He resigned in August
1862. *Courtesy of John Kuhl.*

FIGURE 6. Alfred Torbert, initially the commander
of the First NJV, became the third commander of
the First New Jersey Brigade. He left the brigade
to command a cavalry division. *Courtesy of John
Kuhl.*

FIGURE 7. Samuel Fowler was the initial com-
mander of the Fifteenth NJV. He resigned in
March 1863. *Courtesy of the New Jersey
Archives.*

FIGURE 8. Henry Brown took command of the Third NJV when George Taylor was elevated to brigade command. He commanded the First New Jersey Brigade during several campaigns. *Courtesy of the New Jersey Archives.*

FIGURE 9. William Penrose commanded the Fifteenth NJV and was the last commander of the First New Jersey Brigade. *Courtesy of John Kuhl.*

FIGURE 10. Henry Ryerson had the distinction of commanding, at one time or another, the Second, Tenth, and Twenty-third NJV. He died of wounds sustained at the Battle of the Wilderness, May 12, 1864. *Courtesy of John Kuhl.*

FIGURE 11. Ellis Hamilton (Fifteenth NJV) died of wounds sustained at the Battle of the Wilderness, May 16, 1864. *Courtesy of the New Jersey Archives.*

FIGURE 12. Paul Kuhl (Fifteenth NJV) was killed at Spotsylvania, May 12, 1864. *Courtesy of John Kuhl.*

FIGURE 13. Benjamin Hough (Fifteenth NJV) was killed at Spotsylvania, May 12, 1864. *Courtesy of Martha Hough Brenzel.*

FIGURE 14. A company of the Fourth NJV, probably in 1861. *From Camille Baquet, History of Kearny's First New Jersey Brigade (Trenton, N.J.: MacCrellish and Quigley, State Printers, 1910).*

FIGURE 15. Oscar Westlake (Third NJV) was killed at Cold Harbor, June 2, 1864. *Courtesy of John Kuhl.*

FIGURE 16. Edward Campbell, second in command of the Fifteenth NJV, led the regiment during several campaigns. *Courtesy of John Kuhl.*

FIGURE 17. Dayton Flint (Fifteenth NJV) rose to command a company. *Courtesy of John Kuhl.*

FIGURE 18. Edmund Halsey rose to adjutant of the Fifteenth NJV. He resigned in December 1864. *Courtesy of John Kuhl.*

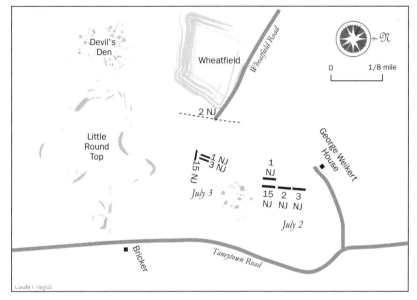

MAP 8. Battle of Gettysburg (July 2–3, 1863).

on the ground in front of them and waited. Some of the men picked up additional muskets. The quiet concerned the men. This ended with the massive cannonade that preceded the Pickett-Pettigrew-Trimble charge. A Jerseyman recalled that "most of the missiles passed over our heads harmlessly, bursting in the rear, or going too low, struck in the hill below us." Less than five men were wounded, as the troops ground their bodies into the dirt. When the cannon fire ended, the Jersey boys watched the awesome charge and awaited orders to move to the right to take on Pickett's Division. A soldier wrote, "with strange emotion we watched their coming; it was not fear, it was not surprise, but every man was silent, and grasped his weapon more closely." Charles Harrison called it "one of the grandest sights of the war . . . the Round Shot whistles through the air and the sharp crack of the Rifle is heard on all sides. The enemy charge our front but are cut down by hundreds and obliged to fall back in great confusion." The New Jerseyans were not needed to repel the charge, as the Federal troops to the right handled the reduced masses of Confederates. The Third NJV replaced the Second NJV on the picket line later in the afternoon.

The Fourth NJV was missing from the brigade, as it was still on guard duty. Six of its companies were on the battlefield with the artillery reserve near Little Round Top; and the remaining companies were with the wagon train at Westminister. The regiment would not rejoin the brigade until November.[32]

The men slept better that night knowing that Lee's massive charge had failed and that it was unlikely he would try his hand against this sector again. The brigade's losses during the battle were minimal—ten wounded (Second NJV: six; Third NJV: one; Fifteenth NJV: three). Knowing the importance of this battle and learning of the heroic actions of the Second New Jersey Brigade, many men were disappointed in their minor role. Lieutenant Ellis Hamilton wrote home that his brigade "was not engaged at all being, by a singular freak by Gen. Sedgwick, on the reserve."

Taking his Fifteenth NJV out on picket duty on July 4, Colonel Penrose ordered his men to stack their Enfield-type muskets and pick up Springfields that lay about the field in abundance. The latter rifles were considered superior, but some of the men grumbled that their Enfields "could shoot farther, and with more certainty of aim." Being on a battlefield after a fight was a new experience for the men. Dayton Flint wrote home, "it was a scene I hope never to witness again, and a sad 4th of July it was to us." The men spent considerable time burying the dead. Lucien Voorhees of the same regiment wrote home, "the pen cannot perform its duties in describing the horrible, ghastly scenes there visible." Sergeant Phineas Skellenger noted that the "battelfiedl [*sic*] was the awfullest sight I ever saw—some of the dead lay 3 or 4 days before they was [*sic*] buried." The bodies turned black and became bloated under the hot July sun, polluting the air and sickening the men. Lieutenant Ellis Hamilton also reported on the numerous "pools of blood lying all around the ground." Heavy rains settling into the area that afternoon helped dissipate the smell and clean the landscape somewhat.[33]

The brigade was roused at 2:00 A.M. on July 5 with news that Lee's army was in full retreat. There was less enthusiasm about the rest of the news—the VI Corps would lead the effort to bag them before they could reach Virginia. The brigade began the march at 11:00 A.M. at the van of the corps. Cautiously advancing in line of battle, with a heavy line of skirmishers in front of them, the Jerseyans approached the now-vacated enemy positions in the Wheatfield, picking up an enemy straggler here and there. They came upon Lee's rearguard about two miles from Fairfield. The brigade's skirmish line was initially thrown back on the line of battle, but when the entire line swept forward, it drove "the enemy from the woods and across the field beyond," recalled Reverend Haines. The Confederates were driven two miles before Sedgwick halted the advance. The Third NJV, which was the principal aggressor, had one man killed and two wounded, and a Rebel bullet tore off one of General Torbert's buttons. The enemy lost two killed and six captured.

The usual rotation occurred on July 6, so the First New Jersey Brigade was now in the rear of the corps. Finding the enemy in heavy numbers, the Second Division deployed while the First Division rested behind it. The march continued at 6:00 P.M., and the brigade marched all night to make up for lost time, arriving at Emmitsburg, Maryland, at daylight. After a short rest for breakfast, the pursuit of Lee's army continued at 6:00 A.M. on July 7. Marching along the foot of South Mountain, the column used a road described as "muddy, rocky, narrow." It was an interminable march that continued all day and into the night. The night was pitch dark and rain fell in torrents, drenching the men and forcing them to inch forward. They began wondering if their officers were confused and lost, but finally received orders at 10:00 P.M. to halt for the rest of the night. "It was a hard march[.] I never thought men could stand so much[.] Our rations run out the day before," reported Benjamin Hough. Without shelter tents, the men sought nonexistent cover, and lay down in the mud as the rains continued. A lack of supper and coffee added to their misery. "The men considered the past two days as *rough* as any in the service, all things considered," noted Edmund Halsey in his diary. July 8 was somewhat easier, as the brigade did not break camp until late morning, and then marched only eight miles over the mountains to Middletown. The rain continued, and with each step the roads worsened. The Jerseyans rested in camp until 4:00 P.M. on July 9, when they made another eight-mile march, this time to Boonsborough. The column marched only three miles on July 10, and then deployed in line of battle, as the enemy was near. The corps remained here the next day. Many took the opportunity to bathe in Antietam Creek. The corps marched about six miles on July 12, to within two miles of Hagerstown, Maryland. Torbert deployed his brigade in line of battle and aggressively advanced his skirmish line. When within 175 yards of the enemy, Torbert ordered a charge. The enemy pickets occupied rifle pits on a hill but quickly scrambled out of them and beat a hasty retreat. "You had oughte [*sic*] a have seen the rebs run," wrote Hough. Ellis Hamilton noted that the fight was a short one—twenty minutes, after which the "Rebs took to their heels." Three officers and four enlisted men were wounded at this action near Funkstown.[34]

The corps remained here on July 13, as the two picket lines constantly fired at each other. A unofficial truce was called that evening, and the opposing soldiers chatted and exchanged goods. A soldier in the Fifteenth NJV explained it as "such is war—one minute trying to take life and the next, perhaps, shaking hands." The officers discouraged these activities and, when observed, quickly put an end to them.

The brigade was on the road again on July 14, this time to Williamsport, about six miles away. Lee's army was here with its back to the Potomac River, as its pontoon bridge was destroyed and recent rains had raised the water levels. The Confederates quickly built fortifications and awaited the enemy's attack. Meade took his time in bringing up his army. Oscar Westlake wrote home, "I think we will have a fight with them yet before they all get across the Potomac." However, Lee quickly crossed his men to safety prior to the attack. The VI Corps marched back to Boonsborough on July 15, taking all day to make the sixteen-mile march. The intense heat caused many to drop by the side of the road, but most caught up later that night. There was no rest for the weary, as the corps marched twenty miles the next day to Berlin via Middletown and Petersville. The heat was intense during these marches. Chaplain Haines wrote, "it seemed as if it was the intention of our general officers to kill us by hard marching." In reality, there was no need for these forced marches. Upon reaching Berlin, the corps was given a well-deserved three-day rest. The Jersey Brigade crossed the Potomac River on July 19 and marched eight miles to Wheatland, finally concluding the Gettysburg Campaign. Although the Jerseymen had played but a small role, they knew it was an important reserve one. According to General Torbert's report, the brigade had one killed and seventeen wounded during the campaign.

While in Wheatland, General Torbert filed a brigade strength report that included 106 officers and 1,557 enlisted men, for a total of 1,663. The report did not include the Fourth NJV, which was still on detached service.[35]

First NJV–356
Second NJV–448
Third NJV–367
Fifteenth NJV–492
Total–1,663

Most of the men were content that the army had decisively defeated Lee, but it was not until later that they learned that Meade had squandered a wonderful opportunity. Josiah Brown of the Second NJV wrote after the war that Lee's army was "permitted to recross to the 'sacred soil' thus resigning an opportunity of crushing the rebellion and closing the war. . . . True our force was exhausted and weakened and ill fitted to re-engage the enemy, yet were not we the victors and they the flying foe? They had no way of retreat. . . . But the bird had soon flown and we were booked for two more years of exhausting sacrifice and struggle."

While the begrimed men of the First New Jersey Brigade waited to face Lee's army again, the Twenty-third NJV was still not home. Paul Kuhl had written to his sister on June 18, 1863, that the enemy's invasion of Pennsylvania was the time for the "nine months men to prove that they are not cowards. I say if they do not respond to the call to repel the invaders, they will prove themselves cowards." The Twenty-third NJV proved to be anything but. After reaching Beverly, New Jersey, the regiment was not immediately mustered out, as it took time to prepare the discharge papers and to rectify the sutlers' accounts. The men pitched their tents and waited. Colonel Grubb permitted about half the men to go on leave at a time while waiting there.[36]

The delay tested Grubb's patience. Finally journeying to Trenton on June 17, he implored the governor to hasten the discharge process. Although his men's discipline remained perfect, he was concerned that a nearby military hospital could cause the spread of disease. While here, a telegram arrived for Governor Parker with the news that the Rebels were in Pennsylvania. "Will your men go?" Grubb was asked, and he immediately responded, "Of course they will." Riding back to Beverly with Grubb, the governor gave an impassioned speech to the men of the Twenty-third NJV. Praising them for their service, he recognized that the Federal and state governments had no further claim on their time, but told them that the capital of Pennsylvania was in imminent danger. Parker ended his remarks by saying, "Now every man who will go to Harrisburg to-night, step three paces to the front." Every man stepped forward.

Grabbing their knapsacks and muskets, the men hopped aboard the trains bound for Philadelphia, arriving there about dusk that evening. They were greeted by cheering Philadelphians who feared that Lee's army was about to capture the city. The column marched to another train station to board trains bound for Harrisburg. None were there, so Grubb quartered his 369 men in the police station. The colonel was able to secure a train of open coal cars the following day, June 18, and the regiment finally arrived in Harrisburg at 1:00 P.M. that afternoon. The troops were surprised by the cool reception they received by the local citizens whose city was in danger. Meeting General Darius Couch, commander of this military district, Grubb was told to take his men to the Cumberland Valley Railroad Bridge over the Susquehanna River. Couch was concerned that the enemy would attempt to cross here, so he had the Twenty-third NJV dig rifle pits along the river. The regiment manned the pits for three days and then Couch again appeared and told Grubb that the enemy was falling back and the Army of the Potomac was advancing, so the Twenty-third could return to New Jersey to be mustered out. One veteran wrote that he, "without regret, quitted the inhospitable capital." The regiment reached Beverly and was mustered out of service on June 27. Although merely a nine-month regiment, it had distinguished itself on the battlefields of Fredericksburg and Chancellorsville. Many of the men later joined the Thirty-seventh and Fortieth NJV.[37]

Back on the front lines, the men of the First New Jersey Brigade reflected on the most recent campaign. Losses were minimal, but the long marches and other physical exertions had taken their toll. Sergeant Paul Kuhl wrote home, "such privations as we have undergone for the past month I did not think it in the power of man to stand. I never saw anything to compare with it, and hope I never will again, for it takes a person of iron constitution to stand it. I can very plainly feel the effects on myself, but a few weeks rest will bring me all right again."[38]

CHAPTER 7

The Fall Campaign of 1863 and the Winter of 1863–1864

$\mathcal{T}$reading back on Virginia soil did not end the long marches for the Army of the Potomac. The criticisms of Meade for not destroying Lee's army continued, so he hotly pursued the Rebels toward the Shenandoah Valley. Get the III Corps in front of Lee while the other corps came in from behind and the criticisms would stop, reasoned Meade. The III Corps, however, was tardy and Lee got away. The next day, July 20, the VI Corps left Wheatland and marched fourteen miles, through Aldie and Purcellsville, camping opposite Snicker's Gap near Philomont. The Jerseymen's spirits soared when told they would remain in camp the following day, and they were filled with a newfound optimism. "We are all in high hopes of a speedy end of the war, everything looks so much brighter than it has for a long time," wrote Paul Kuhl. The move south continued on July 22, and the corps reached Carrville, opposite Ashby's Gap, that night. The men were in line at daybreak on July 23 for the march toward Rectortown and White Plains, where the First Division was detailed to protect Thoroughfare Gap and the railroad there. The division remained here all of July 24, occupying a high hill overlooking the railroad. As darkness fell, the trek continued, this time on an "awful road" that ran six miles to New Baltimore. The exhausted Jerseyans arrived at midnight. The countryside was full of blackberries and guerillas, causing the men to be watchful for both. Day by day the men became weaker from more than a month of incessant marching, which had begun on June 12 when the VI Corps started moving north to Gettysburg.

Meade now concentrated his army near Warrenton, which the brigade reached at noon on July 25. The men immediately began throwing up tents on a hill a mile southwest of town. With the enemy just in front of them, the men were on alert all night. When daylight broke on July 26 the enemy was gone. The brigade established a new camp about a mile west of Warrenton and, at the same time, learned that it would remain here for some time. Paul Kuhl wrote home, "us boys are beginning to think it is about time they rest us a few weeks. I never was so completely worn out in my life, a day or twos rest will not do." Phineas Skellenger added, "tis a great wonder that Uncle Sam's men are not half dead[.] [W]e often march nearly all night then lay down in the wet grass and then go two [*sic*] sleep all wet with sweat." Bugles sounded and tents were struck at 6:00 P.M. on July 31, but the order to move out never arrived, so the men put up their tents again. They were used to the uncertainties of being a foot soldier. The brigade broke camp again on August 1, but this time to move its camp about two hundred yards east of Warrenton. Although the town was so close, the enlisted men could not visit without a pass. The weather was so hot that the men only wanted to lay in the shade of the trees. Lieutenant Colonel Campbell, who had been commanding the Third NJV, returned to the Fifteenth NJV when Colonel Henry Brown returned. The brigade performed provost duty here; Colonel Brown became provost marshal and General Torbert was military governor.[1]

With the end of active campaigning, at least for awhile, church services could again be held. The first occurred on July 26, followed by another on August 2. The latter was special, for the chaplains found an abandoned church, and they brought in extra benches and pews from other churches to completely fill it. Led by its band, the brigade marched to the church at 11:00 A.M. The church overflowed with men hungry for spiritual refreshment, and a second service was conducted at 4:00 P.M. "Denominational differences were forgotten in the presence of common spiritual needs. Methodists, Presbyterians and Baptists, united their voices in prayer and praise," noted Josiah Brown of the Second NJV. Not all of the men participated in these spiritual pursuits. "Many preferred to remain in their tents and spend the time in card playing, and reading trashy literature," noted Brown, who later entered the clergy. The church was also used for special ceremonies. For example, when Lincoln designated August 6 as a day of Thanksgiving, the church was decorated with the regimental flags, and over a thousand men congregated to sing patriotic hymns and hear speeches.

Rest and recuperation was the order of most days while at Warrenton. One soldier noted that by the end of the campaign "we were ragged, tired and dirty, in persons, arms and accoutrements. Now the Regiment is in splendid condition. Fully equipped and clothed with arms bright and accoutrements in perfect order." The men also basked in the knowledge that Lee's men were beatable. Samuel Cavileer of the still detached Fourth NJV wrote home, "our troops are in the best of spirits and believe they can whip Lee anywhere knowing that his army is in a manner demoralized."[2]

Twenty pounds returned to Dayton Flint's body during his stay here because of the inactivity and better food. Fresh bread and beef were daily rations. Deeply tanned by the sun, the men no longer burned. "As to our clothing, we go upon the principle that that which keeps the cold out will keep the heat out also, consequently we wear the same apparel winter and summer, with the exception of overcoats," wrote one soldier. Sutlers did a bustling business, and what they did not have in stock, such as fresh vegetables and potatoes, the men could purchase in town.

Because it was the start of the "sickly" season, the officers ordered better personal hygiene. The men also raised their tents off the ground and built bunks. No longer could food be kept in the tents, as it was unsanitary. Despite these actions, scores of men fell victim to chronic diarrhea. Paul Kuhl was probably correct when he wrote, "it is probable that the water does not agree with us."[3]

There were other frustrations. "Our officers are getting very particular again about our appearance," Kuhl wrote home. The men washed and cleaned on Saturdays, because regimental inspections of arms and general appearance occurred the following day. The latter were unpleasant affairs, as the men underwent the "scrutiny of the Col's eager eye, who quickly detects the least dirt on our guns or untidiness on our part."

Drilling became fashionable again, particularly in the Fifteenth NJV, which Colonel Penrose drove with a passion. Kuhl noted that "our Col. is a regular, and of course he must be a little ahead of the other Cols." The discontent only worsened with time for Kuhl, who wrote a few weeks later, "the Col is getting *more regular* every day. The boys are all getting down on him. He is very unpopular amongst the men, and not any too popular amongst the officers." To make matters worse, Penrose formed a school for the officers, as he was not happy with their abilities. He convened the training for an hour every afternoon on the topics of drill, tactics, and discipline. "As books are very scarce, our knowledge is derived from experience, and we are not to be expected to recite *verbatim* from books that we seldom see," wrote Lucien Voorhees, who participated in the training later in the winter. Penrose showed his wrath when an officer fell asleep during a session and when another inadvertently turned his back on his commanding officer. A third officer was disciplined for refusing to participate in a dress parade.[4]

The enlisted men also expressed their dislike of Penrose. "We have got a regular devil for a Colonel out of the regular armey [*sic*] . . . he is trying two [*sic*] make regulars out of the 15th," noted Skellenger. The situation was quite different for General Torbert. Skellenger called him the "gayest looking Genl in the 6th Corps[.] He dresses a great deal finer than Genl. Mead," who Phineas Skellenger called "a good man[.] He is a very tall commanding looking officer[.] He generally looks as though he was in a deep study."

The First New Jersey Brigade had become a fine, veteran unit by now. Paul Kuhl proudly wrote home that the brigade "has the reputation in the army as being one of the best looking, as well as the best fighting brigades in the service. And we are proud of that name." Voohees added, "with white gloves and collars, blackened shoes and belts, glittering plates and buttons, what *can* imagination picture more imposing."[5]

The Jerseymen sought ways to avoid physical labor, and one way was by impressing local African Americans into service. "Whenever there is any work to do, such as sweeping the Court House where our men are quartered, burying the dead horses, they start a squad of men out who stop every colored man they come to and impress him into the service . . . but the negroes are getting too smart for them when they see a soldier coming they skedaddle in double quick time, and don't show themselves until the soldiers are well out of the way," noted Sergeant Kuhl.

Promotions and discipline were meted out. One officer resigned with Penrose's blessing because, as the latter wrote, "this officer is entirely unreliable and unfit for his position by reason of too free use of intoxicating liquor." An enlisted man in the Fifteenth NJV was drummed out of the service and given two years of hard labor for desertion.[6]

There were other hazards. This was Colonel John Mosby country, and the Jerseymen were always on the lookout for partisans, who attacked isolated wagons and men. The men found contentment in the confines of Warrenton, populated by fine homes and amicable citizens. Wallace Struble wrote home, "Warrenton is like home to me, and the people like our brigade." This was not initially the case, as several fearful citizens requested and received guards to protect their homes, but as time went on they grudgingly admitted that the invaders generally behaved themselves. The townspeople soon realized that the visitors also brought the potential for economic gain. Many sold goods to the soldiers, and Struble was pleased that a family would wash his clothes at a modest price.

The men soon became bored from the long period of inactivity. "Camp life, well enough for a time, became at length wearisome to the Union volunteer. . . . There were many hours of leisure in camp life and these must be filled somehow," recalled Brown. Voorhees agreed, "life in camp seldom presents anything exciting, for then our duties are monotonous, consisting of inspections, drills, and parades." When not drilling or cleaning up their camp, the men rested, read, played games, and wrote letters home. Many were frustrated when letters did not arrive as frequently as they would have liked.

"I have not received a letter from home for nearly two weeks and I wish you would write oftener. You don't know how anxiously I look for news from you at home as I think you would write oftener," wrote Oscar Westlake to his father. With spare time on their hands, a day sometimes felt like a week, so when a friend or loved one did not write for two or three weeks, the men showed their displeasure. Most were gentle in suggesting that they receive more frequent mail. For example, Phineas Skellenger wrote to his brother, "I dont [*sic*] think my friends in N Jersey have forgotten me[.] I suppose it is some mismanagement in the mail."

Enterprising members of the Second NJV styled themselves the "Union Opera Troupe" and put on minstrel shows for the entire brigade. The officers occupied the church's upstairs galleries and the enlisted men sat in the main sanctuary. "The performances are quite credible and highly appreciated by the audience," noted Halsey. Lucien Voorhees enjoyed August 22, when the head of a deserter from the Second NJV was shaved, the Letter "D" was branded on his hip with indelible ink, and he was sentenced to two years of hard labor and drummed out of camp with the tune of the "Rogues' March."[7]

Most men continued resenting the Copperheads, or Southern sympathizers, back home. "They are easily known, as they always hiss when they hear about preserving the Union; they shake their whole body in rage and splutter out 'Linkum has broken the Constitution,' and the 'South could not get her rights,' even when they cannot repeat a single paragraph of that instrument, and many never read it; and they foam terribly about emancipating the 'niggers,' while at the same time the negro is the superior copperhead," sputtered Voorhees.

The men heard the ominous sounds of cannon fire in the distance on September 8, and wondered if their quiet days might soon be ending. Sure enough, the brigade received orders on September 15 to pack up and prepare to break camp. Realizing that Lee had sent two of his powerful divisions west to fight in Tennessee, Meade immediately planned a new campaign to take advantage of his weakened enemy. The VI Corps left Warrenton by

6:00 P.M. on September 15, heading toward the Rappahannock River. The six-mile march brought the corps within a mile of White Sulphur Springs, where the First New Jersey Brigade went into camp in a weedy field without their tents. Up early the following day, the brigade marched eighteen miles through Jefferson and Rockyville. Reaching the Hazel River, the Jerseymen removed their shoes and socks and rolled up their pant legs before crossing. "It was fun for the boys[.] Some Fell down[,] gun & all going Under," wrote Benjamin Hough to his parents. All were exhausted when they finally reached their stopping point near Stone House Mountain at 10:00 that night. The unit might have traveled farther, but it was so dark, and the terrain so foreign to General Torbert, that he decided to wait until morning to continue the trek. The brigade reunited with the division the following day, September 17, about three miles north of Culpeper Court House. Here the Jerseyans learned that the II Corps had driven Lee's men across the Rapidan River, and the rest of the Army of the Potomac was concentrating there. The VI Corps guarded the railroad bridge across the Rapidan and remained there until October 10. The men knew they would remain for awhile because of the careful way their officers laid out the campground.[8]

Next to the camp was a large field, splendid for parades. General Torbert, who Captain Henry Callan of the Second NJV called "the most fancy, or stylish Genl. in the army," made good use of the field to display his men and his own appearance. "Officers used to come from the other Corps to witness them, they were very fine affairs, once we were reviewed by Genl's Sdegwick & Wright," Callan noted. The region was most bountiful. Sergeant Eugene Forbes of the still detached but nearby Fourth NJV noted that "this part of Virginia does not look as if any troops had ever been here. Corn and fence rails are very plentiful, but the supply is fast diminishing before the inroads of the Northern barbarians."

September 22 found the men of the Fifteenth NJV standing at attention, watching General Torbert present a set of flags to their unit. They came from the state of New Jersey and, according to the unit's historian, included the Fifteenth's first national flag. The state flag was inscribed with the words, "Fredericksburg, December 13 and May 3, Salem Heights May 3, Gettysburg, Fairfield and Hagerstown." General Torbert and Colonel Penrose gave short speeches. Torbert's was spoken with "fervor, a heart full of patriotism, and was indeed eloquent. . . . He strongly admonished us 'never to surrender our colors' as long as an arm remained to defend them. . . . The Colonel's reply was brief, but truly patriotic. He pledged that the colors would never be lowered to the enemy, his men would defend them, and in death they could only be taken," recalled John Thompson. Edmund Halsey characterized Torbert's speech as "a very good one and the Col.'s in reply was good for him." The men cut a piece from the old flag and sent it to the mother of Eugene Hicks, who had died carrying the banner on May 3, 1863. The rest of the flag went to Trenton for preservation.[9]

The men of the brigade awoke every morning along the Rapidan to the sound of fifes and drums. Sergeant Thompson painted a word picture— "just imagine how it would sound to hear about twenty fifes, at least thirty tenor drums and four or five bass drums, all making music at once.—There is not much danger of anyone sleeping when they open their 'Sheepskin Artillery' as the soldiers term it." Much of the brigade's time was spent in brigade drills and parades, and on the picket line. "We have about two hours [of] drill daily—skirmish drill an hour in the forenoon, and battalion drill an hour and a half in the afternoon—just enough to keep us from becoming too lazy," wrote Thompson. A veteran of the Second NJV wrote home, "we go out every day, and walk and run around the drill ground two or three hours, just as if there was any movement laid down in the tactics that we had not executed a hundred and one times before." He agreed with Thompson, though. "It is necessary as a part of the system of discipline by which great armies are held together and governed, as we will grin and bear it good-naturedly eight months longer, and then—well, then we'll see." In addition to drilling, there was a brigade parade every morning at 8:00 A.M. and a regimental dress parade in the evening. With the increasingly cold nights, the sick list grew in length. Chronic diarrhea was a common ailment.

The picket lines of the two armies were within seventy-five yards of each other in some places, causing much fraternizing. The Virginians in front of the Third NJV offered $30–$40 for a pair of boots and $25–$30 for overcoats. These items could be readily purchased in the Federal army for about $7.50. "We don't allow them to sell anything to them although they offer to pay in Gold or Greenbacks," wrote Oscar Westlake.[10]

Another soldier was executed for desertion on October 9. John Connelly of the still detached but nearby Fourth NJV had deserted once before and received a pardon. There would be no such leniency this time, as the division formed three sides of a square to witness the execution. Seated on his coffin in the rear of a wagon, the men could see and hear Connelly loudly crying as the band played the "Dead March." He was shot by members of his own regiment and then the division paraded past his prone body. William

Thompson noted that it was a "sad scene, and I trust such may be few, and that men who swear to perform a duty will fulfill all its obligations." Henry Callan added that it was a "sight I do not care to witness again."

The VI Corps received orders to break camp on October 5, 1863, and at 6:00 A.M. began a long sixteen-mile march to just south of Mitchell's Station. This movement brought the corps to the army's left, where it relieved the II Corps near the Rapidan River. Because their cavalry had driven the enemy across the river on October 6, the men were under arms, waiting to be called into battle. They could see the strong enemy works across the river being further strengthened each day. Because of the proximity of the enemy's artillery, no fires could be built. Constant rains soaked the area, making the Yankees even more miserable. The attack never came, and on October 9 the Jerseyans received five days' rations and word that they would move out the following day. Under arms all day on October 10 waiting for orders to move out, the corps finally pulled back at 9:00 P.M., but not before firing the depot at Mitchell's Station. Benjamin Hough called it a "skedadel [*sic*] at dark."[11]

Captain Callan of the Second NJV recalled receiving orders at about 7:45 P.M. to form his men into line. Everything was to be left in place as though they still occupied their camps. While waiting for the entire brigade to form, the men heard several drum corps beating tattoo at 8:30 P.M., and then taps about fifteen minutes later. The bands then serenaded headquarters, as usual, for half an hour. It was now time to move out. "Not a word was spoken or a sound to be heard, save an occasional muttered curse as a man would trip in the briars and fall or sink to the knee in a rut filled with mud and water," recalled Callan. It was so dark that the men could barely see those in front of them, and the rutted road was extremely hazardous. Callan had trouble not laughing when a "poor Dutchman, who marched in front of me . . . every few minutes would go heels over head in the mud and maybe someone else over him. I believe the poor fellow tumbled at least twenty times that night." The brigade became so strung out at one point that the first two regiments in the column were told to rest in a field until the others caught up. The exhausted men threw themselves down and quickly fell asleep. It was a mistake, for the perspiration, combined with the biting wind, made them miserable. They were actually happy to be on the road again, warmed by their exertions. The brigade finally reached Culpeper Court House between 3:00 and 4:00 A.M. Hoards of troops crowded the small town, and at daybreak the men were permitted to build fires and prepare breakfast. The Jerseymen were off again by 8:00 A.M., this time bound for Rappahannock Station.

The Confederate victory at Chickamauga, Georgia, worried the Federal high command, so they detached the XI and XII Corps from the Army of the Potomac and sent them to Tennessee. Lee took advantage of the weakened Yankee army by sliding around its right flank on October 9. Not knowing Lee's actual location, Meade sent several corps to Brandy Station on the Orange and Alexandria Railroad on the morning of October 11. The VI Corps now marched along the east-side of the tracks, while the V Corps marched along the opposite side to Rappahannock Station, which they reached by midafternoon after recrossing the Rappahannock River at the United States Ford. Learning that Lee was at Culpeper Court House, Meade sent the V, VI, and part of the II Corps back in that direction on October 12. The thirty thousand men reached Brandy Station that night and bivouacked. Tired and ready to eat, the Federals were annoyed to find little firewood. Two or three empty houses loomed nearby, and "such a clattering and banging never was heard before. Heels and stones were used in place of axes, and in less time than it takes for me to write it, hundreds of fires were burning along the line, making the sky red with their flames," wrote Dayton Flint to his sister. Henry Callan, also writing to his sister, noted "boards from them began to walk off in all directions, houses and barns disappeared like dew before the morning sun."[12]

Lee was actually moving quickly north toward Warrenton, also on the Orange and Alexandria Railroad, so the Jerseyans were roused at midnight and marched back to Rappahannock Station, which they reached at about 3:00 A.M. on October 13. Callan was impressed by his men's commitment to duty. "I wish you could see a Regt of [men] awakened out of a sound sleep and told to pack up, it would surprise you [to] see every man get up and without asking a question or saying a word, take down his tent, if up, roll up his blanket, pack his knapsack, put on his accouterment[s] take his Rifle and be ready." Many a soldier must have grumbled about the back and forth movements they had made over the past few days. Marching along the railroad, the VI Corps reached Warrenton at noon and rested for a couple of hours before continuing the trek along the line. The corps passed Catlett's Station, crossed Cedar Run, and finally halted at Kettle Run near Bristoe Station at midnight, having marched over twenty-five miles in twenty-four hours. "We were all played out and could not have gone much further if the Johnnies had been after us or we after them," Callan declared. Like the Gettysburg Campaign, Lee's army had gained a step on the Union army and the latter needed to rush to save Washington.

There was no time for rest, and the men were up at daybreak and on the march a short time later on October 14, as the VI Corps cautiously approached Manassas Junction. Turning to their left, the corps crossed Bull Run at Blackburn's Ford and reached Centreville by noon. As the men marched across the old battlefields, they could still see the devastation wrought to flesh and flora. Lieutenant Ellis Hamilton noted that "there still remains a smell of dead flesh there." Climbing the heights, they observed the bloody fight at Bristoe Station, where a portion of Lee's army was destroyed. Captain Callan was surprised to see the change in his men as soon as they took position behind the strong defensive embankments. "They would sight their pieces over the pit and wish for the Johnnies to come now." They had been much less aggressive prior to taking these positions. That evening, the brigade marched about six miles toward Chantilly, halting at the Aldie Cross Roads to prevent an attack from that direction. The brigade reached its destination by 9:00 P.M., and the men slept in line of battle. It was soon clear that Meade's army had won the race toward Washington, and was strongly entrenched around Centreville. The brigade moved just north of the crossroads on October 15 and dug rifle pits. Cannon and small arms fire could be heard all day. The Jerseymen were called back into the pits several times over the next few days to repel an attack that never came.[13]

Realizing that he had nothing to gain by attacking the strong Federal positions, Lee abandoned his offensive. It was a rainy morning on October 19 when the VI Corps began its movement after Lee. The corps halted for the night at Gainesville, and the pursuit continued the following day when the column passed through Buckland Mills. The men finally took position on a hill just west of New Baltimore in the afternoon. They remained here until nightfall, when they moved to Warrenton, bivouacking in their old campsite. John Thompson reported, "after a cruise of nearly 'all round Virginia,' we have again made a halt in this noted place. . . . When the Gen. filed us up the hill . . . there was a loud hurrahing throughout the Brigade at the knowledge that we could have our old spot again." The enemy had vacated the town only an hour before they arrived, but the officers realized their men were exhausted, so they broke off the pursuit and allowed them to camp for the night. The brigade remained here until October 25, when it moved two miles toward Fayetteville, closer to sources of wood. The officers were unhappy with the move because it was more difficult for them to get to Warrenton. The corps remained in camp until the morning of November 7. "As every storm is followed by a calm, so is every campaign followed by a rest, and again we have sunk into the monotony of camp life," wrote Thompson. Talk of winter quarters permeated the camps, and many men became discouraged. "The past season has been marked with many bloody engagements. . . . We are no nearer Richmond than we were shortly after this time last year, thousands of lives have been sacrificed by disease and carnage, and what has been gained," noted a soldier.

One potentially dangerous and rewarding activity was a given—picket duty. Here the men could do as they wished. There was always the prospect of good-natured ribbing and exchange of goods if the Rebs were about. There was also the prospect of foraging. Officers also participated in the latter activity. For example, Lieutenant Ellis Hamilton wrote home that he "had a good time as usual on such occasions." He described how "we did a little foraging on our own account. Killed (no 'confiscated') a calf and two pigs and burned five government wagon-wheels which we found concealed in the barn of one old Secesh."[14]

Meade was not content to let the autumn die without another thrust at Lee. Dividing his army into two wings, Meade again moved against his adversary. General Sedgwick commanded the right wing, composed of the V and VI Corps, and moved it toward Rappahannock Station on November 7. Meanwhile, the left wing, with the I, II, and III Corps, approached Kelly's Ford, about four miles below Rappahannock Station. Sedgwick's troops encountered enemy pickets at noon, and after driving them back he deployed his artillery. Sedgwick's entire wing of thirty thousand men assaulted the Confederate lines north of the Rappahannock River, composed of two thousand men of Harry Hays' and Robert Hoke's brigades. The Second and Third Brigades of the First Division attacked Hays' Louisianians from the north, while Torbert's First Brigade supported them. The Jerseymen had been in the first attacking line, but because the Fourth NJV was still guarding the wagons, its line of battle of was not long enough to be effective, so the brigade was pulled back to a supportive role. The First and Fifteenth NJV occupied the brigade's first line; the Second and Third NJV formed the second. Speeding forward, the two brigades threw themselves on the enemy positions, taking twelve hundred prisoners, four cannon, and eight battle flags. The losses to the two attacking brigades were heavy, but the First New Jersey Brigade had none. The Louisianians marching to the rear were "tall, athletic men, and were decently clad in butternut suits recently drawn, though the greater part had rather poor shoes," noted a Jerseyman.

The men expected to be attacked during the night, but when the sun appeared Lee's army was gone. Sedgwick quickly moved his two corps across the river and then three more miles before going into camp on November 8.

The men could hear firing all day but were content to rest in camp. The brigade moved its camp closer to Freeman's Ford, not far from Brandy Station, on November 10. They did not know it, but except for one excursion against the enemy, the Jerseyans would remain there until May 1864. A number of commissions arrived while the brigade rested here in mid-November. The paymaster also arrived, with piles of greenbacks for the men. Lucien Voorhees groused that "the absence of sutlers or purveyors tend to keep our pockets lined with 'greenbacks,' and right welcome would a few of the little necessaries of life be among us just now."[15]

Lieutenant Colonel Campbell left the Fifteenth NJV again, this time to temporarily command the Fourth NJV. Voorhees noted that "we are sorry to be deprived (though temporarily) of so valuable an officer. He has won the admiration and good will of his men for his attention to them in camp and undaunted bravery on the field of battle." The Jerseymen's viewpoint of their second in command had radically changed since the unit formed.

The weather turned cold, and the men grumbled because the brigade had not yet gone into winter quarters. Captain Callan wrote home, "we have our fires outside and keep the doors open to admit the warmth instead of shutting them to keep the cold out, as you at home do."[16]

It became apparent that a new thrust against Lee was about to begin when five days' rations were issued on November 23. Violent storms hit the area the next day, drenching the men as they pulled down their tents; there was a good deal of grousing when they were told to erect them again, because they would not move out as planned. The brigade remained in camp on November 25, but was on the road at 6:00 A.M. the next morning. The going was slow and difficult, as the Jersey Brigade was in the rear of the army. The long column snaked past Brandy Station and headed toward Jacob's Ford on the Rapidan River, behind which Lee had massed his army. The Jerseyans had bivouacked by midnight and expected to be up at dawn, but the march did not resume until mid-afternoon on November 27. Firing could be heard to the front, and the men were ordered to load their rifles and double-quick to the front as masses of stragglers and wounded walked and limped past. The firing in the front grew in intensity, and the Jerseyans knew only too well what this meant. They could soon see units of the III Corps breaking and running to the rear. Darkness descended before the brigade was called into battle, so the men rested on their arms at 10:00 P.M. "We lay down not having the least doubt but that we would have a heavy battle next day," according to Paul Kuhl.

The men did not have to wait until morning, for two hours later they were roused and ordered to fall in. The weary men marched all night through the Wilderness, halting at Robinson's Tavern. The march was made more difficult by the meandering road that cut through thick forest. Sounds of battle intensified in their front, and after marching another couple of miles the column turned to the right and made its way through the brush and woods to a ridge, where it connected with the II Corps on the left. Up ahead, across Mine Run stream, Confederate general Richard Ewell's Corps was strongly posted on a hill. The rain intensified, adding additional grief. General Torbert threw out a skirmish line, which began to take casualties. The division remained here all through the remainder of November 28 and 29. It was a tense period, as an order to advance was expected at any moment.[17]

The Jerseymen went to sleep early on the night of November 29, for they suspected they would be awoken long before the sun rose. Sure enough, they were ordered up at midnight and told to make coffee, then marched two miles to the right, to where the attack was to be made. The brigade was in position in a thick pine woods at about 4:00 A.M. on November 30. Throwing their knapsacks in a heap, the Jerseyans were told to lie down and wait for the attack to begin. The officers constantly reassured the men and reminded them to remain quiet, as the attack was to be a surprise—perhaps the only way the works could be taken. Colonel Penrose, whom the men disliked because he was a tough disciplinarian, was, however, respected by them in battle. He walked along the Fifteenth NJV lines, saying, "let your battle cry be Salem Heights, and avenge your comrades who fell there last May." Two brigades of Howe's Division formed on the Jerseymen's right, and Russell's Brigade formed on the left. The men sensed that any attack would be disastrous. Before reaching the waist-deep, eleven-foot-wide Mine Run, which had only begun to freeze, the brigade would have to traverse a cedar forest whose trunks had been cut off, breast-high, with the downed trees strewn in every direction. The enemy had created these defenses several days earlier to retard a Federal attack. After crossing the river and the downed trees, the attacking line would have to traverse a half-mile-wide meadow leading up to the heavily manned Confederate position on the hills. Rebel artillery was also strategically placed to sweep the open ground. And then there were "the pleasant prospects of freezing to death should we get wounded," recalled Dayton Flint. According to a soldier in the Fifteenth NJV, Colonel Brown of the Third NJV "shed tears in anticipation of the almost total annihilation of the Jersey Brigade, though a braver man cannot be found in the army."

The men were not cheered to see R. B. Yard, the First NJV's chaplain, walking along the line giving each man a slip of paper and a pin with instructions to write his name, regiment, company, and home address on it before pinning it to his lapel. Yard also collected any valuables the men wanted to send home in case of their death. Most did not have much to give the chaplain, as they had left their knapsacks behind. After the chaplain passed, the men exchanged handshakes and bid each other a fond goodbye. The bitter cold penetrated and numbed the Jerseymen, for they had left their blankets behind and could not build fires, so they resorted to "vigorous exercise" to keep warm.[18]

The Yankee artillery was to open fire at 8:00 A.M. to soften up the enemy's defenses, and the infantry would attack an hour later. The artillery barrage began at the appointed time as the men gripped their rifles and tried to see the effects on the enemy line. Nine o'clock arrived and the Jerseyans were ordered to rise and form into line of battle. They answered roll call and then waited. "Each man stood silently waiting for the order forward to be given, stern determination was written on every face, to do their best and if it need be die for their Country that day," recalled Kuhl. The tension was palpable, and then the men heard whispers that the attack had been cancelled. They later learned that General Warren of the II Corps, who had suggested the attack to Meade, realized that the enemy's position was just too strong to be carried. The joy was overwhelming. Lieutenant Ellis Hamilton predicted that "not 50 men out of 1200 in our Brigade would have 'lived to tell the tale'" had an attack been launched. Some men fell to the ground and immediately went to sleep; others scrounged around for something to eat. Later that day they were assembled and marched to their original position. Retrieving their knapsacks, they rummaged through them for hardtack while wrapping blankets around their bodies for warmth against the bitter cold. Best of all, they were permitted to build fires for heat and to brew coffee. Unfortunately, food, save those hardtack crumbs, was in short supply. The night was so cold that few men were able to sleep.

December 1 found the I, III, and V Corps marching back across the Rapidan River. The VI Corps followed after dark. It was bitter cold and the men were unhappy about the frequent halts that did not allow their blood to circulate and their muscles to generate heat. Reaching Robinson's Tavern at 10:00 P.M., the Jerseyans could see bright flames from a tannery and other buildings that had been fired during the retreat. The column finally turned left and crossed the river at Germanna Ford just before daylight on December 2, and continued marching several miles before halting. The brigade, with the rest of the corps, remained here through the rest of the day and night. "We laid still all day and rested, out of rations, very hungry," Ellis Hamilton wrote to his aunt. The men were back on the road before daylight on December 3, passing through Stevensburg and Brandy Station, finally reaching their old camps in the early afternoon. The wagons arrived after dark, carrying rations for the men. So ended the Mine Run Campaign. Not much was accomplished, but at least the brigade was not destroyed.[19]

The men finally settled into winter quarters, and many grumbled that it was none too soon. Permanent structures now arose. "We had stockaded, mudded, laid up, dove-tailed, &c., till a complete city of modern architecture has been erected," wrote Lucien Voorhees. The brigade's camp was near the river, with its abundance of water. Thick forests also abounded in the area, delighting those who remembered the long treks to gather firewood the year before. Each company occupied both sides of a "street." Every hut had a fireplace and places to hang accoutrements, and was roofed with shelter tent canvas.

The Jerseymen also built company mess houses and received nourishing meals. Mail arrived on a more regular basis, and many received packages loaded with clothes and goodies from home. The men generally shared the contents with their hut mates. Sometimes the food in the boxes was too rich, sickening those accustomed to an army diet.[20]

In letters home, the Jerseyans begged for reading materials. "Forward literature, no matter how old, that our minds may not relax into comparative indifference." noted a soldier. Camp life was dreary, so the men appreciated anything that helped pass the time.

New Year's Day was uneventful, except for the whisky ration provided for the holiday. "Some are slightly inebriated, and with a 'hic' wish you a 'Happy New Year,'" wrote Lucien Voorhees.[21]

Cold weather often prevented the soldiers from washing their clothes and bodies. This was not always the case, however. On January 26, Paul Kuhl walked down to the Hazel River, undressed, and took a bath. "It was rather cold but the best I could do under the circumstances." He could not bring himself to wait "months without washing [as some do]," he told his sister.

The resignation of Chaplain Yard of the First NJV saddened his regiment. As he prepared to leave for home, the First NJV paraded in front of him, then formed a hollow square. Yard entered, gave a speech, and was presented with a gold watch. It was rumored that Yard was disillusioned. He had saved five deserters from death, but when his attempts to save a sixth one from his own brigade failed and the man was executed, a dejected Yard decided to end his army career and return home.[22]

Confederate colonel John Singleton Mosby's battalion of irregulars continued scooping up isolated Federal soldiers and staging raids on wagons, bridges, and railroads during the winter. It was a minor nuisance, but it helped keep the men in camp and brought relief from the drudgery of camp life.

Around Christmas, the men of the First through Fourth NJV were asked to make the difficult decision about reenlisting for another three years prior to the end of their original three-year hitch. The enticements were great—a $402 Federal bounty, a thirty-day furlough, and the title of "Veteran Volunteer." Some New Jersey communities, wishing to avoid a draft, offered additional compensation. For example, Bergen, Essex, and Passaic counties offered an additional $300. Almost the entire Fourth NJV reenlisted, but although most hailed from southern New Jersey, they reenlisted in Essex County to take advantage of its high bounty. The numbers reenlisting were less impressive in the First, Second, and Third NJV, as most of their men had had their fill of war. Paul Kuhl wrote home, "the 4th Regt left today for Jersey. They are anticipating a glorious time for the next thirty days, after which they will return to Dixie."[23]

Captain Oscar Westlake explained that his company of the Third NJV "don't seem to go in for it much [reenlisting] as yet but they may change their minds—in fact none of the regiment would hear of it at first but the 6 Companies remaining in camp last night seemed to change their minds as some 40 or 50 put their names down so the rest may do the same thing."

Years later, in his memory, Josiah Brown of the Second NJV summed up the position of the men who decided not to enlist. "I do not think that the veterans of three years service were wanting in patriotism: yet they looked at it in an extremely practical way. They had endured every privation for the term of three years and they longed for a change . . . I think . . . if an emergency like that of 1861 should arise in this our beloved land, hundreds of the broken and decrepit veterans of the war of the rebellion old as they are would be seen offering themselves for the service of their country."[24]

The initial phases of the Fourth NJV's trip home were not pleasant. The weather turned warm on January 1 when the men left, thawing the ground and turning the roads into muck. By the time the Jerseyans reached the railroad at Brandy Station their shoes were sodden and mud-encased. The only transportation were recently used cattle cars that had not been thoroughly cleaned. As the cars made their way to Washington, the night turned bitterly cold, and heavy winds made frostbite a problem. Several men subsequently lost some fingers and toes, which ended their military careers.

Not all Jerseymen were willing to wait until the end of their enlistments to leave the army, and several deserters were court-martialed during this period. Justice was sometimes erratic, according to the influence and position of the accused. For example, Private George Adams of the First NJV, charged with desertion, brought five captains as character witnesses to his trial and got off with a sentence of an extra month of service and loss of four months' pay. Adams, who had reenlisted, would never serve his penalty, as he was later killed at the Wilderness on May 5, 1864. There were other trials, some amusing. One involved Private Peter Clancy, an aide to General Torbert. Both shared a sweet tooth, and when the general saw Clancy stealing some candy from his "stash" under his bed, Torbert immediately had him arrested. Torbert testified that this was symbolic of the declining discipline in the army, and Clancy must be penalized to the fullest extent. The court-martial board convicted Clancy, but gave him a light sentence. An enraged Torbert dismissed the board and sought to retry Clancy. Edmund Halsey reminded Torbert that the laws forbid a person being tried twice, but the general insisted. However, every time that Clancy's file made its way to the top of the pile, Halsey put it back on the bottom and continued making excuses until Torbert was promoted and left the unit.[25]

A number of officers were overjoyed to receive ten-day furloughs to see their loved ones. The enlisted men were not considered for furloughs, causing considerable grumbling. Sometimes the enlisted men benefitted even when they did not get a furlough. Paul Kuhl wrote home, "Col. Penrose has not returned from Jersey yet, and we all earnestly hope that his stay may be long, we are getting along so nicely now that I hate to see him come back, for the machine will run rough when he is around."

As the officers left for short visits home, other men arrived in camp for longer stays. Among these were new recruits attracted by the bounties now being paid, or were substitutes for draftees. For example, the Fifteenth NJV received thirty-two recruits during early January and another twenty-two on January 21. Many of these men were older and ill-fitted for service. Many quickly fell ill. Acting Surgeon Levi Miller of the First NJV complained that the replacements included "men over 50 . . . boys under 18, men recently discharged . . . on account of disease or disability from wounds" and "men afflicted with various diseases." An arm of one volunteer was useless, and so was he. Of the fifty-four new recruits in the Fifteenth NJV, fifteen were rejected by the regimental surgeons as unfit for duty and sent home. Colonel

Penrose complained that "four were over sixty-five years of age, some boys of fourteen, some with one eye, and various other faults."[26]

Some men from Fifteenth NJV built a twenty-foot by thirty-foot chapel, roofed with a canvas fly, that opened on January 17, 1864. A sheet-iron stove, donated by the Christian Commission, kept the men warm. Candles lit the structure, and later the men even built a chandelier. The chapel could hold only two hundred soldiers, so two services were held each Sabbath and another service was held every evening, except Wednesdays. A number of men "found religion" during the winter. The historian of the Fifteenth NJV grimly wrote that "before the month of May 1864 ended, two-thirds of them [the regiment] had been slain, or were disabled from wounds on the battlefield."

Wednesday night was not a prayer night because that evening the chapel was used by the Adelphi Literary Society. The organization's preamble read: "Whereas, It is evident that the evenings with many of us are spent in comparative idleness, and with a desire for the cultivation of our minds, and the furtherance of religious and moral good, we have agreed to form ourselves into a Literary Association." Some of the themes debated by the society were: "Should capital punishment be prohibited by law," and "Which exerts the most pernicious influence in society—the Slanderer or the Flatterer?"[27]

Many men who "found religion" discarded the cards and dice so abundant in the tents of the prior winter. "Now, scarcely a game of chance is indulged in—books and newspapers, both secular and religious, are to be found where cards and dominoes were wont to be," noted Lucien Voorhees.

Colonel Penrose resurrected his "school" and extended it to the noncommissioned officers as well. The commissioned officers met every Monday and Thursday evening, and the noncommissioned officers met every Tuesday and Friday evening. Many attended Wednesday evening's Literary Society meetings. Penrose also gave his officers additional reasons to despise him. At a regimental dress parade on February 10, Penrose had an order read "censoring his line officers for gross and continued neglect of duty, attending to their own comfort [rather] than to the welfare of the men and ending with a new list of duties [for them]." This was a vicious circle, as Penrose was angry at his officers for snubbing him by giving his second in command, Lieutenant Colonel Campbell, a sash, and this was one of his ways of lashing back at them.[28]

Unlike the prior winter, relatively few men took sick. Paul Kuhl noted that "our regiment is in fine condition, very different from our case this time last year, when early every day and sometimes twice per day we would hear the solemn strains of the band, as some one of our Regt were carried to their last resting place." The rolls of the ill did increase as the winter wore on, but there were relatively few deaths. Captain Hamilton noted that the first death in the Fifteenth NJV was on February 22. Chronic diarrhea was again a major problem, sending scores to the hospitals. It appears that a disproportionate number of new recruits became ill, "and now and then one of them gets planted," wrote Sergeant Phineas Skellenger to his brother.

Many officers secured the services of African Americans as their personal servants during this period. Captain Ellis Hamilton wrote home on February 11, "George makes a very good servant thus far," and noted on February 24, "my nigger is 'bully,' in fact, tip top, the best servant in the Brigade." Although paid, they were especially reliant on the Union soldiers for protection and sustenance.[29]

With their three-year enlistments about to end in June, many men did not relish the prospect of being involved in combat. Captain Oscar Westlake of the Third NJV wrote home in early February that there was a "small prospect of having any *fighting* to do which would suit me very well as you know that I am not anxious to do any more of that than I can possibly help."

The monotony was broken at 3:00 A.M. on February 6 when the brigade received orders to prepare to move out in light marching order with three days' rations. "Speculation was rife and excitement high," recorded Edmund Halsey in his diary. Phineas Skellenger wrote home that "as usual in all winter campaigns it is raining two [*sic*] day and I am fearful of another Burnside and march." The new recruits had the hardest time of it. "They roll[ed] up their eyes two [*sic*] be waked up so early this morning[.] They did some tall Jersey swaring [*sic*]," Skellenger continued. Two cavalry divisions crossed the Rapidan River the next day amid heavy cannonading. The Jerseymen were to support the horsemen, but were not needed, so they never left their camps. While the movement would have been a distraction for the men, they did not savor leaving their snug, warm quarters for the rainy, muddy roads.[30]

Orders arrived again on February 26 to prepare to march with five days' rations the following day. The men were in column by 10:00 A.M. on February 27 and soon on the march. Five miles brought them to Culpeper Court House, and then another ten to James City, where they bivouacked. "This march of 15 or 16 miles being the first for a long time was rather hard on the men who had been so long in camp and there was more straggling than usual," admitted Edmund Halsey. Alanson Haines called the troops "tender-footed," but noted that "they carried, also, considerable extra clothing, and were loaded down with their rations and forty rounds of ammunition." A trail of coats and other articles soon littered the road. The new recruits were the worst stragglers. The men did not know it, but they were supporting a daring cavalry dash into Richmond by fellow Jerseyman General Judson Kilpatrick to rescue prisoners from Libby Prison.

With the Second NJV thrown out as skirmishers, the brigade led the VI Corps' march, which continued at 8:00 A.M. on February 28. After fording the three-foot-deep Rappahannock River, the Jerseyans pushed on rapidly for another two miles to Madison Court House, where General Torbert threw the First and Second NJV out as skirmishers to the left, and the Third and Fourth NJV to the right. The Fifteenth moved straight ahead through the town. Few slept that night, because the enemy was near. General George Custer rode through the picket line at about 2:00 A.M. on February 29 with about fifteen hundred troopers. Dayton Flint recalled that it was a "grand sight . . . with a rumble like distant thunder, the riders whistling, singing and laughing as they went out." The men expected to hear an explosion of carbines as Custer met the enemy, but the front remained quiet. Rained drenched the area on February 29 and March 1, making life miserable.[31]

Custer's force returned during the afternoon of March 1, "presenting a very sorry appearance." The mud-splattered men and their mounts were barely able to stay awake after their long journey. Along with his wounded, Custer brought in hundreds of African Americans fleeing slavery. The First New Jersey Brigade, with the rest of the corps, began the trek back to its camps that night in the darkness, rain, and mud. The men were soaked to the skin and could not make fires because of the wet conditions. The march continued on March 2 as the weather turned cold again, freezing the ground. The officers now set a fast pace on the harder road surface. "Once in a while a man would fall shivering and speechless but an application of cold water would bring him up and ambulances in the rear would take him in," noted Edmund Halsey in his diary. Straggling was heavy, and as the temperatures again rose a steady rain hit the area, further soaking the troops and making the roads almost impassible. According to Dayton Flint, "now and then some man would lose his balance and tumble flat in the deep mud, his gun flying out of his hands, taking him some time to find it and fish it out." The men received whisky rations when the column finally reached their camps that night after the long and exhausting twenty-mile march. Lucian Voorhees angrily wrote, "to march 21 miles, in the condition that we were, seemed cruel and in the extreme." Paul Kuhl noted that when he reached camp, he was "so completely worn out that I could scarcely stand up." Kuhl could report after a few days rest, "I begin to feel first rate with the exception of being a little lame and sore."

Perhaps because of the exertions of this march, the rolls of the sick quickly increased. Several men died; others were discharged for disabilities.[32]

Drilling continued to be a daily component of the soldiers' lives. There were two-hours of company drill in the morning and two hours of battalion or regimental drill in the afternoon. The new recruits had additional drills, conducted by the sergeants, who rotated this responsibility. Dayton Flint wrote home that "it does not seem possible that we were once just as awkward as they." A rapidly moving snowstorm hit the area about noon in mid-March, causing the cancellation of all drilling for the day, and Paul Kuhl wrote "I would not mind it if we should have a squall every day, about drill time."

The men played baseball and football as the weather moderated. "The exercise will do more toward restoring health in the regiment than all the blue pills in the medical department," noted Lucien Voorhees. Some men secured boxing gloves, and daily fights were all the rage. Sometimes the fights were not in jest. A captain and a lieutenant in the Fourth NJV got into a disagreement, and although everyone thought the matter was resolved, the latter challenged the former to a duel. The captain accepted, with rifles as the weapon of choice. One of the seconds informed the colonel of the impending duel, and he arrested both of them, thus ending the matter.[33]

A major change occurred on April 10 when General Torbert, newly assigned to command a cavalry division, left the brigade. With the regiments drawn up into a square, Torbert gave his farewell speech, noting that he would retain his love for the brigade and continue watching it with a "zealous eye." The men were sad to see him leave. "The general looked quite down & hated to leave as bad as we hate to see him," noted Benjamin Hough. "He is an excellent officer, as well as a friend to the soldier," Paul Kuhl noted. Phineas Skellenger added, "we have sometimes spoke harshly of Genl. Torbert on the march and drilling, but this afternoon when he bid us farewell we all felt more like crying than laughing[.] He is a soldier every inch of him." Colonel Henry Brown of the Third NJV assumed command of the brigade. The men were not happy, as "he keeps us drilling too much," noted Jonathan Hutchinson.

The men of the Fifteenth NJV's dislike of Colonel Penrose continued. While Penrose was on leave, his second in command, Lieutenant Colonel Campbell, received an elegant sword from his enlisted men. "the Col (Penrose) may well look upon it as a cut on him," wrote Edmund Halsey to his sister. "[H]e has given some of them just cause of provocation."[34]

Further evidence that they would be campaigning soon came in the form of target practice in early April, and orders to the sutlers to pack up and leave by April 20. Paul Kuhl wrote to his sister, "it will go almost like leaving home, to go away from here where we have spent to [sic] many happy hours."

While Meade retained command of the Army of the Potomac, Lieutenant General U. S. Grant joined the army in his new capacity as commander of all Federal forces. Upon hearing the news, Oscar Westlake wrote, "I suppose there will be a chance for the Army of the Potomac to distinguish itself this Summer." The men got their first look at Grant on April 18, when he reviewed the VI Corps with General Sedgwick. Paul Kuhl wrote that "I will willingly undergo a little fatigue for the sake of seeing the hero of so many battles and so many victories." To Edmund Halsey, Grant "looks just like his pictures, very plain and unpretending." Phineas Skellenger called him a "rather small man and quite good looking." Paul Kuhl added that "I was rather disappointed . . . he was a very common looking man for one who has won so many laurels . . . still it is not always those that make the most show that are made of the best stuff."[35]

The following day, April 19, the size of the brigade significantly increased with the arrival of the eight hundred-man Tenth New Jersey Volunteers. Commanded by Colonel Henry Ryerson, formerly of the Second and Twenty-third NJV, the regiment had not seen much action. Watching the unit march into camp, Sergeant Phineas Skellenger noted, "they are underdisciplined and I am afraid they will do us no good right away." The Fifteenth NJV, which had been the newest unit, could boast only 429 men at this stage of the war.

The Tenth NJV's history was very unusual, as it was initially recruited under the authority of the War Department without the "consent and against the wishes of the Governor of New Jersey." First known as the "Olden Legion," its first commander was Colonel William Bryan, who assembled the regiment at Beverly. Ordered to Washington in December 1861, the regiment was "of little service, falling almost immediately indeed, into disrepute, owing to its defective organization and the absence of all proper discipline," according to historian John Foster. A month later, the secretary of war asked Governor Olden to accept the regiment as part of New Jersey's quota and whip it into shape. A proud Olden respectfully refused, but the secretary sent him another plea in late January, stating that if the regiment was not accepted it would be disbanded. After a conference with Colonel William Murphy of Trenton, Olden reluctantly accepted the regiment, with Murphy as its commander.[36]

Murphy reached the regiment on February 19, 1862, and was distressed by what he saw. Not only was the regiment nothing more than a rowdy mob, but one company had openly rebelled. Recruited as cavalry, the men in this company threatened mutiny when told they would become infantry. Murphy arrested the entire company and mustered them out of the service, and he did the same with other men considered to be unworthy. New recruits, and a new company, G, swelled the ranks of the regiment. Most of the commissioned officers were also relieved of their duties, as Murphy brought in his own officers, most with combat experience.

The appearance and discipline of the regiment was so improved by the summer of 1862 that it was called to Washington to perform provost duty. Most of the men were not anxious to experience battle and were happy with their quiet existence. Private William Cazier believed that the regiment would remain in Washington "as long as we behave ourselves and do our duty." Colonel Murphy was not of the same mind. He wanted to see action, so he requested the regiment's transfer to the Army of the Potomac, but every request was denied. A permanent barracks for the regiment was built in early 1863. Distraught by the regiment's inactivity, Colonel Murphy resigned his commission on March 12, 1863, and was replaced by Colonel Henry Ryerson, originally of the Second NJV, but most immediately of the Twenty-third NJV. The regiment finally received orders on April 12, 1863, to move to Suffolk, Virginia, then under siege by a Confederate force commanded by General James Longstreet. The Tenth NJV was engaged in several skirmishes and did well. The regiment's first fatality occurred when the One Hundred and Seventieth New York, thinking it was defending itself against guerrillas, fired into the Jerseymen during a march from Carrville, Virginia.[37]

With the siege lifted, the Tenth was ordered to join the Army of the Potomac in July. These orders were countermanded, as Federal authorities believed the imposition of the draft would cause riots in Philadelphia. Accustomed to provost marshal duty, the regiment was sent to the city, where it remained for two months. The unit became a favorite of the local citizens, who enjoyed watching their dress parades. New bouts of disorder were expected in the mining regions of eastern Pennsylvania, so the Tenth NJV was sent to Pottsville in September. After a short stay, the regiment journeyed south to perform picket duty at Shepherdstown, Maryland. It remained there for about a month, guarding against a Confederate raid. By November, riots had finally broken out in Pennsylvania's coal mining regions, and the regiment was sent to Mauch Chunk. During its time there, the Tenth NJV was broken up and its companies dispersed to various locations in Carbon and Luzerne counties. The Jerseymen helped quell further riots by rounding up the draft dodgers. The regiment remained here during the winter of 1863–

1864, when most of the men reenlisted, as they enjoyed their fairly quiet chores.

Fearing the loss of his men to desertion and eager to distinguish himself, Colonel Ryerson petitioned the War Department to send the regiment to the Army of the Potomac. Ryerson was ecstatic, but his regiment less so, when he got his wish on April 10, 1864. Nine days later the Tenth NJV joined the First New Jersey Brigade at Brandy Station. Ryerson was incorrect in thinking that the change in venue would reduce the number of desertions, as Lieutenant Edmund Halsey wrote home on April 30, "since they have been ordered to the front they have lost heavily by desertion. Still there is more of them than two of our regiments."[38]

The Fifteenth NJV received a new addition on April 26—an experimental accoutrement. Developed by a Colonel Mann, the cartridge box hung in front of a soldier, rather than on his side. By placing the box in front, it counterbalanced the knapsack. The straps crossed behind the soldier, like a pair of suspenders, and the knapsack was suspended on them with hooks. Most of the men liked this new design, as it better distributed the weight, there was no chafing, it permitted a greater range of arm movement, and they were able to double-quick "with no uneasiness, the box being held firmly in it place," noted Colonel Penrose. The improved design proved so popular that during the upcoming campaign men of other units scoured the battlefield, exchanging their boxes with those of the Fifteenth's dead and mortally wounded. Penrose reported later in the summer that the matching knapsacks had been mistakenly sent to New Orleans and that he hoped they would soon arrive. They never did.

The brigade assembled on April 30 to receive a new brigade flag, presented by its late commander, General Torbert. Formed into a square, Torbert told the men that he was presenting the flag "as a memorial of the esteem and favor in which you shall ever be held . . . [I] trust you will ever care for it and defend it, aye, if need be, even hallow it with your blood."[39]

As the end of April arrived, the signs of a new campaign became even more evident. Jonathan Hutchinson wrote home that the indicators were "sick going to the rear, all surplus bagage [*sic*] being sent away, and there is no end to the reviews and inspections." He also ominously wrote, "today [May 1] I see the pontoon train." Edmund Halsey wrote home "a battle will be fought which will equal Gettysburg in severity. . . . The army was never larger or in better condition." He did not know that the future held a spring of endless battles that would result in the majority of his comrades in the Fifteenth NJV being killed or maimed before the summer arrived.[40]

CHAPTER 8

The Wilderness and Spotsylvania

When Colonel Henry Ryerson's sister opened his letter of May 3, 1864, she already knew that he was dead. The letter began with the sentence, "We have all been surprised by an order to move tomorrow morning at 4 o'clock . . . of course I know nothing or our direction except that it will be an offensive toward Richmond." Ryerson also noted "I dread going into a fight on account of the arms of my Regt," which he considered worthless. "I shall have to depend on the bayonet."

The men of the reinforced First New Jersey Brigade, packed and ready to go, stood in line at 5:00 A.M. on May 4, 1864. After waiting four hours, the march began to Germanna Ford on the Rapidan River. The brigade was part of the reorganized and enlarged Army of the Potomac. Now about 120,000 strong, it was consolidated and contained new units.[1]

Lee's 65,000-man Army of Northern Virginia was still full of fight, despite the hard winter on an almost starvation diet. Grant's plan was simple—slide around Lee's right flank, halt between the Confederate army and Richmond, and force Lee out of his defenses and into the open, where the vastly superior numbers of the Army of the Potomac could destroy him. The dense ten-mile by fifteen-mile Wilderness stood between Grant and his destination. The area was described as "a broken table-land, covered with a dense under growth of hazel, with but few clearings, and intersected by numerous cross-roads, generally narrow, and bounded on either side by a thick growth of low-limbed and scraggy pines, stiff and bristling chinckapins, and scrub oaks." Grant decided to divide his army into two wings so he could quickly traverse this difficult area that had already seen heavy fighting within the past year. Crossing the Rapidan at Germanna Ford, the VI Corps would march southwest toward Robertson's Tavern and then to Verdiersville. To catch Lee by surprise, Grant hoped to have the Wilderness behind him by sunset on May 4. The plan changed when the infantry halted within the Wilderness to permit the wagons to catch up with them.

The regimental commanders of the First New Jersey Brigade for this campaign were: First NJV—Lieutenant Colonel William Henry Jr.; Second NJV—Lieutenant Colonel Charles Wiebecke; Third NJV—Captain Samuel DuBois; Fourth NJV—Lieutenant Colonel Charles Ewing; Tenth NJV—Colonel Henry Ryerson; Fifteenth NJV—Colonel William Penrose.[2]

The Jerseymen experienced a mixture of emotions. The delightful weather and the sight of thousands of other soldiers made them optimistic about the future. But they had traveled in this direction before, and it usually meant heavy fighting and additional loss of comrades. They knew that Lee was just ahead and that he was not about to let the Federal army march on Richmond without a fight. Because of road congestion, the brigade did not reach the Rapidan ford until late afternoon, when it crossed on pontoon bridges. Reaching just beyond the Spottswood house, near Flat Run Brook at about 5:00 P.M., the men halted for the night after the sixteen-mile march. Camping near a saw mill, they went looking for firewood. Not finding any, they pulled the mill to pieces and roaring fires could soon be seen throughout the area.

The long march was exhausting, as the Jerseyans were softened by months of inactivity. John Hoffman of the Tenth NJV wrote home that he and his comrades were "tired, sore, dirty and hungry." Charles Hopkins of the First NJV noted that because the new men were from the "strike region, they were supplied with all kinds of wearing gear and everything that a soldier in a permanent camp could wish for . . . or could use." This did not bode well for the new troops, for Hopkins continued, "this march tried them as never before—loaded like 'jackmules'—and being placed in line between Regiments of hardened veterans they soon displayed their weakness in hard gruelling [*sic*] and marching . . . the old Vets would laugh and jeer at them for carrying so much while the knapsack and blanket roll for the Vet was like a wallet, the day after the circus was in town." The veterans finally convinced them to discard all but their most important belongings. "It was like pulling teeth to part with some things," he noted.[3]

Most men were content to lie by their fires that night, but some participated in prayer meetings, knowing that it was just a matter of time before they would face the enemy again. Few realized that it would be as soon as tomorrow. Reverend Alanson Haines recalled that it was a "repose on the eve of the most terrible conflict known in American history."

Up at 3:00 A.M. on May 5, the brigade ate breakfast and was on the road two hours later. Looking back, the men could see enough belongings strewn around their campsite to fill several wagons. These included playing cards, razors, folding stoves, shoes, socks, and books—items they had tenaciously carried during their first day's march but, with prospects of another long march, now decided to ditch to lighten their loads.[4]

Now leading the VI Corps, the New Jersey Brigade marched two miles, halted, then countermarched awhile, and halted again. This second halt lasted until noon. The Jerseymen stayed off the road because artillery continually flew by at a roaring gallop. The large number of guns did not make the men feel safer, and no one could have known that they would play no significant role in the coming battle because of the terrain. Gunfire ripped through the air, first a few scattered shots, then some ragged volleys, and finally the sounds of a heated battle up ahead as the V Corps engaged the enemy. That did not make much sense to some, as they were supposed to be sliding around Lee's flank. They were wrong. Concentrating his army, Lee put it on a collision course with the V and VI Corps on the Orange Plank Road and the Orange Turnpike. An inadequately deployed Federal cavalry screen failed to provide Meade with this vital information.

General Charles Griffin's Division of the V Corps encountered the enemy first, and immediately took the offensive, driving them back. Charge and countercharge characterized this vicious and prolonged fight. Convinced that Lee was trying to crush his right flank, at about noon Grant called up the VI Corps, which took Spottswood Road toward the scene of the fighting. Like the first day at Gettysburg, additional troops were fed into the battle as they arrived.[5]

The brigade immediately deployed to the right of the Orange Turnpike and, with the rest of Wright's Division, advanced a mile and a half through the scraggly pines to make contact with Griffin's beleaguered division. Adjutant Edmund Halsey noted that the brigade's commander, Colonel Brown, issued no orders—"Col. Penrose moved us up and Col. Ryerson, the 10th on our right followed by the rest of the Brigade in the direction of the firing under orders from Gen. Wright." Only one brief official report was filed by a Jersey Brigade officer about the battle, but Colonel Emory Upton of the nearby Second Brigade left this account of the movement: "The advance was made by the right of wings, it being impossible to march in line of battle on account of the dense pine and nearly impenetrable thickets which met us on every hand." The division's assistant adjutant-general, Major Henry Dalton, noted that the line "was moved with the greatest difficulty on account of the

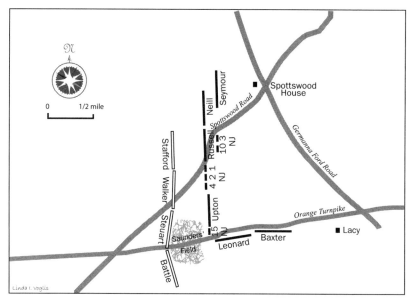

MAP 9. Battle of the Wilderness (May 5, 1864).

thick and tangled underbrush, which necessarily impeded the progress of a line, and often breaking it completely." What should have taken an hour took more than three because of a variety of factors. The impenetrable terrain was a problem, as were enemy skirmishers who contested all movements and, when that failed, set fire to the parched vegetation, forcing the Federal troops to halt to stamp the blaze out. This type of terrain advantages the defense.

The Jerseymen passed wounded soldiers making their way to the rear, and then encountered dead and dying lying scattered along the field where the first contact occurred. As the brigade rushed onward, the sounds of battle intensified. When they reached their assigned position, Brown deployed them into line of battle, but this was a difficult process given the tangles of the Wilderness. The briars were so thick in some places that the men had to stamp them down before proceeding. According to historian John Foster, the Jersey Brigade was deployed with its left "resting on Warren, and the right curving off to the rear, winding up as a skirmish line." The brigade was deployed in two lines, with the Fifteenth NJV on the left of the first line and the Tenth NJV to its right. The veteran regiments, at least what was left of them, formed the second line. Colonel Emory Upton's Brigade was on the left of the Fifteenth NJV, and General David Russell's was on the right of the Tenth NJV. Lieutenant Halsey noted that the Fifteenth's orders were to "guide left." The problem was that Upton's were to "guide right," causing a collision between the two brigades. Colonel Brown, who was sitting on a log with his staff, told an aide that he would come up shortly to reconcile the problem.[6]

Lieutenant Halsey was stationed between Ryerson's and Penrose's regiments during the advance to ensure that the two units lined up properly and advanced in unison, an almost impossible task in the thick vegetation. The two commanders knew that someone needed to lead the advance in Brown's absence, but neither would accept responsibility for the demibrigade. The two men apparently argued about it during a short halt.

As the brigade approached the front, the Fifteenth NJV was detached and sent to a hill near the Orange Turnpike to the left, where the Second Brigade was attempting to make contact with the V Corps. Saunders' Field loomed in front of them—the site of heavy fighting earlier in the afternoon. Gathering stones and scraping earth, the men built a crude breastwork. Spades arrived, allowing the men to dig in earnest. Enemy bullets passed in showers over their heads, occasionally felling a soldier. According to Charles Paul, a brigade staff officer, the Third and Tenth NJV were sent to the right, where they took position behind Russell's Brigade. John Judd believed that his Third NJV was in the third line. The location of the First, Second, and Fourth NJV are in question, but they probably remained between Upton's and Russell's brigades. Colonel John Horn, whose Sixth Maryland formed the right of Upton's Brigade, noted that the Fourth NJV was on his right.[7]

Color Sergeant Theodore Phillips of the First NJV was the first man killed. Struck through the heart, he died instantly; Color Sergeant Peter Brobson caught the flag before it fell and advanced about a hundred yards. Colonel Brown halted the brigade here, and while he aligned its ranks Brobson fell dead. Color Sergeant C. A. Pettie caught the colors. The line finally reformed, but with men falling like autumn leaves, Brown ordered his unit to lie down.

The enemy could not be seen, and the gunfire soon died down. Like the Fifteenth NJV to their left, the Jerseymen were ordered to entrench, and they clawed the ground with whatever they could find. Occasional volleys flew harmlessly over the men in their prone positions. They intermittently fired, but could not see the effect of their efforts. The enemy brought up artillery, and shells screamed overhead. "The shells flew over our heads at a lively rate. The trees rattled and the branches fell; but though we bowed our heads low to the ground and knew not what was to follow, no man left his place," recalled Alanson Haines.[8]

At least one of the regiments, the Third NJV, never engaged the enemy on May 5. According to John Judd, the regiment "maneuvered around through the woods and bushes all day under a heavy fire but was not actually engaged." That night the regiment bedded down within three hundred yards of the enemy line.

Captain Baldwin Hufty of the Fourth NJV reported that the brigade's main body advanced and attacked the enemy twice: first at 3:15 P.M. and again at 7:00 P.M. Between these two charges, probably just before 5:00 P.M., his regiment moved to the right, which was under attack. After gaining its assigned position, attached to Neill's Brigade, at about 6:45 P.M. the men heard explosions of gunfire up ahead, and then Federal skirmishers from a Maine regiment came tumbling back yelling that the rebels were right behind them. Lieutenant Colonel Charles Ewing ordered his men to "Fix bayonets," then "Double quick march!" and the Jerseymen dashed forward. Sergeant Eugene Forbes estimated that the Fourth NJV charged quite a distance before the men were halted and told to reform their ranks on the colors because the line of attack had become so ragged. Charles Paul noted that the Fourth NJV "made a gallant charge capturing a number of prisoners and forcing back a Brigade of Louisiana troops." The enemy to the left of the regiment had halted Upton's advance by setting the woods on fire, and the men of General Leroy Stafford's Brigade were probably doing the same to the woods in front of them. One enemy soldier wrote after the battle that the fighting "raged with inconceivable violence along the whole front of the brigade." Sergeant Forbes noted that his regiment made several charges during the evening hours.[9]

Not all of the soldiers would be cited for their bravery. Ewing of the Fourth NJV was charged with cowardice after the battle, for he "did leave his regiment, when they were engaging the enemy and lie down and hide behind a tree and so remain until taken by the collar by Captain Channing, 7th Maine Vols., and with kicks and cuffs driven up toward the position then occupied by his regiment." No trial would be held for Ewing, as he was badly wounded at Spotsylvania on May 12.

After the Fourth NJV moved to the right, the First, Second, and Tenth NJV came under attack. "The Confederates came on with great dash and spirit, charging right up to the low breastworks that the Jerseymen had thrown up, and which were on fire in several places," noted the brigade's historian. With losses mounting and not making any discernable gains in position, the remaining enemy soldiers reluctantly fell back. A Louisiana soldier wrote that the retreat "was executed in perfect order under a most galling fire from the enemy who were pressing the line heavily at all points." The deadly fight lasted about twenty minutes.[10]

As dusk settled on the battlefield, the begrimed Jerseymen gripped their muskets, expecting another attack. None came, which relieved them, as their ammunition was running low. Many of their comrades lie dead or wounded all around them. Because of the dense vegetation, most of the wounds were to the head or upper body. Arms were also frequently hit while the men rammed home the minié balls in their rifled muskets. A volley was fired to the left of the brigade as the last light faded, and like a row of dominos, it cascaded toward them, until, despite orders from their officers, the Jerseymen also opened fire at the unseen enemy. Later, another rolling series of volleys also reached them from the right. There was constant picket firing throughout the night, making the men apprehensive and unable to sleep. Only the whip-poor-wills seemed unperturbed. Eugene Forbes noted that there were three alarms during the night, "none of which amounted to anything." But at about 3:00 A.M. on May 6, when most of the men had finally succumbed to sleep, something caused a portion of the brigade to rush to the rear with nothing but their rifles. These men had progressed about twenty steps when they abruptly stopped and returned to their former positions.

The fighting began anew on May 6. Roused at 4:00 A.M., "the day was ushered in at five o'clock this morning by the Enemy making a spirited attack upon our front. After a sharp fight of fifteen minutes duration, they were handsomely repulsed," noted Charles Paul. The men then ate a quick breakfast in their uncomfortable surroundings. The thick forest prevented air flow, causing an intense feeling of closeness. Mules carrying ammunition arrived to replenish cartridge boxes. In addition to filling their cartridge boxes, the men were told to grab another fifty rounds for their knapsacks. This order indicated that their officers expected the worst. The Third Division, which had been guarding Germanna Ford, arrived and took position to the right of the brigade, causing a measure of reassurance. The Fourth NJV moved to the left—closer to brigade, but it was still attached to Neill's Brigade. The Third NJV, which had moved about the day before, was now in Neill's Brigade's second line. The men actively built breastworks, and several were hit in the process.[11]

Deadly sharpshooting was the order of the day, and many officers went down, including Captain Ellis Hamilton of the Fifteenth NJV. Out on the picket line, he was an easy mark to enemy sharpshooters that morning. One in a tree fired a bullet that passed through both his thighs. Quickly sent to the rear and then back to Washington, eighteen-year-old Hamilton eventually succumbed to his wound. One of his comrades noted, "though one of the most youthful officers in the regiment, he was distinguished for bravery and efficiency, and universally beloved as having gone into the service from the purest sense of duty."

The two sides exchanged gunfire through the day, igniting the tangles and indiscriminately consuming friend and foe alike. The screams of the affected were heart rending. At about 4:00 P.M., the Fourth NJV was ordered to build breastworks out of old logs, covering them with dirt, but the regiment was moved to the third line soon after. News that the enemy was advancing in force caused the men of the First, Second, and Tenth NJV to prepare for action at about 6:00 P.M. An explosion of musketry suddenly broke out on the right. The men looked at each other, not knowing what it meant. They would soon learn that part of General Jubal Early's Division had fallen on the Federal right flank, quickly rolling it up. General Truman Seymour's Brigade was overrun, and then General Alexander Shaler's was flanked, resulting in the capture of hundreds of men and both commanders.[12]

Several units of the First New Jersey Brigade, including the First, Second, Fourth, and Tenth NJV, rushed to the right to help stem the tide. The still inexperienced Tenth NJV fell into disorder and nearly an entire company was gobbled up by the enemy. Colonel Ryerson quickly rallied his men and ordered them to lie down and fire into the advancing Confederates. Ryerson joined his troops in their prone position. Men soon began bolting from the line, and the colonel got up on one knee to try to stop them. At that moment a bullet crashed into the bugle insignia on his cap, fracturing his skull. Ryerson, the highly ambitious son of an influential Sussex County family, died on May 12 in a Confederate hospital. The historian of the Fifteenth NJV wrote of his "remarkable bravery and ardent devotion to his country, and forgetfulness of himself." Charles Harrison noted that the brigade's musket fire initially halted the enemy charge but "there is so much confusion. We are obliged to fall back." The First NJV was also overwhelmed, and the enemy captured forty of that regiment's men.

The Fourth NJV, still operating independently of the rest of the brigade, was ordered to move to a position perpendicular to the Federal line, where it could stop runaways and help form a new defensive line. However, the dense vegetation, coupled with the growing darkness, caused the regiment to lose its direction, and instead it approached General Sedgwick's headquarters. "The tears were rolling down Sedgwick's face, as he tried to rally the men, crying 'Shame! Shame!' but to no avail," recalled Eugene Forbes.

The approaching enemy shot several members of the Fourth, and many others, like Sergeant Forbes, were captured.[13]

The rest of the brigade attempted to hold its position. "We were subjected to a terrible fire from front, flank and rear for half an hour," Charles Paul recalled. Darkness and growing Federal resistance finally ended the Confederate attacks.

Over to the left, the Fifteenth NJV was still attached to Upton's Second Brigade. The men could hear Early's attack to the right, but they were more concerned about the enemy in front of them. They could hear "Confederate officers trying to get their men to charge, but in vain," recalled Alanson Haines. To do so would have meant climbing the hill on which the Fifteenth was posted. Meanwhile, bullets were finding their way to the position's right flank. The regiment continued to hold until it was pulled out at 2:00 A.M. on May 7 and marched to the rear on the turnpike. Because the enemy was so near, the men were told to secure all accoutrements and make no noise. The regiment finally rejoined the reconstituted brigade a short time later.[14]

The brigade spent May 7 on a gravelly knoll on the right of the VI Corps' newly formed line about a mile behind its former position. The men again threw up breastworks and awaited another attack. The enemy again approached at noon, but whether it was the strong appearance of the defensive line or the Federal artillery throwing shells at them, the Confederates never mounted an attack. The Jerseymen suffered from the intense sun on the exposed hill, and none were upset when ordered to move out at 10:00 P.M. Their destination was Spotsylvania Court House, where Grant was attempting to slide around Lee's flank.

The brigade lost 364 men, or approximately 13 percent of its total strength, in the Wilderness. The First NJV and Fourth NJV, which were on the brigade's right, suffered the highest losses (162 and 96, respectively). According to Edmund Halsey, the First repelled six attacks in the two days it was engaged. The lowest losses were in the Third NJV (8), which merely played a supporting role, and in the Fifteenth NJV (14), which was on the left. Appendix B contains the regimental breakdowns of losses.[15]

In addition to Colonel Ryerson and Captain Hamilton, two other men whose letters home have been used in this work were also killed. Captain Henry Callan, who served on General Kearny's and Taylor's staffs and later commanded a company in the Second NJV, was killed on the skirmish line on the afternoon of May 5. According to Reverend Robert Proudfit, "a rebel bullet entered his neck below the right ear and passing through, severed the carotid artery, causing death in about two minutes." Proudfit continued, "his men, stimulated by high respect and warm affection for him, impetuously charged forward and recovered his body which they brought safely away." Josiah Brown called Callan a "Christian and a soldier" who left a "noble record."[16]

The Battle of the Wilderness was very confused, and because only one officer left an official account, the brigade's actions are even more so. It appears that the men did as good a job as they could, given the difficult conditions. Colonel Upton, who oversaw the activities of the Fifteenth NJV, wrote that the "regiment behaved under all circumstances with a steadiness indicative of the highest state of discipline."[17]

Wishing to again slide around Lee's right flank, Grant eyed Spotsylvania Court House. General Gouverneur Warren's V Corps led the advance down Brock Road, and the VI Corps moved along the Orange Turnpike. The latter corps began its march at 8:30 P.M. on May 7 and marched all night, halting for a half hour for breakfast at about 10:00 A.M. on May 8. The march was very difficult, as the men were exhausted after the Battle of the Wilderness, and this was compounded by the heat and dust of the endless trek. As the column traversed the old Chancellorsville battlefield, the Jerseyans could easily see the effects of that deadly battle waged a year before. The old rifle pits were still in good shape, and at least one human skull lay along the side of the road. The V Corps was engaging the enemy when the VI Corps arrived near the court house. General Warren was in a foul mood because the Confederates had beaten him to the destination and now held a strong position on Laurel Hill that barred his path.

The First New Jersey Brigade led the VI Corps' march on May 8. Upon reaching a crossroads at about noon, the men could see a highly excited General Warren approaching. Warren screamed at Edmund Halsey of the Fifteenth NJV, "Whose brigade is that?" Halsey replied, "Col. Brown—The N. J. Brigade." Warren continued, "Who will show me this Col. Brown—where is this Col. Brown?" Halsey found Lieutenant Charles Paul and said, "Here is one of his staff." Without waiting to locate Brown, General Warren took over and moved the brigade into position to the right of Brock Road. The men were not pleased by this sudden turn of events, as they had been under arms and almost without sleep for three days. Warren intended to launch the V and VI against the Confederates on Laurel Hill, but needed to first "develop the enemy's strength and position."[18]

Confederate artillery opened fire on the brigade as it advanced to the Spindle farm, injuring some men of the Second NJV. All was quiet when they arrived, as most of the enemy could be seen quickly entrenching. Orders arrived at 6:00 P.M. for a reconnaissance in force to determine the strength of the Confederates' position on Laurel Hill. The brigade apparently did not move fast enough for General Warren, for he rode up and demanded to know the whereabouts of Colonel Brown. Not finding him, Warren said to Colonel Penrose, "I ordered this brigade into action an hour ago. Colonel form your brigade and charge; I want to develop that hill." Penrose threw the Third NJV out as a skirmish line, followed by the Fifteenth NJV. The rest of the brigade was told to lie down and await future developments.

A hundred-yard open field lay between the two combatants, and the Third NJV was surprised when its approach did not draw enemy fire. That changed as they neared Laurel Hill and the enemy positions composed of hastily constructed earth and logs. Realizing that the Fifteenth NJV's line of battle was too short and should be extended to the left, Colonel Penrose sent Halsey to Colonel Brown for reinforcements. In a very strange exchange, Brown asked Halsey which regiment he should send. Looking around, Halsey replied, "The First," as it was "the only one nearby." Meanwhile, the Third and Fifteenth NJV had reached a marshy strip within fifty yards of the Confederate works, and the enemy muskets opened fire as one. The Jerseymen were mowed down by frontal fire from Bratton's Brigade and enfilade fire from DuBose's and Wofford's brigades on both flanks. "With hideous yells the Confederates poured in a deadly shower of bullets," recalled Alanson Haines. "Whole companies seemed to melt away," wrote historian John Foster. Realizing that they could not go back across the open ground, the men tried to cross the muddy area and reach the enemy's line. Behind the marshy area, the Rebels had felled timber to form a more formidable position. Scrambling atop this barrier, the Jerseymen blazed away at the Confederates, forcing them from their works. Haines characterized the breach as "going through it like a slug."[19]

The men could not savor their victory for long, as they heard enemy drums beating assembly. A glance to either side of them also showed long lines of enemy infantry beginning to stir and move in their direction to seal the breach. The relatively small number of men from the two regiments knew their only hope was to abandon the works and traverse the field of fire again. About halfway into its rapid retreat, the Fifteenth NJV encountered the First NJV moving forward, led by Edmund Halsey—too late to do any good. Lieutenant Colonel Campbell, who apparently led the Fifteenth NJV, was pinned to the ground when his horse was wounded. Extracting himself, Campbell realized it was too risky to try to escape during daylight, so he waited until after dark, when he literally crawled back to the Union lines. The brigade spent the night on the edge of the open field while the Third NJV remained on the picket line. Charles Paul recorded in his diary, "All very much worn out." Haines sadly related, "all this dash, so costly to us, accomplished nothing." He bitterly continued, "it was a terrible thing to lay some of our best and bravest men in a long row on the blankets, waiting their turn for the surgeon's care." The Fifteenth NJV lost 101 men in this charge, and could now muster a mere 306 muskets. Among the dead was Sergeant Lucian Voohees, a frequent contributor to the *Hunterdon Republican.* The *Trenton Gazette* called Voorhees "a young man of more than ordinary intelligence. Had he lived, he would, without a doubt, have reached a much higher rank in the service." Reverend Haines added, "he was a very attractive young man, of great nobleness of bearing, and esteemed as one of our best noncommissioned officers." The Third NJV lost about fifty men.

Sergeant Phineas Skellenger of the Fifteenth NJV wrote to his father soon after the battle, "I regret to inform you that I am much wose [*sic*] than wen [*sic*] I last wrote[.] my arm is amputated[.] oh cant you or aunt Martha or aunt Lydia or some of you come to me. . . . I am very weak. . . . I would write more if I could." On May 24, Skellenger's brother wrote from the Washington hospital that Phineas' "stump is doing as well as can be expected but he is very weak yet he says that it pains him but very little." Elias Skellenger wrote again on May 27, "dear father it becomes my painful duty to write you these few lines—your dear son is in heaven."

The Tenth NJV was also involved in a major attack on Laurel Hill that evening. Detached from the brigade and sent to Brigadier General Samuel Crawford's V Corps Division, it participated in the attack on the Confederate line further to the left. The Tenth NJV initially occupied the second line of attack. While they waited to go in, Confederate artillery fire caused tree limbs and branches to rain down on the men. The regiment first charged across a meadow under a galling fire, suffering many casualties, but pushed into the woods on the other side, which harbored the Confederate breastworks. "The balls flew around us with fearful rapidity," recalled John Hoffman. Confusion arose in the dense woods, as night was falling, and the unit attempted to cross a "swampy thicket." The regiment on the left wandered off, as did some companies of the Tenth. Lieutenant Colonel Charles Tay pressed the attack with three or four companies, and was pounced upon by the enemy. According to Hoffman, "our officers thought it was our own men ahead and commanded us to cease firing." Tay and more than eighty of his men were scooped up in the confusion. "In a few minutes we found the rebels had flanked and surrounded us entire," noted Hoffman. Those who refused to surrender were shot down, and the rest were marched to the rear. The remaining scattered companies "came back disorganized, without an officer of experience to command them," stated Alanson Haines. The remnant of the regiment eventually reformed in the rear and would remain detached from the brigade for most of the campaign. As a result, it was spared much of the destruction realized by its comrades.[20]

The brigade, minus the Tenth NJV, moved about a mile to the left on May 9, where it formed a reserve in the center of the Federal line. The First Division was on the left of the VI Corps, with Upton's and Eustis' brigades in the first line and Penrose's and Cross' brigades in the rear. Prior to making this movement, the men collected surplus muskets and, laying them against a stump, smashed them with their feet, lest the enemy capture them. Most of the action on this day occurred on the skirmish line, "pressing the enemy, developing his position, and seeking points of attack for the deadly struggle," noted John Foster. The brigade, already forming the VI Corps' left flank, moved about another mile to the left at 3:00 P.M. to participate in a demonstration against the enemy.

Sniper and artillery fire racked the entire line during the day, killing and wounding a number of men. In his last diary entry before being killed a few days later, John Judd of the Third NJV wrote, "Sergt. Frankish had his head taken off by a shell." As the Fifteenth NJV moved into a new position, a sniper caught sight of the unit's flag, carried by Sergeant Samuel Rubadeau. The subsequent minié ball found his breast, killing him a short time later. The bullet passed through Rubadeau and wounded another soldier in the thigh. General Sedgwick was hit in the face a short time later. Falling from his horse, he died within a half hour. "We mourned his loss as irreparable, and of all the wounds which tore our hearts, the most painful was caused by this unexpected fall of our commander," wrote Alanson Haines. Sedgwick's last order was to the men of the First New Jersey Brigade. Believing the men to be needlessly exposed, he moved them back into the woods, where they dug rifle pits for protection. Sedgwick was making fun of some of the men who were dodging enemy bullets when he was hit. Colonel Penrose, who was nearby, told Halsey about the incident, putting his finger to his lips to keep it quiet and shaking his head to indicate that the wound was fatal. Sedgwick was replaced by First Division commander General H. B. Wright, and General David Russell took over the division.[21]

In one day, the brigade had lost its corps and division commanders. It soon lost its brigade commander, as Colonel Henry Brown was relieved of duty. Brigade staff officer Charles Paul merely recorded in his diary that the change was made "by authority from Hd Qs Army of Potomac." The Union high command was upset that Brown was not at the head of the column as it approached Spotsylvania the day before, and his fate was sealed when he was slow getting his brigade into position for the reconnaissance toward Laurel Hill. Brown returned to the Third NJV and was replaced by Colonel Penrose. Lieutenant Colonel Campbell took over the Fifteenth NJV.

Later in the afternoon of May 9, Campbell was dispatched with the First and Fifteenth NJV to advance as far as the "Block House and Alsop Road," if possible. The latter destination did not exist—Meade's headquarters was probably referring to Brock Road in front of the brigade. He really wanted the two regiments to "feel around the enemy's right and get to the Brock Road if possible," according to Halsey. This was to the left of the army. Pushing the enemy picket line before them and taking several losses, the two regiments splashed across a swamp and entered some woods. Ascending a ridge that commanded the road, the men spent the night near the Brown house, about three-quarters of a mile from the entrenched Confederate positions. Halsey complained in his diary, "No supper and no breakfast."[22]

Two divisions from the II and V Corps attacked the enemy lines to the right of the New Jersey Brigade on the morning of May 10, but they were quickly repulsed. A second attack was mounted, but it too met with failure. Later in the afternoon, the remainder of the New Jersey Brigade was attached to Upton's Brigade and ordered to assail the Confederate line at dusk. They were probably thrown out on the skirmish line. A distinguished historian wrote of this attack, which also included two other brigades: "Heading the advance, the Jerseymen dash up with headlong courage to the enemy's works, and leaping over into the midst of the rebels, took over a thousand prisoners, together with several guns." Charles Paul observed that the "works were carried at the point of the bayonet without a shot being fired from our side—altho [*sic*] they gave us a very warm reception." The attack could not continue because the expected support from Mott's Division never materialized. Reluctantly leaving the captured cannon behind, the men quickly retreated with their prisoners. Only the Third NJV's losses have been reported—seventy-five men. The Fourth NJV was thrown out on the picket line after the Federal units returned to their former positions.

While the brigade's Second, Third, and Fourth NJV were successfully assaulting the Confederate positions, the First and Fifteenth NJV were ordered forward to find the enemy's flank. Driving the enemy skirmish line, composed of the Twenty-first Virginia of Witcher's Brigade, before them, the two regiments finally struck the right of the enemy line at the Mule Shoe Salient, but it was too strong to be taken with two regiments. General Gershom Mott arrived with two New York regiments from the Excelsior Brigade, who with the First NJV continued the attack. The New Yorkers, burnt out from long service, broke and ran to the rear at the first enemy volley, forcing the First NJV to break off the attack. The two New Jersey regiments with their New York comrades tried the attack again, but again the New Yorkers ran at first fire. Later in the afternoon, after a series of Federal attacks were repulsed, the First and Fifteenth NJV helped repel a determined Confederate counterattack. The Fifteenth NJV lost twenty-two men during these encounters; the First's losses are unknown.[23]

May 11 was a relatively quiet day as the Federal high command plotted its next actions. The Fourth NJV out on the picket line sustained several casualties before being relieved by the Second NJV that evening. The brigade, now reunited, except for the Tenth NJV, was moved from the right of the line to the left and then, after nightfall, back again.

May 12 dawned gray and foggy, with the sound of heavy gunfire as the Federal II Corps attempted to break the Confederate line at the Mule Shoe Salient in the same manner as Upton's smaller force had on May 10. The historian of the Fifteenth NJV described the day differently—"Terrific day of awful, murderous conflict! Combine the horrors of many battle-fields, bring them into a single day and night of twenty-four hours, and the one of May 12th includes them all."[24]

The Jerseymen were up at 3:30 A.M. and, following Upton's Brigade to the left of the corps, formed part of its front line. Over to their left, the II Corps launched its attack at 4:30 A.M., catching the Confederates unprepared behind their strong works. General Edward Johnson's Confederate division was almost entirely captured (over four thousand men) and, eventually, over twenty cannon fell into Federal hands. The II Corps surged on to exploit the breech in the Confederate line, but the men soon realized that there was yet another strong Confederate breastwork about half a mile behind the first. Enemy reinforcements descended upon the area, forcing the Federal troops to abandon their attack and return to the captured entrenchments. While the brigade's band played patriotic tunes, General Hancock realized that he needed reinforcements, and soon the VI Corps, including the First New Jersey Brigade, readied for action. But first they were read an order about the successes of the II Corps. The men cheered until they were "interrupted by rebel shells which showed they were still in position," reported Halsey. Moving along a small back road, the men passed thick lines of wounded men from the II Corps making their way to the rear. The musketry was continuous and at a high intensity.

As the Jerseymen attempted to deploy to the right of Upton's men, Penrose realized that the space was already occupied by other brigades, so he moved his men another quarter-mile to the right through the scraggly pines. Theirs was now the right-most brigade on the Federal line, and they formed into line of battle. The First NJV was on the left, the Fourth NJV in the center and the Fifteenth NJV on the right of the first line. Behind it were four companies of the Second NJV (the other six were out on the picket line) on the left and the Third NJV on the right. The belt of pines was thin here, so the men were plainly visible to the enemy, who opened fire and inflicted some casualties. Penrose now ordered the brigade forward. It was raining furiously and the Jerseymen were soaked to the skin. Upon reaching the edge of an open field, they could see that the Confederate positions were about a quarter of a mile away. It was about 10:00 A.M., and the men were ordered to charge with a cheer. The officers emphatically told the men not to fire their muskets, as they must quickly traverse the open space. It was folly to fire anyway, as no enemy troops could be seen—they were hidden behind a bank of earth with logs piled on top and three-inch openings between them to fire through with little exposure.[25]

Because of the terrain and troop deposition, the brigade approached the Confederate line at an oblique angle, actually moving perpendicular across part of it. The center of the brigade was oriented to hit the right of Harris' Brigade and the left of McGowan's on the northwestern portion of the Mule Shoe. The Fifteenth NJV's right flank presented an inviting target to Ramseur's Brigade and literally moved across its front from left to right.

No man in the Fifteenth NJV who survived could ever forget what happened next. Halsey reported that the "next twenty minutes were horribly fatal to the 15th." As it approached the enemy works, the line was hit with a "deadly, concentrated fire," and scores of men fell dead or wounded. The right companies of the Fifteenth NJV literally disappeared—essentially annihilated under the intense flank fire. But the attack continued. Because of the angle of the attack, the left portion of the Fifteenth NJV broke through the line first, followed by the Fourth NJV and part of the First. What was left of the right side of the Fifteenth NJV never made it to the works, as they were just too close to the defensive fire and were instead ordered to lie down to save themselves.[26]

After a short but deadly period of hand-to-hand combat, the breastworks fell to the Jerseymen. The brigade captured almost three hundred prisoners

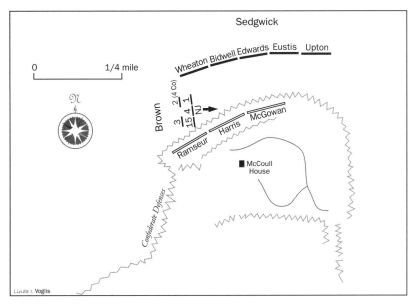

Map 10. Battle of Spotsylvania (May 12, 1864).

and the flag of the Fourteenth Georgia. Some enemy soldiers threw down their weapons and raised their hands in surrender, only to quickly pick up them up again when the victors were preoccupied and shoot the Federals in the back. Such was the fate of Lieutenant George Justice, who had jumped on the ramparts and was waving his hat when he was killed. He left behind a wife and seven children. An enraged enlisted man bayoneted the Confederate soldier who killed Justice.

The Jerseymen did not have time to savor their victory, for they received a deadly fire from both sides as the enemy tried to seal the breech. Bullets descended on the area in torrents, hitting the unwounded, wounded, and dead alike. The dead and wounded fell in heaps, ground into the mud by their still-fighting comrades. "Forty bodies, or near one-fifth of the whole [Fifteenth NJV] regiment, lay on the breastwork, in the ditch or the narrow open space in front. Numbers had crawled away to expire in the woods, and others were carried to the hospital, there to have their sufferings prolonged for a few days more, and then expire," noted a period historian. These losses were in addition to those sustained during the charge. "No experience during the whole time the Fifteenth was in the service was more destructive than the half hour from ten o'clock to half-past ten of the morning of May 12th."[27]

The heroism and horror of that day cannot be adequately recounted, and the survivors never healed from their dreadful experiences. Corporal Jim Bullock wrote home that "the horrors of the last few days cannot be imagined, let alone be described." Corporal Joseph Runkle carried the Fifteenth NJV's flag until his right arm was pierced by bullets and paralyzed. Runkle picked up the flag and carried it forward in his other hand, refusing to relinquish his precious charge. He died in Washington on June 7. Luckier was Lieutenant Colonel William Henry of the First NJV, who leaped onto the captured breastworks and waved his sword to encourage his men. When it was time to fall back, Henry was the last member of his regiment to leave, "and coolly turned about and walked off, his hat and clothes pierced with balls," a New Jersey newspaper reported.

The Fourth and part of the First NJV jumped down from the fieldworks and continued to push toward the enemy's second line. Corporal John Beach of the Fourth NJV recounted that the men "received a murderous fire from the oak woods, and from the enemy advancing through the clearing, and we had to beat a hasty retreat back to the works, but the Johnnies were right on top of us and captured several of our regiment." Lieutenant James Gilliss' battery rolled up to the front line to support the attack, but within seconds most of the cannoneers were killed or wounded. Beach threw down his rifle and helped serve the battery by bringing ammunition to each gun, but it was ultimately overrun by the Mississippians of Harris' Brigade. Five-foot four-inch Beach, once considered too small to be a soldier, won the Medal of Honor for his exploits, although it did not arrive for thirty years.[28]

Colonel Penrose realized a forlorn situation when he saw one and ordered the shattered brigade back to its starting point. Many men refused to relinquish the captured enemy rifle positions. Charles Paul noted that the men were "firing heedless of danger. In fact neither side seemed to know what fear was." It rained throughout the day, thoroughly soaking the men, but "the roar of Artillery and musketry drowned the thunder of heaven" and they never realized how wet they were.

The losses were horrendous, particularly in the Fifteenth NJV—45 killed, 85 wounded, and 21 missing. More than half of the regiment that had begun the attack had been lost. Only four line officers remained, and only one of the nine-man color guard rallied with the rest of the regiment. The regiment, which had entered the Wilderness with 429 men and 14 line officers, now numbered 153 men. So devastating were the losses that the regiment was consolidated into four companies, each commanded by one of the surviving line officers. Corporal Jim Bullock wrote to his father, "our regiment is like a company this morning. Another such fight, and the country will be a vast hospital." The Fourth NJV lost about a hundred men during the charge. The Third NJV had entered the Wilderness with 280 men and was down to 130 after May 12.[29]

The brigade's terrible losses can be directly attributed to Colonel Penrose. Moving the brigade to the right of the VI Corps attacking the lines, Penrose apparently did not reconnoiter his front to determine the Confederate position. If he had, he may have shifted his point of attack and sustained fewer losses.

The Fifteenth NJV's chaplain wrote, "the brave, the generous, and the good lay slaughtered on the ground of our charge, in close proximity—the most precious gifts which our State ever gave to the sacred cause of the country." Among the dead was John MacKenzie Thompson of the Fifteenth NJV, who, along with Lucien Voorhees, had been a loyal correspondent to several New Jersey newspapers, including the *Hunterdon Republican.* Lying in front of the Confederate works, Sergeant Paul Kuhl examined his wounded right leg. Pulling himself up, Kuhl took out his bayonet to fashion a tourniquet, but before he could use it he was hit again and again by enemy bullets, falling flat on his back, dead. "He had, in his military life, given his young heart to his Saviour, and was loved and respected, for his manly piety, by all who knew him," wrote his chaplain. Lying dead not far away was Lieutenant William Vanvoy, who had been harshly disciplined by Colonel Penrose and had taken his case to the newspapers. Also dead was Benjamin Hough, who frequently wrote letters to his parents. Several of these men died after their initial wounding because, with no healthy soldiers to fire at, the enraged Confederates took aim at any wounded soldier that moved.

The brigade's survivors, still stunned by the day's events, pulled back through the scraggly pine thickets and moved to the right. They were finally permitted rest when they reached the Shelton house. Heavy rain pelted the men, but their minds were elsewhere. An occasional thud of artillery told them that the enemy was still active. "It was a grievous day for the 15th," wrote Halsey.[30]

Although stunned by the loss of so many of his friends and colleagues, Lieutenant Halsey believed that the tide had shifted in favor of the Federal army. However, as he recorded in his diary, "the army is almost exhausted and I am afraid that a slight reverse would be terrible in its consequences."

The wayward Tenth NJV was sent by General Russell during the late afternoon to reinforce Edwards' Brigade, which was to the left of the First New Jersey Brigade. The former brigade was expected to hold its position, despite the withdrawal of Upton's, Bidwell's, and Eustis' brigades next to it. When the Tenth NJV arrived they were ordered to fire to their left oblique and help relieve some of the pressure on Edwards' men.[31]

Roused at daybreak on May 13, the Jersey Brigade was told to stand to arms, and after breakfast they moved several times during the day. The regiments took turns manning the captured rifle pits at the Mule Shoe Salient. For example, the Fifteenth relieved the Tenth there during the afternoon. Here they saw the enemy's dead lying three feet deep. Some of the men requested permission to return to the spot where the brigade had breached the Confederate line to bring off their dead for proper burial. Reverend Alanson Haines brought off eleven, who were buried in an open field with cracker box boards marking their graves. Veteran Charles Paul rode over the battlefield and recorded in his diary, "I have never before, and I hope I never shall again witness such a sight—The dead were piled in places three and four deep, wounded and dead together, in all manner of positions. Some with muskets clasped in their hands others with hands clasped together in the agony of death, and some had taken their bibles out to read, and died in the act." The brigade moved again with the corps, this time three miles to the extreme left of the army, where the IX Corps was to its right and the Ny River to its left.

The Jerseymen were up at 3:00 A.M. on May 14 and told to prepare for another assault on the Confederate positions. The VI Corps marched to the left to support the V and IX Corps' attacks, but difficulties in getting the troops into position delayed the corps' participation. That afternoon, the Second and Tenth NJV were thrown across the Ny River with Upton's Second Brigade to seize Myers' Hill to the left-front of the V Corps. These units took position near the Gayle house. Worried that enemy sharpshooters might occupy the woods near the house, Upton dispatched the Ninety-sixth Pennsylvania and two companies of the Second NJV to secure the woods. As they approached, the men could see two full brigades (probably Wright's and Harris') of enemy infantry preparing to attack the hill. The Tenth NJV and the Ninety-fifth Pennsylvania were immediately sent to reinforce the picket line while Upton quickly deployed his men around the Myers house. The Confederates hurled the three regiments and part of the Second NJV back toward the house with heavy losses. While Upton's initial fire stopped the advance, there were just too many Rebels approaching, so he ordered the hill abandoned. Upton lost more than 160 during this engagement—many were prisoners from the Tenth NJV. Among the dead was Lieutenant Colonel

Charles Wiebecke, commander of the Second NJV. Upton called him a "brave officer and thorough soldier." Too good a soldier for his fate, for when his men finally retrieved his body, they found it was stripped naked. The entire division crossed the Ny later that afternoon and, with the First New Jersey Brigade deployed as skirmishers, retook the hill.[32]

Still in position at the Gayle house on May 15, the men could see enemy troops massing for an assault, but the attack never came. Toward dark the Jerseymen were told that they would make a night attack on the enemy's rifle pits. None were upset when the orders never arrived, and they quietly spent the night in heavy sleep. They were essentially shells of their former selves by this time. According to Haines, "the terrible losses sustained, and the continual checks we met, combined with the effects of this marching and countermarching . . . produced a feeling of listlessness and discouragement, which extended throughout the army. The men felt that they were doomed to slaughter." The Federal high command understood the destructiveness of these feelings and issued an order, "exhorting them, by the memory of their losses and what they had already suffered, not to be discouraged, but to crown their efforts with victory," recalled an historian.

May 16 was quiet, and the men participated in prayer services throughout the day that included songs. They provided a measure of relief to the living who would never recover from the ordeal they had experienced. May 17 was also quiet. One of General Wright's aides galloped up at 4:00 P.M. with news that part of the picket line had withdrawn without orders, and the division commander wanted the First and Fifteenth NJV out on the line immediately. The Fifteenth NJV subsequently sustained two additional casualties on the picket line.[33]

Tempers flared on the picket line during the early morning hours of May 18 when a "sudden dash of the rebels" resulted in "the 1 Regt. Running without a shot," noted Edmund Halsey. A group of Rebel pickets sneaked up on the First NJV and delivered a volley, causing the Jerseymen to stampede for the rear. Colonel Penrose "called them a lot of cowards which Col Henry [commander of the First NJV] resented." The Fifteenth NJV took the First's place on the picket line, and a short time later the enemy repeated their actions, and this time the Fifteenth NJV fled. According to the regiment's historian, Joseph Bilby, this was the first and last time the unit "broke and ran." The corps moved yet again at sunset that day, this time to support the II Corps, which was to attack the Confederate salient the following day. All but the Third and Tenth NJV were left behind to man the skirmish line. These two regiments formed in support of the Second Division. It did not matter, as the Federal attack was repulsed yet again. The corps marched back to the vicinity of the Gayle house that night, where the men went to sleep without supper, as the wagons had not arrived to bring supplies. Added to their discomfort were the Confederate volleys whizzing over their heads in the growing darkness.

Roused at 3:00 A.M. on May 19, the men ate breakfast and then marched a half-mile to the front, where they were ordered to fortify their positions in anticipation of a Confederate attack. The Confederates attacked, but not in this sector. The officers quickly formed the men into column at 10:30 P.M. and marched them toward the scene of the action, arriving there at 2:30 A.M. on May 20. The attack was repulsed by that time, so the men were permitted to lie down in a plowed field and get some rest until daylight, when they were roused and ordered to prepare coffee. Moving again, the brigade halted and was again ordered to throw up entrenchments. The men expected an attack, but it never came.[34]

The men were told on May 21 that the army was finally abandoning the area in favor of another slide around Lee's right flank. This time, the VI Corps would bring up the rear. The brigade moved to the left, back to the Gayle house, at 10:00 A.M. that day. The house was gone—torn down by the desperate troops who defended the area after them. The materials and contents had been used to build barricades against yet another expected Confederate attack. The rest of the army marched past the Jerseyans all through the day. Part of the VI Corps was attacked at about 5:00 P.M. by General A. P. Hill's Corps, probably to determine if the entire army had vacated its positions. "They found out," wrote Lieutenant Paul, "but not likely to their satisfaction," as the attack was easily repulsed. The men could see a storm brewing, and soon a tremendous thunderstorm thoroughly drenched them. When it dissipated, the Confederates threw themselves at the VI Corps' picket line, driving it in. The Jerseyans could see long lines of Confederates approaching their positions, and they resolutely fingered their weapons and prepared to fire. The Federal artillery pounded the advancing enemy troops, and in the growing darkness the enemy line halted and then returned the way it had come. The brigade formed in column at 11:00 P.M. and began its march toward Richmond again. The Jerseymen would be the last to leave the Spotsylvania battlefield. The woods that they traveled through were so thick and entangling that the brigade had progressed only a mile and a half by dawn.

The Spotsylvania Campaign was now over. It had changed the face of the war, but was only the beginning of what would become an increasingly grim experience for the survivors of the First New Jersey Brigade.

The brigade's casualties at Spotsylvania (788) were more than double those of the Wilderness Campaign (364). The greatest losses were sustained by the Fifteenth NJV, which lost 272, followed by the Tenth NJV (149) and the Third NJV (148). The Fifteenth and Third regiments had attacked the Confederate positions on Laurel Hill on May 8 and had had the misfortune of being on the brigade's right flank (the Fifteenth in the first line; the Third in the second) during the attack on the Mule Shoe Salient on May 12. Captain Dayton Flint wrote home that "the gallant 15th Regiment is no more a regiment and it brings tears to one's eyes as he looks upon the little band which now gather around our colors . . . the whole Jersey Brigade, comprising six regiments will not make more than one good-sized regiment when it is consolidated." Only one other regiment, the One Hundred and Forty-eighth Pennsylvania, lost more men than the Fifteenth NJV. The high losses of the Tenth were a result of its rough handling on May 8 and 14.[35]

Losses were particularly high among the officers. The commanders of the Second, Third, and Fourth regiments were all killed or wounded at Spotsylvania. Added to the loss of Colonel Ryerson at the Battle of the Wilderness, the brigade had lost four of its six regimental commanders within two weeks. The proud First New Jersey Brigade, which mustered twenty-eight hundred men when it entered the spring campaign, now fielded barely eleven hundred.[36]

CHAPTER 9

To Petersburg

The Army of the Potomac continued its sliding movement toward Richmond. Although General Meade remained in command, it was now Grant's army, imbued with a resolve never witnessed in prior years. The losses were terrible—more than forty thousand since May 4, and gone was the illusion of a quick victory with few casualties. The Jerseymen now realized that the war had turned grim and that Grant would take Richmond, even if it meant the lives of every one of them.

The VI Corps was the last Federal unit to leave Spotsylvania, departing at 11:00 P.M. on May 21. The brigade left Myers' Hill and marched most of the night, reaching Guinea Station before 1:00 P.M. on May 22. The Jerseyans rested here until 6:00 P.M., and then made a "miserable and fatiguing" march that finally ended at midnight. Bringing up the rear, the brigade made only six miles in those six hours, as artillery and wagon-trains choked the road. Darkness compounded the problems, as did the thickets that lined the road, and the ever-present mud and water, but for the first time in many days they were not under or near enemy fire. Alanson Haines believed that it was more difficult than a "clear march of four times the distance by daylight." Worrying about an enemy attack, Colonel Penrose threw out flankers on both sides of the road. Lack of rations was becoming a problem. Penrose, Reverend Haines, and Adjutant Halsey had coffee and popped corn for their midday meal, but had nothing for supper.[1]

The thoroughly exhausted men threw themselves to the ground in a plowed field near Slapper's Store and slept until 3:00 A.M. on May 23. They groaned and complained when told to be ready to move at any time. Three hours of rest was not nearly enough for their weary bodies. However, the roads were still so congested that they did not receive orders to resume the march until 10:00 A.M. After marching eight miles, the brigade halted and moved to the side of the road to receive rations. It was 3:00 P.M. After eating and resting for two and a half hours, the Jerseyans were back on the road. They continued their march until midnight.

The army, moving in two columns, approached the North Anna River as Lee's troops quickly maneuvered into position on the opposite side. The Federal engineers threw pontoon bridges across the river, and units of the II and V Corps crossed and engaged the enemy. The VI Corps halted for the night of May 23 at Jericho Mill.[2]

Lee again skillfully used the terrain to his advantage. Aligning his army to resemble a wedge, Lee dug in and waited for Grant and Meade's next move. The Yankees were at a distinct disadvantage because the two wings of their army were separated from each other by Lee's wedge and the North Anna River.

The Jersey Brigade, with the rest of the corps, crossed the river during the early morning hours of May 24, and several regiments performed picket duty. May 25 found the brigade and most of the others from the corps destroying four miles of the Virginia Central Railroad near Noel's Station. The men first pulled off the rails and burned the ties in a pile. They used the fires to heat the rails until they were red hot and easily twisted. Lieutenant Paul noted that "the men enjoyed the work." Destroying the railroad was crucial because it was a vital supply link between Lee's army and the Shenandoah Valley.[3]

After a long day of destruction, the Jerseymen grumbled when ordered to dig entrenchments all night near the station. The importance of that protection became evident when the sun rose and the enemy opened fire and bullets whizzed by all day. The men were ordered out of their entrenchments at 8:00 A.M. on May 26 during a pouring rain that quickly soaked them. The First Division marched eight miles back to the North Anna River and, crossing it, arrived at Chesterfield Station at noon. The brigade then waited there until dark, when the supply wagons arrived. Because food was in short supply, the men received half rations the next three days. Fortunately for the soldiers, this part of Virginia had escaped the ravages of war and food was fairly plentiful. "Whenever we had access to a house before a guard was established, our men made bargains for corn-bread, chickens, potatoes, and onions," recalled Alanson Haines. The area also had a bounty of hogs, sheep, corn, and oats.

Upon receiving its rations, the division was off again at 8:00 P.M., this time on a forced march toward the Pamunkey River. The corps' new mission was to support General Phil Sheridan's cavalry, which had split up in an effort to confuse Lee about Grant's next grand movement. The corps marched all night, making twenty miles before daybreak. Realizing that their men were almost spent, the officers halted the column soon after sunrise and gave them ninety minutes for breakfast and rest. The march then continued. The pace was fast, as the foot soldiers were following the cavalry. The blazing sun beat down on the column, causing scores of men to fall by the wayside with heatstroke. The rest continued on, marching eight miles by noon. Reaching the Pamunkey River at Hanovertown, the corps quickly crossed without opposition and remained there on May 28.[4]

The entire army was now reunited near the Pamunkey River—within easy reach of its new supply base at White House. Lee was also active, again swinging into position between Grant and Richmond. This time he gathered his forces on the high ground north of the Chickahominy River. Entrenching his army, he awaited Grant's next move. After several Federal maneuvers, Grant again forced Lee to shift his army, this time behind Totopotomoy Creek. The VI Corps received the assignment of locating the new Rebel position on the morning of May 29. The First New Jersey Brigade, in the van, cautiously approached Hanover Court House. According to staff officer Charles Paul, the brigade moved "by the flank, in the following order—10th Regt. right in front, 4th Reg. left in front, 3d Regt. right in front." The Fifteenth NJV and three companies of the Tenth NJV were thrown out as skirmishers. They drove away Rebel cavalry outside of Hanover Court House and took possession of the hamlet at 3:00 P.M. The Jerseymen were again out of rations, but African American women at the Winstead house busily baked corn cakes, selling them to the Yankees at "good round prices." The Jersey boys found sheep and potatoes to help sate their hunger later that day.

May 29 was a special day for the Second NJV. With their terms of enlistment expired, the 315 men of that regiment who had not reenlisted were pulled back in preparation for their trip home. Only one officer and sixty-four men had reenlisted, and they were sent to the Fifteenth NJV, swelling their numbers. The actual number reenlisting was 138, but half of them were "absent, wounded," or on detailed duty. The men of the Fifteenth NJV were not overjoyed to receive these new veterans. Sergeant Andrew Yeomans wrote home that the men of the Second transferred to his regiment were "unused to our more strict discipline [and] create much trouble." The homeward bound were first sent to White House, where they guarded the growing mountain of supplies.[5]

The brigade, with the rest of the corps, left Hanover Court House at 6:00 A.M. on May 30, marching parallel to the railroad, halting near an old church at 10:00 A.M. After waiting four hours, the supply wagons arrived with rations. Back on the road at 2:00 P.M., the Jerseymen marched rapidly toward Mechanicsville, halting about seven miles from it after a six-mile trek. The march ended when it was ascertained that Lee's army was in front of the corps. The men spent the next several hours marching and countermarching as units maneuvered into position. It was only a matter of time before the brigade again engaged Lee's veterans.

Roused at 4:00 A.M. on May 31 amid heavy picket line fire, the Jersey Brigade moved a quarter of a mile to the left, where the men learned they would assault Lee's lines behind Totopotomoy Creek. As the day brightened, they realized that they faced an impossible task. Lee's troops were entrenching in what was an already strong position, and to make matters worse, a swamp intervened between them and the enemy's positions. Ordered forward, the brigade moved to the edge of the swamp and waited. The men did not know that the army's corps commanders had convinced Grant not to attack the impregnable Confederate defenses. Ordered back into the woods, the corps took a circuitous route to a new position.[6]

As the army angled toward Richmond, it could tally its losses during the short and indecisive North Anna Campaign. The First New Jersey Brigade's losses were minor—seventeen. The First NJV's eight casualties were the highest in the brigade.

The men were up at 2:30 A.M. on June 1 and, with the rest of the VI Corps, marched six miles beyond Totopotomoy Creek before breakfast. Another march, this time eight miles in length, brought the corps to Cold Harbor at noon. The day was hot and dust hung in dense clouds over the columns, making the march difficult. Soon everything had the same brown color—the men, their clothes, the horses. Dismounted Federal cavalry skirmished with the enemy as the VI Corps arrived.[7]

Seeing this movement, Lee again dispatched his army southward to get between Grant and Richmond. General Wright quickly deployed his corps. To its right was General William Smith's XVIII Corps, and the II Corps was to its left. The New Jersey Brigade deployed in an apple orchard to the south of Cold Harbor Road, with the First Division's Fourth Brigade on its left and the Second and Third Brigades to its right.

The brigade deployed in column of regiments, with the First NJV in the first line, the Third in the second, the Fifteenth in the third and the Tenth in the fourth line. The Fourth NJV was on the skirmish line. The men were ordered to lie down as the Federal artillery rolled up, and for an hour the guns of both armies banged away at each other. Being between these two sets of guns was a harrowing experience, even though few men were hit. One

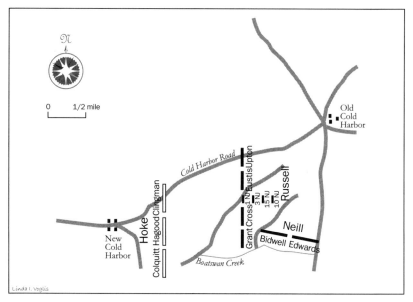

Map 11. Battle of Cold Harbor (June 1, 1864).

unfortunate soldier in the Fifteenth NJV was struck in the head by a shell, which tossed his lifeless body into the air.[8]

Many men in the First and Third NJV openly showed their hostility about the pending action, for their terms of enlistments had expired on this day. Instead of being sent to the rear, they were ordered into line of battle with their comrades, and they were none too happy about it.

The men hoped that attack orders against the fortified Confederate positions would not come, and as the afternoon wore on it looked as though they might get their wish. But the Federal high command had other ideas, for the VI Corps and XVIII Corps (six divisions, numbering about thirty thousand men) would take on parts of two Confederate divisions (or about ten thousand men). On paper it seemed like a mismatch, but two of the Federal divisions did not participate in the charge, lowering the Union number to twenty thousand, and these attackers had to traverse an open field against the well-fortified Confederate positions. Grant's plan was to push Lee's army back onto the Chickahominy River, causing panic and the Confederate force's destruction, no matter how many men he lost in the process.[9]

Penrose received orders at approximately 4:00 P.M. to advance his first two lines of battle. The First and Third NJV rose to their feet, but they were veteran enough to know an impossible order when they heard one. Some complained that their terms of enlistment were up, and they made other excuses, but the two regiments eventually advanced against Clingman's Brigade on their right-front and Hagood's Brigade on their left front. Both brigades were part of Robert Hoke's hastily deployed division. The Tenth and Fifteenth NJV remained behind in the orchard. It was three-quarters of a mile across the open field to the Confederate positions. Heavy artillery and small arms fire ripped into their lines, forcing them to veer to the right at a quick time pace. "They raked us terribly with canister, but we went within 200 yards of their works, when we had to halt," Charles Paul reported. "The ground was, within a brief space of time, strewn with the fallen; but the charging force swept on through the death-dealing artillery fire, and met the still more destructive discharge of musketry as it passed through a little skirt of woods," observed the historian of the Fifteenth NJV. Because of the thick smoke, the men of the Fifteenth could only hear what was happening.

The intense fire, especially from the Thirty-first North Carolina of Clingman's Brigade, quickly blew apart the First NJV, forcing its survivors into retreat. Among the wounded was Lieutenant Colonel Henry, who had led his regiment so heroically at Spotsylvania. The Third NJV in the second line veered to the right and took shelter behind a small knoll between the two hostile lines and opened fire on the enemy. An officer appeared and ordered the Fifteenth NJV into the fray. As the regiment advanced through the woods toward the open field, it could see the First NJV moving to the rear. An enemy battery on the left opened fire almost as soon as the regiment halted at the edge of the woods. Lieutenant Colonel Campbell ordered the Fifteenth NJV to perform a half wheel to the left and then quickly advance to a knoll about 150 feet from the battery, where they opened fire and soon silenced it. Ahead of them and to their right was the Third NJV with Captain Charles Wahl, part of his hat destroyed by enemy bullets, conspicuously waving his sword.[10]

With their advance stalled behind a knoll, about a hundred yards from the Confederate line, the men looked to their left and were dismayed to see no Federal troops there, leaving them vulnerable to being flanked by Martin's brigade of North Carolinians. To make matters worse, a Federal battery in the rear periodically dropped shells among the Jerseymen. A soldier was sent back to the battery commander with a request to exercise more care, "but the stupid or frightened Captain insisted upon his fratricidal work." Another messenger was sent, this time with word that if the firing did not stop, the regiment would open fire on the battery. That seemed to work, for the shells stopped slamming into the knoll.

Looking back, the men were relieved to see several regiments from Cross' Brigade moving to their support. Among the units was the Twenty-third Pennsylvania in their colorful Zouave uniforms. This attack also failed, and the Pennsylvanians were soon streaming to the rear. The attacks to the north, or right, of Penrose's Brigade initially met with success, but they too were repulsed with bloody losses. Grant lost about twenty-two hundred men that evening, with nothing to show for it.[11]

It was a stalemate, as the Third and Fifteenth NJV could not advance, nor could they go back. The Tenth NJV was sent forward, forming behind the Fifteenth, and the three regiments maintained a steady fire against the enemy line until dark. The men fired their rifles so rapidly that they grew too hot to handle and had to be dropped. Among the dead and wounded were several members of the First and Third NJV whose terms of enlistment had expired. The Fifteenth NJV lost twenty-five men on June 1.

The Jerseyans quickly dug rifle pits using their bayonets, tin plates, and cups. Spades arrived, and they made better progress in the darkness. It was a very difficult period, for, according to Alanson Haines, the enemy "in front seemed to take special pleasure in making us uncomfortable," firing periodic volleys toward the Federal positions day and night, making sleep impossible. The two lines remained remarkably close together. "We replied to their cries with our cheers. Within easy speaking distance, we returned their words of defiance, and answered their volleys by the return fire of our rifles," recalled Haines.[12]

In addition to the enemy volleys, Rebel sharpshooters constantly watched for exposed Federal soldiers. John Hoffman of the Tenth NJV noted that "whenever a man raised his head over the breastworks, a shower of bullets greeted him." Casualties mounted until the men adapted to this threat. "There was a constant fire from the rebel sharpshooters, that hit almost every man who exposed himself," noted Haines. It was folly to try to go to the rear during the daylight hours, so nightfall brought supplies and allowed movement. The remedy was to continue deepening the trenches to ensure that no body parts were exposed. The Jerseymen still worried about the area to their left, for if occupied by the enemy, they would make their position untenable. Lieutenant Colonel Campbell's headquarters was a deep hole covered by a piece of shelter tent. While enemy bullets occasionally put holes in the fabric, it protected Campbell and his staff from the sun and dust. The misguided Federal battery sent a shell screaming into the hole on June 3, but it was unoccupied at the time. The shell was brought to the battery commander to show him that he was hitting the Fifteenth's positions, but apparently to no avail. The Jerseymen did not have problems with the nearby Confederate battery, however. According to Captain Paul, "the 10th & 15th Regts. have dead range of a battery in their front, and have not allowed a man to come near the battery to day."

Grant planned another assault on the Confederate works on June 3. Sixty thousand men advanced, and while they breeched part of the enemy line, the attack finally failed with bloody losses. The VI Corps' First Division commander, General David Russell, approached the Jersey Brigade and told Lieutenant Colonel Campbell to prepare to attack. Campbell, referring to the II Corps troops attacking on their left, replied, "We will when the line gets up to us." Almost as soon as the Federal troops hit the open field they were engulfed in a maelstrom of gunfire that broke their ranks. The Eighth New York Heavy Artillery, new to war, rushed forward only to be sacrificed well before it reached the enemy positions. "These men were in bright new uniforms and went into the fight with all their knapsacks on," noted Haines. Edmund Halsey added, "it was the most sickening sight of the war—and the sight of these bodies showered over the ground for a quarter of a mile and in our sight for days will never fade from our recollections." A veteran Massachusetts regiment veered to the right, taking cover near the Fifteenth's positions. The Bay State men had seen too much of the war and knew that the charge was folly, so they broke it off and took shelter. Seeing the devastation, General Russell quickly revoked his orders to charge, "for it would certainly have resulted in our destruction, and losing the hold we had," noted Chaplain Haines.[13]

The men breathed a sense of relief when told they would not be called upon to charge the Confederate entrenchments. They were not out of trouble, however, as a shell from the misguided Federal battery exploded overhead, wounding five men in the Fifteenth NJV. Thousands of soldiers had been lost in the morning assault on June 3, including a number from the Tenth NJV— the only regiment in the Jersey Brigade directly involved. Little is known about that regiment's activities, but it lost about seventy men in the failed assault. One period historian wrote, "the regiment charged alone at a peculiarly exposed point and sustained heavy loss." A modern historian believed that the regiment had at least partially redeemed itself as a result of this charge. Grant decided to attack again in the afternoon, this time with his entire line, including the First New Jersey Brigade. Cooler heads prevailed and the attack was cancelled.

The Fifteenth NJV advanced after dark and relieved the Tenth NJV to its right. While still exposed to the enemy, the men of the Fifteenth NJV were pleased to see Federal troops now on their left. They remained here during the night, eating meals delivered in the dark—supper and breakfast the following day. Expecting a counterattack, the officers did not permit their men to sleep.[14]

Daybreak of June 4 brought good news to the First and Third NJV—those men who had not reenlisted, a total of 340, would be pulled back and sent home. The reenlistees were integrated into the ranks of the Fourth and Fifteenth NJV, joining their new regiments after dark. To avoid confusion, and to quickly distribute the men, they were told to join the same company designation that they had occupied in their former regiments. With the 118 men from the Third NJV, the Fifteenth NJV now numbered 233 muskets, after the losses at Cold Harbor are considered.

The Jerseymen continued digging parallel trenches that brought the Federal troops closer to the Confederate positions. By the end of June 4, the Yankees were within seventy-five yards of the enemy fortifications.[15]

Crazy with thirst, Corporal David Husted, formerly of the Third NJV, ran to the rear for water. He halted behind an apple tree when the Confederate sharpshooters opened fire on him. The bark on the tree was almost entirely shot off and Husted would have surely been hit except his new comrades in the Fifteenth rose and opened up a covering fire, allowing Husted to continue his journey. According to Adjutant Halsey, "he understood what his comrades were doing for him."

June 5 found the brigade's three remaining regiments still occupying their positions and exchanging shots with the enemy, less than fifty feet away in some places. Trench construction was continuous, and an interconnecting network developed that was used to move troops and supplies. The periodic rain made the men even more miserable. John Hoffman recorded in his diary, "we are covered with mud from head to foot." During the next week or so, the regiments rotated every day through the lines of trenches.[16]

Cold Harbor became a hell on earth, as the men were largely unsheltered from the hot sun in cramped trenches. Because a truce could not be arranged, dead bodies littering the no-man's-land between the two armies decayed, attracting insects and emitting noxious odors. John Hoffman of the Tenth NJV wrote home, "we are a dirty set of fellows, I can tell you that; black, dirty, and sunburned."

When the Jerseymen rotated to the rear, they finally gained a measure of safety and could wash themselves and their clothing, clean their equipment, and rest. Many also attended prayer services. For example, fifty-three men attended the hour-long service of the Fifteenth NJV at 7:00 A.M. on June 7. Other services were held in the afternoon and evening. "It was a service in a rifle-pit, on a field of battle, with the sounds of whistling bullets mingling with our songs and prayers," recalled Reverend Haines. All around them were recently dug graves holding their comrades. "Tears fell from the eyes of brave men, and there was sincerity in our thanksgiving for our own preservation amid so many scenes of danger," he continued.[17]

June 7 was also notable for the short truce to allow the wounded to be brought in for treatment and burial of the dead. Most of the men were able to finally leave their trenches and stretch their legs and arms. The truce was all too short, and that night the brigade returned to the first line of trenches. While the rest of the First New Jersey Brigade toiled in front of Cold Harbor, the mustered out veterans from the First and Third NJV reached Trenton.

The First New Jersey Brigade, now composed of the Fourth, Tenth, and Fifteenth NJV, welcomed the temporary addition of the First Delaware Cavalry. The unit was horseless, so the men received Springfield rifles instead of sabers. Training as infantrymen followed, much to the horse soldiers' disdain.[18]

Despite being on the first line again, June 8 was quiet for the brigade, which forged an unofficial truce with the Georgians in Colquitt's Brigade, now facing it. As a result, the men were able to sit atop their trenches and move around freely. Newspapers and other goods were also exchanged. Not so pleasant was the court-martial of two officers of the former Third NJV. When Charles Wahl and Ridgway Poinsett had been promoted to the rank of captain, their papers had stated that their term of service was to be three additional years. However, all had agreed that the papers were incorrect and that the men would be able to leave with their regiment, as they had not reenlisted. Colonel Penrose, who needed seasoned officers, was not so sure, and he convened the court proceedings against them. The verdict went against Wahl and Poinsett, holding them to the papers and finding them guilty of disobedience of orders and neglect of duty. The court ruled that the defendants should be "reprimanded privately by his [their] division commander and the court is thus lenient on account of the confusion and misunderstanding of orders." They continued to fight the verdict by refusing to take command of their companies.

The Georgians' officers put an end to the truce on June 9, and the enlisted men yelled, "Hey, Yanks! You better git inter yer holes!" The firing resumed soon after. A couple of men were hit on June 10 as the regiments exchanged positions.[19]

The Jersey Brigade pulled out of the front line and moved to the rear at 9:00 P.M. on June 12, except for 140 men of the Fourth NJV, and waited until after midnight for the road to clear of other troops and wagons. The detachment of the Fourth NJV rejoined the brigade at 2:00 A.M. The Jerseyans marched until sunup, covering only two miles on the clogged road. None of them were sorry to leave the trenches at Cold Harbor, but all worried about what Grant had in store for them next.

The brigade's losses at Cold Harbor were fairly minor (184), despite the charge on June 1 and maintaining their exposed positions for several days under almost constant enemy gunfire. Almost half of the losses were sustained by the Tenth NJV (eighty), which had the dubious honor of participating in the attacks on June 1 and 3. The losses in the rest of the regiments ranged from sixteen in the Third NJV to thirty-six in the Fifteenth NJV. Appendix B contains the regimental breakdowns of losses. Only one officer was killed at Cold Harbor—Captain Oscar Westlake of the Third NJV died on June 2. He was to be mustered out on June 4. In an earlier letter to his father, Westlake wrote, "should I have my usual good luck I will soon be home once more to stay for awhile."

Grant had failed yet again to drive Lee from his front. He always regretted his actions at Cold Harbor and vowed never to pursue that tactic again. He now decided on a new approach to capture Richmond. While he continued sliding around Lee's left, his new objective would be Petersburg, a vital railroad center. Its capture would strangle Richmond into submission. Grant had determined to transfer his army to the south side of the James River on June 5, but it took about a week to plan the massive army's movements.[20]

The army's march to the James River turned into a sixteen-hour ordeal for the Jerseymen, beginning when the brigade broke camp shortly after midnight, during the first few minutes of June 13. "The country seemed to be a continuous pine thicket with here and there a clearing," noted Halsey. Halting in one of these clearings at Summit Station at 8:00 A.M., the men ate breakfast, and then moved southward again. With the large number of men on the march, thick, suffocating clouds of dust filled the air. After marching through the pine barren countryside and through Hopkins Mills and Beulah Church, the column finally reached the Chickahominy River at Long Bridge and, marching east for several miles, approached the pontoon at Jones' Bridge. The brigade marched two additional miles before camping for the night, about six miles from Charles City Court House. It was now 4:00 P.M. and the Jerseyans had marched a total of twenty miles.

Roused at 4:30 A.M. on June 14, the brigade did not move out until 7:30 A.M., as its division formed the VI Corps' rearguard and, therefore, had to wait for the other divisions to pass. After marching six miles through the steamy bottomland country, the column bivouacked at Longwood Plantation at 2:00 P.M., by the James River. Several regiments conducted prayer meetings that evening, and the men were pleased to learn that the VI Corps would remain in the area the next day to protect the wagon train that was now making its way across the James River. The brigade spent June 15 in a cornfield, where it threw up earthworks, and moved again on June 16, this time about a mile closer to the James, where it again entrenched. This chore completed, many men bathed and swam in the river. The last wagon finally passed at about 4:00 that afternoon, and the Jerseyans formed into column and marched to the James, where they saw the Third Division embarking on transports. Still awake at midnight, the First Division climbed aboard the boats. The small First New Jersey Brigade could be accommodated in two transports—far fewer than when last transported in this manner.[21]

The two-hour journey up the James River toward Petersburg ended at 3:00 A.M. on June 17, when the troops disembarked at Bermuda Hundred. Marching along the Appomattox River, the VI Corps passed General Ben Butler's Army of the James, which had been bottled up by the Confederates until Grant came to his rescue. The Jerseymen were not impressed with the fighting abilities of Butler's army. Edmund Halsey recorded in his diary that Butler's men were "as neat and clean and fresh as if in summer quarters." The brigade spent a very uncomfortable five hours in the open, under a broiling hot sun until 5:00 P.M., when they moved to a pine woods. The men remained here until midnight, resting, eating, and participating in prayer services. The sound of bugles halted these activities, and the brigade prepared to move out. Midnight found the men in light marching order—any belongings not needed in battle were left behind under guard.

The men marched a short distance, then halted and remained on alert all night. With daylight, they returned to camp and slept until late morning. Firing could be heard in the direction of Petersburg, where General William Smith's XVIII Corps slugged it out with the enemy. On June 19 at 2:00 A.M., the Jersey Brigade was ordered to break camp, and two hours later was on the march to Petersburg. Crossing the Appomattox River on a pontoon bridge, the VI Corps relieved the XVIII Corps at about noon. The Confederate defenders opened fire on the fresh Federal troops with artillery and small arms fire, but few casualties resulted. The Jerseymen could easily see the outer defenses of Petersburg and the church steeples marking its boundaries. There was not enough space for the entire brigade to occupy the available earthwork defenses, so the Tenth NJV formed the front line and the rest of the brigade remained in the woods behind the works.[22]

Shells flew over the men's heads, and some occasionally dropped down on them, causing several casualties. The Tenth and Fifteenth NJV lost men on June 20. Lieutenant Halsey noted that "our safety depended on the enemy not seeing us—we had no works but were partially covered by a skirt of wood." The artillery barrage continued on June 21. Chaplain Haines and Adjutant Halsey had a close call when a shell landed between their two horses but did not explode. The XVIII Corps arrived that night to relieve the Jerseyans, and they marched four miles all night in a southeasterly direction to the Jerusalem Plank Road on the left of the Federal line. Reaching some woods, the brigade threw out a skirmish line to determine if they were occupied by the enemy.

Two Confederate divisions hit the Federal II Corps in the gap between it and the VI Corps on June 22, driving the Yanks back and capturing hundreds of prisoners. The Jerseymen formed into line of battle at 7:00 P.M. and were told they would charge after dark. Ordered to advance, the line quickly lost its direction and cohesiveness in the darkness and the thick forest undergrowth with many downed trees. The First Delaware Cavalry had the most trouble. Halsey characterized them as "a flock of sheep—not even the semblance of a line." The Second Division also charged, but it found the II Corps instead, and fired into it in the confusion. The following day, the VI Corps finally connected with the II Corps on the right and both dug trenches. The First Division moved to the left and the men were told they would again attack. Orders never arrived, so the division returned to the position it had occupied the night before. These types of confused movements characterized the next five days as Grant's army jockeyed for position against Lee's. The Jerseymen spent most of the time digging trenches.[23]

General Wright inspected the brigade on June 29. "With our worn and soiled clothes, [we] presented a very shabby appearance," Reverend Haines recalled. Bugles sounded at noon for the men to prepare to march, but they did not move out until 3:00 P.M. The trek down the Jerusalem Plank Road was hot and dusty, made worse by the scarcity of water. Reaching their destination at Ream's Station at 11:00 P.M., the men of the brigade dropped their belongings and by midnight were actively destroying the Weldon Railroad. Disruption of the rail service into Richmond was one of Grant's goals, and the Jersey boys went about their task with a vengeance.

They worked through the night and into the morning destroying about three miles of track, and began a return to their camp at about 4:00 P.M., marching about halfway before bivouacking for the night. They remained there on July 1, improvising brush shelters to protect themselves from the blazing sun.[24]

After waiting for the road to clear of other troops, the division marched back to its camp on July 2, arriving at noon. This was not a direct march, as the column marched back and forth for six hours, making only three miles in the process. The men camped in a large cornfield that had been pulverized by many feet. As a result, the least amount of wind stirred up swirls of fine granules that coated the men, and they named the camp the "Dust Hole." Water availability was a problem, as safe supplies were too far away. However, five or six feet of digging produced a source of fresh water. Because of the water scarcity, the field officers' horses could not use these wells; instead the officers had to take their mounts a distance away to drink in muddy pools. To Edmund Halsey, "the whole country seems a swamp with no streams in it." Halsey also noted that officers received permission to draw their rations with the men, "owing to their inability to pay." Normally, the officers used their higher pay to purchase food, but they had not been paid in four months and, to Halsey, this "added insult to injury."

The men remained in the Dust Hole until July 7, when they were permitted to move into the woods to avoid the dust that made their existence miserable. They heard that miners were digging a shaft under a portion of the Confederate defenses. After the dynamite exploded, a massive infantry charge would follow. More unsettling was the fact that the Third Division had embarked on transports at City Point for a rapid transport to Maryland. General Jubal Early's Confederate corps had invaded Maryland, and Washington was in danger.

Captain Wahl was tried by a military court on July 9 for again refusing to take command of his company. The verdict was the same—guilty, with discipline to be a private matter. Some of the units created makeshift chapels to conduct prayer meetings. Such a meeting was about to begin in the afternoon, when the brigade was ordered to break camp. The men were on the march by midnight and continued through thick dust until 9:00 A.M. on July 10, when the First Division reached City Point. Reinforcements were needed against Early's raid, so the rest of the VI Corps was being sent north. The brigade camped in a flat field inside an old earthwork while awaiting transportation. Horses arrived for the First Delaware Cavalry, which mounted them and said goodbye to the Jersey Brigade.[25]

Climbing aboard the transports, the Jerseymen bid farewell to Virginia and began a new adventure to the north.

CHAPTER 10

Washington and the Shenandoah Valley Campaign

The First New Jersey Brigade embarked on transports at City Point at about 10:00 A.M. on July 11 and was on its way toward Fort Monroe within an hour. Many men probably pulled out their new bibles, given them the day before by the Christian Commission. They heard that a pick-up army under General Lew Wallace had delayed General Jubal Early's march on Washington on July 9 at the Battle of the Monocacy. The VI Corps' Third Division had participated in the fight and lost about half its men in the process. More troops were desperately needed, so the remainder of the VI Corps was tapped to provide the reinforcements. The men were not aware that Early's small army of seventeen thousand men was within sight of Washington.

Early's small corps was initially dispatched to the Shenandoah Valley to halt a Federal thrust. Driving up the Valley, Union general David Hunter's men had burned and pillaged, forcing Lee to send Early to check him. Early drove Hunter into West Virginia, and then moved north toward Washington. Crossing into Maryland, Early caused a panic, forcing the VI Corps' recall to the defense of the capital.[1]

The Jerseymen had a gay time during their passage, as flags flew, bands played, and gunboats saluted them. "The Sailors manned the rigging, and cheered us lustily as we passed which was heartily returned by our men," noted Charles Paul. Edmund Halsey happily wrote in his diary, "a good dinner, an opportunity to dress up and *no dust.*"

The men reflected on their past ordeals during the quiet hours. Many of the veterans of the First, Second, Third, and Fourth NJV who had reenlisted the previous winter probably regretted their decisions, now that the war had turned especially deadly with Grant's arrival. They could not believe that only slightly more than two months had passed since they marched into the Wilderness. In that time they had participated in several pitched battles in four campaigns. None could sail north without thinking of their dead and maimed comrades. So few remained. Then there was the future. What would it hold for them? Would they join their comrades in a cold, hard grave? Now they faced the unknown, which was always difficult for soldiers. Gone was the feeling that the war would soon be over. In fact, many may have worried that the capture of Washington would prolong the war and their ordeal.

The transports dropped anchor at Washington at noon on July 12. The Fourth and Fifteenth NJV disembarked and waited for the Tenth NJV by the docks. Sutlers appeared, relieving many men of their hard-won dollars. Not able to wait beyond 4:00 P.M., the two regiments formed into column and marched through the city, where the townspeople hailed them as heroes. According to Reverend Haines, the men were received as "deliverers from a great peril . . . on every side the heartiest expression of good will." Flags were everywhere and cheering citizens thronged the streets waving handkerchiefs. If the warm reception was not enough, the men were thrilled to receive rations of fresh bread.[2]

Fort Stevens, now under attack by Early's Confederates, was the First Division's destination. The Second Division arrived there first and helped repulse Early's attack. As the Jerseymen arrived, they could see the enemy about three-quarters of a mile from the fort in the fading light. "The tremendous Siege Guns of the Forts ruined the monotony by their deep booming," noted Captain Charles Paul. Realizing that Washington was now heavily reinforced by the VI and XIX Corps, Early wisely decided to withdraw from Washington on the night of July 12. Paul wrote, "the rebs left in a hurry last night, leaving their dead and wounded behind." Marching all night, Early's men recrossed the Potomac River at Edwards Ferry, ending the immediate threat. Not content to leave Early alone to terrorize Maryland, the VI Corps followed for about twelve miles on June 13, camping about six miles from Rockville, Maryland. The Tenth NJV rejoined the brigade here. The original members of the Fifteenth NJV were excited when they passed Fort Kearny, which they had helped construct during the summer of 1862. Not much had changed except for the installation of heavier guns and greater protection for the men serving them.

On the road again at 5:00 A.M. on July 14, the Jerseymen marched two hours before halting. The Second Division led the VI Corps, and the Fifteenth NJV was ordered out on a reconnaissance to investigate a rumor that the enemy was on the corps' right flank. Advancing with the cavalry, the Jerseymen quickly learned that the enemy had withdrawn across the Potomac to Leesburg. The column continued its trek, marching about fourteen miles to Poolesville, Maryland. Because the Fifteenth NJV was in advance of the corps, it took a different return route. The men of that regiment were rewarded for their efforts, as they encountered farmers more than willing to sell milk, eggs, and biscuits.[3]

After the long journey north by ship and two days of hard marching, the Jerseyans were allowed July 15 as a day to rest. Edmund Halsey wrote his sister comparing Maryland with what the men had recently experienced in Virginia: "no one is anxious to go back at least not until he has had time to breathe fresh air."

Early was still dangerous, so General Wright was ordered after him with the VI Corps on July 16. The XIX Corps, fresh from Louisiana, joined the hunt. The men were in column at 5:00 A.M. and reached the Potomac River at White's Ford after a short march. Enemy cavalry were on the opposite bank but posed no serious opposition. Without pontoon bridges, the men waded the Potomac—the first time they had ever done so. It was a difficult cross-ing, as the river was wide, the current strong, the bottom stony and slippery, and the water waist-deep, forcing the men to hold their cartridge boxes above the water. "The sight of the river, alive with shouting men, was a novel one," recalled Haines. Wet below the waist, the Jerseymen quickly reformed and pressed on to Leesburg, Virginia, where they rested for an hour. They could see the enemy here, retreating with Federal troops in pursuit. The march con-tinued another five miles before the column bivouacked on the opposite side of Chester Gap in the Blue Ridge Mountains. The men had marched fifteen miles that day. Early was now moving south. Expedition commander Gen-eral Wright thought the ten thousand men available to him in the two VI Corps divisions and the roughly three thousand men of the XIX Corps were too meager to confront Early, who probably commanded in excess of fifteen thou-sand men at this time. Wright knew, however, that General Hunter's men were marching quickly north, so the possibility of bagging Early was very good. Early sensed the trap and pulled his men back out of harm's way.[4]

Wright's force, now linked with Hunter's, continued after Early at 4:30 A.M. on July 18. The Rebels were in the Shenandoah Valley, while the Fed-eral pursuers followed on the east side of the Blue Ridge Mountains. The men passed through Hamilton, where some of the citizens waved American flags, then Purcellville, and at about 4:00 p.m. entered the Shenandoah Val-ley through Snicker's Gap. Rich farmland abounded, causing Lieutenant

Halsey to write, "our men could not resist the many temptations to straggle." The men waited here while some of General Hunter's men tried unsuccessfully to clear a Shenandoah River ford of Confederates. As the New Jersey Brigade arrived at the river after its ten-mile march, its men could see enemy batteries in position across the river. The Fourth and Tenth NJV halted and stacked arms behind a Federal battery and the Fifteenth was in the process of doing so when the enemy artillery opened fire. Some of the shells overshot the Federal battery, causing nine casualties in the Fourth and Tenth NJV. Some of those not injured "felt the glow of heat from the shells that passed by us unpleasantly near," recalled Chaplain Haines. The brigade shifted its position to the protective belt of woods to its left until Federal batteries neutralized the Confederate challenge.

Burying the three men killed during the artillery barrage was the first order of business for July 19. Thick clouds of dust in the distance revealed that the enemy was again on the march in the direction of vital Harper's Ferry. The Jerseyans expected to be ordered into column, but were surprised that they remained in camp all day. Division commander General David Russell decided to make a reconnaissance, and he selected the always-reliable Fifteenth NJV and two companies of the Tenth NJV to accompany him. Although honored, the men were not happy with the pace he set toward the river. Halsey wrote, "Gen. Russell was with us all the way and a little ahead of anything." Seeing heavy enemy activity on the opposite side of the river, Russell wisely decided not to force a crossing with the depleted Fifteenth NJV.[5]

Meanwhile, Early's small army, menaced by General William Averill's cavalry division, retreated toward its stronghold at Strasburg. The VI Corps finally crossed the waist-deep Shenandoah River on July 20 and marched cautiously two or three miles toward Berryville, halting until 10:00 P.M. During this march, the men saw how poorly the dead from the July 18 skirmish had been buried by the anxious-to-retreat enemy. The brigade's historian wrote, "the grewsome [sic] sight of heads, legs and arms of the Union dead, sticking out from under the few shovelfuls of earth thrown upon them, gave rise to bitter denunciation, by the Union soldiers, of Confederate inhumanity."

Grant needed his troops back, and believing that General Hunter's men could handle Early, the VI and XIX Corps prepared for their return trek to the Army of the Potomac. Assembly sounded in the pouring rain, and the Jerseymen heard orders that the VI Corps would undertake the fifty-mile forced march back to Washington. Their recently issued rations were to last two additional days, and straggling would not be tolerated. If the men had not been so miserable, they would have stared at each other in disbelief, as they had never been read this type of information before—usually they just marched in blissful ignorance.[6]

The brigade was on the road, forming the rearguard, an hour after hearing their orders. Fording the Shenandoah River again, the Federal column left the Valley the way it had entered, through Snicker's Gap. Marching all night in the drenching rain, the Jersey Brigade reached Chester Gap at noon on July 21. The twenty-two-mile march left the men bone tired, and no one complained that they rested here until the next morning. Captain Paul recorded in his diary, "Good many of the men have very sore feet." This was Confederate partisan Colonel John Mosby's territory, and he took advantage of the Federal invaders by raiding supply wagons and capturing stragglers. The march toward Washington resumed at 7:30 A.M. on July 22, and the column soon reached Drainesville, where the men were given an hour to prepare their morning coffee. The subsequent march did not go well, for the brigade got lost while making a detour to find a better place to ford a stream, and did not go into camp until 9:00 that night near Lewisburg. The fifteen-mile march left the Jerseyans only twelve miles from Chain Bridge over the Potomac River. Again on the road at 4:00 A.M. on July 23, the brigade crossed the bridge and went into camp with the rest of the corps three miles into Maryland, at Tenallytown.

Although warned that they could be again on the march at anytime, the corps remained around Tenallytown until July 26. A number of visitors from Washington descended on the camps. Some of the VI Corps regiments received clothing and accoutrements, and most importantly, the paymaster arrived. The spirits also flowed freely. Riding back to camp from a day in Washington, Adjutant Halsey noted the "road was lined with drunken soldiers walking the best of their way back."[7]

With Early's army inactive at Strasburg, it appeared to the Jerseymen that the worst was over. Halsey wrote in his diary, "so ends the Maryland campaign." He was wrong. Learning that the VI and XIX Corps had left his front and were in the process of returning to Washington and then to the Army of the Potomac, Early attacked General George Crook at Kernstown on July 23, inflicting severe losses on the Federal troops and driving them from the Valley. Early next sent General John McCausland's Brigade north to capture and ransom Chambersburg. When his demands were not met, he burned the town, causing hysteria in Maryland and Pennsylvania. Meanwhile, Early moved his small army back across the Potomac River into Maryland.

Early's renewed threat prevented the VI Corps' return to the Army of the Potomac. It was time to destroy Early's army once and for all. The VI Corps broke camp at around noon on July 26. Its destination was Harper's

Ferry. The men marched through Tenallytown and Rockville that day, halting about five miles beyond the latter town at midnight. It was a killing fifteen-mile march.[8]

Permitted only a four-hour rest, the men were back on the road at 4:00 A.M. on July 27, marching twelve miles through Middleburg, Clarksburg, and finally halting near Hyattstown at about noon. While there, the much-awaited promotions from Governor Parker arrived to fill some of the vacancies in the officer ranks. The following day, the corps marched through the towns of Urbana and Monocacy Bridge. The men rested at the latter town until 3:00 P.M., and then forded the Monocacy River, crossed over Catoctin Mountain, and camped at midnight, just south of Jefferson, Maryland, after a seventeen-mile march.

The seemingly endless marches continued at 6:00 A.M. on July 29, and the weary Jerseymen trudged through Jefferson, Petersville, and Knoxville. All were relieved to see a pontoon bridge over the Potomac River, which they used to reach Harper's Ferry. It was hot and dusty, and the men were exhausted after their sixteen-mile march. Adjutant Halsey wrote, "the heat painfully intense." Many men limped along because of sore feet. After a short rest in the town, the brigade continued two more miles, finally camping on Bolivar Heights. July 30 was quiet until the bugles sounded late in the day. "Down came the tents and baggage was repacked. The little white houses of the soldiers disappeared as if by magic," wrote Captain Dayton Flint of the Fifteenth NJV. The column marched back to Harper's Ferry. Scores fell from the ranks because of the exceptional heat and grueling pace. The brigade finally reached the Potomac River again, but other troops clogged the crossing, so the men waited their turn to cross. No one complained about the rest, but they did not realize that they would have to make up the time, for they finally crossed at 10:00 P.M. and marched four hours through the darkness to Petersville on July 31.[9]

The men expected to be on the march again at dawn, but the bugles did not sound until late morning. The heat was again intolerable, forcing a halt in the early afternoon, when the brigade was granted a few hours' rest in the shade. The march toward Frederick continued at 4:00 P.M. Many grumbled that they were marching back in the same direction they had come. The march finally ground to a halt about a mile from Frederick at about 7:00 P.M. The men did not know it, but they would remain here until August 3. During this reprieve, Adjutant Halsey convened courts-martial for twenty-two stragglers. Each was sentenced to ninety days of fatigue duty and loss of $25 in pay. The brigade finally moved out at 4:00 P.M. on August 3 and marched with the wagon train to Buckeystown, camping near the Monocacy River. Many men went swimming and washed their clothes and bodies.

General Grant ventured up to Washington to confer with his officers, and they all agreed on August 5 to concentrate their forces and form an impregnable defensive line around Hallstown and Harper's Ferry. Russell's Division of the VI Corps was on the march that evening—back to Harper's Ferry. The Second and Third Divisions got to take trains to their destination, while the First Division marched. After halting for breakfast at 8:00 A.M. on August 6, the brigade guarded the slow-moving wagon train. As a result, the Jerseymen did not reach their bivouac site, three miles beyond Harper's Ferry, until 10:00 that night. The men were bone weary from the twenty-four miles of marching and countermarching. They remained here until August 10. Despite the hard marches, the men liked being away from Grant's army. Wallace Struble of the Fourth NJV wrote home, "we are encamped on the banks of the Potomac and a more healthy spot does not exist. Grants Army lay in low marshy sickly swamps and the soldiers are dieing off very fast."[10]

Feeling unable to cope with Early's threat, General Hunter offered his resignation to General Grant, who quickly accepted it. Grant immediately sent for General Phil Sheridan to assume command of the new Army of the Shenandoah. News that General Sheridan now commanded the army reached the men during the march. The army included the three divisions from the VI Corps, two divisions from the VIII Corps, two more from the XIX Corps, and three cavalry divisions, including two crack ones from the Army of the Potomac, all totaling sixty-eight thousand men. When the troops assumed their designated positions, the defensive Federal line was twenty-miles long.

Lieutenant Colonel Campbell later recalled his first interaction with Sheridan:

> Seeing what appeared to be a troop of cavalry about to make its way through the column, between the Fifteenth and the regiment in front of it, thus increasing its interval and interfering with the leg-weary men in the hard task of keeping 'closed up,' I put spurs to my horse and dashed back toward the little chap at the head of it, with tongue and teeth ready charged with a message designed to let him know, in terms easily understood, my opinion of such a proceeding. Just before opening on him, I noticed a pair of stars on his shoulders and the headquarters flag of Phil Sheridan. I did not deliver the message.

Sheridan was too aggressive to assume a defensive posture, particularly against an outnumbered foe, so he decided to take the offensive. Russell's

Division broke camp at 7:30 A.M. and moved south to near Summit Point on August 10, passing through Charleston at 9:00 A.M., where the bands struck up "John Brown's Body" to pay tribute to the man and location of his trial and execution. The Jersey Brigade went into camp at 5:00 P.M. in an area abundant in corn, green apples, and mutton.[11]

The march after Early continued for the next few days. August 11 found the Jerseymen marching twelve miles, camping close to Berryville; August 12 through Newtown and Middletown; August 13 across Cedar Creek to within two miles of Hupp's Hill, which overlooked Strasburg. They could see the strong Confederate positions on nearby Fisher's Hill. That night, the division recrossed Cedar Creek and returned to its camp of August 12, where the Jerseyans received three days' rations and were told to make them last, as they would not receive additional food for four days. The men did not really care because of the abundance of corn and apples in the region. "We lived pretty well on the march," wrote John Hoffman of the Tenth NJV, "for the corn is now old enough to boil and we can eat of it. We strip whole fields in a short time of all that is fit to boil." The Fifteenth NJV filed a return on August 13 reporting 234 men present for duty. This slim number included the reenlisted men from the Second and Third NJV.

On August 14, Sheridan decided to test Early's position by sending a strong skirmish line from the VIII Corps toward Fisher's Hill, while another from the VI Corps advanced toward Strasburg. He received unwelcome news that Early's army was reinforced and now boasted forty thousand muskets. The following day, Colonel Penrose assembled the Fifteenth NJV and conducted a reconnaissance toward Strasburg. Splitting his regiment into two wings, Penrose cautiously advanced on the town. He found plenty of Rebels and wisely withdrew, his mission accomplished. Lieutenant Halsey was happy with the order, as he could see enemy soldiers "crawling around our right." Instead of returning to his original position, Penrose halted the regiment on a hill in front of it, where his men could see the enemy picket line approaching. The Jerseymen opened fire, causing the enemy to dash for cover. Confederate sharpshooters in houses returned the fire, and it was a hot time for awhile. Penrose finally received orders to return the regiment to its original position, and the men complied without a complaint. They thought the rest of the day would be quiet, but shouts of "here come the Rebs" echoed down the line at 3:00 P.M. Jumping to their feet, the men could see a long line of battle advancing toward the Federal position. The Yankee picket line gradually fell back, and soon Confederate artillery opened fire on the Union positions. The Fifteenth NJV lost nine men during this cannonade. Fearing an all-out attack, Penrose ordered the Tenth NJV up from the rear to form on the right of the Fifteenth. Almost as suddenly as the enemy had appeared, they halted and then retreated back toward the town. After the skirmish, Captain Charles Paul reported that the Fifteenth NJV "stood firm as a rock."[12]

Resting until just before midnight on the night of August 16–17, the Jerseymen were ordered back into column because of Sheridan's concern about Early's growing numbers. The three Federal corps abandoned their positions under cover of darkness, with the New Jersey Brigade acting as rearguard. The army marched all night, and daylight found the men at Newtown sixteen miles from their starting point. When Early learned of the Federal army's withdrawal at daylight, he quickly put his army on the road after it. Meanwhile, the New Jersey Brigade reached Winchester at about noon on August 17. Sheridan deemed the town indefensible, so he continued the retreat toward Berryville. Left behind were two cavalry divisions, commanded by General Torbert. Realizing that he needed infantry support, Torbert requested his old unit, so the small, 850-man brigade reluctantly watched the rest of the infantry march off to safety. Torbert's orders were to delay Early's troops long enough for the army to reach safely. The three New Jersey infantry regiments immediately deployed as an extended skirmish line behind Abram's Creek, south of Winchester. The Fifteenth NJV was deployed on the right across the Martinsburg Turnpike. The Fourth NJV, still under Captain Baldwin Hufty, formed on the left of the Fifteenth, and then came the Tenth NJV, which covered Front Royal Pike. The line to be defended was about two miles long, but because there were so few Jerseymen, each was about fifteen paces from the next. The men took cover behind whatever could stop a bullet—the bank of the creek, rocks, stones, fences, trees, etc., causing Captain Hufty to report, "our line was well protected by the nature of the country." The orders were to "hold our positions at all hazards."

The veterans grimly awaited Early's army. Clumps of Federal cavalry, then whole regiments, galloped from the front beginning at 2:00 P.M., and the men knew it was just a matter of time before the enemy appeared. Sure enough, enemy cavalry quickly rode into view and, seeing the deployed Jerseymen, dismounted and began testing the Federal position. The first advance was against the Fifteenth NJV and part of the Fourth on the right of the line, but they could not budge the Jerseymen. Big trouble was brewing, however. "All the afternoon large columns of the enemy could be seen moving both to our right and left, evidently forming for an attack," noted Captain Hufty. Their skirmish line advanced between 4:00 and 5:00 P.M., only to meet the same fate as the one before. Reinforcements were thrown forward with little success. The entire brigade was now engaged. Colonel Campbell recalled that "it was a beautiful, though unequal, skirmish fight. The enemy crowded forward with fearless determination, and kept up an uninterrupted, cool, well-directed fire; but they were advancing chiefly over open ground, whilst every rock and tree on the line confronting them seemed animated with a personality of flame and smoke." Some troopers from the Third New Jersey Cavalry helped strengthen the line by forming on the right flank; other cavalry units helped defend the left.[13]

Thinking that Sheridan's entire army was making a stand, Early deployed for an attack. The Jerseymen quickly saw the enemy line extending beyond each flank. "There was a grim kind of unsought amusement about the sight," reported Campbell. He summed up the situation as "a thin [Federal] skirmish line along a small creek, visible from the rear, but chiefly invisible from the front, except by its line of fire. No supports of any kind—the cavalry had moved to the rear of the city. In front of this attenuated line a veteran army moved deliberately and rapidly up, and division after division went into position for assault. Whilst the formation was going on, the stubborn skirmish line continued, our little brigade not yielding an inch." Penrose's veterans grimly gripped their rifles and waited, but Early decided not to attack.

General John Breckenridge, commanding the division on the Confederate left, did not agree with Early's assessment of the strength of the Federal force in front of him. Gaining permission from Early to feel the Federal force at 8:00 P.M., Breckenridge sent his division against the right of the Fifteenth NJV in the growing darkness. With the Federal cavalry on both flanks pulled back because they were low on ammunition, Breckenridge's men went through the outnumbered Jerseymen like a warm knife through butter. Hearing of the success of this movement, Early immediately ordered an en echelon attack on the rest of the New Jersey Brigade's position, from his left to his right. Captain Paul estimated that the brigade held the enemy at bay for about forty-five minutes. "They came in our rear on our right and left flanks, and almost completely surrounded us[—]in fact the conflict was hand to hand," Paul wrote. It was time to retreat. The brigade broke into two pieces. The Tenth and part of the Fourth NJV on the left retired via the Berryville Pike, while the right of the Fourth NJV and the Fifteenth eventually pulled back via the Martinsburg Pike. It appears that the Fifteenth on the right of the latter pike remained in position to cover its comrades' retreat. Some claimed that the Tenth NJV never received orders to pull back, but did so when the men realized that they were almost surrounded. John Beach of the

Fourth NJV noted that the situation was becoming precarious. "The Tenth on the left and the Fifteenth on the right, retiring, the bullets whistling from both flanks. It was either be captured or run. With bent forms we broke for the rear."[14]

Beach was probably on the left-center of the line, so he did not realize that part of the Fifteenth and perhaps some of his own Fourth NJV had fallen back a bit but were holding their ground while the left wing and the center retreated. Colonel Campbell ordered a stout resistance in the darkness. As he reordered his defensive line, he rode forward, but he could not understand why the number of troops seemed greater than earlier in the day. They also appeared to be firing in the wrong direction. It was only then that Campbell realized that he was amongst enemy soldiers, so he quickly retreated before his identity became known. This kind of confusion also occurred several times with the enlisted men, and some, like Josiah Brown, previously of the Second NJV, and now with the Fifteenth, were captured. "When we found the greycoats almost upon us and when there seemed no other sensible thing to do we simply surrendered[,] gave up our arms and passed within their lines," he wrote.

The last organized resistance was made by a group of about a dozen Jerseymen from the Fifteenth NJV who took position on a hill on the right of Winchester at about 11:00 P.M. Seeing a solid mass of men approaching, the Northerners yelled out, "Don't fire on your friends! Don't fire on your friends!" The handful of men then fired their weapons almost into the faces of the approaching enemy troops and quickly took off for the rear, taking advantage of the confusion they had caused. There was so much disorganization that night that no one knew exactly where anyone else was. Almost 240 were captured. The number of casualties was slight, however, because the men were so well protected during the initial fight. Some Jerseymen were killed or wounded when townspeople opened fire on them in the darkness as they retreated through Winchester. The Fourth NJV lost the fewest men—three wounded and thirty-seven missing/captured. The Fifteenth NJV was next with nine killed or wounded and fifty-one missing/captured. The unlucky Tenth NJV lost Lieutenant Colonel Tay and 150 men missing/captured. They had become lost in the darkness and were taken en masse. According to a history of the Tenth NJV, "no order was sent to the regiment to withdraw, and the result necessarily was, that holding on from moment to moment, fighting and waiting, it was gradually surrounded, so that when at last the attempt was made to fall back, it only fell into the snare set for it." Lieutenant Colonel Edward Campbell of the Fifteenth disagreed, noting that Tay "reached

Winchester, but instead of keeping on, halted there, and was surrounded, with a large portion of the Tenth Regiment." Why Tay halted his men rather than continuing the retreat remains a mystery. The remainder of the regiment was now a mere skeleton of its former self, numbering a mere eighty men. John Hoffman was surprised that anyone escaped. "I think we should not if it had not been for darkness coming on and hiding us from view of the enemy. They had overlapped both of our flanks and were rapidly closing upon our rear." The survivors were placed under the command of Major Lambert Boeman of the Fifteenth NJV. Only one company commander made it out of the fight. The enemy's losses are not known, but one Confederate lieutenant became confused and fell into the hands of the Fifteenth NJV.[15]

The men had reason to be proud. Fewer than nine hundred men had held up Early's forty thousand soldiers and inflicted many casualties. Wallace Struble noted the "brigade was in good fighting order and we slew a good many rebs." Captain Paul believed that "the rebs will feel cheap when they find they employed all of one of their corps (Breckenridge's) to dislodge a Skirmish line of 800 men." Colonel Penrose told General Wright, tongue in cheek, that he could have whipped the enemy with two more regiments.

Realizing that the enemy was not following, Lieutenant Colonel Campbell halted the retreat of the four hundred men with him at Summit Point and permitted them to sleep through the rest of the night. A steady stream of stragglers joined the brigade. The men were back in line at 10:00 A.M. on August 18 and on the march in a drenching rain. They finally reunited with the remainder of the brigade, 150 men, at noon. These men had made their way to safety with Colonel Penrose and Captain Robert Johnson of the Fourth NJV. Although the brigade's losses were heavy, they were not as great as previously feared. When the brigade finally linked up with the First Division, the latter's bands played and men cheered, as they thought the brigade had been destroyed. Some might say it had, for it now numbered under 550 men. The division was on the road at 2:30 P.M. after a three-hour rest. Its destination was Charlestown, where it camped after the sixteen-mile march. Adjutant Halsey noted that it was "our 5th day of 3 day rations."[16]

The men rested in Charlestown on August 19 and August 20 while Early probed toward Shepherdstown. Many were participating in church services on Sunday, August 21, when Early attacked the VI Corps' picket line at about 9:00 A.M. They quickly learned of the attack because the Federal pickets were equipped with repeating Spencer rifles, permitting them to fire faster and make more noise than traditional rifles. The Jerseymen immediately entrenched. As luck would have it, the brigade's only casualties were to the already decimated Tenth NJV, which lost about nine men. A sharp counter-attack dimmed the Confederates' enthusiasm, and the skirmish ended by nightfall. Not wishing to take on Early, Sheridan withdrew his army to Halltown on the night of August 21, deploying it between two rivers that protected each flank. Leaving at midnight, the New Jersey Brigade reached its designated position at 6:00 A.M. on August 22. The ninety-one men of the Fourth NJV who had not reenlisted left for home during this period. "As they marched out of camp on their journey towards home, there were many who envied them," noted the brigade historian.

Early followed Sheridan, and the two forces skirmished through the morning as the Rebels tested the Federal position. Worried that Early intended to force the issue, Sheridan sent the First Division to the left of Hallstown at about noon to help support the XIX Corps. A tremendous storm hit the area, halting hostilities and the movement of the division, which went into camp and remained there for five days. During this period the brigade's three regiments rotated duty on the picket line. Reinforcements also arrived to swell the regiments' depleted ranks. For example, thirty-four recruits were assigned to the Fifteenth NJV—four of them had served in the Confederate army before deserting.[17]

Realizing the strength of Sheridan's position, Early decided to feign another invasion of the North by sending some of his units north to Shepherdstown on the Potomac River. Sheridan prepared to move if Early crossed the river, but the latter was content to halt his men at Bunker Hill, with his line running south to Stephenson's Depot. Sheridan moved his army again on August 28, this time closer to Charlestown. Marching through the town, the bands again played "John Brown's Body," to the disgust of the local citizens. The brigade went into camp two miles beyond the town and remained here until September 3. Any soldier not possessing a Springfield rifle was given one during the brigade's stay here, and a sixteen-man sharpshooter unit was formed and equipped with Spencer repeating rifles. Captain Paul of the brigade staff commanded the detachment.

The Jerseymen were up early on September 3 for the march to Berryville, but they did not move out until 5:30 A.M. because other troops clogged the road. The brigade remained at Berryville until 5:00 P.M. the next day, when ordered to entrench due to an enemy advance. Springing to work, "we carried rails, piling them four feet high and driving stakes to hold them in place," recalled Alanson Haines. Spades and picks arrived about an hour later, and within in a short time a formidable breastwork was constructed. If the men had had time to look around, they would have seen the same construction was being completed over a five-mile front. Seeing the strength of the fortifications, Early wisely decided not to attack. "They were not willing to adopt the mode of fighting we had pursued in the overland campaign," a disappointed Haines wrote. Wild cheering erupted when the Jerseyans learned about Atlanta's fall to Sherman.[18]

The army remained near Berryville from September 3 through 18, to the satisfaction of soldiers whose feet ached from the constant marching. Reinforcements arrived daily. Most were formerly wounded comrades who were now sufficiently recovered to rejoin their units. New recruits also arrived during this period, many of them substitutes. For example, fifty-three recruits were distributed among the companies of the Fifteenth NJV on September 2. Halsey called them "a bad lot," and many deserted within twenty-four hours of arriving. The new recruits arrived unarmed, without tents, and hungry, as they had not been provided with rations. It was an inauspicious start to their military careers, as they were without food for two days and soaked to the skin by the cold rainstorms that socked the area after their arrival. Another batch of recruits arrived on September 8, and these were "a better lot." By the end of that day, the Fifteenth NJV numbered a mere 175 men—a skeleton of its former self. A total of 123 recruits had arrived since the end of August, but many had already deserted. Those who remained learned quickly from the veterans and spent considerable time drilling. The almost daily evening religious service was a favorite activity during this period.

Despite the horrendous casualties sustained by the Federal forces, most of the men believed that the end to the war could be achieved "only by bullets and bayonets," according to Samuel Cavileer of the Fourth NJV. He was confident that Lincoln could beat the Democratic candidate, former Army of the Potomac commander George McClellan. "The election of our old Chieftain Abe is sure," he wrote, and he criticized the New Jersey Democrats who wished to vie for peace as "sons of bitches."[19]

The usually aggressive General Sheridan patiently waited for the right time to launch his offensive against Early. He would not have to wait long.

CHAPTER 11

Defeating General Early

$\mathcal{B}$oth Lee and Grant looked to the Shenandoah Valley for needed troops as the summer waned. Early was sent to protect Lynchburg and the Valley against marauding Federal forces and to pull Federal troops from Petersburg. He was successful in both assignments, but this did not dissuade Grant from continuing his operations against Lee. Grant wanted to envelop Petersburg, but he needed additional troops to do so. The VI Corps had been recalled at least once, but Early's aggressiveness cancelled those orders. Now, on September 2, Joseph Kershaw's Division of Richard Anderson's Corps began its movement toward Richmond but engaged in a firefight with the Federal VIII Corps and returned to Early's army. Since Sheridan was showing no signs of aggressiveness, the division again tried to return to Lee's army on September 14. Grant visited Sheridan the following day to review the army's position and plan for the future.

Learning that two of Early's divisions were chasing Federal cavalry toward Martinsburg, north of Winchester, and a third was moving east to return to Lee's army, Sheridan realized the enemy forces at Fisher's Hill were just too vulnerable to pass up. He quickly prepared attack plans that had two corps and his cavalry looping around Winchester to attack from behind, while another corps approached from the south. As Sheridan plotted and planned on Sunday, September 18, the Jerseymen spent a quiet morning resting. Their participation in afternoon prayer services, however, were interrupted by orders to prepare to march. The order was soon suspended and the men put their tents back up and resumed their prayer service.[1]

The men were up at 1:00 A.M. on September 19 but did not move for almost two hours, when the army marched along Berryville Pike toward Winchester, preceded by Wilson's cavalry division. It was ten miles to Winchester and another six east to Early's army at Opequon Creek. Sheridan wanted his army ready to pounce on Early before he had time to recall his missing troops. This would be difficult, as the road to Winchester was clogged with Federal troops, artillery, and wagons, which hindered the march. The men halted frequently, then jogged forward to make up for lost time. After crossing Opequon Creek, Sheridan deployed the XIX Corps and then brought up the Second and Third Divisions of the VI Corps; Russell's First Division was held in reserve.

The army was finally deployed by noon—far later than Sheridan anticipated. If he had been able to carry out his plan, Ramseur's lone division near Winchester would have been overwhelmed. Seeing Sheridan's approach, Early quickly recalled John Gordon's and Robert Rodes' divisions and deployed them against the Federal assault. The two VI Corps divisions advanced against Ramseur's and Rodes' divisions shortly before noon, pressing them back toward Winchester. The XIX Corps on the right was having similar success against Gordon's Division. General Cullen Battle's fresh brigade from Rodes' Division counterattacked in the gap between the two Federal corps and, with other Confederate units, drove back Ricketts' Division of the VI Corps and Cuvier Grover's of the XIX Corps. The remaining Federal divisions also began wavering. The Third Battle of Winchester had changed very quickly.[2]

The New Jersey Brigade, now barely six hundred strong, occupying a hollow, moved by the right flank into some woods. "Change front forward on first company," the men were told, and they quickly obeyed. Colonel Penrose was on leave, so Lieutenant Colonel Campbell commanded the brigade, and Captain William Cornish commanded the Fifteenth NJV. The Tenth NJV was on the left, the Fourth NJV in the center, and the Fifteenth NJV on the right. The latter was the right-most unit of the VI Corps' reserve. Heavy artillery fire blasted the brigade, so Campbell moved slightly to the right. Emerging from the woods, the Jerseymen could see the Third Division to its left-front advancing against the enemy. Seeing Colonel Oliver Edwards forming his Third Brigade into line of battle, Campbell issued the same order to his men, with the center of the brigade resting on the Berryville Turnpike. The Third Brigade was just in front of the Jerseymen, and its right half covered the left of the New Jersey Brigade. Both brigades had advanced a few hundred yards when Ricketts' Division broke for the rear.

Seeing a hill just in front of his position, Campbell ordered his men to advance and occupy it before the Confederates could do the same. The movement ended quickly when Campbell, "seeing the Third Brigade on my left halt, and retire a little to higher ground, I also halted my left." An aide to General George Getty, commander of the Second Division, rode up to

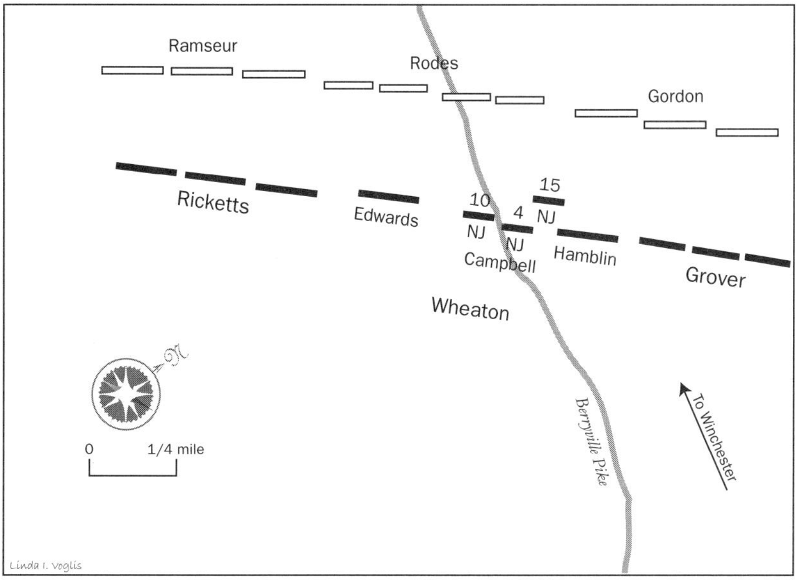

Map 12. Third Battle of Winchester (September 19, 1864).

Campbell and ordered him to "detach my right battalion and send it forward in the front lines to drive the enemy from a corn-field through which he was advancing." Campbell selected the Fifteenth NJV on the right and sent it forward with fixed bayonets and orders to hold the enemy "as long as possible." This was a tall order, as there were no Federal troops on its left or right and a mass of victorious Confederates was rapidly approaching. It appears that Campbell personally accompanied the regiment to its new position. In his absence, Colonel Edwards assumed command of the remaining two regiments, which were having their share of problems. According to Campbell, "the retiring front lines [Ricketts' Division] crowded into the ravine and came in such dense unorganized masses upon the front of my remaining two battalions [Fourth and Tenth NJV] that it was with the utmost difficulty they were arrested." The officers and men of the two veteran regiments pushed and harangued the fleeing men into a new defensive line. A number of Jerseymen apparently fixed bayonets to drive their point across. Campbell, now back with the rest of the brigade, received an order from General Russell to move his two regiments to the right, and form on the right of the Third Brigade, which had shifted in that direction.[3]

The First New Jersey Brigade, at least the Fourth and Tenth NJV, was now between the Third Brigade on its left and the Second Brigade on its right. Russell ordered the three brigades to open fire on the enemy troops appearing on a hill in front of them. The concentrated fire drove the enemy from view, causing Russell to order a charge that took the hill and gave the division a commanding position. The Tenth NJV captured between twenty and thirty enemy soldiers during this charge. Russell would not enjoy the fruits of this great victory. Wounded in the left part of the chest earlier in the day, he had kept it a secret. Now a shell fragment tore into his breast, piercing his heart and killing him instantly. General Emory Upton assumed command of the First Division.

Just prior to this charge, the Fifteenth NJV clung to its isolated position in front of the main Federal line. Their journey to this position was hazardous, as they had to charge through a hail of bullets. Reaching the edge of the cornfield, the regiment halted to redress its lines, then began firing at the unseen Rebs in front of them. The return fire caused men to fall here and there. Hearing a Rebel yell, the men looked to their right, where they saw enemy soldiers through the smoke resting their muskets on fence rails as they prepared to fire. Halsey estimated that the enemy was not more than half a dozen yards away. The Fifteenth's position was untenable and, according to the regiment's historian, "Captain Cornish . . . after a little, ordered us to fall back, as we were a mere handful by this time, and apparently unsupported." Never commanding the regiment before, it appears that Cornish momentarily froze, then regained his senses and quickly moved his men to the rear. During this movement the Jerseymen captured a number of enemy soldiers who were trying to get into their rear.[4]

While the Fifteenth was buying time, Upton reorganized his division, sending the Second and Third Brigades to the right to meet the growing threat. As the Fifteenth NJV returned to the Federal line, General Upton quickly moved it to the right to fill a gap between the Second and Third Brigades.

With the VI Corps on the left, the XIX Corps in the center, the VIII Corps on the right, and then Torbert's two cavalry divisions, Sheridan ordered a general advance at about 5:00 P.M. that swept the remaining Confederates from the field. During this advance the Second Brigade was on the right of the division, with the Fifteenth NJV on its left. Next came the Third Brigade, with the Tenth and Fourth NJV on its right. "It was a beautiful sight when the charging army, four miles in breadth from wing to wing, moved over the plain," wrote Alanson Haines. "They offered but little resistance, and fell back at the first onset." In his report, Upton singled out the Fifteenth NJV for its gallant final charge in conjunction with Edwards' Brigade, capturing a number of enemy troops in the process. Upton fell wounded at this time, forcing Colonel Edwards to take command of the division until General Wheaton arrived. A Federal cavalry charge against Early's left flank turned the retreat into a rout. Captain Paul noted the cavalry "driving them before them like Sheep." John Beach of the Fourth NJV noted in his diary, "every damn thing in the shape of a rebel is on the run!"[5]

After playing the game of cat and mouse for several weeks, Sheridan had finally engaged Early's army and sent it packing. Edmund Halsey wrote home, "I never saw troops feel better than ours or an army in more complete rout than the rebels." Riding along his lines that evening with his corps commanders, Sheridan was wildly cheered by his men. The First Division camped for the night northeast of Winchester.

The brigade had played an important role in the battle, along with the rest of the First Division. Its losses were modest, however—ninety-three. The Fifteenth NJV's fifty-five casualties were more than the other two regiments' combined, probably because it was ordered to occupy the exposed hill for part of the battle. The regimental breakdowns can be found in Appendix B.[6]

The Federals were back on the march after Early's army at about 5:00 A.M. the following day, September 20. Marching through Winchester, the Jerseymen saw about sixteen hundred Confederate prisoners being held in the town square. To one Federal observer, "they were in appearance able-bodied, active men, with long hair and shabby clothes, and bronzed by exposure to air and sun. They bore their changed fortunes with great stolidity."

The march took the Jerseymen south, toward Strasburg, where Early's troops were making a stand. With the VI Corps on one side of the Valley Turnpike, the XIX Corps on the other, and the officers and wheeled vehicles on the road, the column trudged through Newton and Middletown, waded Cedar Creek, and reached Strasburg at about 3:00 P.M. after a long, hot, eighteen-mile march. During the advance, "rebel flags captured from the enemy were carried in triumph behind the different generals and all were in high spirits over the victory," wrote Halsey. The men could see Early's men entrenched in a strong position on Fisher's Hill.[7]

As the mists parted during the morning of September 21, the Tenth NJV and half of the Fifteenth NJV on the picket line could make out the diminutive figure of Sheridan reconnoitering the front with General Wright. There was some action that morning, but it did not involve the Jersey Brigade. The brigade moved to the west about a mile and a half at about 2:00 that afternoon, and then was ordered to close on the enemy's position on Fisher's Hill. The brigade was deployed in two lines, with its right resting on the Manassas

Gap Railroad. The Second Division was on the opposite side of the railroad; the Second Brigade was to the Jerseymen's left. The men remained here until 1:30 A.M. on September 22, when they moved again to the right, this time to occupy a wooded hill. As the brigade deployed, it again made contact with the Second Division on its right, which had departed for its new position the night before. The Jerseyans were ordered to immediately entrench. The Fourth NJV occupied the first line; the Tenth and Fifteenth NJV occupied the second.

Heavy skirmishing occurred all day, while the Jerseymen lay in their trenches, trying to sleep or talk with their comrades. Campbell received orders at about 3:00 P.M. to watch the Second Division, and when it moved forward, he was to do so as well. The Second Division began its attack soon after, and, with the Jersey Brigade, it slowly drove back the enemy's skirmish line. The Confederate artillery opened fire, pounding the Federal advance, spraying the men with dirt. Some fell from the ear-shattering concussions or from shell fragments tearing into them, but most of the projectiles screamed harmlessly over their heads. Veteran Edmund Halsey honestly wrote, "we were so scared—but no big loss was experienced." Reaching a deep ravine, the men gratefully hopped into it to get away from the hostile artillery fire.[8]

General Crook's VIII Corps had formed on the enemy's left flank, and its surprise attack caused the enemy line to collapse toward the center. It was now time for the VI Corps, in the center of the line, to attack. After lying in the ravine for about an hour, Campbell received orders from his new division commander, General Wheaton, to throw out a skirmish line, followed by the rest of his meager brigade. This time, he would operate on his own without watching out for the Second Division. A two-company detachment of the Tenth NJV formed the skirmish line, followed by the Fourth NJV. The Fifteenth NJV and the rest of the Tenth NJV followed in the third line. Campbell was reassured to see the Second Division on his right and the Second Brigade on his left also advancing. The Confederate artillery again opened fire with devastating effect. The Jerseymen realized that their only hope was speed. Campbell proudly noted in his report, "so rapidly did the men dash up the hill that the enemy had no time to reload their pieces, after the first discharge, before our men were upon them, and receiving a heavy fire they broke and fled in utter confusion, leaving their artillery, which was promptly prevented from getting away by our skirmishers, who were led by Captain Paul." Halsey wrote that "as we approached, the rebels ran, leaving [their] guns in position." The Tenth NJV's skirmishers led the advance and were the first to capture the ridgeline, thus getting some redemption for the horrific

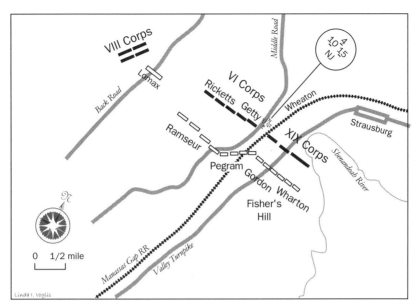

MAP 13. Battle of Fisher's Hill (September 22, 1864).

losses they had suffered earlier in the campaign. Upon reaching the enemy cannon, now theirs, the men danced, shouted, and slapped each other's backs.

In actuality, the charge at the Battle of Fisher's Hill was assisted in large measure by the successes of General Crook's men on their right, who were rolling up the Confederate line. Still, it was a magnificent charge. Long after the war, some of the men still remembered the sight of a Fourth NJV officer, his head bandaged, encouraging his men forward while holding a stick. Arrested for a minor offense, the officer had relinquished his sword but was not about to be absent when his men needed him most. His sword was restored to him the following day.[9]

Crazed with victory, the men ignored Campbell's orders to halt to re-form at the crest of the hill. Instead, they dashed after the fleeing enemy, capturing "quite a number of prisoners," according to their commanding officer. Twice the enemy soldiers tried to rally, and twice the Federals forced them to retreat. General Wheaton finally got his men to halt. All were famished, so they gladly accepted orders to stop to prepare supper before continuing the pursuit of the flying enemy.

As night descended upon the fields, most of the units were jumbled together. Men yelled constantly, "This way, Eighth Corps . . . Sixth Corps, this way." One exception was the First NJV Brigade, which resolutely marched to the front to guard against an enemy attack while the rest of the army sorted itself out.[10]

The brigade's losses were insignificant—fourteen—and the capture of a number of Confederate cannon more than made up for them. The men were furious when they learned that they were not credited with the capture of the battery, for as they swept on after the flying enemy, a support unit advanced and claimed it. Although disappointed, Campbell could not contain his excitement about his men's actions. His General Order #20, contained the statement, "prompt at the word of command they dashed impetuously forward, very first in the charge, first in the enemy works, capturing his artillery, first everywhere, and finally, the first reorganized command after the battle was over."

There was no rest that night, as the Jerseymen marched toward Woodstock, frequently scooping up prisoners along the way. Arriving at the small town at daylight, the men rested through the morning until rations arrived.[11]

Losses to the brigade on September 19, 21, and 22 totaled eight officers and a hundred enlisted men. These seemingly modest numbers actually amounted to a fourth of the officers and a fifth of enlisted men. The brigade strength was now hovering around five hundred—the size of a well-stocked regiment. A large number of the men were unarmed or were convalescents still unable to shoulder arms.

The army received a message from Secretary of War Stanton a few days after the Battle of Fisher's Hill describing his enthusiasm and relating how a hundred guns were fired in honor of its accomplishments. Most of the men cheered at the news, but not the Tenth NJV. Instead of cheering, its chaplain took off his hat and asked the men to join him in a fervent prayer. According to John Hoffman, the men thanked God "for the victory and praying for the future success of our army 'without much effusion of blood.' . . . How much more Christian like to give God the thanks."[12]

The brigade, with the rest of the First Division, was back on the road again between noon and 1:00 P.M. on September 23 after receiving rations and ammunition. The men could not complain about the short five-mile march to Edinburg, where they bivouacked that night on a high hill just west of the town. Groups of Confederate stragglers continued to be scooped up by the victorious Federal troops during this short march. Back on the road at 8:00 A.M. on September 24, the brigade marched sixteen miles to Mount Jackson, where the men could easily see Early's forces across the Shenandoah River on Rude's Hill. The Rebel army was down to six thousand men, so Early had to use the topography to his best advantage. According to Reverend Haines, it was a "splendid position. There was every indication that they had halted with the determination of making a stand." The men marveled at the countryside. "The valley through which we passed . . . [has] splendid rich farms, large handsome farmhouses and everything to correspond," noted John Hoffman.

Determined to destroy Early's army, Sheridan immediately prepared to attack both enemy flanks with his cavalry while the infantry attacked the center. The Federal batteries were in place, throwing shells at the enemy by noon. The brigade, with the rest of the division, then crossed the North Fork of the Shenandoah River and formed line of battle at right angles to the turnpike. Cavalry thundering past captured their attention, as the men knew that it was just a matter of time before they would be engaged. Early had learned to respect Sheridan, so he withdrew as the Federal cavalry angled into position. "They fled in confusion and our artillery kept shelling them all day. They are getting a good whipping," wrote Hoffman. Ordered forward, the First Division occupied the enemy's former positions on Rude's Hill, finding the view quite spectacular. The men were not permitted to linger, as they could not let Early slip away. They marched rapidly until dark, passing through New Market and Sparta, a distance of twenty miles. Because there were so many troops and wagons on the road, the VI Corps marched adjacent to the turnpike, while the XIX Corps marched on the opposite side. Seeing the enemy's wagon train, the men made haste to capture it, but were halted because the XIX Corps had lagged behind. By the time they came up, the enemy's wagons were out of danger.[13]

While waiting, the Jerseymen could see the enemy's lines of battle in the distance, still formidable, and seemingly ready for another encounter with Sheridan's forces. Early thought better of it, though, and continued his retreat. September 25 was extremely hot, but Sheridan was not about to allow Early to get away, so the men were back on the road at 6:30 A.M., reaching Harrisonburg by the middle of the afternoon after a fourteen-mile march. The men waited here two days for the supply wagons to appear. Hoffman reported that "we are resting in camp after our triumphal march."

An unpleasant incident occurred here that convinced Halsey to be careful of his new recruits. A new soldier was brought in the camp with his throat partially cut. Out collecting apples, he had been attacked from behind by what he thought were local townspeople, who took his $300 bounty money. Halsey was not so sure. "I guess it was some of our own men. Possibly men of our own regiment who knew him to have the money—his recent bounty."[14]

Colonel Penrose, who had been on leave since September 14, returned to the brigade on September 27. Nine recruits also joined the Fifteenth NJV that day. Reveille sounded at 3:00 A.M. on September 28, and the men were ordered to get breakfast and prepare to march by 4:30 A.M. After they waited several hours, the advance was cancelled. The brigade finally moved out at 5:00 A.M. on the following day, and the VI and XIX Corps marched to Mount Crawford, which Adjutant Paul called "a pretty little town." The Fifteenth NJV left the brigade to guard the wagon train during this march. Because of the land's bounty, they relied less on the army for rations and instead actively foraged for poultry, sheep, and apples. Lieutenant Halsey recorded in his diary, "our men were out foraging and some of them I am afraid pillaging." Guerrillas operated in the area, killing, wounding, and capturing many Federal soldiers. The march back to the division's old campground at Harrisonburg began at noon and ended just before dark on September 30.

Realizing the potential of a fully manned First New Jersey Brigade, General Sheridan wrote a letter to Washington on September 30 requesting reinforcements for the decimated unit: "Having understood that there are two new regiments now organized in New Jersey . . . I . . . request that they may be sent to me for the following reasons: The Jersey Brigade in the Sixth Corps has gained a reputation as one of the very best in the service. Its number has, however, become so small because of its terrible losses in battle as to be hardly equal to a regiment. The organization of so good a brigade should not be broken up. . . . The new regiments would soon become effective, in serving with old and tried troops from the same state."[15]

The troops were told to be prepared to move out at any time on October 2. The men of the Fifteenth NJV were saddened to learn that their senior captain, William Cornish, was promoted to the rank of major in the new Thirty-ninth NJV and would leave shortly to join that regiment. Their spirits, however, soared with the paymaster's arrival. John Hoffman of the Tenth NJV received two months pay and his $40 bounty, for a total of $72. He immediately gave $50 to his chaplain for transport home to his wife and children. As a result of the recent infusion of cash, "gambling is the order of the day in camp," Hoffman noted. "Money is won and lost without much effort." A field return filed on October 3 showed that the Fifteenth NJV contained about half the men in the brigade—264 officers and men.

The VI Corps retraced its steps north to Strasburg, beginning at 5:30 A.M. on October 6, finally reaching there on October 8. The corps was under orders to return to the Army of the Potomac. However, General Early, always the aggressor, closely followed the Federal army. The first day's march was particularly difficult, as the men marched twenty-two miles to New Market, halting at about 4:30 P.M. Rations were again short. The men remained in camp until 8:00 A.M. on October 7, when the march continued—fourteen miles to Woodstock. October 8 found the men at Strasburg after a short march that began at 8:00 A.M. There the army received rations of fresh meat, much to the delight of the men. The corps was on the march again on October 10 after a day's rest, slogging through Middletown, crossing the North Fork of the Shenandoah River, and finally reaching Front Royal, where the corps camped and waited for rations to arrive.[16]

The Jerseyans could see how the Federal cavalry was laying the Valley to waste during this series of marches. Captain Paul wrote that the cavalry was "burning Barns, Mills, destroying grain, and thousands of sheep and cattle before them—I imagine for the remainder of the War, this beautiful Valley will be called the Valley of Desolation." John Hoffman said a silent prayer of thanks that his New Jersey farm was out of reach of both armies. "From Stanton [*sic*] back to Washington is hardly a barn left in the Valley." The infantrymen participated in the devastation as well, for during the rest at Front Royal, forager teams scoured the countryside. "We went about 9 miles from camp. The teams were loaded with hay and corn and the boys loaded themselves with turkeys, geese, ducks, chickens, sheep, pigs, honey, butter, lard, flour, potatoes, turnips and apples; in fact everything eatable," noted Hoffman. Edmund Halsey wrote, "everything which they seem to think can be made of use and they are able to carry they bring in—the rest they demolish—beds and womens [*sic*] apparel are ruthlessly torn up and the house ransacked from cellar to garret." He did not feel sorry for the farmers because of their treasonous acts, but he did feel sorry for the women and children. Mosby's partisans captured many of these marauders and brought them to justice.

The march toward Petersburg and the Army of the Potomac began at 7:00 A.M. on October 13. The corps marched fourteen miles northeasterly through White Post before halting close to Millwood, near the foot of the Blue Ridge Mountains, at 4:00 P.M. It was a difficult march, as the brigade brought up the rear of the VI Corps. The men were not pleased to learn that they would retrace their steps back to White Post, beginning at 3:30 A.M. on October 14, reaching that town at sunrise. The brigade passed through Newtown and went into camp near Middletown at 3:00 P.M. Charles Paul ominously recorded in his diary, "the enemy are in position at Fisher's Hill once more." Kershaw's Division had returned to Early's army, allowing it, despite its decimation, to still pose a threat.[17]

Although the Jerseyans were exhausted from the never-ending marching, reinforcements continued to reach the brigade, swelling its ranks. On October 16, for example, the Fifteenth NJV welcomed thirteen of its formerly wounded men and twenty-six new recruits. The brigade now numbered twenty-eight officers and was two shy of six hundred men.

Many of the remaining veterans still fought for noble causes. For example, John Hoffman recorded in his diary during this period, "if through the instrumentality of God I can aid in establishing a free Government and crush out the rebellion and oppression, then I shall be repaid in some measure, for this tedious separation from my family." Hoffman, a "long-termer" in the Tenth NJV, was in the minority—most of the brigade was now composed of newer recruits who had entered the army for the money, and probably did not entertain the same noble motives.[18]

Early had tangled with part of the XIX Corps near Fisher's Hill on October 13, and this was what caused Sheridan to recall the VI Corps. Although his ten thousand–man army was vastly outnumbered by Sheridan's, Early was still full of fight. Climbing Massanutten Mountain on October 18, some of Early's officers looked down on the Federal encampments behind Cedar Creek and perfected their attack plan. The Federal VIII Corps occupied the left of the line, facing south and the creek. To its right was the XIX Corps, which was also entrenched. The newly arrived VI Corps formed the right of the line. While feigning an attack on the Federal right, Early intended to throw most of his men against the left, with three divisions making a flanking movement to get into the VIII Corps' rear, while two other divisions attacked its front. It would be a month to the day of Early's defeat at Fisher's Hill.

As luck would have it, Sheridan was away when the plans were being drafted. Called to Washington to meet with General Halleck to discuss future plans, Sheridan left on October 15 and arrived in Washington on the morning of October 17. The meeting concluded, Sheridan boarded a special train heading for Martinsburg, and then mounted his horse to get back to his army. When he heard the sounds of gunfire on October 19, Sheridan initially thought it was a skirmish. But as the din intensified, the general realized that his army was under attack, and he dashed toward Fisher's Hill.[19]

General Early had wasted no time in getting his troops ready for the assault. Surprise was paramount, so his troops were in motion at 8:00 P.M. on October 18, and in position by dawn the next day. Canteens and other noise-making equipment were left behind to ensure that the movements were not detected. Prior to the attack, the New Jersey Brigade was roused with reveille, and the men assembled for roll call. They shivered on this cold, foggy day and fell out to make coffee and eat breakfast. Firing broke out at either end of the line, but it was dismissed as merely picket fire. A staff officer rode up to Colonel Penrose soon after and said, "Colonel let your men stand to arms." The gunfire had intensified by this time, and the men knew that something more than a skirmish was occurring. No one was surprised when the officer returned with orders to "Move your brigade out at once."

The Confederates could not have hoped for a better outcome. Lying in their tents, or just beginning to move about, the VIII Corps' men were overwhelmed by the fast-moving attack. The Federal troops stampeded to the rear, many of them gobbled up by the whooping and yelling Confederates. Early's men captured the corps' artillery and quickly turned the guns around to fire at the fleeing Yankees. According to Reverend Haines, "in a few moments the whole [VIII] corps was a disorganized and panic-stricken mass. There was nothing for them but flight."[20]

The XIX Corps to the right of the stricken VIII Corps was now attacked along its front, flank, and rear by Early's victorious troops. These men could not hold their positions under such conditions and many fled to the rear, while others assembled behind the VI Corps to the right. The latter corps was now prepared to meet the onslaught. Early's troops had performed masterfully, and their commander's plan was flawless. By taking on each Federal corps individually, Early was able to neutralize Sheridan's numerical superiority.

At the first alarm, General Wheaton ordered the Jerseymen to move to their left, cross Opequon Creek, and form line of battle on a high hill to support Crook's VIII Corps. Because the VIII Corps was so quickly overrun, Penrose received orders to recross the creek and take up a position in the rear and left of the brigade's former camp, which was opposite the town of Middletown, across the Valley Turnpike. Penrose deployed his men with the Fourth NJV on the right, the Fifteenth NJV on the left, and the Tenth NJV in the center. No sooner had the brigade deployed than Penrose received orders to withdraw. The two other Federal corps had been so thoroughly beaten that they were beyond help, and up ahead the irresistible Confederate tide rolled toward them.[21]

The Jerseymen returned to their former camp and grimly waited for the Confederate onslaught. They had bested Early's men twice, but this was different—too many Federal units were in full flight. The men had not been in this position long when they saw Federal troops on their left, probably remnants of the VIII and XIX Corps, breaking to the rear, leaving the artillery behind. Without orders, Penrose "changed front to rear" and moved his brigade up to support the now defenseless batteries. The Confederate gun-

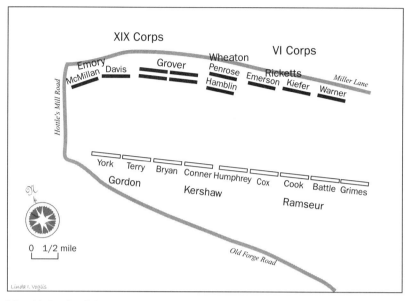

Map 14. Battle of Cedar Creek (October 19, 1864).

fire was extremely heavy during this time, and losses mounted. A bullet passed through Colonel Penrose's boot and killed his horse. Thrown to the ground, Penrose quickly got up, only to be struck by a bullet that shattered his right arm.

The brigade, along with the Tenth Vermont and Sixth Maryland, charged the enemy around the Federal batteries at about 7:30 A.M. Major Boeman, commanding the Tenth NJV, was killed almost instantly by a bullet that entered the lower part of his breast during this attack. "With a single exclamation he fell from his horse to the ground," noted a soldier. Another recalled that he murmured, "Carry me off," and then died. Lieutenant Colonel Campbell, now in command of the brigade, ordered it to retake the lost artillery pieces. The Jerseymen sprang into action, pushing the Confederates back long enough for the artillerymen to pull at least two pieces out of danger. Campbell fell during the charge—his left arm broken by a bullet that traveled from his wrist to his elbow, shattering the bone. He refused to seek medical attention until the brigade was out of danger, and only then rode toward Winchester for treatment. "The boys, in all the excitement of the moment, followed him with their eyes. As he rode away he lifted his unwounded hand and made a motion to them which they understand to mean, 'hold on,'" related Alanson Haines. Captain Baldwin Hufty of the Fourth NJV took command of the brigade. The losses during this part of the fight were especially heavy in the Fifteenth NJV.[22]

With the enemy nearby and the men of the VIII and XIX Corps flying to the rear, the Jerseymen knew they could not hold their position very long. All were relieved when General Wright rode up and ordered them to the rear, and out of harm's way. The men were upset to see that their corps commander was also wounded—a bullet had grazed his chin. Rebel bullets followed the retreat, as did the victorious enemy troops, and more Jerseymen fell or were captured. While withdrawing through a woodlot, Sergeant John Mouder, carrying the unfurled Fifteenth NJV state color, was killed, but no one realized it. It was the first flag lost by the regiment. The brigade, with the rest of the bloodied First Division, moved by the flank about three hundred yards to another hill in the rear. Despite the large number of recruits, the brigade held its formation well during this movement. This was not true of other units, which one soldier characterized as "a herd of buffaloes." Those with watches noted that it was only 8:00 A.M. The Jerseymen were not here long before General Wheaton ordered them back another two thousand yards, where they reformed their lines, then fell back two more miles.

The division then halted, dressed its lines, and turned and advanced about a mile in the direction it had come, halting about a mile north of Middletown. Although the entire corps was with them, the men felt a sense of dread moving back toward the victorious Confederates. The Second Division was on the corps' left, and on its right was the Third Division, and then Wheaton's First Division. A portion of the XIX Corps formed on the right of the VI Corps. With a strong cavalry contingent, General Wright was in a good position to halt the Confederate onslaught. It was only 9:00 A.M.[23]

The Jersey Brigade was in the First Division's second line with the One Hundred and Twenty-first New York of the Second Brigade. Lieutenant Colonel Egbert Olcott commanded this line. The rest of the Second Brigade occupied the first line. The situation was so desperate that no attempt was made to sort the jumble of men into their respective regiments. Instead, the Jerseyans functioned essentially as a regiment. General Sheridan finally appeared on the battlefield during this reprieve, much to the relief of his men. "His appearance was like ten thousand reinforcements," noted Hoffman. Riding along the entire length of the Federal line, Sheridan reassured the men, yelling, "It's all right, we'll flank 'em. . . . We can't be beat. . . . You'll be back in your old camps tonight." A very religious man, Hoffman believed that "God were [*sic*] at work for us, truly I think His hand was visible." The men were permitted to rest and eat here, as Sheridan made plans. Early's men made several feeble attacks on the Federal line during this period.

Thinking they had soundly defeated Sheridan's army, Early's men began plundering the captured Federal camps and supply wagons. They found considerable quantities of whisky, and toasted their great victory. The celebrations were premature, for Sheridan launched his counterattack at 3:00 P.M. Driving toward a hill about four hundred yards ahead with the rest of the VI Corps, the Jerseymen smashed into the confused Confederates, driving them from their positions. The VI Corps was ordered to wait about half an hour until the XIX Corps moved up on its left. "While in this position we were subject to a most galling fire from both artillery and musketry," noted Captain Hufty.[24]

The attack again commenced. Olcott's first line was repulsed, and the second, composed of the First New Jersey Brigade and the One Hundred and Twenty-first New York, "pushed forward with alacrity, leaving the troops on our right and left far in the rear," Hufty reported. "The enemy broke in confusion and scattered in all directions." The two brigades pushed after the retreating Confederates, crushing any units attempting to organize a resistance. As Sheridan had promised, when finally darkness settled on the region, the Federal troops were able to reoccupy their old camps.

The Fifteenth NJV almost lost its national flag in addition to its state colors when a solid shot artillery projectile struck flagbearer Sergeant Peter Gunderman on his right shoulder, breaking the flagstaff, tearing off his sleeve, and throwing him into the air. After rolling down a hill, the stunned Gunderman retrieved the colors and ran forward.[25]

The Jerseyans built large fires to warm themselves that night. They found Major Boeman's body, but it was stripped naked by the enemy. Coffee was soon boiling, which helped rejuvenate the survivors, but the brigade's losses were heavy. Out of a total of 628 men, the brigade lost 164, or 26 percent. As usual, the Fifteenth NJV bore the brunt of the losses, this time 85, or half of the brigade's casualties. The regimental breakdown of the losses is in Appendix B.

Although both Penrose and Campbell received severe arm wounds, neither lost their limbs. Bone splinters were removed from each, and both returned to duty after relatively short recuperation periods. Among the wounded was Sergeant Edwin Ulmer, a frequent letter writer. His leg was amputated at the hip joint; he was one of only eight men in the war to survive this operation. Ulmer would never forget that day at Cedar Creek—his debilitating wound and how the Confederate officers ordered their men to use caution as they moved through the woods, lest they step on the wounded Yankees.[26]

With Captain Hufty commanding the 464-man brigade, the Fourth NJV was led by a lieutenant, William Bechtel. The Tenth NJV was commanded by Captain James McNeely, and the Fifteenth NJV was led by Colonel Penrose's brother, Captain James Penrose.

Under orders to be ready to pursue the enemy on October 20, the men rested all day, helped carry the wounded to hospitals, and buried the dead. Over forty cannon stood silent near Sheridan's headquarters—about half were Federal guns recaptured from the Rebels; the others were Confederate guns captured during the latter phases of the fight. There were many captured wagons and over a thousand Confederate prisoners.[27]

When the euphoria of victory wore off, the men became depressed by the loss of their comrades and from the cold whipping through their insufficient clothing. The men of the Fifteenth NJV were told at noon on October 21 that Generals Wheaton, Torbert, and Custer would visit them at 3:00 P.M., so they spent the next three hours cleaning up and trying to look presentable. The band assembled and prepared a hearty welcome for the guests. The color guard, down to two men and one tattered flag on a splintered pole, stepped to the front. Lieutenant Edmund Halsey noted "the regiment presented a sorry look. Gunderman was in line with his blouse half torn off and holding the other color by its shattered staff." The officers arrived at the appointed hour, carrying the regiment's lost state flag. The men were ecstatic. The flag had been found in one of the captured Confederate wagons. General Torbert, whose men captured the flag, and who had led the New Jersey Brigade for several years, presented the flag to the regiment, proclaiming its loss "was no disgrace, under the circumstances. . . . The Fifteenth New Jersey had ever done its duty. . . . He restored it again by order of General Sheridan, conscious that it was safe in the keeping of those to whom it belonged, and he knew they would never part with it while men remained to draw a sword or fire a musket." Generals Custer and Wheaton then said a few words. "Our boys tried to cheer, but their hurrah was faint and weak compared to what it had been in the regiment's palmier days," sadly recalled Haines. The officers of the Fifteenth NJV collected eighty dollars to cover the expense of shipping Major Boeman's body to New Jersey.

The Jerseyans spent the remainder of October and the first week of November resting in their camps. The brigade was now composed of twenty-five officers, a hundred noncommissioned officers, and 403 men, with an aggregate strength of 528. Many thought they would remain here for the winter, and so began erecting chimneys in their tents, which were reinforced with logs. Each regiment also put up a large tent for a chapel. The brigade, however, broke camp on November 9 and marched seven miles to near Kernstown. "The ground was very slippery and we had a hard march," noted Hoffman. The men went into camp here, at "Camp Russell."[28]

Rumors swirled around the camp that the small brigade would be broken up and its regiments distributed to other units. Lieutenant Halsey learned otherwise on October 26—"it is said to be a fact that the 40th NJ is coming to our Brigade—if so it will relieve our anxiety as to our Brigade being broken up."

Inactivity returned, and with it depression, particularly among those old soldiers who had seen so much—too much—of war. Adjutant Halsey's November 17 journal entry read, "there is but one officer who came out with us [on] May 4 who has not been wounded, killed, detailed or mustered out. I feel like a stranger." Halsey presented his resignation to Captain Hufty on November 22, citing his father's ill health as the reason, but General Wheaton ultimately denied it.[29]

Hard feelings developed over who should command the Fifteenth NJV, as Captain Ebenezer Davis claimed seniority over Captain Penrose. The issue was presented to General Wheaton, who did not seem to care. The officers disliked Penrose enough to write a letter to Governor Parker attempting to derail his promotion, but it did not work.

With its departure imminent from the Valley, General Sheridan reviewed the VI Corps on November 21. According to Haines, "though the rain fell in torrents, the men moved past the General in handsome lines." Halsey complained that the Jerseymen had to wait two hours in formation in the pouring rain before marching past Sheridan's observation post. Thanksgiving brought nineteen turkeys to the commissary sergeant of the Fifteenth NJV, "which will be about a mouthful apiece for the men, I suppose, if they are equally divided," noted Captain Dayton Flint. The Tenth NJV received geese, turkeys, and chicken for its men, but not enough for all of the men to be satiated. It was an exciting day for John Hoffman. A large oak tree fell while his mess was preparing dinner. "It struck our chimney, knocking it to atoms and filling our dinner with mortar and stones. Of course we had to throw it away, so our Thanksgiving dinner went."[30]

The orders for the VI Corps to rejoin the Army of the Potomac finally arrived soon after midnight on December 1. The brigade broke camp and was on the march to Stephenson's Depot beyond Winchester by 7:30 A.M. Because of the throng of troops, the Jerseymen had to wait from noon until dark to board trains at the depot, and finally reached Harper's Ferry at about midnight.

This ended the Shenandoah Valley Campaign for the VI Corps. The Jerseymen had fought in three major battles and one heavy skirmish, and had performed well in all of them. Although bone tired from their exertions, they proudly boasted that they had helped defeat Early's army, thus reducing the threat to Washington. They tried not to think what awaited them around Petersburg.[31]

CHAPTER 12

Back to Petersburg

$\mathcal{A}$s the train sped toward Washington, the Jerseymen dreaded what the horrible war would bring. "Unpleasant anticipations of what awaited us intruded upon our thoughts and entered into our conversation," recalled Alanson Haines.

Passing Ellicott's Mills, Maryland, at daybreak, the train finally arrived in Washington at noon on December 2, 1864. Their reception shocked the men. During the summer citizens had lined the streets and cheered their arrival. No one was present now, and "we were treated more as a band of convicts than as victorious troops who had saved the national capital, and routed the enemy wherever we had met them," sadly noted Haines. The men could not leave the train until the steamboats, *Thomas A. Morgan* and *Monitor,* were ready, and even then they had to stand in the pouring rain for two hours. During this time they were "guarded" by "[General] Halleck's mounted provost guard—cavalrymen who had never saw a battle—rode up and down, with new uniforms and drawn sabers, ordering us as though we were prisoners of war, and, as we stood waiting . . . it required no great stretch of the imagination to suppose ourselves as such. Any officer or man transgressing the limits assigned us was rushed upon by a horseman with naked sword or drawn pistol and ordered back," continued Haines.[1]

The steamboats cast off on December 3 and sailed down the Potomac River, reaching the Chesapeake Bay by evening. The morning of December 4 found the ships in the James River, and docked at City Point by 10:00 A.M. that day. Disembarking, the brigade marched about a mile and encamped—the field and staff officers remained near the docks awaiting the arrival of the steam tug *Idaho,* which carried their horses. The night was bitter cold and few slept, as their tents had not arrived and wood was scarce, so most men merely wrapped their blankets around their overcoats and shivered all night.

The brigade marched to the military railroad the next morning and boarded trains for the five-mile ride to Park's Station. There they relieved the Twenty-fourth Michigan of the V Corps in their trenches. The men were pleasantly surprised to see how well the Twenty-fourth's huts were constructed. "They were as handsome as though made of sawed lumber, with floors and chimneys," Haines recalled. John Hoffman of the Tenth NJV described his quarters as being six by ten feet in size, "standing with the end to the street. In the front end is the door. On the right side as you enter near the end is the fireplace. In the back end is the bunk, which is about three feet high from the ground. The walls are about five feet high which makes a nice little room. It is plastered outside which makes it very warm." Dayton Flint of the Fifteenth NJV added, "the walls inside are hewn smooth and papered with old blank muster rolls, which are two feet square, thus giving the wall a neat appearance, and being white, they make the tent very light. We need no windows, as the white tent roofing lets in plenty of light." Pegs driven into the logs made it easy to hang muskets and accoutrements. There were also shelves and rudimentary furniture. Nearby wells provided adequate water. The IX Corps was to the VI Corps' right, and the II Corps to their left. The men spent the next few days quietly resting in their new quarters.[2]

Fort Howard, Battery Number 26, and the line of rifle pits between them was now the responsibility of the New Jersey Brigade. In the event of enemy movements, the Jerseymen were to man the fort and battery position with 150 men in each.

The Jerseymen were told on December 9 that the VI Corps was moving to the left to support the II and V Corps, but they were to be left behind to picket the entire First Division's former position. The brigade was too small for this chore, so a Third Brigade regiment was left behind to assist. Those men not on the picket line manned the forts. There was no sleep that night, as the men expected an enemy attack. Snow fell and the men tried to keep warm. The First Division's remaining brigades returned during the evening of December 10, but were immediately sent to the right, where an attack on the IX Corps was expected.[3]

The V Corps, which had torn up about thirty miles of the Weldon Railroad, returned on December 12 to strengthen the line. This reassured the men, as they expected an attack at any time, and there was continuous firing on the picket line to their right. "The boys call it 'Fort Hell' . . . they keep up an everlasting fire of musketry during the day and night," wrote Lieutenant Dayton Flint. The Confederate fort opposite it was dubbed "Fort Damnation." It was fairly quiet in their own sector, though, as the Jerseymen struck a deal with the enemy not to fire on each other. Confederate deserters entered the Federal lines almost daily, responding to Grant's promise of good clothes, adequate rations, and high wages. The greatest number arrived on dark, moonless nights. The rest of the VI Corps returned on December 15, so "we shall have it some what easier than before," noted John Hoffman of the Tenth NJV.

Adjutant Edmund Halsey received orders on December 17 that the men from the former Second and Third NJV were being removed from the Fifteenth NJV to form separate battalions. "I feel quite anxious to see what will be left," he wrote in his diary that day. The action reduced the Fifteenth NJV to thirteen officers and 250 men. Similarly, the First Battalion NJV was formed from the Fourth NJV. Each of these battalions contained up to three companies of men.[4]

Upon reaching what seemed to be their permanent quarters, the chaplains of the Tenth and Fifteenth NJV immediately set to work on a chapel, only to see its roof torn off during a storm in late December. Another setback occurred when soldiers from other regiments stole some wood from the structure. Undeterred, the chaplains rebuilt the chapel, and Captain Hufty, still in command of the brigade, provided a guard to keep it intact. The chapel eventually served the entire brigade.

Camp life was rarely monotonous, for when the men were not on picket, they were out repairing roads or policing their camps. Checkers, chess, and quoits were also popular pastimes. The men received rum on Christmas, and at least the officers dined on roast beef in lieu of turkey. A band of African American minstrels serenaded the men. John Hoffman estimated that about six hundred enemy soldiers came into their lines on Christmas Eve, sloshing through a sea of sticky, deep mud.[5]

Each regiment's huts formed three sides of a square. The men swept the streets daily after roll call, as the officers attempted to maintain clean conditions. Some of the latter, like Flint, hired enlisted men and paid them six dollars a week to keep their quarters clean and provide food. "Today [December 25] he gave us roast beef and some very good mince pies," Flint noted. Wood availability was a problem, forcing men to trudge farther distances to find it as the winter progressed.

The most desired perk, furloughs, were liberally distributed during the winter. Flint, promoted to the rank of captain, estimated that two out of ten officers and five out of a hundred enlisted men were gone at any given time.[6]

The routine was broken on December 30 when the Rebels quietly approached the picket line, capturing several Jerseymen before the alarm was sounded. The Federal picket line was also driven in at 5:00 A.M. the next day. The men grabbed their muskets and rushed to the breastworks, remaining there for about three hours in the pouring rain. Realizing that an attack was not in the offing, the officers permitted the men to return to their camps and eat breakfast. The Fourth NJV, which had been on the picket line, lost ten men in this skirmish.

Captain Baldwin Hufty continued to command the brigade on December 31, 1864. On that date it was composed of:

> First NJV Battalion (three companies)—Lieutenant Jacob Hutt
> Second NJV Battalion (one company)—Lieutenant Adolphus Weiss
> Fourth NJV—Captain Ebenezer Davis
> Tenth NJV—Captain James McNeely
> Fifteenth NJV—Captain James Penrose
> Fortieth NJV (two companies)—Captain John Edelstein

The two companies of the Fortieth NJV were a portion of the last regiment raised by New Jersey for the war effort. Organized at the Trenton Draft Rendezvous (Camp Perrine) shortly after the Thirty-eighth and Thirty-ninth NJV, the regiment was composed of men from every part of the state. Many apparently believed the writer for the *Trenton Gazette,* who wrongly predicted that enlistment in the regiment "will be a good opportunity to join a new regiment that will not probably be called into service for some time to come." Unlike other regiments, its companies were sent to the front as they were formed—the first two arrived on January 12, 1865, and joined the Fourth NJV until enough companies arrived to constitute the regiment. This occurred with the arrival of Company F in early February 1865; the unit formed into a separate battalion under Colonel Stephen Gilkyson, who had seen considerable service with the Sixth NJV. The regiment's last company arrived on March 12. General Sheridan got his wish—the First New Jersey Brigade received its reinforcements.[7]

The $500 bounties offered by some communities attracted men to the Fortieth NJV. As a result, almost half of the recruits were not from New Jersey, and few were enthusiastic soldiers, as they gambled that the war would soon be over. Dayton Flint asked his sisters to discourage his father from joining the army—"Not that we do not need more men, but there are plenty of young men yet, who have nothing to keep them home. He has furnished one son for the war, let that suffice for our family. Besides I do not believe he would withstand the exposure, and what would the paltry sum of $500 be should he return with a broken constitution." Flint also noted that "it is not the strongest nor those that appear most hearty at home that last the longest here. They seem to be the first ones to break down."

Faced with the reality of grim trench warfare, the new recruits deserted in droves. Some companies lost over half their men in this manner. Desertions actually began before the companies left Trenton. For example, thirty-four of the fifty-one men who deserted from Company B were gone before their unit stepped foot on the trains. Many of those who reached the front went over to the enemy, hoping that prison camps were safer than the trenches.[8]

January 1, 1865, dawned clear and cold, and the commanders of both armies ensured that their men had a peaceful day. By January 3, however, the officers objected to the continuing picket line truce and issued orders to the men to stop this practice and open fire when enemy soldiers showed themselves. The men had been exchanging coffee, tea, tobacco, and other commodities with the enemy. They were, however, still permitted to communicate General Grant's desertion incentives to the Confederates across the way.

The division was called together on January 6 to watch the execution of John Cox of the Fourth NJV. He apparently had deserted during the Battle of the Wilderness in May 1864 and joined the enemy. It was rumored that he was captured on a blockade runner. No one sympathized with Cox or bemoaned his fate.[9]

The enemy made a dash on the Jerseymen's picket line during the pre-dawn hour of January 9. The sleeping men heard the long roll and hastily formed into line of battle, but the Rebels retreated before the brigade advanced. To prevent these sudden attacks, the men reinforced their breastworks with abatis of sharpened sticks. The enemy initially only watched these activities, but later opened fire, killing one soldier and wounding several others, including the officer in command of the detail.

Lieutenant Edmund Halsey finally got his wish and left the army on January 10. Growing increasingly ill from his two and a half years of campaigning, Halsey also worried about the failing health of his father, who was responsible for the family farm and for caring for an invalid relative. The regiment's adjutant, Halsey had been ever-present in the camps, on the march, and on the battlefield. He had begun his military career as a private and clerk, rising to sergeant major and then first lieutenant. One by one he had lost his best friends to death and discharge, and he knew it was time to return to New Jersey and resume his life.[10]

Lieutenant Colonel Edward Campbell returned to the brigade on January 12, much to the satisfaction of his men. Captain Hufty, who had provided outstanding leadership during the final phases of the Shenandoah Valley Campaign, returned to the Fourth NJV. Other soldiers joined the brigade, mostly new recruits that swelled its numbers. For example, the Fourth NJV received almost two hundred new men on January 15—increasing its roster to almost six hundred.

"Jan. 31st 1865 was a day long to be remembered by our Nation," wrote John Hoffman. "Our Congress passed the resolution to amend the Constitution abolishing slavery from the United States. Thank God that we are now taking the right direction."[11]

Just before sunrise on February 5, the Jerseyans were ordered to prepare to move out sometime that day. Final orders did not arrive, so they took advantage of the church services conducted on this Sabbath day. However, as darkness fell, the men received new orders to pack up and fall in. They did not know that Grant had sent the Federal II and V Corps, with the VI Corps in support, to cut off a Confederate supply route near Hatcher's Run. The march began by the left flank at 7:30 that night and ended, five miles later, at Squirrel Level Road at midnight, where the men rested. After what must have seemed like minutes, but was actually two hours, the men were back in column and marching another three miles, crossing Hatcher's Run, where they approached the V Corps' positions on the morning of February 6. Gunfire erupted up ahead. "The bullets flew over us briskly, causing our line, with its many recruits, to waver, and a few men threw down their muskets and ran back," noted Alanson Haines. The brigade had become almost a new unit with the infusion of so many new recruits and with so few veterans remaining.

As the Jerseymen were ordered to the left, they heard Rebel cheering up ahead. Several men were hit during this movement. "Just as we came up some of the 5th Corps . . . became panic stricken and broke for the rear but it was only a false alarm," reported Hoffman. John Beach noted that many of the new recruits threw away their rifles as they thundered to the rear. Reaching a line of rifle pits abandoned by the V Corps, the men gratefully jumped into them and awaited the expected attack. The attack never came because the enemy realized that the Federal positions were too strong. The brigade was relieved by the V Corps at 8:00 P.M. and pulled back to a field, where it bivouacked. Snow fell continually during the night, changing to rain at daybreak. "We kept from freezing by walking about . . . it rained so hard we were soaked through," Hoffman reported. The brigade shuffled to new locations several times on February 7 in support of the V Corps, but did not engage the enemy. The men were finally ordered back to their old quarters at about 1:00 A.M. on February 8, arriving at 4:30 A.M. It was a hard march, for the wet roads had turned icy as the temperatures fell. After several weeks in camp, the veterans were not accustomed to hard marching. This, coupled with the number of inexperienced recruits, made the mission very difficult. Many would remember the hardships during the Battle of Hatcher's Run.[12]

The men were furious to find that many of their belongings had been stolen during their absence, but the brigade continued to grow in strength. Waiting for the Tenth NJV in the camp were fifty-one recruits, most of whom where foreign-born. The Fortieth NJV was composed of four companies at this time.

Promoted to the rank of major, Ebenezer Davis took over the Fifteenth NJV in early February. Colonel Penrose, now promoted to brevet brigadier general, returned in February. His arm had not completely healed, but he could not stay away from his command any longer. Campbell was offered a promotion to full colonel and command of the Fourth NJV. He declined, instead deciding to accept an appointment as a judge advocate general of the army. With the influx of new recruits and several companies of the Fortieth NJV, the brigade's strength had swelled from under five hundred men to over twenty-two hundred.[13]

The rest of February and all of March were fairly routine. Hordes of enemy soldiers approached periodically with their arms in the air. Sometimes alarms sounded that the enemy was approaching without their hands raised, so the men rushed to the breastworks. These were usually false alarms. Picket duty rotated, so each man was exposed to danger periodically, but the rest of the time was spent whiling away the hours. Most of the men were sick from time to time, primarily with colds and respiratory problems because of the cold, wet conditions. As with the prior winter, singing clubs and debating organizations formed. "Consequently time does not hang so heavy on our hands," wrote Flint. On March 19, the men were issued white gloves because they were to be reviewed by Generals Meade and Wheaton the following day.

The quiet ended on March 25, when the enemy attacked Fort Steadman to the Jerseymen's right. Lee hoped to roll up Grant's flank, permitting his army's retreat to North Carolina, if needed. It was a desperate gamble, but he also hoped that by punching a hole in the Federal line his cavalry could raid the huge supply depot at City Point, and maybe even capture General Grant. The attack was brilliant, and the Southerners captured the fort and about five hundred men. The Jerseymen heard bugles sounding at 4:00 A.M. and gunfire exploded to their right. After breakfast, they waited another half hour for orders, and many were surprised that they were not already on the move. Orders finally arrived at 11:00 A.M. and the division moved to the right, but by this time the IX Corps had counterattacked, pushing back the enemy and inflicting heavy casualties. The men marched back to their camps at about noon and, after a short ten-minute rest, marched another mile beyond it, where they were surprised to see not only General Grant, but also President and Mrs. Lincoln.[14]

Continuing another two miles to the left, the VI Corps moved into position to attack the Confederate lines between Petersburg and Hatcher's Run, opposite Fort Fisher. The First Division's Second and Third Brigades successfully punched a hole in the Confederate lines in the late afternoon, but the New Jersey Brigade merely acted as a reserve. The Jerseymen finally advanced at 5:00 P.M. to help guard the captured positions. The men remained here in the relative quiet until 10:00 P.M., when they were ordered back to camp.

March 26 was filled with false alarms. The brigade received orders to fall in line at 4:00 A.M., and remained in readiness until 6:30 A.M. Heavy fire on the picket line twice caused the Jerseyans to form to repel an enemy advance. They also spent March 27 through April 1 in readiness, but remained in camp or manned the picket line. Small arms and artillery fire frequently broke out during this period. Watching a mortar bombardment on March 30, John Hoffman wrote, "the shells were thrown almost perpendicular[,] turning and coming down[,] they looked like balls of fire flying through the air. At times 25 of them could be seen at once making beautiful curves."[15]

The First Division was ordered into line at 10:00 P.M. on April 1 and marched to the Weldon Railroad and was massed outside of Fort Fisher by 2:00 A.M. on April 2. General Wheaton deployed his First Division en echelon to the right and slightly behind the Second Division. Colonel Oliver Edwards' Third Brigade was on the left in three lines, thirty paces behind the Second Division. The First New Jersey Brigade was to the right in four lines, thirty paces behind the Third Brigade. General Joseph Hamblin's Brigade was on the right, deployed in two lines, thirty paces behind the Jerseymen. Probably because he was afraid that the green troops of the Fortieth NJV would run in their first real action, Penrose placed them in the first line of attack. The Fourth NJV occupied the second line; the Tenth NJV the third line, and the Fifteenth NJV the fourth. The First, Second, and Third Battalions acted as tactical parts of the Fourth and Fifteenth NJV.

Lee's flank had recently been devastated at Five Forks, so the Union men knew that this would be a desperate assault that could seal the Confederacy's fate. All were somber as they waited for the signal to advance—two shots fired from Fort Fisher. The men had to first traverse open ground before taking on the defenses. The brigade's historian recalled the latter—"two lines of abattis and slashings, that is, trees cut partly through and felled in such a way that they crossed and interlaced, the butts being held by uncut fibre, making it extremely difficult to remove them." Each brigade received additional pioneers equipped with sharp axes.[16]

The men heard the two shots at about 4:15 A.M. The Fourth NJV in the second line moved forward, only to bump into large numbers of the Fortieth NJV, who refused to advance. Wheaton's orders were for the division to move "forward with its 'guide left,' each brigade taking up the movement toward the enemy's lines as soon as the troops on its left had gained their prescribed distance of 100 paces between brigade lines." It was still dark, but the Fourth NJV continued moving past the prone green troops and began their advance. They soon caught up with those members of the Fortieth NJV advancing under the leadership of Major Augustus Fay. According to General Penrose, his brigade "had gone but a short distance before the first and second lines became one, owing to the fact that the pickets which were to have advanced simultaneously with us did not, and the first line received the fire of the enemy's pickets, which was very severe." This shocked the new troops, causing them to halt in confusion. As a result, the Fourth now joined the first line, and the Tenth and Fifteenth NJV crowded the line from behind. The advance continued, and the Jerseyans scooped up a number of enemy solders on the picket line.

The darkness caused additional confusion in the division. "In the dark each command became more or less disordered, the lines naturally merging in each other, on account of the enemy's opposition and the natural physical obstacles—abatis, frise-work, &c.—encountered," noted General Wheaton. The Fourth NJV split into two parts. One part halted to reform, while the rest, under Lieutenant Colonel Hufty, continued their advance. The pioneers hacked at the abattis, clearing a way for the infantry to hit the breastworks. According to Wheaton, "all were astonished to find these obstructions such serious obstacles and so difficult to remove; openings were made in them, however, under a severe canister and musketry fire, and all along our front officers and men pushed through and captured the enemy's strong works in the most dashing and gallant manner." It was actually a bit more difficult than that. The shattering gunfire halted the brigade in its tracks. Gathering troops from the various commands around him, Major Fay stormed the works with the assistance of the Thirty-seventh Massachusetts, who were armed with Spencer repeating rifles. After the battle, the various commands fought for the right to claim the greatest glory. For example, Hufty reported that "my colors [Fourth NJV] . . . the first in the brigade to enter the works." The men also had to contend with another threat—friendly fire from the Federal troops behind them. Frank Beach noted, "we had nearly reached the rebel works when the fire in our rear was so severe that I had to go back and try to stop their firing upon us." Beach noted that these were men from the Fortieth NJV who had refused to charge.[17]

There were not many Confederate defenders in the breastworks, but those present fought like tigers. Some refused to surrender or retreat and were gunned down or bayoneted. According to Beach, the greatest danger was not Confederate infantry, but their artillery to the right, which fired into the Jerseyans' right flank. "As we saw the flash we dropped, and in a moment we were on our feet, and before they fired many shots we were up to and over their works in double-quick order, capturing the guns with quite a number of prisoners, without much opposition and with comparatively little loss." Private Frank Fesq of the Fortieth NJV captured a Confederate battle flag at the works. Major Augustus Fay also performed magnificently. Although not wounded, his clothing was perforated by bullets. General Penrose was unable to report the exact number of Confederate prisoners taken by his men, as many were sent to the rear without guards. He estimated that the total number was at least two hundred. The Jerseymen continued to their left, clearing over a mile and a half of the works and capturing portions of three batteries in the process.

Two artillery pieces became the center of contention between the Jerseyans and the Thirty-seventh Massachusetts. The guns were captured by Major Paul, Captain James Penrose, now acting aide-de-camp to his brother, and a few men. Penrose had the guns loaded and ready to fire at the fleeing Rebels, but primers could not be found, so he went looking for them. Two companies of the Thirty-seventh Massachusetts arrived and, in the words of General Penrose, "wished to remove them, which Captain Penrose refused to allow them to do. They then formed around the platforms. . . . In the meantime his attention was directed elsewhere, when the men of the Thirty-seventh Massachusetts drove my guard from the guns, claiming them as their capture. As this has occurred once before I am not disposed to allow it to pass this time without notice, as the command is entitled to the credit of the capture."[18]

General Wright wanted the First Division to continue advancing toward Petersburg after taking the works, but this was difficult. According to General Wheaton, "the troops were perfectly wild with delight at their success in this grand assault, and with difficulty could be restrained and the brigades reformed after the works, guns, prisoners, and camps were indisputably ours."

The lines were finally reformed, but before the division could advance again, Wright wanted two brigades sent to Hatcher's Run on the left to assist the Second and Third Divisions in their attempts to take the enemy's breastworks. Wheaton sent the Jerseymen and the Third Brigade to assist, leaving the Second Brigade to hold the captured works. The latter unit thought it would have its hands full, as a signal officer reported seeing a column of at least six hundred troops approaching. However, a division from the XXIV Corps arrived to bolster the line.

The two brigades were not needed, so they returned to their positions in the captured breastworks at about 9:45 A.M. Forming again on the right of the Second Division, and the left of the XXIV, Wheaton sent his division toward Petersburg. The Third Brigade formed the first line, with the New Jersey Brigade, again en echelon, on its left, with its left refused, or pulled back. The Fourth NJV formed the left of the first line and the Fifteenth NJV was on its right, with the First NJV Battalion acting as skirmishers. The division advanced for nearly three miles, "exposed to a constant front and flank artillery and occasional musketry fire," reported Wheaton. The advance halted at 1:00 P.M. at the South Side Railroad, within two miles of the city. Penrose now swung his left to reach the Appomattox River. Wheaton was told to halt until reinforcements arrived before entering the city. The men received orders at 5:00 P.M. to begin entrenching, a task they completed five hours later.[19]

General Wheaton was enthusiastic about the actions of his men on April 2. "The work accomplished by the division on this day was the most difficult I had ever seen troops called upon to perform. Massing and advancing in the dark they successfully assaulted strongly entrenched and elaborately obstructed lines with a determination and gallantry that could never be excelled."

While Penrose was not enthusiastic about the confusion during the assault, he found no fault in the brigade's afternoon actions. He wrote in his report, "the men and officers behaved to my entire satisfaction, especially as two-thirds of them were new men, and had not been in the army three months."[20]

The brigade's losses of seventy-six men on April 2 were insignificant, compared with other charges during the war. As expected, the Fortieth NJV on the first line and the Fourth on the second line, which mingled together, sustained the heaviest casualties (twenty-three and twenty-one, respectively). The Tenth and Fifteenth NJV each had nine casualties.

The men slept just outside of Petersburg that night but were abruptly awakened by massive explosions before daybreak. They soon learned that the enemy had exploded the magazines in their remaining forts, "one fort following the other in slow succession," recalled Alanson Haines. The men rejoiced at the news that the Confederates had evacuated Petersburg during the night, leaving the road to Richmond open. Lee now desperately moved south in an attempt to link with General Joseph Johnston's army in North Carolina. Major Fay of the Fortieth NJV observed a carriage approaching his picket line at 5:00 A.M. and told his men to prepare for action, but after seeing a white flag they relaxed. It was the mayor and some prominent citizens wishing to surrender the city.[21]

A second battle flag was captured in as many days on April 3, this one from the Forty-sixth North Carolina. Lieutenant William Brant of the Fourth NJV simply picked it up while on the picket line. He received the Medal of Honor for his act.

The men were not permitted to savor their victory, or even to visit the city they had struggled to capture for more than seven months. Instead, the brigade moved out at 7:30 A.M. in pursuit of the enemy. The VI Corps reached Sutherland's Station on the South Side Railroad at 5:00 P.M., where the Jerseymen bivouacked after the eleven-mile march. Signs of Lee's hasty retreat were evident everywhere along the route—overturned wagons, caissons, and discarded shells. The march continued at 5:00 A.M. on April 4, and during a halt the men heard General Grant's announcement that Richmond had fallen. Wild cheering broke out along the line. The brigade was now designated as the rearguard, which considerably slowed its movements. The roads were in terrible condition, forcing the men to corduroy them so the wagons could pass through the worst spots. The march ended four miles beyond Mainsboro. The trek continued on April 5, except that when night fell the column continued marching—all night long until noon on April 6, when the brigade was about three miles from Burkesville Junction. The men rested here with the wagons until 9:30 that night, when the march resumed. "We marched like the very devil all night. During the march the Fortieth got frightened at something and formed line of battle, and had the whole Brigade about face, but nothing could be seen," wrote John Beach.[22]

Since they were in the rear, the brigade missed the seminal action at Sayler's Creek on April 6 that resulted in thousands of Lee's men falling into Federal hands. The march finally ended at 5:30 A.M. on April 7, when the brigade caught up with the VI Corps at Saylor's Creek. "The field presented such a spectacle as we have never seen before; small arms and accoutrements lay strewn all over the fields and along the road," noted Beach. After a two-hour rest, the men were on the move again with the rest of the VI Corps as they followed Lee's battered and bleeding army. The corps halted about a mile from Farmville at 4:30 P.M. The men could see a gray line of battle facing Sheridan's cavalry up ahead. The Rebels were driven off by nightfall, and the column continued southward. Because the enemy had burned the bridges before retreating, the men forded the Appomattox River. The thoroughly exhausted Jerseymen finally bivouacked at 10:00 P.M.

The march resumed at 9:30 A.M. on April 8. The men rested for half an hour at 11:30 A.M. and then, according to Beach, "marched as we never marched before, for all there was in us, till midnight, when we went into camp." The brigade traveled eighteen miles, but it did not seem so long because of the constant news of Lee's men being driven back with a steady string of captures. At one point the officers read a dispatch that the enemy was surrounded and the cavalry was capturing large numbers of prisoners. The men were not surprised, for they were definitely following a defeated enemy. "The road that we pass over is strewn with wagons, dead horses, boxes, cooking utensils, paper records of the army, etc." wrote John Hoffman in his diary.[23]

The relentless pursuit of the remnants of the Army of Northern Virginia continued on April 9 at 5:30 A.M. This was an easier march with frequent stops. The column halted at 1:30 P.M. amid rumors that a flag of truce had been seen and that Lee and Grant were meeting at Appomattox Court House. Later than afternoon, news arrived that Lee had indeed surrendered to Grant. General Wheaton wrote in his report that this caused "the wildest enthusiasm and heartfelt joy among the troops." Hoffman captured the scene very well: "the wildest enthusiasm prevailed. All the officers and men were nearly crazy. Bands commenced to play wildly, caps and haversacks flew in the air. Both officers and men jumped and stamped, laughed and cried, flags were waving and cheers rose on high till it became one continuous yell." According to Beach, "the men were perfectly wild with delight. The batteries belched forth salutes, and the air was rent with cheers and black with caps thrown high in the air. It was a sight never to be forgotten." Beach was one of the men who did not cheer. "There seemed to rise before me a full realization of all the surrender implied, our sufferings and our sacrifices for the last four years, and as I tried to cheer, a lump seemed to rise in my throat, and it was some time before I could give vent to my delight."

Camille Baquet, the brigade's historian, wrote, "Every man felt a pardonable pride in having assisted so successfully in terminating the destructive and desolating war. The fighting was over, the strategic marches finished and all that they could now be called upon to do was to help in cleaning up the disrupted Confederacy. The four years of drilling, marching and fighting had come to a glorious end, and the men, tired of the soldier life, yearned for home and loved ones."[24]

The men of the two armies fraternized, now brothers again. Food was a serious concern for the Confederate soldiers. "Our boys opened their haversacks to give to the hungry rebels, and soon full rations were distributed to them," noted Haines. One of the soldiers receiving the rations called out, "Say, Yanks! You're mighty glad the war's over, but ye're hain't half so glad as us are." The men assembled at 4:00 P.M. to hear the order announcing the surrender. The officers intended to make speeches, but the men would hear none of it, as they were too busy screaming and celebrating. The Jersey Brigade went into camp at 5:00 P.M. and each man received a whiskey ration. Many men attended prayer services that evening. They had much to be thankful for, as few had thought they would survive the ordeal.

The men rested on April 10, when John Hoffman noted, "nothing is thought, heard, or talked of in camp but the surrender of Lee." The VI Corps was ordered back to Petersburg the following day, and the following few days were filled with hard marches—twenty-three miles on April 11 and fifteen miles on April 12. The men rested at Burksville Junction when they arrived there at noon on April 13. Hoffman was officer of the day on April 15, and apparently had his hands full, recounting that "in the afternoon whiskey became pretty plentiful and several of our officers are drunk to say the least. . . . So much for rum, the destroyer of the human race."[25]

News of President Lincoln's assassination at Ford's Theatre arrived on April 16. "We could not credit the horrid story and all day it was the theme of conversation," wrote Hoffman. The men became "much incensed and depressed in consequence," recalled Beach. The Fourth NJV received a new state flag on April 18, to the wild cheers of the entire brigade. Meanwhile, new recruits continued arriving. For example, one hundred arrived on April 20 for the Fifteenth NJV.

The men were told to pack up on April 23 and prepare for a long seventy-mile march to Danville, Virginia, near the North Carolina line. General W. T. Sherman was maneuvering Confederate general Joseph Johnston into submission in the Carolinas, but needed help to box him in, and the VI Corps was quickly selected for the mission. The men marched through Keysville and past Halifax Court House, finally reaching Danville on the afternoon of April 27. They unfurled their flags and, with bands playing, marched through the town. Crossing the bridge into North Carolina, the corps camped about two miles farther south. Almost as soon as they arrived, the men heard that Johnston had surrendered, so they rested here until May 2, when the corps began its return to Virginia. Rations were short.[26]

The Jerseymen marched to the train depot at 7:00 A.M. on May 5, where they boarded cars for the trip back to Burksville Junction, arriving there at 7:00 P.M. Beach noted that "the inhabitants along the road have undergone a great change in their sentiments, and appear to be perfectly satisfied to return under the old flag once more." The men were back on the road at 6:00 A.M. on May 7, this time marching toward Sutherland's Station, about forty-two miles away, which they reached the following evening. They remained here for ten days, guarding the railroad and telegraph lines from Keysville to Scottsville Station. This was finally a time when the men could dream about the future and begin mentally preparing to become civilians once more.

Now that the rebellion was over, the military authorities began the difficult task of mustering out hundreds of thousands of men. With so much time on the soldiers' hands, property owners worried about marauding troops, so the officers placed strict restrictions on travel. None of the troops could go farther than half a mile from camp without a pass, which were not frequently issued.[27]

Reveille sounded at 3:00 A.M. on May 18, and the men were on the road to Petersburg by 4:30 A.M. Reaching the outskirts four hours later, they rested for ninety minutes and then marched through the city. Hoffman noted that the brigade "formed and marched through the town in platoons, with our colors unfurled and bands playing." This was a special time for the men, as they had spent so much time outside of Petersburg but had never been inside. They admired the enemy fortifications and toured the city before getting back in column on May 19 to move to the outskirts of Richmond. The march continued at 5:00 A.M. on May 24, and officers were told to wear their dress coats to make a good impression as they marched through Manchester and Richmond. Then it was on to Hanover Court House, which they reached that night after a difficult twenty-mile march. The day was hot, and men fell out of ranks by the score. Many questioned the need for such a forced march.

The Jerseyans were up early again at 2:15 A.M. on May 25, and on the road just over two hours later. "Marched like the devil was after us from 8 A.M. to 2:30 P.M., when we went into camp," John Beach recorded in his diary. This was another difficult march—sixteen miles. Many grumbled when noon came and went without a halt for their midday meal, and they did not eat until they stopped for the night around mid-afternoon. Rumors circulated that several men had died during these two severe marches. There was one encouraging feature of the movements—the Jerseymen were rapidly heading north toward Washington. The men awoke at 4:30 A.M. on May 26, but because of the heavy rains they were permitted to rest in their tents for several additional hours. The rains broke the heat, but knee-deep mud replaced it in some places. After the brigade moved out at 9:30 A.M., it took seven hours to muck through ten miles of mud.[28]

The marches continued for the next several days, bringing the Jersey Brigade through many past battlefields. Most sobering was Spotsylvania Court House. Here the survivors of the Fifteenth NJV visited the sites where so many of their comrades had fallen. Salem Church and Fredericksburg also brought bittersweet memories. The long marches of the VI Corps finally ended at Hall's Hill, outside of Washington, on June 2. The men knew they would remain here for awhile, as their officers told them to raise their tents eighteen inches off the ground. They just had to find axes to build the platforms. General Wright knew that a horde of visitors would descend upon his camps, so he insisted that they be laid out properly and kept clean. One of the first visitors to the Jerseymen's camps was New Jersey governor Marcus Ward.

New clothing began arriving on June 6, and the men were told to clean all of their equipment, as they would be reviewed by the president in a parade that would outdo all others. Because they had been guarding government property to the south, the VI Corps had not participated in the army's Grand Review on May 22 and 23, so this was their opportunity. Reveille sounded at 2:00 A.M. on June 8, and the march to Washington began at 4:00 A.M. Crossing the Potomac, the brigade and the rest of the VI Corps took position at 9:00 A.M. on Maryland Avenue. The day was very hot, and after the review the men marched back to their camps, where they waited to be mustered out of the Federal army. Josiah Brown, now released from Confederate captivity, rightfully recalled, "the Government probably was just as anxious that the troops should be discharged as were the men themselves," but there were many details to be settled before such an immense army could be returned to civilian life. The original members of the Fifteenth NJV were finally mustered out on June 22. The rest of the regiment was transferred to the Second NJV, now restored to regimental status. The Tenth NJV was also mustered out that day.[29]

The Jerseymen's frustrations boiled over on June 23. The Fourth NJV conducted a torchlight parade after taps. Some of the men carried crude banners saying, "We want our rights." Colonel Hufty and his officers tried to stop the demonstration, but the men were too upset to be dissuaded. "About two hundred had candles tucked in their bayonets and the rest marched in the rear. The whole drum corps was out. We marched through the Brigade, passed headquarters, cheered for some of the officers, and groaned others," noted John Beach. After returning to their camps, the men heard the Second Division's demonstrations, which "made more noise and racket than all of the corps put together."

Preparations were made on June 27 for mustering out of some units, and this began occurring on June 29. The First and Third NJV Battalions entrained for home on June 30; the Tenth NJV, approximately 450 strong, followed the next day. Prior to leaving for the train station, each unit marched to the brigade headquarters, where General Penrose gave a short speech. The Fourth NJV was mustered out on July 9. The men packed up their knapsacks at 4:00 A.M. on July 10, loaded them into wagons, and were on the road to Washington a half hour later. Entraining in Washington at 10:00 that morning, they reached Philadelphia at 6:00 A.M. on July 11. Leaving the trains, the men marched to the Cooper Shop Volunteer Refreshment Saloon, where they received breakfast and were able to wash up and prepare for the last leg home. Many visited barber shops. John Beach was one of them, having his mustache dyed. Large crowds greeted the trains in Trenton, and the men of the Fourth NJV finally received their final pay and discharges on July 18.[30]

The final units of the Jersey Brigade were mustered out a short time later. The Second NJV Battalion was mustered out on July 11 and the Fortieth NJV on July 13, formally ending the existence of the First New Jersey Brigade.

The war was finally over for the men of the Jersey Brigade. None returned the same as he had entered. The scars were both physical and emotional, but all shared a common sense of pride that they had preserved the Union. For many, being home began the healing process. John Hoffman recorded in his diary on July 6, "at home all day getting well and enjoying myself hugely. My appetite is returning. Being home is better than tons of medicine." After the years faded some of the bitter memories, the men glorified their days fighting for their country. Josiah Brown ended his 1885 war recollections with the sentence that the war years were "the proudest periods of my life, and shall deem it my highest glory and privilege to have fought for the flag, and all that it represents."[31]

APPENDIX A

Regimental Losses in the First Half of the War

Regiment	Gaines' Mill	Second Bull Run	Crampton's Gap	Fredericks- burg	Chancellors- ville
First NJV					
Killed	21	1	7	?	7
Wounded	80	46	33	?	71
Missing	58	85	–	?	27
Total	159	132	40	?	105
Second NJV					
Killed	15	7	10	–	4
Wounded	55	58	45	1	36
Missing	43	64	–	–	9
Total	113[a]	129	55	1	49
Third NJV					
Killed	35	–	11	–	11
Wounded	136	14	29	2	69
Missing	44	50	–	–	15
Total	215	64	40	2	95
Fourth NJV					
Killed	45	–	10	9	–[b]
Wounded	103	6	26	35	–
Missing	437	5	–	36	–
Total	585	11	36	80	–
Fifteenth NJV					
Killed				4	24
Wounded				20	126
Missing				5	4
Total				29	154

Regiment	Gaines' Mill	Second Bull Run	Crampton's Gap	Fredericks- burg	Chancellors- ville
Twenty-third NJV					
Killed				5	20
Wounded				36	57
Missing				9	31
Total				50	108
Brigade Totals					
Killed	116	8	38	18	66
Wounded	374	124	133	94	359
Missing	582	204	–	50	86
Total	1,072	336	171	162	511

Notes: a. Only three companies were present at Gaines' Mill.
      b. On detached duty and not present at Chancellorsville.

Regimental Losses in the Second Half of the War

Regiment	Wilderness	Spotsylvania	Cold Harbor	Third Winchester	Cedar Creek
First NJV					
Killed	17	3	5		
Wounded	106	50	25		
Missing	39	9	3		
Total	162	62	33		
Second NJV					
Killed	5	4			
Wounded	18	37			
Missing	23	27			
Total	46	68			
Third NJV					
Killed	–	20	3		
Wounded	7	98	12		
Missing	1	30	1		
Total	8	148	16		
Fourth NJV					
Killed	8	15	2	2	1
Wounded	73	66	15	19	29
Missing	15	8	2	1	4
Total	96	89	19	22	34
Tenth NJV					
Killed	3	15	18	1	3
Wounded	16	80	62	14	42
Missing	19	54	–	1	–
Total	38	149	80	16	45

Regiment	Wilderness	Spotsylvania	Cold Harbor	Third Winchester	Cedar Creek
Fifteenth NJV					
Killed	3	75	12	4	13
Wounded	9	159	24	44	57
Missing	2	38	–	7	15
Total	14	272	36	55	85
Brigade Totals					
Killed	36	132	40	7	17
Wounded	229	490	138	77	128
Missing	99	166	6	9	19
Total	364	788	184	93	164

Numbers and Losses of the First New Jersey Brigade

The First New Jersey Brigade fought with distinction throughout the war without being disbanded. Such was not the case of most other brigades, including the Philadelphia Brigade and the Iron Brigade, which were disbanded in 1864 when their core regiments' enlistments expired and the men went home. The brigade also, with the exception of the brief assignment of the First Delaware Cavalry in 1864, remained a single state brigade throughout the war, which was highly unusual.

The brigade participated in countless battles and skirmishes. Some were pitched, with the brigade playing a major role, including West Point, Gaines' Mill, White Oak Swamp, Second Bull Run, Crampton's Pass, Fredericksburg, Salem Church (Chancellorsville), Fairfield, Wilderness, Spotsylvania Court House, Cold Harbor, Third Winchester (Opequon), Fisher's Hill, Cedar Creek, and Petersburg. On several occasions they were on or near battlefields but did not play a major role, such as at First Bull Run, Antietam, Gettysburg, Mine Run, and Hatcher's Run.

William Fox compiled a list of statistics relating to selected Federal regiments during the Civil War. His analysis includes four regiments in the First New Jersey Brigade: First, Third, Fourth, and Fifteenth NJV. His major results are summarized in Table C.1.[1]

While all four regiments began their service with more than nine hundred men, the Fourth and Fifteenth NJV enlisted more men than the First and Third NJV because a flood of new recruits swelled their ranks after the latter regiments were mustered out. This has a profound effect on the percentages listed above, as most of these men joined after the major battles were fought. Therefore, the Fourth and Fifteenth NJV's percentages are artificially

TABLE C.1   *Strengths and Losses of First New Jersey Brigade*
Regiments Included in Fox's Analysis

Regiment	Total serving	Killed(%)	Died/Disease(%)	Wounded(%)
First NJV	1,324	153(11.5)	91(6.9)	393(29.7)
Third NJV	1,238	157(12.7)	81(6.5)	380(30.7)
Fourth NJV	1,867	131(7.0)	105(5.6)	457(24.5)
Fifteenth NJV	1,702	240(14.1)	132(7.8)	616(36.2)

Source: William F. Fox, *Regimental Losses in the American Civil War* (Albany, N.Y.: J. McDonaugh, 1898), 243–245, 253.

lowered and would be significantly higher if the new recruits were not included. Even with the new recruits added, the 14 percent killed in the Fifteenth NJV is significantly higher than that of the other regiments (see below).

As expected, the greatest casualties in each regiment were due to wounds, followed by battle mortality and death through disease, in that order. With regard to battle deaths, Fox found that the greatest number of deaths in the First NJV (44), Third NJV (58), and Fourth NJV (52) were at Gaines' Mill; it was Spotsylvania Court House for the Fifteenth NJV (116).[2]

In his review of the Federal regiments with the greatest number of men killed in battle, Fox noted that the Fifteenth NJV's loss of 240 men placed it in twelfth place on a list of over two thousand Federal regiments. He found a total of forty-five regiments losing over two hundred men, but no other New Jersey regiment populated this list. Fox also identified four New Jersey regiments whose mortalities exceeded 10 percent, and three of them were in the First New Jersey Brigade. The First NJV's mortality rates were 11.5 percent, the Third NJV's were 12.7 percent and the Fifteenth NJV's were 14.1 percent. The Fourteenth NJV was the other New Jersey regiment to make this list.

Fox also examined the number of men killed during specific battles and found that only one regiment lost more than the Fifteenth NJV's 116 at Spotsylvania. That was the Fifth New York, which lost 117 at Second Bull Run. Also making the high mortality list were the Third NJV and Fourth NJV at Gaines' Mill.[3]

When comparing total percentage casualties in a specific battle, Fox found that the Fifteenth NJV's losses of 62.9 percent at Spotsylvania were seventeenth on the list. Only one other New Jersey regiment, the Eleventh NJV at Gettysburg, was on this list.

These statistics further illustrate the sacrifice of the First New Jersey Brigade.[4]

Fate of the Men Whose Diaries/Letters Were Quoted

*F*orty-nine soldiers were quoted in this book. The fates of each are listed below, along with their regiment in parentheses. Almost half, twenty-three, never returned from the war: ten were killed in battle, eight died of their wounds, four died of disease, and one was missing in action. Of the remaining men, two resigned their commissions and left the army, three transferred to other units, three were wounded and later discharged, and eighteen were mustered out at the end of the war.

Robert Aitken (Fourth NJV)	Died December 15, 1864, of wounds sustained at Fredericksburg.
Jacob Apgar (Fifteenth NJV)	Died May 20, 1863, of wounds sustained at Salem Church.
John Beach (Fourth NJV)	Survived the war, mustered out July 9, 1865.
Edwin Bishop (Second NJV)	Captain, resigned January 7, 1863.
Reuben Brooks (Third NJV)	Survived the war, mustered out June 23, 1864.
Josiah Brown (Second, Fifteenth NJV)	Survived the war, mustered out July 11, 1865.
James Bullock (Fifteenth NJV)	Survived the war, mustered out June 22, 1865.
Henry Callan (Third NJV)	Killed at the Wilderness, May 5, 1864.

Samuel Cavileer (Fourth NJV)   Survived the war, mustered out July 9, 1865.

William Cazier (Tenth NJV)   Died of diarrhea and pneumonia, August 19, 1864.

Isaac Clark (Third NJV)   Discharged October 26, 1862, to join regular army.

Charles Currie (Fourth NJV)   Transferred to signal corps and survived the war.

E. L. Dobbins (Twenty-third NJV)   Survived the war, mustered out June 27, 1863.

Robert Elmer (Twenty-third NJV)   Survived the war, mustered out June 27, 1863.

Dayton Flint (Fifteenth NJV)   Survived the war, mustered out June 22, 1865.

Eugene Forbes (Fourth NJV)   Died of scurvy and starvation at Andersonville Prison Camp.

Frank Gaul (Fourth NJV)   Survived the war, mustered out July 9, 1865.

Peter Goetschins (First NJV)   Discharged for disability, December 31, 1862.

Martin Grassman (Fifteenth NJV)   Died of chronic diarrhea, May 4, 1863.

Quincy Grimes (Fifteenth NJV)   Died of chronic diarrhea, September 8, 1863.

Edmund Halsey (Fifteenth NJV)   Resigned from the army, January 10, 1865.

Ellis Hamilton (Fifteenth NJV)   Died May 16, 1864, of wounds sustained at the Wilderness.

Charles Harrison (Second NJV)   Survived the war, mustered out June 21, 1864.

David Hatfield (First NJV)   Died July 30, 1862, of wounds sustained at Gaines' Mill.

John Hoffman (Tenth NJV)	Survived the war, mustered out July 1, 1865.
Edward Hollinger (First NJV)	Transferred to Veteran Reserve Corps on November 1, 1863, and survived the war.
Charles Hopkins (First NJV)	Survived the war, mustered out April 21, 1865.
Benjamin Hough (Fifteenth NJV)	Killed at Spotsylvania, May 12, 1864.
Jonathan Hutchinson (Fifteenth NJV)	Killed at Salem Church, May 3, 1863.
John Judd (Third NJV)	Died May 30, 1864, of wounds sustained at Spotsylvania.
Paul Kuhl (Fifteenth NJV)	Killed at Spotsylvania, May 12, 1864.
John Laughton (Fifteenth NJV)	Disabled, discharged April 11, 1863, died that month.
Robert McAllister (First NJV)	Transferred to Eleventh NJV, survived the war.
Robert McCreight (First NJV)	Missing in action at Salem Church, May 3, 1863.
Charles Paul (Fifteenth NJV)	Survived the war, mustered out June 22, 1865.
Abram Paxton (Second NJV)	Survived the war, mustered out June 21, 1864.
John Pedrick (Third NJV)	Killed during Chancellorsville Campaign, May 3, 1863.
Charles Reid (Third NJV)	Killed at Gaines' Mill, June 27, 1862.
Henry Ryerson (Second, Tenth, Twenty-third NJV)	Died May 12, 1864, of wounds sustained at the Wilderness.
David Samson (Second NJV)	Wounded and transferred to the Veteran Reserve Corps on September 1, 1863.

Phineas Skellenger (Fifteenth NJV)   Died May 27, 1864, of wounds sus-
                                     tained at Laurel Hill, May 8, 1864.

Wallace Struble (First NJV)   Survived the war, mustered out June 29,
                                     1865.

Forrester Taylor   Survived war, mustered out June 27,
(Twenty-third NJV)   1863; reenlisted in the Thirty-Fourth
                                     NJV, rising to rank of major.

John Thompson (Fifteenth NJV)   Killed at Spotsylvania, May 12, 1864.

Edwin Ulmer (Fifteenth NJV)   Severely wounded at Cedar Creek,
                                     discharged May 29, 1865.

Lucien Voorhees (Fifteenth NJV)   Killed at Laurel Hill, May 8, 1864.

Oscar Westlake (Third NJV)   Killed at Cold Harbor, June 2, 1864.

Jacob Wycoff (First NJV)   Killed at Spotsylvania, May 12, 1864.

Andrew Yeoman (Fifteenth NJV)   Survived the war, mustered out May 22,
                                     1865.

Notes

Archival Sources

Jacob Apgar (Fifteenth NJV), William Apgar Papers, Hunterdon County Historical Society, 114 Main Street, Flemington, N.J.

Joseph Bilby Collection (private).

Reuben Brooks (Third NJV), Brooks Papers, Special Collections, Alexander Library, Rutgers University, New Brunswick, N.J.

James Bullock (Fifteenth NJV), Bullock Papers, John Kuhl Collection (private).

Henry Callan (Third NJV), Henry Callan Papers, Special Collections, Alexander Library, Rutgers University, New Brunswick, N.J.

Samuel Cavileer (Fourth NJV), Cavileer Papers, Atlantic County Historical Society, 903 Shore Road, Somers Point, N.J.

William Cazier (Tenth NJV), Gandy Collection, Atlantic County Historical Society, 903 Shore Road, Somers Point, N.J.

Isaac Clark (Third NJV), Gloucester Historical Society, 17 Hunter Street, Woodbury, N.J.

J. L. Conklin (Second NJV), Conklin and Jones Papers, Special Collections, Alexander Library, Rutgers University, New Brunswick, N.J.

Ebenezer W. Davis (Fifteenth NJV), "Campaigns in Maryland and Virginia with the 6th Corps," A. P. Young Papers, New Jersey Historical Society, 52 Park Place, Newark, N.J.

Robert Elmer (Twenty-third NJV), Elmer Papers, John Kuhl Collection (private).

Edmund English (Second NJV), Papers of Edmund English, Huntington Library, 1151 Oxford Road, San Marino, California.

Eugene Forbes (Fourth NJV), Eugene Forbes Papers, Special Collections, Alexander Library, Rutgers University, New Brunswick, N.J.

Peter Goetschins (First NJV), Peter Goetschins to George Scott, May 12, 1862, Marcus Wood Collection, Special Collections, Alexander Library, Rutgers University, New Brunswick, N.J.

Martin Grassman (Fifteenth NJV), Martin Grassman to Mary Ewing, October 30, 1862, New Jersey Historical Society, 52 Park Place, Newark, N.J.

Quincy Grimes (Fifteenth NJV), Quincy Grimes Papers, John Kuhl Collection (private).

Edmund Halsey (Fifteenth NJV), Edmund Halsey Diary, U.S. Army Military History Institute, 950 Soldiers Drive, Carlisle, Pa.; Letters—Rockaway Borough Library, 82 E. Main Street, Rockaway, N.J.

Ellis Hamilton (Fifteenth NJV), Hamilton Papers, Special Collections, Alexander Library, Rutgers University, New Brunswick, N.J.

Charles Harrison (Second NJV), Charles Alexander Harrison Diary, U.S. Army Military History Institute, 950 Soldiers Drive, Carlisle, Pa.

Jonathan Hutchinson (Fifteenth NJV), Norwich Civil War Round Table Collection, U.S. Army Military History Institute, 950 Soldiers Drive, Carlisle, Pa.

John Judd (Third NJV), John Judd Diary, Kansas State Historical Society, 6425 Sixth Avenue, Topeka, Kans.

Philip Kearny (First New Jersey Brigade), Philip Kearny Papers, Library of Congress.

Paul Kuhl (Fifteenth NJV), Paul Kuhl Papers, John Kuhl Collection (private).

John Laughton (Fifteenth NJV), John Laughton Papers, John Kuhl Collection (private).

Robert McCreight (First NJV), Robert McCreight Papers, U.S. Army Military Institute, 950 Soldiers Drive, Carlisle, Pa.

Charles Olden (New Jersey governor), Nathaniel Banks Papers, Library of Congress.

James Park (First NJV), Robert McCreight Collection, U.S. Army Military History Institute, 950 Soldiers Drive, Carlisle, Pa.

Charles Paul (Fifteenth NJV), Charles R. Paul, "Campaign of 1864" and "Diary," Murray S. Smith Collection, U.S. Army Military History Institute, 950 Soldiers Drive, Carlisle, Pa.

William Penrose (Fifteenth NJV), Bound Regimental Records, 15th N.J., National Archives.

John Perdrick (Third NJV), Gloucester Historical Society, 17 Hunter St., Woodbury, N.J.

Robert Proudfit (Second and Tenth NJV), Proudfit Letters, Special Collections, Alexander Library, Rutgers University, New Brunswick, N.J.

Charles Reid (Third NJV), Charles Reid Collection, New Jersey Historical Society, 52 Park Place, Newark, N.J.

Henry Ryerson (Second, Tenth, and Twenty-third NJV), W. J. Anderson Family Papers, New Jersey Historical Society, 52 Park Place, Newark, N.J.

David Samson (Second NJV), Civil War Miscellaneous Collection, U.S. Army Military History Institute, 950 Soldiers Drive, Carlisle, Pa.

James Simpson (Fourth NJV), Olden Family Papers, Historical Society of Princeton, Bainbridge House, 158 Nassau Street, Princeton, N.J.

Phineas Skellenger (Fifteenth NJV), Phineas Shellenger Papers, John Kuhl Collection (private).

Wallace Struble (First NJV), Wallace Struble Papers, Wayne McCabe Collection (private).

Joseph Sullivan (Fifteenth NJV), Mary Ewing Papers, Special Collections, Alexander Library, Rutgers University, New Brunswick, N.J.

Edwin Ulmer (Fifteenth NJV), Edwin Ulmer Papers, John Kuhl Collection (private).

Oscar Westlake (Third NJV), Oscar Westlake Papers, John Kuhl Collection (private).
Montreville Williams (Third NJV), diary, Museum Collection, Antietam National
    Battlefield, Sharpsburg, Maryland.
Jacob Wycoff (First NJV), Wycoff Papers, Special Collections, Alexander Library,
    Rutgers University, New Brunswick, N.J.
Andrew Yeoman (Fifteenth NJV), A.C. Yeoman Papers, New Jersey Historical Soci-
    ety, 52 Park Place, Newark, N.J.

CHAPTER 1   *Forming the First New Jersey Brigade*

1. Camille Baquet, *History of Kearny's First New Jersey Brigade* (Trenton, N.J.:
   MacCrellish and Quigley, State Printers, 1910), 353–354; Joseph Bilby, *"Remember You Are Jerseymen!"* (Hightstown, N.J.: Longstreet House, 1998), 3–4.
2. William B. Styple and John J. Fitzpatrick, ed., *The Andersonville Diary and Mem-
   oirs of Charles Hopkins* (Kearny, N.J.: Belle Grove, 1988), 29–30; James I.
   Robertson, ed., *The Civil War Letters of General Robert McAllister* (New
   Brunswick, N.J.: Rutgers Univ. Press, 1965), 29, 30.
       As many as 1,200 New Jerseymen joined New York's Excelsior Brigade,
   and a total of 8,957 served in units from other states (Bilby, *Remember,* 7–8).
3. *The War of the Rebellion: A Compilation of the Official Records of the Union
   and Confederate Armies* (Washington: U.S. Government Printing Office, 1880–
   1901), ser. 3, vol. 1, pp. 142–143, 150. (Hereafter cited as *OR.*)
4. Robertson, *McAllister,* 31; Oscar Westlake to brother, May 25, 1861, John Kuhl
   Collection; Styple and Fitzpatrick, ed., *Hopkins,* 31.
       Although the brigade's historian, Camille Baquet, and modern historian
   James Robertson wrote that this facility was Camp Olden, noted New Jersey historian Joseph Bilby believes that it was really a militia camp at the state arsenal.
   Indeed, at the top of McAllister's letter describing this facility is "State Arsenal,
   Trenton, May 6, 1861" (Bilby, personal communication).
5. Baquet, *Kearny's,* 4, 12; *Newark Daily Advertiser,* June 5, 1861.
6. Bilby, *Remember,* 5–6; Robertson, *McAllister,* 31, 32.
7. *OR,* ser. 3, vol. 1, p. 188.
8. *OR,* ser. 3, vol. 1, pp. 204, 214–215; John Y. Foster, *New Jersey and the Rebellion* (Newark, N.J.: M. R. Dennis, 1868), 65; Robertson, *McAllister,* 32–33.
9. Baquet, *Kearny's,* 6; Robertson, *McAllister,* 33, 38; Bilby, *Remember,* 665; John
   Perdick to parents, June 27, 1861, Gloucester Historical Society; William S.
   Stryker, *Record of Officers and Men of New Jersey in the Civil War, 1861–1865*
   (Trenton, N.J.: John L. Murphy, 1876), 69; Edmund Raus Jr., *A Generation on
   the March* (Gettysburg, Pa.: Thomas Publications, 1996), 53.
10. Charles Olden to General Patterson, May 31, 1861, Nathaniel Banks Papers, Li-
    brary of Congress; Stryker, *Record,* 102, 150; Baquet, *Kearny's,* 6; Raus, *Gen-
    eration,* 53; Bilby, *Remember,* 667, 669; William J. Jackson, *New Jerseyans in
    the Civil War* (New Brunswick, N.J.: Rutgers Univ. Press, 2000), 67.
11. Wallace Struble to Hannah, June 13, 1861, Wayne McCabe Collection; Jackson,
    New Jerseyans, 37–54; Oscar Westlake to brother, May 25, 1861. Lieu-
        One reason why so many men wished to become officers was the pay. Lieu-

tenant Colonel McAllister received $212 a month, but with that he had to pay for his uniforms, rations, and upkeep of his horse.

12. Charles Reid to wife and children, June 5, 1861, Reid Collection, New Jersey Historical Society, Newark; John Perdick to parents, May 26, 1861; Robertson, *McAllister,* 54; Reid to wife and children, June 5, 1861.

13. Styple and Fitzpatrick, ed., *Hopkins,* 31–33; *New-Brunswick Fredonian,* May 30, 1861; *Newark Daily Advertiser,* June 5, 19, 1861; Struble to Hannah, June 13, 1861.

14. *Newark Daily Advertiser,* June 19, 1861; Struble to Hannah, June 13, 1861.

15. Styple and Fitzpatrick, ed., *Hopkins,* 31.
    The guns were actually .69 caliber (Joseph Bilby, personal communication).

16. *OR*, ser. 3, vol. 1, pp. 287, 288.

17. *Trenton State Gazette and Republican,* June 28, 1861; *Newark Daily Mercury,* Friday, June 28, 1861; Charles Alexander Harrison diary, June 28, 1861, U.S. Army Military History Institute.

18. Alan A. Siegel, *Beneath the Starry Flag* (New Brunswick, N.J.: Rutgers Univ. Press, 2001), 32; Struble to Hannah, no date; *Trenton State Gazette and Republican,* July 5, 1861; *Newark Daily Mercury,* Friday, June 28, 1861; Oscar Westlake to brother, July 4, 1861.

19. Siegel, *Beneath,* 32.

20. *Trenton State Gazette and Republican,* July 5, 1861; Robertson, *McAllister,* 36; Wallace Struble to Hannah, no date.
    Civil unrest in Baltimore resulted in an attack on the Sixth Massachusetts on April 19, 1861. Four soldiers and twelve civilians were killed in the fighting.

21. *Trenton State Gazette and Republican,* July 5, 1861; Robertson, *McAllister,* 36–38; Styple and Fitzpatrick, ed., *Hopkins,* 32.

22. *Trenton State Gazette and Republican,* July 5, 19, 1861; Siegel, *Beneath,* 34; Oscar Westlake to brother, July 4, 1861.

23. George Brewster to his sister, July 9, 1861, Joseph Bilby Collection; Oscar Westlake to brother, July 4, 1861; Siegel, *Beneath,* 33; Baquet, *Kearny's,* 7, 413; *Trenton State Gazette and Republican,* July 13, 1861.

24. Baquet, *Kearney's,* 414.

25. *Princeton Standard,* July 12, 1861; Robertson, *McAllister,* 39.

CHAPTER 2   *Into Virginia*

1. Reid to wife and children, July 14, 1861; Robertson, *McAllister,* 40; Bilby, *Remember,* 64; Baquet, *Kearny's,* 7.

2. Oscar Westlake to brother, July 4, 1861; Oscar Westlake to mother, July 10, 1961.

3. Robertson, *McAllister,* 41–44; John Perdick to parents, July 30, 1861.

4. Robert McCreight to mother, July 21, 1861, U.S. Army Military Institute; Baquet, *Kearny's,* 359–360; Robertson, *McAllister,* 45.
   Middleton was severely wounded at the Battle of Gaines' Mill and discharged from the army.

5. Robertson, *McAllister,* 45, 55; Baquet, *Kearny's,* 415; Reid to wife and children,

July 14, 1861; Robert McCreight to mother, July 21, 1861; Wallace Struble to Hannah, August 7, 1861.

6. *Trenton State Gazette and Republican,* July 26, 1861; Robert McCreight to mother, July 21, 1861; Robertson, *McAllister,* 45; *OR,* ser. 1, vol. 2, p. 321; Henry Ryerson to sister, July 24, 1861, W. J. Anderson Family Papers, New Jersey Historical Society.

7. *OR*, ser. 1, vol. 2, p. 438; Baquet, *Kearny's,* 415.

According to Major David Hatfield, the men made "preparations at once," but it apparently took four hours for Montgomery to gather the fifteen companies and begin the march. The delay was probably related to the men's inexperience and the necessity of gathering some companies on detached reconnaissance duty. The Third NJV was at Fairfax and not ordered to join the relief column (Robertson, *McAllister,* 50, 56; *Trenton State Gazette and Republican,* July 26, 1861).

The Battle of Bull Run had started well for the Federals, but when General McDowell realized that he could not win the battle, he ordered a withdrawal, which became a rout.

8. Baquet, *Kearny's,* 4, 16; *OR,* ser. 1, vol. 2, p. 438; Bilby, *Remember,* 65; Henry Ryerson to sister, July 24, 1861.

9. Baquet, *Kearny's,* 4, 16; Bilby, *Remember,* 65; Robertson, *McAllister,* 47.

Lieutenant Colonel Isaac Tucker sent two messengers to General McDowell for orders. Neither found the army's commanding officer, and they reported that the "whole army was retreating thoroughly demoralized and disorganized" (*Newark Daily Mercury,* July 25, 1861).

In attempting to defend the Second NJV's honor, an enlisted man reported to his local newspaper that the First NJV was "so eager to do something, that their Colonel led them almost into the hands of the enemy *before he knew it.* . . . *We* retreated in *order* and *covered* the retreat of the others" (*Newark Daily Advertiser,* August 5, 1861).

10. *OR,* ser. 1, vol. 2, pp. 425, 438; Robertson, *McAllister,* 47, 48, 52; Baquet, *Kearny's,* 8, 346, 417; Wallace Struble to Hannah, July 27, 1861.

11. *New Jersey Mirror and Burlington County Advertiser,* August 6, 1861; John Perdick to Family, July 30, 1861; Robertson, *McAllister,* 49–50, 54, 56.

12. Robertson, *McAllister,* 54–55, 57; Bilby, *Remember,* 65.

One of McLean's men wrote: "If *he* is a coward, there are a *thousand cowards to back him*" (*Newark Daily Advertiser,* August 5, 1861).

13. Bilby, *Remember,* 6; *OR,* ser. 3, vol. 1, p. 365.

14. *Princeton Standard,* August 2, 1861; *Trenton State Gazette and Republican,* August 2, 1861; *Somerset Messenger,* August 29, 1861; Bilby, *Remember,* 7; Baquet, *Kearny's,* 387, 390; Stryker, *Record,* 182.

15. *Somerset Messenger,* July 18, 1861; Bilby, *Remember,* 66, 662–663; Robertson, *McAllister,* 60; Jackson, *New Jerseyans,* 67.

16. Baquet, *Kearny's,* 9, 10, 418; Jackson, *New Jerseyans,* 68; Styple and Fitzpatrick, ed., *Hopkins,* 40.

A soldier indicated that the men only had two or three pieces of hardtack during the march, which was so hard "you could not put a bullet through them at fifty yards distance!" (*Princeton Standard,* August 16, 1861).

Not all of the men received Kearny's wrath. Charles Hopkins' company commander recognized Kearny and ordered his men to march by as if on parade, and their new commander complimented them (Styple and Fitzpatrick, ed., *Hopkins,* 39–40).

According to Orderly Henry Callan, Kearny called the men "thieves" because they were breaking into private homes to steal personal belongings (Callan to sister, August 19, 1861, Henry Callan Papers, Rutgers University).

17. Styple and Fitzpatrick, ed., *Hopkins,* 40; Robertson, *McAllister,* 74, 76; Philip Kearny to Jerome Parker, August 29, 1861, New Jersey Historical Society; Henry Callan to sister, August 14, 1861.

18. Robertson, *McAllister,* 62, 65; Oscar Westlake to mother, August 8, 1861; McCreight to brother, November 18, 1861; Henry Ryerson to sister, August 20, 1861.

19. Baquet, *Kearny's,* 11; John Perdick to parents, August 16, 1861; Isaac Clark to family, November 30, 1861, Gloucester Historical Society; Henry Callan to sister, August 19, 1861.

20. Henry Ryerson to sister, August 20, 1861; Foster, *Rebellion,* 807; Styple and Fitzpatrick, ed., *Hopkins,* 40; *Newark Daily Advertiser,* August 21, 1861; Baquet, *Kearny's,* 390–392; *Trenton State Gazette and Republican,* August 30, 1861.

Forty-eight-year-old Colonel Simpson was a West Point graduate who had served in the Indian Wars and came equipped with extensive experience in the topographical engineer corps. With his appointment, Governor Olden continued the trend of placing experienced soldiers at the head of his regiments (*Newark Daily Advertiser,* September 25, 1861).

21. Wallace Struble to Hannah, August 24, 1861; Robertson, *McAllister,* 70, 71; *Trenton State Gazette and Republican,* September 6, 1861; Kearny to Parker, August 29, 1861.

Montgomery would serve almost three years at Arlington. He finally resigned his commission on April 4, 1864, and returned home to Pennsylvania (Stewart Sifakis, *Who Was Who in the Civil War* [New York: Facts on File, 1988], 453).

22. Robertson, *McAllister,* 72, 73; Kearny to Parker, August 29, 1861.

23. Styple and Fitzpatrick, ed., *Hopkins,* 43; Edward N. Hollinger letter, *New Jersey History* 106, nos. 3–4 (fall/winter 1988): 74; *Paterson Daily Guardian,* August 26, 1861.

24. Kearny to Parker, August 29, 1861; Robertson, *McAllister,* 66, 68, 110.

25. *Paterson Daily Guardian,* September 2, 1861; Charles Reid to children, September 15, 1861; Oscar Westlake to mother, August 27, 1861; Henry Callan to sister, September 7, 1861; Jackson, *New Jerseyans,* 59; Robertson, *McAllister,* 77, 105; McCreight to brother, October 9, 1861.

26. Bilby, *Remember,* 67–68; Harrison diary, August 23, 1861; Kearny to Parker, August 29, 1861.

27. Robert McCreight to brother, August 29, 1861; Robertson, *McAllister,* 70–71.

28. *OR,* ser. 1, vol. 5, p. 122; *Trenton State Gazette and Republican,* September 6,

1861; *OR,* ser. 1, vol. 5, p. 238; *Somerset Messenger,* September 19, 1861; Baquet, *Kearny's,* 12–13, 420; Oscar Westlake to mother, September 20, 1861.

29. Robertson, *McAllister,* 75–76, 81–83; *Trenton State Gazette and Republican,* October 4, 1861; Baquet, *Kearny's,* 14; Charles Meves to wife, October 15, 1861, John Kuhl Collection.

 McAllister questioned whether the half dozen men on the picket line could have killed three of the New Yorkers and wounded six others. He hypothesized that a band of Rebels was in the area (Robertson, *McAllister,* 82).

30. *Trenton State Gazette and Republican,* October 11, 1861; Robertson, *McAllister,* 89, 100–101, McCreight to brother, November 5, 1861.

31. *Princeton Standard,* October 25, 1861; Charles Reid to wife and children, November 17, 1861; *Paterson Daily Guardian,* August 26, 1861; Jacob Wycoff to parents, October 29, 1861, Special Collections, Alexander Library, Rutgers University, New Brunswick, N.J.; David Samson to friend, October 3, 1861, Civil War Miscellaneous Collection, U.S. Army Military History Institute.

32. Oscar Westlake to mother, October 27, 1861; Robertson, *McAllister,* 91; David Samson to friend, September 4, 1861.

33. McCreight to brother, November 1861; Oscar Westlake to mother, November 7, 1861; Oscar Westlake to brother, November 12, 1861, Oscar Westlake to father, December 3, 1861; John Judd diary, November 2, 1861, Kansas State Historical Society.

34. Baquet, *Kearny's,* 393, 421; Robertson, *McAllister,* 97.

35. *Somerset Messenger,* September 26, 1861; Bilby, *Remember,* 65; Kearny to Parker, August 29, 1861; Judd diary, November 28, 1861.

 Because of McLean's "incapacity or indifference," Tucker had in actuality commanded the regiment since its inception. He was not a strong disciplinarian, and was highly respected by his men (Foster, *Rebellion,* 81).

36. Robertson, *McAllister,* 99, 104; Baquet, *Kearny's,* 421, 422.

37. Robertson, *McAllister,* 101; David Samson to friend, January 9, 1862; Henry Callan to sister, December 15, 1861; McCreight to brother, November 1861, January 3, February 12, 1862; Josiah Brown, "Record of My Experiences during the Civil War From October 1, 1862 to July, 1865" (typed transcript) (Newark: New Jersey Historical Society), 3; Baquet, *Kearny's,* 14–15.

38. McCreight to brother, January 13, 20, 28, 1862; Robertson, *McAllister,* 103, 117, 118; Henry Callan to sister, February 2, 1862; Baquet, *Kearny's,* 15, 421; McCreight to brother, February 6, 12, 1862; *Trenton State Gazette and Republican,* February 12, 1862; Brown, "Experiences," 4

39. Robertson, *McAllister,* 113–114; Henry Callan to sister, February 2, 1862.

40. Judd diary, February 7, 22, 1862; *OR,* ser. 1, vol. 5, pp. 713–714, 719.

CHAPTER 3 *On to Richmond!*

1. Robertson, *McAllister,* 121; Oscar Westlake to mother, March 1, 1862; Stephen W. Sears, *To the Gates of Richmond* (New York: Ticknor and Fields, 1992), 12–14.

2. *Somerset Messenger,* March 20, 1862; Baquet, *Kearny's,* 15, 423; *OR,* ser. 1, vol. 5, pp. 537, 538, 541, 542; Bilby, *Remember,* 68.

3. Baquet, *Kearny's,* 16, 407; *OR,* ser. 1, vol. 5, pp. 542, 537, 640, 539, 545; Robertson, *McAllister,* 124; McCreight to brother, March 16, 1862; Oscar Westlake to father, March 20, 1862.

4. *OR,* ser. 1, vol. 5, pp. 539, 541–543, 545; Baquet, *Kearny's,* 423; Oscar Westlake to father, March 20, 1862.

5. Douglas S. Freeman, *Lee's Lieutenants,* 3 vols. (New York: Charles Scribner's Sons, 1942), 1:139–141; Robertson, *McAllister,* 124; Sears, *Gates,* 14; *OR,* ser. 1, vol. 5, p. 542.

6. Robertson, *McAllister,* 129; McCreight to brother, March 26, April 2, 1862; Judd diary, April 4, 1862.

7. Robertson, *McAllister,* 127; *OR,* ser. 1, vol. 5, p. 46; Baquet, *Kearny's,* 17.

8. Oscar Westlake to father, March 28, 1862; Foster, *Rebellion,* 72; Baquet, *Kearny's,* 17; Wallace Struble to Hannah, April 11, 1862; Peter Goetschins to George Scott, May 12, 1862, Marcus Wood Collection, Rutgers University; Robertson, *McAllister,* 130–133; McCreight to brother, April 15, 1862; Judd diary, April 10, 1862.

9. Baquet, *Kearny's,* 17, 425; Wallace Struble to Hannah, April 15, 1862; Robertson, *McAllister,* 135–136; *Trenton Gazette and Republican,* March 9, 1862; J. L. Conklin letter, April 20, 1861, Conklin and Jones Papers, Rutgers University; Judd diary, April 17, 1862.

10. Robertson, *McAllister,* 136–140; Baquet, *Kearny's,* 425–426; McCreight to brother, May 1, 1862; Bradley M. Gottfried, *Stopping Pickett: The History of the Philadelphia Brigade* (Shippensburg, Pa.: White Mane, 1999), 58.

11. Judd diary, April 25, 1862; Sears, *Gates,* 65.

12. Robertson, *McAllister,* 136, 150, 158; Robert McCreight to brother, June 7, 1862; Foster, *Rebellion,* 73.

13. Sears, *Gates,* 65; Robertson, *McAllister,* 150–151.

14. Sears, *Gates,* 85–86; *OR,* ser. 1, vol. 11, pt. 1, pp. 615–616; Baquet, *Kearny's,* 428.

15. *OR,* ser. 1, vol. 11, pt. 1, p. 616; Wallace Struble to Hannah, May 20, 1862; Robertson, *McAllister,* 152–153.

16. *OR,* ser. 1, vol. 12, pt. 2, p. 624; Baquet, *Kearny's,* 22; Harrison diary, May 8, 1862.

17. Baquet, *Kearny's,* 23–24; Robertson, *McAllister,* 155, 156, 160; Judd diary, May 15, 1862; *West Jersey Press,* May 28, 1862.

18. Harrison diary, May 29, 1862; Sears, *Gates,* 124, 149–150.

19. Foster, *Rebellion,* 74; Robertson, *McAllister,* 169–176, 178–180, 182; William Styple, ed., *Death before Dishonor: The Andersonville Diary of Eugene Forbes: 4th New Jersey Infantry* (Belle Grove, N.J.: Belle Grove, 1995), 16; Judd diary, June 19, 1862.

20. Sears, *Gates,* 184–189, 200–208; Baquet, *Kearny's,* 432.

21. Sears, *Gates,* 214–215; Baquet, *Kearny's,* 311–312; *Newark Daily Advertiser,* July 9, 1862; Brian Burton, *Extraordinary Circumstances* (Bloomington: Indiana Univ. Press, 2001), 91–99.

22. *OR,* ser. 1, vol. 11, pt. 2, pp. 40, 432, 442–444, 461, 467; Reuben Brooks to brother, July 8, 1862, Rutgers University; Burton, *Extraordinary,* 123–124.

Brown's account of the battle is, unfortunately, quite short and inadequate (*OR,* ser. 1, vol. 11, pt. 2, pp. 443–444).

23. Burton, *Extraordinary,* 124–126; *OR,* ser. 1, vol. 11, pt. 2, pp. 438, 439; Baquet, *Kearny's,* 317; Robert McCreight to sister, July 14, 1862.

    In a letter to his brother on July 14, McCreight noted that when Torbert finally appeared at the end of the battle, "he was almost crying when he asked if the colors was [*sic*] safe."

24. Baquet, *Kearny's,* 317–319; *OR,* ser. 1, vol. 11, pt. 2, pp. 313, 438, 442–443; *Paterson Daily Register,* July 12, 1862; Joseph Bilby, "Some of Us Will Never Come Out," *Military Images* (November–December 1992): 12; Foster, *Rebellion,* 75.

    The Fourth Michigan may have believed that the Second NJV was to relieve it, not support it.

25. *OR,* ser. 1, vol. 11, pt. 2, pp. 442–443, 437; *Paterson Daily Register,* July 12, 1862; Burton, *Extraordinary,* 124.

    There were two other stories about the flag. E. Burd Grubb insisted that the wounded flagbearer gave him the standard (Baquet, *Kearny's,* 320), and Foster believed that the flagbearer buried the flag rather than allow its capture (Foster, *Rebellion,* 81).

26. Baquet, *Kearny's,* 314–316; Bilby, *Remember,* 69–71; *Newark Daily Advertiser,* July 9, 1862; *OR,* ser. 1, vol. 11, pt. 2, p. 444.

    According to Grubb, Taylor asked him, "Where is the Fourth?" Grubb replied, "Gone to Richmond, sir." Taylor then snapped, "Young man, this is no place for levity," but Grubb quickly added, "They are captured, every man of them." Taylor wringed his hands and repeated the phrase, "My God, My God." This account, written years after the battle, cannot be correct, as Grubb could not have known the regiment's fate that early in the fight (Baquet, *Kearny's,* 317).

27. *OR,* ser. 1, vol. 11, pt. 2, p. 445.

28. *OR,* ser. 1, vol. 11, pt. 2, pp. 389, 446, 604; Burton, *Extraordinary,* 125–126; Bilby, "Some," 13.

29. *OR,* ser. 1, vol. 11, pt. 2, p. 446; Baquet, *Kearny's,* 311; Harrison diary, June 29, 1862; Burton, *Extraordinary,* 134–135.

30. *OR,* ser. 1, vol. 11, pt. 2, pp. 40, 438, 442; Robertson, *McAllister,* 186; Bilby, *Remember,* 72; *Elizabeth New Jersey Journal,* July 15, 1862; *Newark Daily Advertiser,* July 9, 1862.

31. *New Jersey—A Historical, Industrial, and Commercial Review* (Elizabeth, 1906), 40; Baquet, *Kearny's,* 321; Bilby, *Remember,* 71.

32. *OR,* ser. 1, vol. 11, pt. 2, pp. 434, 443; James Park letter, undated, Robert McCreight Collection, U.S. Army Military History Institute; Foster, *Rebellion,* 84; *Newark Daily Advertiser,* July 9, 1862; Judd diary, June 29, 1862.

33. *OR,* ser. 1, vol. 11, pt. 2, pp. 434–435; Sears, *Gates,* 293; Burton, *Extraordinary,* 296; Foster, *Rebellion,* 84; *Newark Daily Advertiser,* July 9, 1862; Robertson, *McAllister,* 187.

34. Robertson, *McAllister,* 189; Baquet, *Kearny's,* 327–328.

35. *OR,* ser. 1, vol. 11, pt. 2, pp. 435, 443; *Newark Daily Advertiser,* July 9, 1862; Harrison diary, July 2, 3, 1862.

36. *Belvidere Intelligencer,* July 18, 1862; Robertson, *McAllister,* 188, 192.

37. Styple, ed., *Andersonville,* 18–19; James Simpson to Charles Olden, August 27, 1862, Olden Family Papers, Historical Society of Princeton; Baquet, *Kearny's,* 395.

CHAPTER 4   *The Summer and Fall of 1862*

1. Foster, *Rebellion,* 85–86; *Trenton Gazette and Republican,* March 10, 1862; *OR,* ser. 1, vol. 12, pt. 2, pp. 537, 541.

2. Baquet, *Kearny's,* 35; *OR,* ser. 1, vol. 12, pt. 2, p. 541; David Samson to friend, November 22, 1862; Robert McCreight to brother, September 6, 1862; *OR,* ser. 1, vol. 12, pt. 2, p. 541; Brown, "Experiences," 7; Baquet, *Kearny's,* 34.

    According to Foster (*Rebellion,* 87), Jackson's men used Federal flags and fired blanks to deceive Taylor into believing that they were "friendly."

3. John J. Hennessy, *Return to Bull Run* (New York: Simon and Schuster, 1993), 125–126; Brown, "Experiences," 7; Freeman, *Lee's Lieutenants,* 2:98–99.

4. Brown, "Experiences," 7; John W. Kuhl, "General George William Taylor— Hunterdon County's Only Civil War General," *Hunterdon Historical Newsletter* (winter 1980): 301–302; *OR,* ser. 1, vol. 12, pt. 2, pp. 539, 644; Hennessy, *Return,* 126; Baquet, *Kearny's,* 35.

5. *OR,* ser. 1, 12, pt. 2, pp. 408, 539, 542, 543; Hennessy, *Return,* 126–127; Baquet, *Kearny's,* 35–36; Kuhl, "Taylor," 302.

6. Baquet, *Kearny's,* 36–37, 41; *OR,* ser. 1, vol. 12, pt. 2, pp. 410, 541; Hennessy, *Return,* 127; Kuhl, "Taylor," 299–300; Jack D. Welsh, *Medical Histories of Union Generals* (Kent, Ohio: Kent State Univ. Press, 1996), 332.

    The brigade's strength is estimated. Colonel Torbert reported that it numbered sixteen hundred on August 29, 1862 (*OR,* ser. 1, vol. 12, pt. 2, p. 537).

7. McCreight to brother, September 6, 1862; Baquet, *Kearny's,* 36; Foster, *Rebellion,* 88.

8. *OR,* ser. 1, vol. 12, pt. 2, pp. 537–538; David A. Welker, *Tempest at Ox Hill* (New York: DaCapo Press, 2002), 32.

9. *OR,* ser. 1, vol. 12, pt. 2, pp. 537–538; Baquet, *Kearny's* 43.

10. *OR,* ser. 1, vol. 19, pt. 1, pp. 378, 380, 382; Stephen Sears, *Landscape Turned Red* (New Haven, Conn.: Ticknor and Fields, 1983), 119.

11. John Michael Priest, *Before Antietam* (Shippensburg, Pa.: White Mane, 1992), 285, 289, 291; J. Shaw, "Crampton's Gap," *National Tribune,* October 1, 1891; *OR,* ser. 1, vol. 19, pt. 1, p. 380.

12. *OR,* ser. 1, vol. 19, pt. 1, pp. 382–383, 389; *Elizabeth New Jersey Journal,* September 23, 1862; Oscar Westlake to father, September 15, 1862.

    Colonel Torbert told a slightly different story, indicating that it was General Newton who ordered the charge (*OR,* ser. 1, vol. 19, pt. 1, p. 382).

13. *OR,* ser. 1, vol. 19, pt. 1, pp. 384, 387; *Newark Daily Advertiser,* September 20, 1862; *Paterson Guardian,* October 15, 1862.

14. Eugene Forbes to friend, September 16, 1862, Rutgers University; *OR,* ser. 1, vol. 19, pt. 1, pp. 386, 861, 870–871.

15. *OR,* ser. 1, vol. 19, pt. 1, p. 385; Forbes to friend, September 16, 1862; Henry Ryerson to sister, September 29, 1862.

16. *OR,* ser. 1, vol. 19, pt. 1, pp. 826–827; *Paterson Guardian,* September 20, 1862; *Newark Daily Advertiser,* September 20, 1862; *Camden West Jersey Press,* September 24, 1862; Montreville Williams diary, September 14, 1862, Museum Collection, Antietam National Battlefield, Sharpsburg, Maryland.

17. *OR,* ser. 1, vol. 19, pt. 1, pp. 183, 854.

18. *OR,* ser. 1, vol. 19, pt. 1, pp. 383, 387, 388; Baquet, *Kearny's,* 47; Foster, *Rebellion,* 93.

19. Baquet, *Kearny's,* 51; Bilby, *Remember,* 75–76; Baquet, *Kearny's,* 54; Oscar Westlake to father and mother, September 21, 1862; Reuben Brooks to brother, September 28, 1862, Rutgers University; John P. Beach, "Crampton's Pass," *National Tribune,* May 8, 1881; *OR,* ser. 1, vol. 19, pt. 1, pp. 195, 381–382.

20. Reuben Brooks to brother, September 28, 1862; Ryerson to sister, September 29, 1862, October 14, 1862; Oscar Westlake to father, October 25, 1862.

21. *Phillipsburg Standard,* August 7, 1862.

22. Alanson A. Haines, *History of the Fifteenth Regiment New Jersey Volunteers* (New York: Jenkins and Thomas, 1883), 8–9; Joseph Bilby, *Three Rousing Cheers* (Hightstown, N.J.: Longstreet House, 1993), 4; Bilby, *Remember,* 271; Baquet, *Kearny's,* 57.

    The other rendezvous sites were Freehold, Newark, and Woodbury.

23. Ellis Hamilton to father, August 8, 1862, Hamilton Papers, Rutgers University; Haines, *Fifteenth,* 10–11, 16; Bilby, *Three,* 3, 5; Quincy Grimes to sister, August 28, 1862, John Kuhl Collection; Jonathan Hutchinson to cousin, September 3, 1862, Norwich Civil War Round Table Collection, U.S. Army Military History Institute.

    Ellis Hamilton was sixteen years and ten months old when he received his commission. This unusual action was probably prompted by Colonel's Fowler's friendship with Hamilton's father, for Ellis wrote him, "he [Fowler] says he would very much like to accommodate you and me too" (Hamilton to father, August 8, 1862; Bilby, *Three,* 3).

24. *Hunterdon Gazette,* September 3, 1862; Baquet, *Kearny's,* 222; E. L. Dobbins, "Fragments from the History of a Quaker Regiment," *War Talks by Morristown Veterans* (Morristown, N.J.: Vogt Brothers, 1887), 30.

25. *History of the Re-Union Society of the Twenty-third N.J. Volunteers* (Philadelphia: Keystone Printing Co., 1890), 8; Haines, *Fifteenth,* 12; Richard T. Hoober, "Volunteer Refreshment Saloons," *Numismatist* 81, no. 2 (February 1968): 152; Jonathan Hutchinson to cousin, September 3, 1862, Norwich Civil War Round Table Collection, U.S. Army Military History Institute; *Hackettstown Gazette,* September 25, 1862; Quincy Grimes to sister, September 7, 1862.

26. Hoober, "Volunteer Refreshment Saloons," 149; Edmund Halsey diary, August 30, 1862; Haines, *Fifteenth,* 12–13; Hoober, "Volunteer Refreshment Saloons," 149; *Washington Star,* January 19, 1911; Hutchinson to cousin, September 3, 1862; Halsey diary, September 1, 1862; Robert Elmer diary, September 27, 1862, John Kuhl Collection; *Trenton Daily Gazette,* September 23, 1862.

27. *Washington Star,* January 19, 1911; Halsey diary, September 3, 1861; Haines, *Fifteenth,* 14, 15.

28. Hamilton Ellis to father, September 8, 21, 1862; *Hunterdon Gazette,* September

10, 17, 1862; Martin Grassman to Mary Ewing, October 30, 1862, New Jersey Historical Society; Quincy Grimes to sister, September 7, 1862.

29. Quincy Grimes to father, September 20, 1862; Grimes to mother, September 21, 1862.

30. Paul Kuhl to sister, September 22, 1862; John Laughton to father, September 20, 1862, John Kuhl Collection; Halsey diary, September 28, October 1, 1862; Haines, *Fifteenth,* 17; Hamilton Ellis to father, October 2, 1862; *Hunterdon Gazette,* September 30, October 15, 1862; *Millstone Mirror,* October 9, 1862.

31. Halsey diary, September 2, 3, 1862; Phineas Skellenger to family, October 7, 1862, John Kuhl Collection; *Hunterdon Gazette,* October 15, 22, 1862; Ellis to father, October 2, 1862; Benjamin Hough, *Letters from Home,* ed. Edna Raymond (Westtown, N.Y.: The Town of Minisink Archives, 1988), 4.

32. Hoober, "Volunteer Refreshment Saloons," 150–151; Elmer diary, October 6, 1862; Dobbins, "Fragments," 31; Bilby, *Remember,* 309; Inspection Report of Twenty-third Rgt. N.J. Vols., December 23, 1862; First Division, VI Corps, General Order #25, Joseph Bilby Private Collection; Baquet, *Kearny's,* 57.

33. Wallace Struble to Hannah, November 8, 1862; Ryerson to sister, October 14, 1862.

34. *Washington Sun,* January 19, 1911; Edmund Halsey to brother, October 28, 1862; Jonathan Hutchinson to cousin, October 15, 1862; *Hunterdon Gazette,* October 29, 1862.

35. *Washington Sun,* January 19, 1911; John Laughton to brother, October 26, 1862; Edmund Halsey to sister, October 18, 1862; Jonathan Hutchinson to relatives, October 23, 1862.

There is confusion about the date the knapsacks arrived. Hutchinson thought it was on October 18 and Flint recalled it was October 20.

CHAPTER 5   *Fredericksburg, Terrible Weather, and Sickness*

1. *Millstone Mirror,* November 20, 1862; Henry Callan to brother and sister, November 2, 1862; Haines, *Fifteenth,* 19; *Washington Star,* January 19, 1911; *Hunterdon Gazette,* November 12, 1862.

2. Wallace Struble to Hannah, November 8, 1862; *Millstone Mirror,* November 20, 1862; Haines, *Fifteenth,* 19–20.

3. Haines, *Fifteenth,* 19–20; *Millstone Mirror,* November 20, 1862; Bilby, *Three,* 26; *Newton Register,* November 21, 1862; Paul Kuhn to brother, November 10, 1862; *Hunterdon Gazette,* November 19, December 2, 1862; Elmer diary, November 7, 9, 1862; Halsey diary, November 9, 10, 11, 1862; Oscar Westlake to father, November 10, 1862; Quincy Grimes to sister, undated.

4. Baquet, *Kearny's,* 58, 59; Halsey diary, November 16, 18, 1862; Haines, *Fifteenth,* 21; David Anthony to William Apgar, November 6, 1863, Hunterdon County Historical Society; Judd diary, November 16, 1862; Harrison diary, November 17, 1862; Bilby, *Three,* 31.

5. Baquet, *Kearny's,* 58, 59; Haines, *Fifteenth,* 21; Kuhn to brother, November 10, 1862; Judd diary, November 23, 27, December 5, 1862; Halsey diary, November 27, 1862.

6. Judd diary, December 8, 1862; Haines, *Fifteenth,* 22; Halsey diary, December 4, 1862; Jonathan Hutchinson to cousin, December 11, 1862; David Anthony to William Apgar, December 9, 1862; Henry Ryerson to sister, December 7, 1862.
   Assistant Surgeon Robert Elmer reported 122 sick men in the brigade on December 11 (Elmer diary, December 11, 1862).

7. *Hunterdon Gazette,* December 10, 1862; Baquet, *Kearny's,* 59; Halsey diary, December 10, 1862; "The 4th N. J. at Fredericksburg," *West Philadelphia Hospital Register,* April 11, 1863, 33.

8. *OR,* ser. 1, vol. 21, p. 59; Haines, *Fifteenth,* 25–27.

9. George C. Rable, *Fredericksburg! Fredericksburg!* (Chapel Hill: Univ. of North Carolina Press, 2002), 157, 191; Baquet, *Kearny's,* 63–64; Henry Ryerson to sister, November 21, 1862; Henry Callan to sister, December 9, 1862.

10. Judd diary, December 11, 1862; Baquest, *Kearny's,* 22, 60; Haines, *Fifteenth,* 28–29, 26–27; Judd diary, December 11, 12, 1862; Halsey diary, December 12, 1862; *Newton Register,* December 26, 1862; Henry Callan to sister, October 2, 1862; Charles Lockwood to parents, December 24, 1862, Joseph Bilby Private Collection.

11. "The 4th N. J. at Fredericksburg," *West Philadelphia Hospital Register,* 33; *Hunterdon Republican,* December 26, 1862; Haines, *Fifteenth,* 29–30; Oscar Westlake to father, December 17, 1862; John Laughton to brother, December 14, 1862; Henry Ryerson to sister, December 19, 1862; Baquet, *Kearny's,* 224; *OR,* ser. 1, vol. 31, pp. 526–528, 662; *Newton Register,* December 26, 1862; Henry Callan to sister, December 24, 1862; Frank O'Reilly, *Stonewall Jackson at Fredericksburg* (Lynchburg, Va.: H. E. Howard, 1993), 168–169; Bilby, *Three,* 37.

12. *OR,* ser. 1, vol. 31, pp. 526, 528; Bilby, *Three,* 37; O'Reilly, *Stonewall,* 169.

13. Baquet, *Kearny's,* 227–228; Joseph G. Bilby, "Sunshine Soldiers," *Military Images* (January–February 1982): 23; Ryerson to sister, December 19, 1862; O'Reilly, *Stonewall,* 170.

14. Ryerson to sister, December 19, 1862; *OR,* ser. 1, vol. 31, pp. 526, 528, 624; Bilby, "Sunshine Soldiers," 23; O'Reilly, *Stonewall,* 172; Oscar Westlake to father, December 17, 1862; Judd diary, December 13, 1862.

15. *OR,* ser. 1, vol. 31, pp. 140, 528; Judd diary, December 14, 16, 1862; Halsey diary, December 16, 1862; Callan to sister, December 24, 1862; *Newton Register,* February 20, 1863.

16. *OR,* ser. 1, vol. 31, p. 624; "The 4th N. J. at Fredericksburg," *West Philadelphia Hospital Register,* 40; Wallace Struble to Hannah, December 27, 1862.

17. Ryerson to sister, December 19, 1862; *Newton Register,* February 20, 1863; Halsey diary, December 3, 19, 1862.

18. Baquet, *Kearny's,* 69, 229; Haines, *Fifteenth,* 37; *Hunterdon Gazette,* January 9, 16, 1863; Jonathan Hutchinson to cousin, January 7, 1863; Oscar Westlake to brother, December 26, 1862; Judd diary, December 25, 26, 1862; John Laughton to friend John, January 1, 1863; Edmund Halsey to sister, January 3, February 14, 1863; Halsey diary, January 2, 1863.

19. *Hunterdon Republican,* January 16, 23, 1863; Edmund Halsey to sister, January 3, 1863; Baquet, *Kearny's,* 71; Quincy Grimes to mother, January 11, 1863; Dayton Flint to sister, December 28, 1862.

20. Haines, *Fifteenth,* 38; *Hunterdon Republican,* February 6, 1863; Dayton Flint to sister, December 28, 1862; Halsey diary, January 20, 1863; *Newton Register,* February 20, 1863.
21. Rable, *Fredericksburg!* 409, 413; Haines, *Fifteenth,* 38–40; *Newton Register,* February 20, 1863; Baquet, *Kearny's,* 229; John Laughton to brother, undated.
22. *Newton Register,* February 20, 1863; Haines, *Fifteenth,* 40; Edmund Halsey to sister, January 28, 1863; Dayton Flint to sister, January 27, February 1, 1863; *Hunterdon Republican,* February 27, 1863.
23. Quincy Grimes to mother, March 11, 1863; Henry Ryerson to sister, January 13, 1863.
24. Dayton Flint to sisters, February 15, 23, 1863.
25. Dayton Flint to sisters, February 23, March 3, 1863; Baquet, *Kearny's,* 71, 74; Quincy Grimes to mother, February 28, 1863; Quincy Grimes to sister, March 22, 1863; *Hunterdon Republican,* February 27, 1863; Halsey diary, April 3, 1863.

    The men were preoccupied with their maneuvers. Jonathan Hutchinson noted "we done our best to keep a straight line when we went past him, and we done it." (Jonathan Hutchinson to cousin, March 6, 1863).
26. *Newton Register,* April 24, 1863; *Paterson Guardian,* February 18, 1863; Halsey diary, February 2, 1863; *Hunterdon Republican,* February 13, 1863.
27. *Hunterdon Republican,* February 13, 1863; Quincy Grimes to sister, February 21, 1863; Wallace Struble to Hannah, March 17, 1863; Quincy Grimes to mother, February 28, 1863; Hough, *Letters,* 16; *Camden Democrat,* January 10, 1863; *Camden Press,* March 11, 1863; *New Jersey Herald,* March 12, 1863; *Sussex Register,* March 27, 1863.
28. Hough, *Letters,* 14, 15, 18, 21, 26; *Paterson Guardian,* February 18, 1863; Dayton Flint to sisters, March 15, 1863; Halsey diary, February 24, 1863; *Hunterdon Republican,* March 20, 27, 1863; John Laughton to father, February 27, 1863; *Newton Register,* April 24, 1863; Baquet, *Kearny's,* 72.
29. Ryerson to sister, January 13, 1863; *Paterson Guardian,* February 18, 1863.
30. Baquet, *Kearny's,* 71, 230; *Newark Daily Advertiser,* April 22, 1863; *Hunterdon Republican,* February 27, March 20, 1863; Hough, *Letters,* 16; Newton *Register,* March 27, April 24, 1863; *Newton Herald,* April 30, 1863.

    Fowler never completely recovered from his illness, finally dying in 1865 (Bilby, *Three,* 43).
31. *Newton Register,* May 1, 1863; Halsey diary, April 21, 1863; *Hunterdon Republican,* May 1, 1863.
32. Sifakis, *Who Was Who,* 228; *Newton Herald,* April 30, 1863; *Newton Register,* April 24, 1863; *Hunterdon Republican,* April 3, 1863; Edmund Halsey to sister, March 25, 1863; Wallace Struble to Hannah, April 26, 1863; Halsey diary, February 24, 1863.
33. Halsey to sister, March 25, 1863; Jonathan Hutchinson to cousin, March 6, 1863; Quincy Grimes to sister, April 9, 1863; Quincy Grimes to brother, March 12, 1863; *Hunterdon Republican,* April 17, 1863.

    Torbert's first attempt to become a general officer was rejected by the Senate, causing Colonel Henry Ryerson to worry that the brigade would lose him. "If any officer ever deserved promotion, Torbert does. He has won it . . . every officer in the Brigade has signed a petition supporting his appointment and confirmation" (Henry Ryerson to sister, March 6, 1863).

34. *Hunterdon Republican,* April 24, 1863; Paul Kuhl to Dick, April 8, 1863; Quincy Grimes to sister, April 9, 1863.

35. Judd diary, April 11, 1863; *The Burlington Dollar Newspaper,* April 25, 1863.

36. Baquet, *Kearny's,* 72; *Newark Daily Advertiser,* April 22, 1863; *Hunterdon Republican,* May 1, 1863; *Sussex Register,* May 8, 1863; Paul Kuhl to Mattie, April 26, 1863.

37. Haines, *Fifteenth,* 48; Baquet, *Kearny's,* 75; *Hunterdon Republican,* May 8, 1863.

CHAPTER 6   *Chancellorsville and Gettysburg*

1. Ernest B. Furgurson, *Chancellorsville 1863* (New York: Vintage Library, 1993), 65; Foster, *Rebellion,* 98; Baquet, *Kearny's,* 75; *Hunterdon Republican,* May 15, 1863.

2. Foster, *Rebellion,* 98, 102; *Hunterdon Republican,* May 8, 1863; Halsey diary, April 29, 30, 1863; *Newton Register,* May 22, 1863; Haines, *Fifteenth,* 49; Baquet, *Kearny's,* 77; Joseph G. Bilby, "Seeing the Elephant," *Military Images* (January–February 1984): 10.

3. *OR,* ser. 1, vol. 25, pt. 1, p. 164; Halsey diary, May 1, 1863.

4. Baquet, *Kearny's,* 77–78; Haines, *Fifteenth,* 50.

5. *OR,* ser. 1, vol. 25, p. 573; Judd diary, May 3, 1863; *Hunterdon Republican,* May 8, 1863.

6. Stephen W. Sears, *Chancellorsville* (Boston: Houghton Mifflin, 1996), 352–357; Phineas Skellenger to brother, May 1863, John Kuhl Collection; *OR,* ser. 1, vol. 25, pp. 570, 574; Baquet, *Kearny's,* 78; Foster, *Rebellion,* 103; *Newark Daily Advertiser,* May 16, 1863.

7. Sears, *Chancellorsville,* 381; *OR,* ser. 1, vol. 25, pp. 570, 856–857; Baquet, *Kearny's,* 231.

8. Baquet, *Kearny's,* 79; Bilby, "Seeing," 8; Quincy Grimes to mother, May 5, 1863; *OR,* ser. 1, vol. 25, pp. 570–571; Judd diary, May 3, 1863; *Newark Daily Advertiser,* May 16, 1863; Baquet, *Kearny's,* 79.

9. *OR,* ser. 1, vol. 25, pt. 1, pp. 568, 571, 581, 858; Sears, *Chancellorsville,* 380–382.

10. *OR,* ser. 1, vol. 25, pt. 1, pp. 571, 575; Judd diary, May 3, 1863; Halsey diary, May 3, 1863.

11. Baquet, *Kearny's,* 79; Sears, *Chancellorsville,* 382; Edmund English to brother, May 6, 1863, Huntington Library, 1151 Oxford Road, San Marino, California; *OR,* ser. 1, vol. 25, pp. 571, 572, 574; Haines, *Fifteenth,* 54; Hamilton to father, May 5, 1863; Halsey diary, May 3, 1863.

12. *OR,* ser. 1, vol. 25, p. 571; Foster, *Rebellion,* 508; *OR,* ser. 1, vol. 25, p. 571; Baquet, *Kearny's,* 79–80, 242, 244.

13. *OR,* ser. 1, vol. 25, pp. 571, 572, 858; Dobbins, "Fragments," 33; Foster, *Rebellion,* 103; David D. Furman, "Ordeal by Fire," An Address by David D. Furman at the Rededication of the Salem Church Battle Monument by the New Jersey Civil War Centennial Commission (Trenton: State of New Jersey Civil War Centennial Commission, May 6, 1961); Baquet, *Kearny's,* 80, 242.

14. Baquet, *Kearny's,* 242–243; *OR,* ser. 1, vol. 25, p. 858; Dobbins, "Fragments," 33; Foster, *Rebellion,* 509.

15. *OR,* ser. 1, vol. 25, pp. 568, 572, 859; Bilby, "Seeing," 11; Judd diary, May 3, 1863; Augustus Woodbury, *The Second Rhode Island Regiment* (Providence, R.I.: Valpey, Angell and Co., 1875), 170; Bilby, *Three,* 70–71.

16. Baquet, *Kearny's,* 82, 245; Halsey, May 3, 1863; Paul Kuhl to brother, May 8, 1863; Bilby, "Seeing," 11; *OR,* ser. 1, vol. 25, pp. 574, 806; Skellenger to brother, May 6, 1863; Judd diary, May 3, 1863.

    The Twenty-third NJV veterans endeared themselves to their old foes when they unveiled their monument on the battlefield on May 3, 1907. One tablet's inscription recognized the "Brave Boys of the South" (Baquet, *Kearny's,* 261).

17. *New York Herald,* May 9, 1863; A. C. Yeomans to pastor, May 17, 1863, New Jersey Historical Society; Paul Kuhl to brother, May 8, 1863; Joseph B. Mitchell, *The Badge of Gallantry* (New York: Macmillan, 1968), 172–176.

18. *OR,* ser. 1, vol. 25, pp. 572, 574, 577; Halsey diary, May 4, 8, 1863; Foster, *Rebellion,* 509; Skellenger to brother, May 1863; Baquet, *Kearny's,* 85; Sears, *Chancellorsville,* 410–419; Bilby, *Three,* 74; Haines, *Fifteenth,* 59–60.

19. Quincy Grimes to sister, Mary 28, June 3, 1863; *Hunterdon Republican,* May 29, 1863; Paul Kuhl to sister, June 2, 1863; Paul Kuhl to brother, May 18, 1863.

20. *Hunterdon Republican,* May 22, 29, June 5, 19, 1863; Paul Kuhl to sister, May 11, 1863; Sifakis, *Who Was Who,* 77, 732.

21. A. C. Yeomans to pastor, May 17, 1863; Oscar Westlake to brother, May 24, 1863; Quincy Grimes to sister, May 28, 1863; Paul Kuhl to sister, May 23, 1863.

22. Bradley M. Gottfried, *Roads to Gettysburg* (Shippensburg, Pa.: White Mane, 2002), 6–19; *OR,* ser. 1, vol. 27, pt. 3, pp. 12–13.

23. *OR,* ser. 1, vol. 27, pt. 3, pp. 12–13; Haines, *Fifteenth,* 68–69; Baquet, *Kearny's,* 89.

24. Foster, *Rebellion,* 511–512; Haines, *Fifteenth,* 69; *Hunterdon Republican,* June 19, 1863; Halsey diary, June 8, 1863.

25. Haines, *Fifteenth,* 69–70; Halsey diary, June 9, 1863; Dobbins, "Fragments," 34; Oscar Westlake to mother, June 12, 1863; Harrison diary, June 18, 1863; Paul Kuhl to brother, May 18, June 9, 1863; Paul Kuhl to sister, June 10, 1863.

26. Halsey diary, June 12, 1863; Hough, *Letters,* 36; Phineas Skellenger to brother, June 21, 1863; Haines, *Fifteenth,* 70–71; Bilby, *Three,* 80–81; Baquet, *Kearny's,* 90; Gottfried, *Roads,* 41–42, 53.

27. Halsey diary, June 14, 15, 1863; Hough, *Letter,* 37; Haines, *Fifteenth,* 72–73; *Hunterdon Republican,* June 26, 1863; Quincy Grimes to father, June 18, 1863.

    This was the last complete letter that Grimes would write. An uncontrollable case of diarrhea in mid-July caused his death on September 8, 1863. Edmund Halsey called him a "quiet well behaved soldier—obedient to orders and much esteemed by all his comrades" (Halsey to sister, September 8, 1863).

28. Haines, *Fifteenth,* 73, 75; Oscar Westlake to mother, June 21, 1863; Gottfried, *Roads,* 143, 151; Halsey diary, June 27, 1863; Hough, *Letters,* 41.

29. Haines, *Fifteenth,* 76, 79, 91; Halsey diary, June 29, 30, 1863; Baquet, *Kearny's,* 91; Bradley M. Gottfried, *Brigades of Gettysburg* (New York: DaCapo Press, 2002), 285–286; *Hunterdon Republican,* July 8, 1863; *OR,* ser. 1, vol. 27, pt. 1, p. 162.

30. Gottfried, *Brigades*, 286; F. W. Morse, *Personal Experiences in the War of the Rebellion* (Albany, N.Y.: Munsell Printer, 1866), 33–34; Halsey diary, July 2, 1863; *OR*, ser. 1, vol. 27, pt. 1, p. 668; *Hunterdon Republican*, July 10, 17, 1863; Haines, *Fifteenth*, 79–80, 98.

31. *Hunterdon Republican*, July 17, 1863; Halsey diary, July 2, 1863; Haines, *Fifteenth*, 85, 87; *OR*, ser. 1, vol. 27, pt. 1, pp. 665, 668; Baquet, *Kearny's*, 91–93.

32. Halsey diary, July 3, 1863; Baquet, *Kearny's*, 91–92, 98, 208, 397–398; *OR*, ser. 1, vol. 27, pt. 1, p. 669; Haines, *Fifteenth*, 92; Harrison diary, July 3, 1863.

33. Haines, *Fifteenth*, 94–95; Ellis Hamilton to father, July 17, 1863; Baquet, *Kearny's*, 97; Dayton Flint to sisters, *Washington Star*, February 22, 1911; Phineas Skellenger to brother, July 10, 1863; *Hunterdon Republican*, July 24, 1863; Ellis Hamilton to mother, July 9, 1863.

34. *OR*, ser. 1, vol. 27, pt. 1, pp. 669–670; Halsey diary, July 5, 6, 8, 1863; Haines, *Fifteenth*, 98, 99–100; Hough, *Letters*, 44, 45; *Hunterdon Republican*, July 31, 1863; Hamilton Ellis to father, July 17, 1863.

35. Haines, *Fifteenth*, 100–101, 102; *OR*, ser. 1, vol. 27, pt. 1, pp. 668–670; Oscar Westlake to mother, July 11, 1863; *Hunterdon Republican*, July 31, 1863.

36. Brown, "Experiences," 14; Paul Kuhl to sister, June 18, 1863; Baquet, *Kearny's*, 278.

37. Baquet, *Kearny's*, 279, 235, 280–281; Foster, *Rebellion*, 512–513.

38. Paul Kuhl to sister, July 11, 1863.

Chapter 7   *The Fall Campaign of 1863 and the Winter of 1863–1864*

1. Haines, *Fifteenth*, 103–104; Paul Kuhl to sister, July 20, 26, 1863; Halsey diary, July 20, 22–26, 31, August 1, 1863; Phineas Skellenger to brother, July 31, 1863; Bilby, *Three*, 93; *Sussex Register*, September 4, 1863; Oscar Westlake to father and mother, July 28, 1863; *Hunterdon Republican*, August 28, 1863.

2. Haines, *Fifteenth*, 104; Halsey diary, August 2, 1863; Brown, "Experiences," 14; *New Jersey Herald*, September 10, 1863; Samuel Cavileer to Mr. Ashley, August 9, 1863, Atlantic County Historical Society.

3. Dayton Flint to sisters, *Washington Star*, February 23, 1911; Halsey diary, August 7, 1863; *Hunterdon Republican*, August 28, 1863; Paul Kuhl to sister, August 26, September 3, 1863.

4. Paul Kuhl to sister, August 3, 5, 19, 1863; *Hunterdon Republican*, September 11, 1863, February 25, 1864; Halsey diary, August 4, 8, 1863.

   Lieutenant William Vanvoy was the officer disciplined for disregarding orders. He forfeited $50 pay per month for six months—a hefty fine in those days when an enlisted man received $15 a month. Vanvoy was so incensed that he took the unusual step of publicizing his side of the story in the *Newton Herald*, calling it "an outrage upon me, and I am willing to submit the matter to the judgment of my friends."

5. Phineas Skellenger to brother, July 31, 1863; Paul Kuhl to sister, September 2, 1863; *Hunterdon Republican*, March 14, 1864.

6. Paul Kuhl to sister, September 3, 1863; Halsey diary, August 5, 10, 14, 1863; *Hunterdon Republican*, August 28, 1863; David Anthony to William Apgar, August 20, 1863.

7. Haines, *Fifteenth*, 107–108; Wallace Struble to Hannah, October 28, 1863; Brown, "Experiences," 14–15; *New Jersey Herald*, September 10, 1863; Oscar Westlake to father, April 16, 1864; Halsey diary, September 3, 1863; *Hunterdon Republican*, August 28, 1863; Phineas Skellenger to brother, July 28, 1863.

8. *Hunterdon Republican*, August 28, 1863; Haines, *Fifteenth*, 109; Hough, *Letters*, 56–57; Bilby, *Three*, 95; Baquet, *Kearny's*, 100; Halsey diary, September 15, 17, 1863.

9. Henry Callan to sister, November 17, 1863; Styple, *Death*, 31; *Hunterdon Republican*, October 2, 1863; Halsey diary, September 22, 23, 1863; Haines, *Fifteenth*, 109; *Camden Press*, October 17, 1863.

10. *Hunterdon Republican*, October 2, 1863; Halsey diary, September 27–31, 1863; *Paterson Press*, October 10, 1863; Haines, *Fifteenth*, 109; Oscar Westlake to mother, October 9, 1863.

11. *Hunterdon Republican*, October 16, 23, 1863; Hough, *Letters*, 60, 61; Callan to sister, November 17, 1863; Bilby, *Three*, 97; Haines, *Fifteenth*, 111; Halsey diary, October 8, 1863.

12. Callan to sister, November 17, 1863; Baquet, *Kearny's*, 100–101; Haines, *Fifteenth*, 112–113; *Washington Star*, February 23, 1911.

13. Baquet, *Kearny's*, 100–101; Callan to sister, November 17, 1863; Haines, *Fifteenth*, 112–113; Ellis Hamilton to mother, October 17, 1863.

14. Haines, *Fifteenth*, 14–15; Paul Kuhl to sister, October 26, 1863; *Hunterdon Republican*, November 6, 13, 1863; Baquet, *Kearny's*, 101; Ellis Hamilton to mother, November 4, 1863.

15. Martin F. Graham and George F. Skoch, *Mine Run* (Lynchburg, Va.: H. E. Howard, 1987), 20–29; Haines, *Fifteenth*, 115–118; *Hunterdon Republican*, November 27, December 4, 1863; Baquet, *Kearny's*, 103.

16. *Hunterdon Republican*, December 4, 1863; Callan to sister, November 17, 1863.

17. Paul Kuhl to sister, November 24, December 4, 1863; Haines, *Fifteenth*, 118; Baquet, *Kearny's*, 103–104; Halsey diary, November 28, 29, 1863; Judd diary, November 28, 1863.

18. Haines, *Fifteenth*, 120; Judd diary, November 30, 1863; *Washington Star*, February 23, 1911; Paul Kuhl to brother, December 4, 1863; *Hunterdon Republican*, December 11, 1863; Baquet, *Kearny's*, 107–108; Halsey diary, November 30, 1863.

19. Baquet, *Kearny's*, 108; Kuhl to brother, December 4, 1863; Ellis Hamilton to aunt, December 6, 1863; Haines, *Fifteenth*, 120–121.

20. *Hunterdon Republican*, December 18, 1863; Haines, *Fifteenth*, 123; Paul Kuhl to sister, February 7, 1864.

According to Reverend Haines, public opinion was against the army going into winter quarters, so no official orders were issued (Haines, *Fifteenth*, 122).

21. *Hunterdon Republican*, December 18, 1863, January 8, 1864.

22. Kuhl to sister, January 27, 1864; Baquet, *Kearny's*, 109.

23. *Hunterdon Republican*, January 1, 1864; Bibly, *Jerseymen*, 82; Baquet, *Kearny's*, 398; Bilby, *Three*, 114–115; Paul Kuhl to sister, January 1, 1864; Halsey diary, January 24, 1864.

24. Oscar Westlake to mother, October 9, 1863; Brown, "Experiences," 16.

25. Baquet, *Kearny's,* 398; Halsey diary, January 7, 8, 1864; Bruce Chadwick, *Brother against Brother* (New York: Carol Group, 1997), 192–193.

26. Paul Kuhl to brother, February 16, 1864; Paul Kuhl to sister, April 13, 1864; *Sussex Register,* March 25, 1864; Halsey diary, January 13, 21, February 12, 1864; *Hunterdon Republican,* January 22, 1864; William Penrose to Adjutant General, February 1, 1864, Bound Regimental Records, 15th N.J., National Archives.

27. Haines, *Fifteenth,* 123–125; Paul Kuhl to sister, March 11, 1864; *Hunterdon Republican,* January 29, 1864.

28. *Hunterdon Republican,* March 18, 1864; Halsey diary, February 7, 10, 1864.

29. Paul Kuhl to sister, January 29, February 21, 1864; Ellis Hamilton to mother, February 11, 24, 1864; Halsey diary, February 12, 1864; Phineas Skellenger to brother, February 26, 1864.

30. Oscar Westlake to mother, February 5, 1864; Haines, *Fifteenth,* 126; Paul Kuhl to sister, February 7, 1864; Halsey diary, February 6, 1864; Phineas Skellenger to brother, February 6, 1864.

31. Halsey diary, February 27–29, 1863; Haines, *Fifteenth,* 126–129; *Washington Star,* March 9, 1911; Paul Kuhl to sister, March 5, 1864.

32. Halsey diary, March 2, 1864; *Washington Star,* March 9, 1911; *Hunterdon Republican,* March 4, 1864; Kuhl to sister, March 5, 1864; Haines, *Fifteenth,* 131.

33. Paul Kuhl to sister, March 15, April 19, 1864; *Washington Star,* February 23, 1911; *Newton Herald,* February 11, 1864; Hough, *Letters,* 90; *Hunterdon Republican,* March 14, 1864; Ellis Hamilton to mother, April 8, 1864.

34. Hough, *Letters,* 86; Halsey diary, April 10, 1864; Paul Kuhl to sister, April 13, 1864; Phineas Skellenger to brother, April 10, 1864; John Hutchinson to cousin, May 1, 1864; Foster, *Rebellion,* 107; Edmund Halsey to sister, April 4, 1864.

35. Ellis Hamilton to mother, April 8, 1864; Paul Kuhl to sister, March 19, April 13, 19, 1864; Oscar Westlake to father, March 19, 1864; Halsey diary, April 18, 1864; Phineas Skellenger to brother, April 24, 1864.

36. Halsey diary, April 19, 1864; Skellenger to brother, April 24, 1864; Haines, *Fifteenth,* 137; Foster, *Rebellion,* 267–268.

37. Joseph G. Bilby, "A Jersey Journey: Being the Perambulations of the 10th New Jersey Infantry, Late Olden's Legion," *Military Images* (March–April 1995): 6, 8; Foster, *Rebellion,* 268–270; William Cazier to Joseph, November 14, 1862, Gandy Collection, Atlantic County Historical Society; *Sussex Register,* June 12, 1863.

38. Bilby, "Journey," 9–10; Foster, *Rebellion,* 270–271; *Trenton True American,* February 2, 1864; Edmund Halsey to sister, April 30, 1864.

39. "Official Report on Colonel Mann's Improved Infantry Accoutrements," copy in the Bilby Collection; Haines, *Fifteenth,* 134–136.

40. Hutchinson to cousin, May 1, 1864; Edmund Halsey to sister, April 29, 1864.

CHAPTER 8   *The Wilderness and Spotsylvania*

1. Henry Ryerson to sister, May 3, 1864; Haines, *Fifteenth,* 140; Baquet, *Kearny's,* 111–112.

2. Gordon C. Rhea, *The Battle of the Wilderness* (Baton Rouge: Louisiana State

Univ. Press, 1994), 51–55; Foster, *Rebellion,* 107; *OR,* ser. 1, vol. 36, pt. 1, p. 111.

3. Baquet, *Kearny's,* 112–113; Haines, *Fifteenth,* 140–141; John B. Hoffman, *The Civil War Diary and Letters of John Bacon Hoffman of Shiloh, New Jersey* (Plainfield, N.J.: Seventh Day Baptist Publishing House, 1979), 6; Styple, *Andersonville,* 52–53.

4. Haines, *Fifteenth,* 141; Baquet, *Kearny's,* 113.

5. Rhea, *Wilderness,* 63–64, 137; Haines, *Fifteenth,* 143.

6. Halsey diary, May 5, 1864; Halsey to sister, May 19, 1864; Rhea, *Wilderness,* 178–179; *OR,* ser. 1, vol. 36, pt. 1, pp. 660, 665; Edward Steere, *The Wilderness Campaign* (Harrisburg, Pa.: Stackpole, 1960), 244; Baquet, *Kearny's,* 114; Unknown Sussex County newspaper, Bilby Collection; Foster, *Rebellion,* 108.

7. Halsey diary, May 5, 1865; Charles R. Paul, "Campaign of 1864," Murray S. Smith Collection, U.S. Army Military History Institute, 1–2; Judd diary, May 5, 1865; *OR,* ser. 1, vol. 36, pt. 1, p. 736.

8. Baquet, *Kearny's,* 114; Haines, *Fifteenth,* 145.

9. Judd diary, May 5, 1865; *OR,* ser. 1, vol. 36, pt. 1, p. 663; Styple, *Death,* 42–43; Paul, "Campaign," 2.

10. Styple, *Death,* 193; *OR,* ser. 1, vol. 36, pt. 1, pp. 664–665; Baquet, *Kearny's,* 115; Rhea, *Wilderness,* 177, 181.

11. Haines, *Fifteenth,* 146; Styple, *Death,* 43; Baquet, *Kearny's,* 115–116, 211; Paul, "Campaign," 2; Judd diary, May 6, 1864.

12. Ellis Hamilton to father, May 13, 1864; Baquet, *Kearny's,* 117, 211.
Ellis was surrounded by adoring family members and initially fared well. His aunt wrote on May 12, "Good news for you; I have seen Ellis at the officer's Hospital [in] Georgetown; he is doing finely and in elegant spirits . . . is full of joke and laughter." Ellis wrote his father that the bullet made four holes "and [I] expect to walk in a week or so when I shall try & get home." That would never happen. On May 16, his aunt again wrote home, "Poor Ellis has gone to Heaven!" An artery began hemorrhaging again, and when efforts failed to staunch its blood flow, the doctors considered amputation. It was too late. Ellis had lost too much blood. His last words were, "Get me a drink of good water before I go," and then after drinking some, he said, "Goodbye," and laid his arms at his sides and died (Fanny to sister, May 12, 16, 1864; Ellis Hamilton to father, May 13, 1864).

13. Haines, *Fifteenth,* 148–149; *OR,* ser. 1, vol. 36, pt. 1, p. 663; Harrison diary, May 6, 1864; Styple, *Death,* 44–45.
There are several versions of Ryerson's wounding. According to Joseph Bilby, Ryerson was merely assessing the situation in front of him when he was struck. John Foster believed that Ryerson was also assessing the situation prior to the Confederate attack, but was struck by a sharpshooter's bullet (Bilby, *Jerseymen,* 170; Foster, *Rebellion,* 271–272).

14. Baquet, *Kearny's,* 117; Haines, *Fifteenth,* 148, 151.

15. *OR,* ser. 1, vol. 36, pt. 1, pp. 126, 663; Haines, *Fifteenth,* 153.

16. Halsey to sister, May 19, 1864; Robert Proudfit to Reverend E. R. Craven, May 7, 1864, Rutgers University; Brown, "Experiences," 17.

17. *OR,* ser. 1, vol. 35, pt. 1, p. 666.

18. Haines, *Fifteenth,* 156–157; Halsey diary, May 8, 1864; Foster, *Rebellion,* 395; Baquet, *Kearny's,* 119; William D. Matter, *If It Takes All Summer* (Chapel Hill: Univ. of North Carolina Press, 1988), 87.

19. Foster, *Rebellion,* 110, 397; Haines, *Fifteenth,* 158, 167; Halsey diary, May 8, 1864; Baquet, *Kearny's,* 119; Halsey diary, May 8, 1864; Gordon C. Rhea, *The Battles for Spotsylvania Court House and the Road to Yellow Tavern, May 7–12, 1864* (Baton Rouge: Louisiana State Univ. Press, 1977), 82.

20. Foster, *Rebellion,* 111, 272–273, 398; Halsey diary, May 8, 1864; Charles Paul diary, U.S. Army Military History Institute, May 8, 1864; Haines, *Fifteenth,* 159, 160–161; *Trenton Gazette,* May 20, 1864; Phineas Skellenger to father, no date; Elias Skellenger to father, May 24, 27, 1864; Baquet, *Kearny's,* 119; Bilby, "Perambulations," 11; Hoffman, *Diary,* 7, 26; Matter, *All Summer,* 91.

    According to historian William Matter, the Tenth NJV was detached and linked up with Crawford's Division. This is doubtful (Matter, *All Summer,* 91).

    The men of the Tenth NJV captured on May 8 were transported south, and when about the entrain for Richmond at Beaver Dam Station, John Hoffman heard the guards yell, "The Yanks are coming." The captors then fled as General Sheridan's cavalry arrived and rescued the men. The former prisoners subsequently returned to their units on May 26 (Foster, *Rebellion,* 111; Hoffman, *Diary,* 7–8).

21. Foster, *Rebellion,* 112; Haines, *Fifteenth,* 161–162; Halsey diary, May 9, 1864; Baquet, *Kearny's,* 121; Judd diary, May 9, 1864.

    The men were unhappy with their new division commander. "when Gen. Wright had command of our Div. we were willing to go anywhere being satisfied that his judgment was good—but since Russell commands it they have been so miserably handled," noted Sergeant Andrew Yeoman of the Fifteenth NJV. Yeoman did like his brigade commander. "Col Penrose . . . is a good soldier & knows his business." He saved his greatest praise for Lieutenant Colonel Campbell, who he felt, "saved the 15th from capture or annihilation" on May 8 (A. C. Yeoman to pastor, July 5, 1864, New Jersey Historical Society).

22. Haines, *Fifteenth,* 161; Paul diary, May 9, 1864; Halsey diary, May 9, 1864; Baquet, *Kearny's,* 121; Matter, *All Summer,* 127.

    Curiously, none of the histories from the period expound on the reasons for Brown's removal.

23. Foster, *Rebellion,* 113; Paul diary, May 10, 1864; Haines, *Fifteenth,* 165; Halsey diary, May 10, 1864; Matter, *All Summer,* 127–128.

    General Upton did not mention the three regiments in his battle report, but the veterans were adamant about their presence. They probably were on the picket line through which Upton's men passed (*OR,* ser. 1, vol. 36, pt. 1, p. 667; Bilby, *Remember,* 85).

24. Baquet, *Kearny's,* 123; Paul diary, May 11, 1864; Haines, *Fifteenth,* 172.

25. Matter, *All Summer,* 219; Foster, *Rebellion,* 114–115, 399; Halsey diary, May 12, 1864; Peter S. Carmichael, "We Respect a *Good* Soldier, No Matter What Flag He Fought Under," in *The Spotsylvania Campaign,* ed. Gary Gallagher (Chapel Hill: Univ. of North Carolina Press, 1998), 209.

    At least some of the men of the First NJV apparently got tangled up and lost in the pine thickets and did not participate in the attack (Bilby, *Remember,* 87).

Edmund Halsey insisted that the brigade attacked in a single line, but the high losses to the Third NJV suggest otherwise (Halsey to sister, May 19, 1864).

26. Carmichael, "Respect," 209; Foster, *Rebellion,* 115, 401; Halsey diary, May 12, 1864; Robert W. Patrick, *Knapsack and Rifle* (New York: W. H. Lewis and Company, 1889), 335.

27. Foster, *Rebellion,* 115, 401–402; Paul diary, May 12, 1864; Haines, *Fifteenth,* 176–178; Carmichael, "Respect," 208.

The Fourteenth Georgia's flag was apparently captured when a German soldier in the Fifteenth NJV turned while returning to the regiment's starting position, stormed back toward the enemy, grabbed the flag, and ran back with it. He returned unhurt, but he had a hole in his hat and three in his shirt. The soldier was later promoted to the rank of lieutenant but was killed in a subsequent battle (John H. White, "He Got the Flag: The Desperate Charge of a Jerseyman at Spotsylvania," *National Tribune,* January 20, 1887).

28. Haines, *Fifteenth,* 180; Jim Bullock to Dick, May 16, 1864, Kuhl Collection; *Belvedere Intelligencer,* June 10, 1864; John P. Beach, "Company B at Spotsylvania," *National Tribune,* in Styple, *Death,* 191–193; Bilby, *Remember,* 87; Matter, *All Summer,* 221–222.

Beach entered the service with his father on August 9, 1861, and fought with him until the latter was mustered out of service on May 11, 1864. Beach was only sixteen years old when he joined the army (*Evening Times,* April 29, 1969).

29. Paul diary, May 12, 1864; Joseph Bilby, "Savage Spring," *Military Images* (September–October, 1979): 10; Haines, *Fifteenth,* 178; Beach, "Company B"; Oscar Westlake to father, May 15, 1864.

The brigade historian wrote that the brigade remained at the breastworks until 2:00 P.M.; other authors have suggested that at least some of the units, like the Fifteenth NJV, were pulled back much sooner (Baquet, *Kearny's,* 125).

Realizing their vulnerability, none of the men would volunteer for the color guard, until they were promised promotion to the rank of corporal (Halsey diary, May 13, 1864).

30. Bullock to Dick, May 16, 1864; *Trenton Gazette,* May 20, 1864; Haines, *Fifteenth,* 179–181; Hough, *Letters,* 12; Patrick, *Knapsack,* 337; Paul diary, May 12, 1864; Halsey diary, May 12, 1864.

Jacob Apgar, whose letters have also been used in this work, was also killed during this action.

31. Chadwick, *Brother,* 227; Halsey diary, May 13, 1863; Matter, *All Summer,* 253.

32. Haines, *Fifteenth,* 181–183; Paul diary, May 13–14, 1864; Baquet, *Kearny's,* 126; *OR,* ser. 1, vol. 36, pt. 1, p. 670; Matter, *All Summer,* 285; Gordon C. Rhea, *To the North Anna* (Baton Rouge, La.: Louisiana State Univ. Press, 2000), 84–87; Harrison diary, May 14, 1864.

33. Haines, *Fifteenth,* 183–184; Halsey diary, May 15, 1863.

34. Halsey diary, May 17, 1863; Halsey to sister, May 19, 1864; Bilby, *Three,* 152; Haines, *Fifteenth,* 184–188; Paul diary, May 18–19, 1864.

35. Haines, *Fifteenth,* 188–189; Paul diary, May 21, 1864; *OR,* ser. 1, vol. 36, pt. 1, p. 144; Baquet, *Kearny's,* 128.

36. *Washington Star,* February 9, 1911; Joseph Sullivan to Mary Ewing, June 27, 1864, Mary Ewing Papers, Special Collections, Alexander Library, Rutgers University, New Brunswick, N.J.; Bilby, *Remember,* 88, 170; *Belvidere Intelligencer,* June 19, 1864; Bilby, *Three,* 152.

CHAPTER 9   *To Petersburg*

1. Haines, *Fifteenth,* 192–193; Bilby, *Three,* 153; Halsey diary, May 22, 1864.

2. Haines, *Fifteenth,* 193–194; Paul diary, May 23, 1864.

3. Gordon Rhea, *Cold Harbor* (Baton Rouge: Louisiana State Univ. Press, 2002), 6; Halsey diary, May 25, 1864; Haines, *Fifteenth,* 194–195; Paul diary, Mary 25, 1864.

4. Paul diary, May 26, 1864; Haines, *Fifteenth,* 195–196; Halsey diary, May 26, 27, 1864; Rhea, *Cold Harbor,* 24–25, 34.

5. Haines, *Fifteenth,* 196–197; Paul diary, May 28, 29, 1864; Foster, *Rebellion,* 117; Halsey diary, May 29, 30, 1864; A. C. Yeomans to pastor, July 5, 1864.

   In summarizing the Second NJV's activities, Corporal Charles Harrison estimated that it had marched 1,450 miles and crossed 11 mountain ranges, 23 rivers, and 118 railroads. It had passed through 130 towns and been in 22 general engagements and numerous skirmishes (Harrison diary).

   The return of the First, Second, and Third NJV created a stir. The Newark town leaders planned an elaborate celebration for the Second NJV. When the regiment appeared, the fire bell tower would be tapped twelve times and a host of dignitaries would guide the parade through the city (*Newark Daily Advertiser,* May 31, 1864). The organizers knew that the regiment reached Trenton on Sunday, June 5, but there was an "unavoidable disarrangement in the plan of transmitting intelligence" and the Second NJV suddenly marched into town at 4:00 P.M. that day. Anxious to see their loved ones, the regiment "did not wait for the formal reception . . . but marched up Broad Street preceded by their drum corps. . . . On reaching the new City Hall the regiment halted and Col. Buck . . . were welcomed home by Mayor Runyon" (*Newark Daily Advertiser,* June 6, 1864). The First and Third NJV reached Trenton at 11:00 P.M. on Tuesday, June 7—too late for a formal reception, save by the mayor of Trenton. The newspaper reported that the two regiments together numbered 340 men (*Hunterdon Republican,* June 10, 1864).

6. Haines, *Fifteenth,* 197–198.

7. *OR,* ser. 1, vol. 36, pt. 1, p. 159; Halsey diary, June 1, 1864; Haines, *Fifteenth,* 201.

8. Rhea, *Cold Harbor,* 225–226; Haines, *Fifteenth,* 201; Paul diary, June 1, 1864; Halsey diary, June 1, 1864.

9. Baquet, *Kearny's,* 131; Rhea, *Cold Harbor,* 254; Thomas J. Howe, *Wasted Valor* (Lynchburg, Va.: H. E. Howard, 1988), 10.

10. Haines, *Fifteenth,* 202; Baquet, *Kearny's,* 351; Rhea, *Cold Harbor,* 235; Louis Baltz, *The Battle of Cold Harbor* (Lynchburg, Va.: H. E. Howard, 1994), 87–88; Halsey diary, June 1, 1864; Paul diary, June 1, 1864.

11. Bilby, *Remember*, 88; Halsey diary, June 1, 1864; Rhea, *Cold Harbor*, 235–242; Howe, *Wasted Valor*, 9.

12. Haines, *Fifteenth*, 202–203, 207; Baquet, *Kearny's*, 131; Foster, *Rebellion*, 403.

13. Hoffman, *Diary*, 31; Haines, *Fifteenth*, 206–209; Halsey diary, June 2–3, 1864; Paul diary, June 2, 1864; Rhea, *Cold Harbor*, 242, 289–290.

14. Bilby, "Peramulations," 12; Foster, *Rebellion*, 272; Haines, *Fifteenth*, 209–210.

15. Baquet, *Kearny's*, 130; Foster, *Rebellion*, 117; Bilby, *Three*, 161; Haines, *Fifteenth*, 211–212; Halsey diary, June 4, 1864; Bilby, *Three*, 162; Paul diary, June 4, 1864.

16. Halsey diary, June 5, 1864; Haines, *Fifteenth*, 210–211; Hoffman, *Diary*, 32.

17. Baquet, *Kearny's*, 217; Foster, *Rebellion*, 403; Hoffman, *Diary*, 9; Haines, *Fifteenth*, 212.

18. Haines, *Fifteenth*, 212–213; Foster, *Rebellion*, 117.

19. Haines, *Fifteenth*, 212–214; Bilby, *Three*, 163; Halsey diary, June 8, 10, 1864.
    The two officers were dishonorably discharged on August 19, 1864 (Halsey diary, August 19, 1864).

20. Haines, *Fifteenth*, 214–215; Halsey diary, June 5, 12, 1864; *OR*, ser. 1, vol. 36, pt. 1, p. 172; Bilby, *Remember*, 88; Oscar Westlake to father, March 30, 1864; Howe, *Wasted Valor*, 10–11.

21. Haines, *Fifteenth*, 216–218; Halsey diary, June 13–16, 1864; Bilby, *Three*, 164; Howe, *Wasted Valor*, 14–15; Paul diary, June 13–14, 1864.

22. Haines, *Fifteenth*, 218–219; Halsey diary, June 17, 19 1864; Paul diary, June 16, 1864.

23. Haines, *Fifteenth*, 219–221; Halsey diary, June 21–24, 1864; John Horn, *Petersburg* (Conshohocken, Pa.: Combined Press, 1993), 75–83.

24. Haines, *Fifteenth*, 221; Halsey diary, June 29–30, July 1, 1864.

25. Haines, *Fifteenth*, 221–223; Halsey diary, July 2–10, 1864.

CHAPTER 10   *Washington and the Shenandoah Valley Campaign*

1. Baquet, *Kearny's*, 136–138; Haines, *Fifteenth*, 223, 226.

2. Haines, *Fifteenth*, 223, 225–226; Paul, "Campaign," 24; Halsey diary, July 11–12, 1864; Bilby, *Three*, 172

3. Paul, "Campaign," 24–25; Haines, *Fifteenth*, 227–228; Halsey diary, July 14, 1864.

4. Edmund Halsey to sister, July 15, 1864; Paul, "Campaign," 25–26; Baquet, *Kearny's*, 140; Halsey diary, July 16, 1864; Haines, *Fifteenth*, 228–229.

5. Haines, *Fifteenth*, 229–231; Halsey diary, July 18–19, 1864; Paul, "Campaign," 26–27.

6. Baquet, *Kearny's*, 141; Haines, *Fifteenth*, 231–232; Halsey diary, July 20, 1864.

7. Haines, *Fifteenth*, 232–234; Baquet, *Kearny's*, 142; Halsey diary, July 22, 25, 1864; Paul, "Campaign," 27–28.

8. Halsey diary, July 23, 1864; Haines, *Fifteenth*, 233–234; Baquet, *Kearny's*, 143; Paul, "Campaign," 28.

9. Paul, "Campaign," 28, 29; Haines, *Fifteenth*, 235–236; Halsey diary, August 27–29, 1864; *Washington Star*, March 23, 1911.

10. Halsey diary, August 30, 31, September 3, 5, 1864; Haines, *Fifteenth,* 237–238; Paul, "Campaign," 31; Wallace Struble to Hannah, August 9, 1864.
11. Haines, *Fifteenth,* 238–240; Halsey diary, August 10, 1864.
12. Haines, *Fifteenth,* 240–242; Hoffman, *Diary,* 10; Halsey diary, September 14–15, 1864; *OR,* ser. 1, vol. 43, pt. 1, p. 165; Paul, "Campaign," 32.
13. Brown, "Experiences," 22; *OR,* ser. 1, vol. 43, pt. 1, pp. 44, 166; Baquet, *Kearny's,* 151; Halsey diary, August 17, 1864; Haines, *Fifteenth,* 242–244; Paul, "Campaign," 34; Hoffman, *Diary,* 11; Ebenezer W. Davis, "Campaigns in Maryland and Virginia with the 6th Corps," A. P. Young Papers, New Jersey Historical Society; *OR,* ser. 1, vol. 43, pt. 1, p. 166.
14. Joseph G. Bilby, "Every Damn Thing in the Shape of a Rebel Is on the Run," *Military Images* 2, no. 3 (November–December 1980): 3, 17; Haines, *Fifteenth,* 244–245; Hoffman, *Diary,* 11; *OR,* ser. 1, vol. 43, pt. 1, p. 166; Baquet, *Kearny's,* 153; Bilby, *Three,* 184.
15. Haines, *Fifteenth,* 245–247; Bilby, "Perambulations," 12; Bilby, *Three,* 185; Baquet, *Kearny's,* 152, 201; *OR,* ser. 1, vol. 43, pt. 1, p. 171; Halsey diary, August 18, 1864; Hoffman, *Diary,* 11–12.

    Among the wounded was Captain Ridgeway Poinsett. The sentence for his unwillingness to continue to serve, a dishonorable discharge, followed him to the hospital, but he never learned of it, as he died of pyemia before it arrived (Bilby, "Every," 19, 21).
16. Wallace Struble to Hannah, August 23, 1864; Paul, "Campaign," 35–37; Halsey diary, August 18, 1864; Baquet, *Kearny's,* 153–154; Haines, *Fifteenth,* 247.

    General Breckinridge allegedly asked the captured Colonel Tay about the number of Federal troops in front of him. Tay replied, "seven hundred." Breckinridge thought him lying, but Tay suggested that he determine the identity of the captured soldiers' units. After checking, Breckinridge supposedly rode up to Tay and apologized, stating, "Why, Colonel, I never seen such a stubborn resistance by such a small body of men. I have buried over 700 of my men . . . and your whole force was not over that" (Baquet, *Kearny's,* 401).
17. Haines, *Fifteenth,* 250–251; Halsey diary, August 21, 1864; Bilby, *Remember,* 90; Baquet, *Kearny's,* 154; Bilby, *Three,* 187.
18. Haines, *Fifteenth,* 251–252; Halsey diary, August 28, 30, 1864; Bilby, *Remember,* 90; Bilby, "Every," 21; Paul, "Campaign," 38.
19. Halsey diary, September 2, 12, 1864; Haines, *Fifteenth,* 252–253; Cavileer to R. M. Ashley, September 7, 1864.

CHAPTER 11   *Defeating General Early*

1. Baquet, *Kearny's,* 156; Haines, *Fifteenth,* 255–256; Bilby, *Three,* 193.
2. Haines, *Fifteenth,* 257–259; Baquet, *Kearny's,* 156–157.
3. *OR,* ser. 1, vol. 43, pt. 1, pp. 107, 164, 168–169; Halsey diary, September 19, 1864; Bilby, *Three,* 196; Bilby, "Every," 23; Haines, *Fifteenth,* 259.

    While Lieutenant Colonel Campbell clearly indicated that the order to attack the cornfield came from Getty, Captain Halsey believed it originated from General Russell (Halsey diary, September 19, 1864).

4. *OR,* ser. 1, vol. 43, pt. 1, pp. 163, 164, 169; Halsey diary, September 19, 1864; Bilby, *Three,* 196–197; Haines, *Fifteenth,* 259.

5. *OR,* ser. 1, vol. 43, pt. 1, pp. 163, 169; Haines, *Fifteenth,* 260; Paul, "Campaign," 40; Bilby, *Three,* 197, 200; John T. Cunningham, "The John Beech Story," *Newark Sunday News Magazine,* January 29, 1961.

6. Edmund Halsey to sister, October 2, 1864; Haines, *Fifteenth,* 264; *OR,* ser. 1, vol. 43, pt. 1, p. 112.

7. Haines, *Fifteenth,* 264; Hoffman, *Diary,* 50; Joseph G. Bilby, "Flight of Crows," *Military Images* 2, no. 6 (May–June 1981): 4; Paul, "Campaign," 41; Halsey diary, September 20, 1864.

8. *OR,* ser. 1, vol. 43, pt. 1, pp. 169, 171; Hoffman, *Diary,* 51; Halsey diary, September 21–22, 1864; Paul, "Campaign," 41; Haines, *Fifteenth,* 266.

9. *OR,* ser. 1, vol. 43, pt. 1, p. 170; Hoffman, *Diary,* 13; Halsey diary, September 22, 1864; Bilby, "Flight," 5; Haines, *Fifteenth,* 266, 267.

10. *OR,* ser. 1, vol. 43, pt. 1, p. 170; Halsey diary, September 22, 1864; Haines, *Fifteenth,* 267.

11. Jeffry D. Wert, *From Winchester to Cedar Creek* (Carlisle, Pa.: South Mountain Press, 1987), 12–13; *OR,* ser. 1, vol. 43, pt. 1, p. 171; Haines, *Fifteenth,* 267, 268.

12. *OR,* ser. 1, vol. 43, pt. 1, p. 170; Hoffman, *Diary,* 13–14, 50.

13. Haines, *Fifteenth,* 268–269; Paul, "Campaign," 42; Hoffman, *Diary,* 13, 51; Halsey diary, September 24, 1864.

14. Hoffman, *Diary,* 12, 52; Paul, "Campaign," 42–43; Halsey diary, September 26, 1864.

15. Halsey diary, September 27, 30, 1864; Haines, *Fifteenth,* 271; Paul, "Campaign," 42–43; Bilby, "Crows," 13.

16. Halsey diary, October 2, 3, 8, 1864; Hoffman, *Diary,* 14, 53, 54; Paul, "Campaign," 43–44; Haines, *Fifteenth,* 272.

17. Paul, "Campaign," 43–45; Hoffman, *Diary,* 14–15; Edmund Halsey to sister, October 2, 1864; Hoffman, *Diary,* 15; Haines, *Fifteenth,* 273.

18. Halsey diary, October 16, 1864; *OR,* ser. 1, vol. 43, pt. 1, p. 167; Hoffman, *Diary,* 55.

19. Haines, *Fifteenth,* 274–275; Baquet, *Kearny's,* 167–168.

20. Haines, *Fifteenth,* 275–276; Halsey diary, October 19, 1864.

21. Haines, *Fifteenth,* 276; *OR,* ser. 1, vol. 43, pt. 1, p. 167.

22. *OR,* ser. 1, vol. 43, pt. 1, p. 167; Haines, *Fifteenth,* 276–277; Bilby, "Crows," 10.

   Although Boeman's tenure as commander of the Tenth NJV was short, he was well liked and respected by his men. John Hoffman called him "our beloved commander" (Hoffman, *Diary,* 17). Edmund Halsey called him "one of the bravest and best loved men in the service" (Halsey diary, October 24, 1864). He left behind a wife and two children.

23. *OR,* ser. 1, vol. 43, pt. 1, p. 167; Hoffman, *Diary,* 56; Bilby, *Three,* 219; Haines, *Fifteenth,* 277.

   Moulder, wounded at Spotsylvania, had only recently returned to the regiment (Chadwick, *Brother,* 283).

24. *OR,* ser. 1, vol. 43, pt. 1, p. 167; Hoffman, *Diary,* 16; Halsey diary, October 19, 1864; Haines, *Fifteenth,* 278–279.
25. *OR,* ser. 1, vol. 43, pt. 1, p. 168; Halsey diary, October 19, 1864.
26. Halsey diary, October 19, 1864; *OR,* ser. 1, vol. 43, pt. 1, p. 131; Haines, *Fifteenth,* 282; Bilby, "Crows," 11, 15.
27. Haines, *Fifteenth,* 282–283; Hoffman, *Diary,* 56.
28. Haines, *Fifteenth,* 283–284, 287; Halsey diary, October 21, 1864; *Newton Register,* November 4, 1864; Hoffman, *Diary,* 58, 60.
29. Halsey diary, October 26, November 17, 22, 23, 25, 1864.
30. Chadwick, *Brother,* 282; Halsey diary, November 18, 21, 1864; Haines, *Fifteenth,* 287; *Washington Star,* March 30, 1911; Hoffman, *Diary,* 60;
31. Halsey diary, November 30, December 1, 1864; Hoffman, *Diary,* 61.

CHAPTER 12   ***Back to Petersburg***

1. Haines, *Fifteenth,* 289; Hoffman, *Diary,* 19.
2. Halsey diary, December 4–6, 1864; Haines, *Fifteenth,* 290; Hoffman, *Diary,* 19; *Washington Star,* April 13, 1911.
3. *OR,* ser. 1, vol. 46, pt. 2, p. 615; Halsey diary, December 9, 10, 1864; Haines, *Fifteenth,* 290.
4. Haines, *Fifteenth,* 291–292; *Hunterdon Republican,* March 10, 1865; *Washington Star,* April 13, 1911; Hoffman, *Diary,* 62; Halsey diary, December 17, 1864; Baquet, *Kearny's,* 363; Bilby, *Three,* 230.
5. Haines, *Fifteenth,* 291; *Washington Star,* April 13, 1911; Halsey diary, December 25, 1865; Baquet, *Kearny's,* 363; Hoffman, *Diary,* 62.
6. *Washington Star,* April 13, 1911.
7. Halsey diary, December 31, 1864; Baquet, *Kearny's,* 176, 363; *OR,* ser. 1, vol. 42, pt. 3, p. 1119; Bilby, *Remember,* 431; *Newark Gazette,* October 4, 1864; *Newark Daily Advertiser,* February 21, 1865.
8. *Washington Star,* April 13, 1911; Bilby, *Three,* 235; Bilby, *Remember,* 431.
9. Haines, *Fifteenth,* 292; Halsey diary, January 6, 1865; Baquet, *Kearny's,* 364, 366; Hoffman, *Diary,* 62.
10. Halsey diary, December 20, 1864, January 9–10, 1865; Hoffman, *Diary,* 63; Baquet, *Kearny's,* 364; Chadwick, *Brother,* 291–292.
    The "attack" on the Federal line was actually a hundred unarmed Confederate soldiers attempting to desert. About twenty were killed (Hoffman, *Diary,* 63).
11. Haines, *Fifteenth,* 292, 294; Baquet, *Kearny's,* 364; Hoffman, *Diary,* 66.
12. John Horn, *The Petersburg Campaign* (Conshohocken, Pa.: Combined Press, 1993; Haines, *Fifteenth,* 293; Hoffman, *Diary,* 66; Baquet, *Kearny's,* 365.
13. Hoffman, *Diary,* 67; Bilby, *Remember,* 433; Haines, *Fifteenth,* 293; *Hunterdon Republican,* March 10, 1865; Paul diary, February 15, 1865.
14. Baquet, *Kearny's,* 367–268; *Washington Star,* April 13, 1911; Horn, *Petersburg,* 212–213.
15. Horn, *Petersburg,* 241; Baquet, *Kearny's,* 181, 368; Hoffman, *Diary,* 71.
16. Baquet, *Kearny's,* 180–182; *OR,* ser. 1, vol. 46, pt. 1, pp. 910, 928.

17. *OR,* ser. 1, vol. 46, pt. 1, pp. 910, 916, 927, 929; Baquet, *Kearny's,* 370, 371; Bilby, *Remember,* 433.

18. Haines, *Fifteenth,* 302; Baquet, *Kearny's,* 370; *OR,* ser. 1, vol. 46, pt. 1, pp. 910, 916, 927, 929.

19. *OR,* ser. 1, vol. 46, pt. 1, pp. 910–911, 927; Baquet, *Kearny's,* 370.

20. *OR,* ser. 1, vol. 46, pt. 1, pp. 911, 927.

21. *OR,* ser. 1, vol. 46, pt. 1, p. 586; Haines, *Fifteenth,* 303; Baquet, *Kearny's,* 182–183, 372.

22. *OR,* ser. 1, vol. 46, pt. 1, pp. 913, 916, 1257; Haines, *Fifteenth,* 305; Hoffman, *Diary,* 72; Baquet, *Kearny's,* 372–373.

23. Baquet, *Kearny's,* 372–373; Haines, *Fifteenth,* 305; Hoffman, *Diary,* 73.

24. *OR,* ser. 1, vol. 46, pt. 1, p. 916; Hoffman, *Diary,* 73; Baquet, *Kearny's,* 185, 373–374.

25. Haines, *Fifteenth,* 309; Baquet, *Kearny's,* 374–375; Hoffman, *Diary,* 73, 74.

26. Hoffman, *Diary,* 74, 76; Haines, *Fifteenth,* 310; Baquet, *Kearny's,* 376–377; *Washington Star,* April 20, 1911.

27. Baquet, *Kearny's,* 379–380; *OR,* ser. 1, vol. 46, pt. 1, p. 1061.

28. Hoffman, *Diary,* 80, 81; Baquet, *Kearny's,* 380–382; Haines, *Kearny's,* 313–314; Bilby, *Three,* 245.

29. Haines, *Fifteenth,* 314–316; Baquet, *Kearny's,* 188, 193, 382, 384; Brown, "Experiences," 36.

30. Baquet, *Kearny's,* 202, 384–385; Hoffman, *Diary,* 83.

31. Baquet, *Kearny's,* 194; Hoffman, *Diary,* 84; Brown, "Experiences," 37.

APPENDIX C   *Numbers and Losses of the First New Jersey Brigade*

1. Baquet, *Kearny's,* 195; William F. Fox, *Regimental Losses in the American Civil War* (Albany, N.Y.: J. McDonaugh, 1898), 243–245, 253.

2. Fox, *Regimental,* 243–245, 253.

   Fox's numbers are uniformly higher than those in Appendices A and B because he included those soldiers who later died of their wounds. The numbers cited in Appendices A and B are from the after-battle reports of each unit and do not include future deaths.

3. Fox, *Regimental,* 3, 12, 17, 20, 21; Bilby, *Three,* 246.

4. Fox, *Regimental,* 36.

INDEX

ABOUT THE AUTHOR

A native of Philadelphia, Bradley M. Gottfried received a Ph.D. in zoology from Miami University and has spent his professional career as a full-time faculty member and administrator in five states. He is currently president of Sussex County Community College in Newton, New Jersey.

Dr. Gottfried's interest in the Civil War began at an early age. Four of his books have been published, including *Stopping Pickett: The History of the Philadelphia Brigade, Roads to Gettysburg,* and *The Brigades of Gettysburg.* He has also written extensively for *Gettysburg Magazine* and *Civil War Times Illustrated.*